15th International Conference Information Systems 2022

Online
12-14 March 2022

ISBN: 978-1-7138-5789-1

Printed from e-media with permission by:

Curran Associates, Inc.
57 Morehouse Lane
Red Hook, NY 12571

Some format issues inherent in the e-media version may also appear in this print version.

International Association for Development of the Information Society (IADIS)
Rua Sao Sebastiao Da Pedreira
No. 100, 30, 1050-209
Lisbon, Portugal

Phone: 351 21 3151373
Fax: 351 21 3151244

secretariat@iadis.org

Additional copies of this publication are available from:

Curran Associates, Inc.
57 Morehouse Lane
Red Hook, NY 12571 USA
Phone: 845-758-0400
Fax: 845-758-2633
Email: curran@proceedings.com
Web: www.proceedings.com

TABLE OF CONTENTS

FULL PAPERS

SHORT PAPERS

FULL PAPERS

LAYOUT-DRIVEN WEBPAGE READING

Koki Tsumura[1], Junko Shirogane[2], Hajime Iwata[3] and Yoshiaki Fukazwa[1]
[1]*Waseda University, Japan*
[2]*Tokyo Woman's Christian University, Japan*
[3]*Kanagawa Institute of Technology, Japan*

ABSTRACT

Most visually impaired people use a screen reader when using a computer. However, numerous problems are encountered when using screen reader. One of the problems is the reading order of a webpage. Current screen readers basically read aloud the webpage from top to bottom, left to right. Webpages have structures, and information is emphasized by color and size. Normally, when sighted people read a webpage, they decide the reading order by referring to nontext information such as color and structure. In this research, we propose a method to determine the reading order on the basis of the saliency of each element of the webpage and the structure information of the webpage, such as menus and layout patterns.

KEYWORDS

Screen Reader, Accessibility, Menu, Saliency, Webpage Layout

1. INTRODUCTION

According to the World Health Organization (Blindness and vision impairment, World Health Organization), 1 billion people are visually impaired worldwide. With the spread of Internet access, the use of the web by the visually impaired is increasing. According to a survey (Watanabe 2013), 96.3% of blind people use computers, mostly for web browsing. Many visually impaired people use a screen reader to navigate on computers, smartphones, and tablets. A screen reader basically reads aloud the text from top to bottom in the HTML file of a webpage visited by a user, which may cause unwanted parts of the page to be read aloud. According to a survey (Lazar 2007), screen-reader users waste an average of 30.4% of their time because of the reading order, images without alt text, etc.

In recent years, the use of various layout patterns in web design that use nontext information such as images, colors, and positions has increased. Layout patterns exist so that users can acquire necessary information as quickly as possible without becoming bored with the content of the webpage. Many designers use layout patterns to guide the eye movement of visitors of a webpage. Users who visit a webpage will skip certain parts of the layout pattern and read certain parts carefully. As a result, their eye movement and reading order will change accordingly. However, current screen readers do not read aloud the webpage in the same order that sighted people read.

To fill the usability gap between how sighted and blind users acquire information when visiting a webpage, we propose a method to determine the reading order of webpages by focusing on menus, saliency, and webpage layout patterns. Specifically, we first classify webpages into two major parts—menus and content—and create saliency rankings of child elements in each part. The reading order of webpages is then determined on the basis of the rankings and the detected layout pattern. We believe that this method will enable more efficient web browsing by visually impaired users, improve users' understanding of each part of a webpage, and provide a reading order similar to that of sighted users.

2. RELATED WORKS

Extensive research has been conducted to fill the computer usability gap between sighted and visually impaired people. Some research has focused on improving screen-reader usability, and some has focused on improving voice user interface usability. In this chapter, some of these approaches are introduced and the difference between these approaches and the method proposed in the present work is discussed.

Authors of long web documents such as wiktionaries, manuals, tutorials, blogs, and scientific literature provide a table of contents (TOC) for users to access the desired content instantaneously. However, screen-reader users cannot exploit the TOC to the same extent as their sighted peers. Screen-reader users need to press a multitude of shortcuts to access the TOC from the beginning of the page as well as from an arbitrary section in the page, which they find tedious and cumbersome. To solve this problem, a method to identify and extract TOC hyperlinks from the web documents and then facilitate on-demand instant screen-reader access to the TOC from anywhere in the webpage has been proposed in previous works. The method has been proposed as a browser extension called iTOC (Lee 2020). Whenever a user presses a special shortcut, the TOC in the current webpage is identified from the document object model and can be accessed from a screen reader on-demand. However, this approach is limited to long documents that include a TOC inside and does not focus on changing the reading order of webpages.

ARIA (Accessible Rich Internet Applications) landmarks serve as reference points that can be conveniently and quickly accessed using keyboard shortcuts. If ARIA landmarks are properly implemented in web pages, screen reader users can jump to content they are interested in. However, in many cases, web developers use landmarks sporadically and inconsistently, and some webpages do not even have landmarks. To solve this problem, Aydin et al. proposed the SaIL system (Aydin 2020), which dynamically injects role landmark attributes into the HTML source using a deep learning model called SalGAN. However, ARIA landmarks are not commonly used, and their research are not providing method to determine reading order of webpages.

3. LAYOUT PATTERN

Numerous layout patterns, including f-patterns, spotted patterns, layer-cake patterns, and zigzag patterns (Text Scanning Patterns: Eyetracking Evidence, Nielsen Norman Group), are intended to guide the eye movement of a user reading a webpage. For example, a layer-cake pattern is a pattern used by a user visiting a webpage to read each heading and subheading; when a heading relevant to the user's interest appears, the user reads the accompanying body text below the heading. The left half of Fig 1 shows an example of a layer-cake pattern. A gaze plot is shown in circles, and the gazes are mainly plotted in the headings. Designers usually use layout patterns to prevent users from becoming bored and to convey information efficiently by locating elements in certain positions.

Zigzag patterns are commonly used patterns in modern webpages. A zigzag pattern is a layout pattern that alternates the placement of images and text on each horizontal row (Zigzag Image-Text Layouts Make Scanning Less Efficient). The right half of Fig 1 shows an example of a zigzag pattern. The image with a house is located on the left-hand side of the gray rectangular text block, and the image with leaves is located on the right-hand side of text block. A zigzag pattern is used to create a rhythm to maintain the reader's interest in the content while also directing attention so that the user can quickly look through each element and grasp its importance. Zigzag patterns are often used in promotion pages and landing pages to communicate the features of the product and the benefits the product offers. Therefore, the images in a zigzag pattern are included for the purpose of adaptation to attract attention. However, in current screen readers, when a zigzag pattern is read aloud, the readings of these images are not skipped. To reduce redundant reading and to follow the scanning pattern of a sighted user when scanning a zigzag pattern, our proposed method skips the reading of the images.

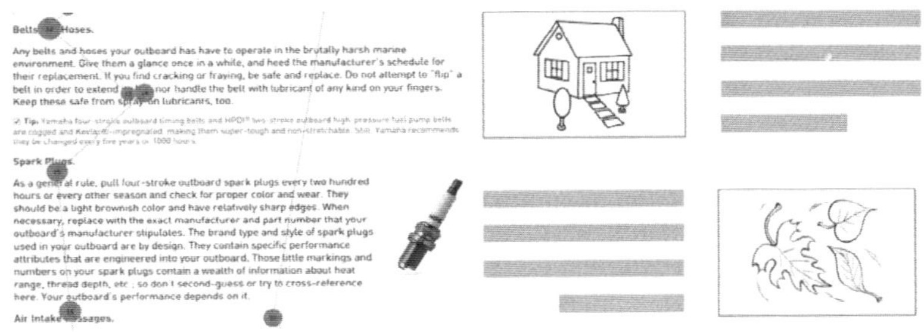

Figure 1. Examples of a layer-cake pattern (left) and a zigzag pattern (right)
(From Nielsen Norman group's Text Scanning Patterns and Zigzag Image-Text Layout)

4. DESIGN

Figure 2 presents an overview of a screen-reader browser extension that implements the proposed method. First, when a user visits a webpage, a URL is given to the saliency prediction system that uses Inagaki's prediction model (Inagaki 2020) and a saliency ranking is generated by the system. The saliency ranking and DOM of the webpage are then passed to the read-order determinator. In the determinator, the menu and zigzag pattern are detected first; after these processes, the reading order of elements in the menu and content parts are determined according to the saliency ranking. In the end, the determinator determines the reading order of all the elements in the webpage and, whenever a user presses a predefined shortcut, it determines the next element to read and reads it aloud.

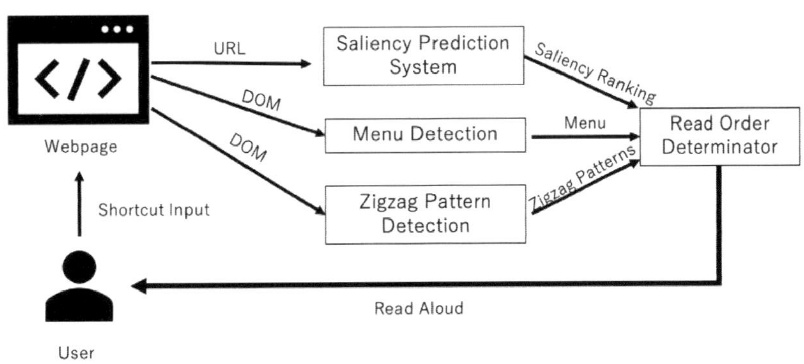

Figure 2. Overview of the screen-reader extension that implements the proposed method

4.1 Menu Detection

For the sake of space, only the nav tag menu detection algorithm is explained here. In the proposed method, other algorithms are also used for menu detection. For parallel navigation, navigation elements are usually in the top one-fourth of the screen height; thus, in the first step, the nav tag elements that satisfy this condition are collected (Fig 3). After this step, each collected element in the same height is grouped to be marked as a single navigation element. In some cases, multiple nav tag elements exist at the same height; for them to be recognized as a menu, nav tag elements at the same height are grouped. For each group, the closest ancestor element is then collected and returned as a menu element. If no menu is detected by the algorithm, other algorithms are used to detect the menu.

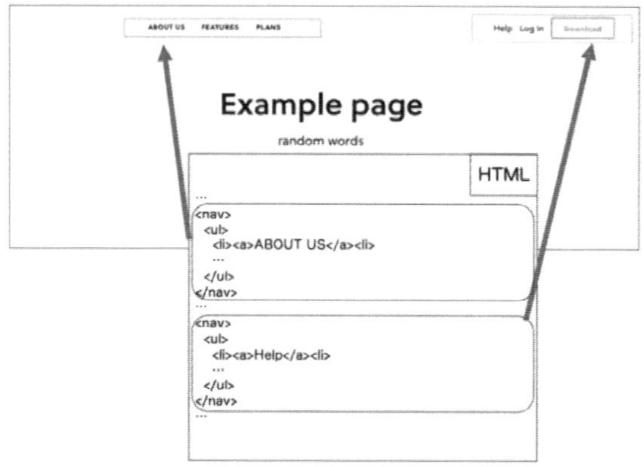

Figure 3. Parallel nav tag menu example and the corresponding HTML entities

4.2 Zigzag Pattern Detection

First, images larger than or equal to 0.2 times the screen width and less than or equal to 0.8 times the screen width are collected. In the next step, the collected images with the same or similar height text neighbor are collected as candidates (Fig 4). Collected images are then grouped by size and distance between each image and returned as zigzag pattern elements.

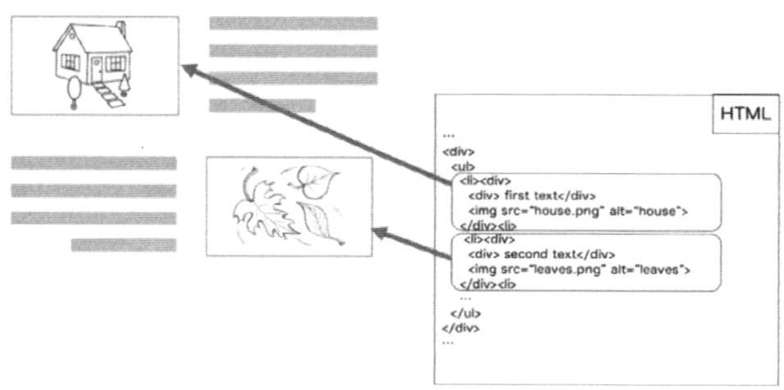

Figure 4. Zigzag example and the corresponding HTML entities

4.3 Menu Reading Order Determination

For each element in a detected menu, the reading order is determined according to a saliency ranking generated by a saliency generation system. Elements' reading order is determined in order of saliency, and, before and after the reading aloud menu, "menu begin" and "menu end" are read aloud. The number of elements inside menu is also read after "reading of menu begin" in the same manner that existing screen readers read list elements.

4.4 Contents Reading Order Determination

For each element in the detected content, the reading order is determined according to saliency ranking generated by a saliency generation system. The reading order of elements is determined in order of saliency; however, for zigzag pattern images, reading orders are not set to skip reading alt text attributed to the image elements. After the reading-order determination steps, whenever the user presses a shortcut key, an element to be read is determined and read aloud by the system.

5. EVALUATION

5.1 Experimental Design

To evaluate our proposed method, we conducted an experiment. Twelve sighted people who usually use a computer in their daily life and work participated. Because of the COVID-19 situation, the experiment was conducted online using Zoom (video communication software). We grouped the 12 participants into 4 groups of 3 participants each and asked them to listen to a reading by the proposed method and to a reading by NonVisual Desktop Access (NV Access), which is a screen reader widely used by visually impaired people; the participants were then asked to answer some questions. In each session, they answered questions using hand signs, which we prepared, or answered via text. To ensure that each participant could not see other participants' answers, the participants were asked to pin the host screen or to close their eyes when answering questions using hand signs.

To determine which reading method was more effective, we asked participants to listen to the menu reading, the zigzag pattern reading, and the reading determined using saliency separately. Otherwise, it would not be possible to determine which reading was most effective. In the experiments, webpages that include a zigzag pattern and a menu were used and we grouped participants into 4 groups (A to D), with 3 participants in each group. Table 1 shows the order in which each group listened to the readings. The participants in group A listened to proposed method's reading first and the NVDA's reading after for the menu reading experiment, whereas the participants in group D listened to the NVDA's reading first and the proposed method's reading after for the same experiment. The orders of the other experiments are also presented in Table 1. The participants participated in the menu reading experiment and subsequently participated in the saliency-sorted reading experiment and then the zigzag-sorted reading experiment. Questions presented in Table 2 were asked during or after the experiments. After each experiment, we asked participants to send comments.

To verify the effectiveness of proposed method's menu reading, we asked participants to listen to the proposed method's reading and the NVDA's reading. To ensure the experiment design did not favor NVDA or the proposed method, 2 groups listened to the proposed method's reading first and the other 2 groups listened to the NVDA's reading first. After or while listening to each reading, participants were asked to answer questions 1–4.

To verify the effectiveness of the proposed method's saliency-sorted reading order, we asked the participants to listen to the proposed method's reading and the unchanged original reading. To ensure the experiment design did not favor the original or the proposed method, 2 groups listened to the proposed method first and the other 2 groups listened to the original first. After listening to each reading, participants were asked to answer questions 5 and 6.

To verify the effectiveness of the proposed method's zigzag pattern reading, we asked the participants to listen to the proposed method's reading and the NVDA's reading. To ensure that the experimental design did not favor NVDA or the proposed method, 2 groups listened to the proposed method's reading first and the other 2 groups listened to the NVDA's reading first. After listening to each reading, participants were asked to answer questions 7 through 9.

Table 1. The order in which each group listened to the readings

Group Name	Menu	Saliency Sort	Zigzag Pattern
A	Proposed, NVDA	Sorted, Original	Proposed, NVDA
B	Proposed, NVDA	Sorted, Original	NVDA, Proposed
C	NVDA, Proposed	Original, Sorted	Proposed, NVDA
D	NVDA, Proposed	Original, Sorted	NVDA, Proposed

Table 2. Questions asked in the experiments

Question Number	Question
1	Raise your hand while the menu is being read
2	Could you understand where the menu started and where it ended? Choose from 5 choices. (1) Completely ununderstandable, (2) Ununderstandable, (3) Neither understandable nor ununderstandable, (4) Understandable, (5) Very understandable.
3	Which reading was easier to understand where the menu started and where it ended?
4	If you were blind, which reading would you prefer to use?
5	Which read necessary information earlier?
6	If you were a visually impaired person, which reading would you prefer to use?
7	How many duplicate readings were there? (1) A very large amount, (2) A large amount, (3) Neither large nor few, (4) A Few, (5) None
8	Which reading had more redundant reading?
9	If you were blind, which reading would you prefer to use?

5.2 Results

Table 3 presents the correct answer rate to question 1. The participants were asked to guess the menu while a webpage was being read, and the correct answer rate was calculated; the answer rate is reported as a percentage calculated as the number of people who answered correctly divided by 12 (the total number of participants). Although every participant correctly answered where the reading of the menu started and where it finished for the proposed method's reading, 1 participant did not correctly guess the start and finish of the menu in the NVDA's reading. Table 4 shows the average answer score for question 2. Eleven participants scored 4 or 5 for the proposed method's reading, corresponding to "understandable" or "very understandable", respectively, whereas 6 participants scored 1 or 2, which correspond to "completely ununderstandable" and "ununderstanble", respectively, for the NVDA's reading.

For the proposed method's reading, participants submitted both positive and negative comments. Two participants wrote that it was understandable to hear the "menu begin" keyword before the start of the reading menu segment and that it was also understandable to hear the "menu end" keyword after the end of the reading menu segment. However, 1 participant mentioned that there should be more time before reading "the number of links in the menu", and some participants mentioned that a more detailed menu explanation should be given because people who do not usually use the Internet might not understand what a menu is.

For the NVDA's reading, participants submitted numerous negative comments. Five participants mentioned that they had no idea when the reading of the menu started and ended. Also, some participants mentioned that they could predict the menu when "link" was read multiple times and when "navigation" was read. However, as the results in Table 3 show, most of the participants failed to guess the answer; thus, even if they made predictions, the predictions were incorrect in most cases.

The results for questions 3 and 4 are shown in Table 5. For both questions, all of the participants preferred the proposed method's reading.

From the results, the NVDA's reading of a menu is insufficient for users to understand the menu. Our proposed method's reading outperformed the NVDA's reading in understanding a menu; the correct rate of guessing the menu from the proposed method's reading was 100%, whereas that from the NVDA's reading was only 8.33%. In addition, the participants preferred the proposed method's reading.

For question 5, 8 participants felt that necessary information was read earlier in the proposed method. For question 6, 6 participants preferred to use the proposed method. From these results, the proposed method's reading was not effective. There were few positive comments and numerous negative comments for the proposed method's reading. The following comments are some excerpted participant comments that seem valuable for our future research:

- The reading of a menu should be skipped first and read whenever the user wants the screen reader to read aloud.
- In most cases, people don't visit a webpage to register a service, so a screen reader should read aloud a menu in the original order.

- When I visit a webpage, I first read the contents and rarely use a menu, so a screen-reader user might want to read like this.

For question 7, as presented in Table 7, 8 participants chose 4 or 5 as their choice for the proposed method's reading, whereas 9 participants scored 1 or 2 for the NVDA's reading. No negative comments were submitted for the proposed method's reading; however, several participants submitted negative comments for the NVDA's reading. Examples include multiple readings of the "image" keyword, which hindered understanding, many duplicate readings, and inability to imagine a webpage from the reading.

The results for questions 8 and 9 are presented in Table 8. For question 8, all participants felt that there were more redundant readings in the NVDA's reading. For question 9, 11 participants preferred the proposed method's reading.

In summary, compared with the NVDA's menu readings, the proposed method's menu readings outperformed with respect to understanding; in addition, all of the participants preferred to use the proposed method rather than the NVDA. Eleven participants preferred to use the proposed method's zigzag pattern readings, and all of the participants felt that the proposed method's reading was less redundant. However, saliency-sorted reading did not perform well.

Table 3. Correct answer rate for question 1

Question	Proposed Correct Rate	NVDA Correct Rate
Raise your hand while menu is being read	100% (12/12)	8.33% (1/12)

Table 4. Average answer score for question 2

Question	Proposed Average Answer Score	NVDA Average Answer Score
Could you understand where the menu started and where it ended? Choose from 5 choices.	3.83 (11 participants answered 4 or 5)	2.42 (6 participants answered 1 or 2)

Table 5. Answers for questions 3 and 4

Question	Proposed	NVDA
Which reading was easier to understand where the menu started and where it ended?	100%	0%
If you were blind, which reading would you prefer to use?	100%	0 %

Table 6. Answers for questions 5 and 6

Question	Proposed	Original
Which read necessary information earlier?	66.7%	33.3%
If you were blind, which reading would you prefer to use?	50.0%	50.0%

Table 7. Average answer score for question 7

Question	Proposed Average Answer Score	NVDA Average Answer Score
How many duplicate readings were there?	3.08 (8 participants answered 4 or 5)	1.83 (9 participants answered 1 or 2)

Table 8. Answers for questions 8 and 9

Question	Proposed	NVDA
Which reading had more redundant reading?	0%	100%
If you were blind, which reading would you prefer to use?	91.7%	8.83% (1/12)

6. CONCLUSION

This paper introduced a new method to determine a reading order of a webpage using saliency, layout pattern, and structure information to convey the intention of the webpage's designer and convey information efficiently. A user study with 12 sighted participants demonstrated the potential of the method in substantially improving usability. We are planning to conduct an experiment with visually impaired people who are screen-reader users. The current method is implemented as a Chrome extension, and the voice implemented in the current method differs from that in NVDA, which is the comparison target; in addition, there are some shortcut keys for participants to remember, which might also influence the experimental results. To solve these problems, we will implement a new system that determines reading order of a given webpage and generates a sorted webpage according to the reading order. Each participant will be asked to perform some tasks using a screen reader on two webpages: an unchanged plain webpage and a webpage produced using our method. The number of shortcut presses will be counted, and the completion time will be measured for each task.

REFERENCES

Ali Selman Aydin, Shrin Feiz, Vikas Ashok, and I V Ramakrishnan. Sail: Saliency-driven injection of aria landmarks. International Conference on Intelligent User Interfaces, pp. 111–115, 2020.

Blindness and vision impairment, World Health Organization, [online] Available at https://www.who.int/news-room/fact-sheets/detail/blindness-and-visual-impairment [Accessed 18 Dec. 2021].

Inagaki et al., Visualization Method of Important Regions by Combination of Webpage Structures and Saliency Maps. ICSOFT 2020. pp 204-211.

Lazar et al., 2007. What frustrates screen reader users on the web: A study of 100 blind users. INTERNATIONAL JOURNAL OF HUMAN-COMPUTER INTERACTION, Vol. 22, No. 3, pp 247-269.

Lee et al., 2020. iTOC: Enabling Efficient Non-Visual Interaction with Long Web Documents. Proceedings of IEEE International Conference on Systems, Man and Cybernetics. Toronto, ON, Canada, pp. 3799-3806.

NV Access, [online] Available at https://www.nvaccess.org/ [Accessed 18 Dec. 2021].

Screen reader user survey #9 results, WebAIM, [online] Available at https://webaim.org/projects/screenreadersurvey9/#landmarks [Accessed 18 Dec. 2021].

Text Scanning Patterns: Eyetracking Evidence, Nielsen Norman Group, [online] Available at https://www.nngroup.com/articles/text-scanning-patterns-eyetracking/ [Accessed 18 Dec. 2021].

Watanabe et al., 2014. A Survey on the Use of Cell Phones, Smartphones, and Tablets among People with Visual Impairments 2013. IEICE technical report. Welfare Information technology, Vol. 113, No. 481, pp 25-30.

Zigzag Image-Text Layouts Make Scanning Less Efficient, Nielsen Norman Group, [online] Available at https://www.nngroup.com/articles/zigzag-page-layout/ [Accessed 18 Dec. 2021].

ANALYSIS AND PREDICTION OF COMPUTER INDUSTRY TALENT DEMAND BASED ON MACHINE LEARNING

Yu Han and Haiyi Zhang
Acadia University, Computer Science, Acadia University, Wolfville, NS, B4P 2R6 Canada

ABSTRACT

From the perspective of enterprise and social demand, this research analyzes the characteristics of talent demand in Canadian computer industries by using big data thinking, text analysis and machine learning. Firstly, through crawler technology, we obtained the recruitment information on mainstream Recruitment websites in Canada and developed a standardized collection process. After processing the data, we used IBM Watson Studio to split the text and constructed the skill keyword dictionary to extract the talent demand. In addition, the time series algorithm was used to predict the changes of the computer skill keyword over time and visualize the results. After analyzing the experiment results, it is found that computer science related jobs are changing over time and require new skills to adapt. Finally, based on the analysis results, suggestions and plans for cultivating talents related to computer science are proposed from the perspectives of enterprises, governments and campuses. The governments should pay attention to policy making, campuses and enterprises should strengthen cooperation and create a new talent training model.

KEYWORDS

Computer Industry, Talent Demand, Text Mining, Machine Learning, Time Series

1. INTRODUCTION

The number of computer-related industries has rapidly increased since computer science emerged as a specialization and associated technology has rapidly developed. At the same time, the demand for talent to fill positions in these new industries has significantly increased. According to Computing Technology Industry Association (CompTIA) reported that 282,000 computer jobs were created since 2011, and the group expects some computing occupations to grow by double-digit percentages between 2019 and 2027 (Computing Technology Industry Association, 2020). Rapidly changing knowledge and skill requirements further aggravates the relationship between supply and demand of trained computer talent in Canada.

In the past decade, research on the characteristics of talent needed by industry and text mining based on Big Data have increasingly attracted attention from researchers. Therefore, taking the perspective of business and organizational enterprise requirements, my research aims to make research on the topic of computer industry talent skills requirements more efficient and by using Big Data and text mining. The intent of this research is to inform the knowledge base of the computer industry so that the industry has a way of tracking changes in talent demand characteristics. Promoting talent training and matching the supply with the demand for computer science talent can ultimately promote the sustainable and healthy development of the computer science industry.

This research used text mining of the web to broadly explore the theory behind unstructured data research. I incorporated online recruitment information as my data source. Then, this research used web crawler technology to collect my data, which extensively saved labour and time and improved efficiency. This research used web text mining technology to construct a multi-dimensional and expandable talent demand skills dictionary from which I extracted features in the recruitment textual data. This research used another text mining algorithm to analyze the invisible knowledge mode of the textual data, which kept my research more systematic. I introduced a time dimension to my data. Using text mining and time series analysis methods allowed my research to comprehensively study the talent demand characteristics of the Canadian computer industry by allowing me to correlate the certain industry jobs with various skills to discover the strength of the relationship between the two and to study how skills keywords changed over time so that I could predict future needs and level of demand.

2. BACKGROUND STUDIES

2.1 Web Text Mining

Text mining is a comprehensive analysis method that intersects multiple fields such as machine learning, data mining, information retrieval, natural language processing, and knowledge management (Feldman and Dagan, 1995). As in the principle of data mining, text mining identifies and explores laws and rules to extract information from data sources sufficient to solve the problem. Web text mining is the process of discovering an implicit pattern, *P*, from a collection, *C*, of a large number of text documents that originate on the web. If *C* is the input and *P* is the output, then web text mining maps σ from input to output: $C \rightarrow P$ (Feldman et al., 1998). The process of web text mining is generally divided into seven steps: text collection, text preprocessing, feature extraction, text representation, text mining, quality evaluation, and visualization of mining results.

2.2 Time Series

Exponential smoothing is a time series forecasting algorithm, generally split into single exponential smoothing, double exponential smoothing, and triple exponential smoothing. The forecast produced by the exponential smoothing method is a weighted average of prior observations. The nearer the observation time, the higher the correlation weight (Bekhradnia, 2007). The exponential smoothing method is sometimes called the ETS model, which refers to the explicit modelling of errors, trends, and seasonality (Hyndman and Athanasopoulos, 2018). Equation 1 describes the process.

Equation 1: $S_t = ay_t+(1-a)S_{t-1}*y$. Where S_t represents the predicted value at time, t (or the value of the exponential). y_t represents the actual value at t, and S_{t-1} represents the predicted value at $t-1$ (or the value of the exponential). a is a smoothing coefficient (Hyndman and Athanasopoulos, 2018). The initial value is the predicted value at the first time step.

When the number of items in the original series is greater than 15, the observed value at the first time step or the observed value at the previous time step is selected as the initial value. When the number of items is less than 15, the average of the observed values at the first three time steps is selected as the initial value.

In performing exponential smoothing, the key is the value of a. When the time series data are relatively stable, a should be a smaller value, generally between 0.05 and 0.1. However, when the time series data fluctuate, and the long-term changes are not large, a slightly larger value for a should be chosen, between 0.2 and 0.5. When the time series data are increasing or decreasing, a should be larger still, between 0.6 and 1.0.

3. THEROY

3.1 Data Collection

For my research, I regularly collected the required data, twice per month, based on defined time nodes using web crawler technology. First, the web crawler selected mainstream recruitment URLs as sub-URLs to form URL categories. Then the software crawled web pages for interpretation and analysis. When crawling, the software continuously obtained new sub-URLs to join the queue and finally crawled all sub-URLs under specific conditions (Amudha and Phil, 2017). The task of the web crawler was to crawl the recruitment information of Canadian computer-related job postings on the three recruitment websites and crawl out my required fields to provide text information regarding the characteristics of talent demand of the industry.

3.2 Data Preprocessing

The collected recruitment information belonged to the unstructured text dataset, including text and symbols. I used the N-gram algorithm to process the recruitment information. I extracted core skills data from the sampled data corresponding to a skill dimension, and I created a skills dictionary as a function of time. The combining text segmentation and N-gram segmentation, a the general search-based morphological analysis method combined with a non-dictionary-based N-gram segmentation, improves the search quality (Rijmenam, 2013).

After preprocessing the recruitment information, I retained the following analysis fields: recruitment position, work location, crawl date, work experience, academic requirements, salary, and job description. To identify the name of the recruiting post, I added a new "job category" field. Because each organization had a different name for its job posting, to facilitate uniformity and standardization, I classified specific posts from a data analysis perspective. The specific classifications are Technology, Product, Design, Operating and Marketing.

3.3 Skill Dictionary

I used relevant software tools extracted the skills keywords. Skills keywords of the same job category were grouped into one category. Semantic skills keywords were also classified into one category. This method only performed feature extraction of skills keywords with the goal of identifying existing skills keywords while simultaneously performing real-time analysis of the data.

The topic classification method of the skills keywords should learn from existing relevant skills keywords and added newly appearing skills keywords. The job skills in computer-related industries are divided into three dimensions: technical skills, business skills, and comprehensive skills (Vassakis, Petrakis & Kopanakis, 2018) and eight first-level skills indicators and thirty second-level skills indicators are constructed, as listed in Table 1.

Table 1. The skill dimensions and indicators of skill dictionary

The dimension	First-level skills indicators	Second-level skill indicators
Technical skills	Basic computer knowledge Website construction and maintenance Search engine optimization	Operating system knowledge, computer protocol knowledge, programming language, database application, website testing, visual perception, graphic design, website architecture/operation, web page production, video clip, search engine application, website ranking
Business skills	The network marketing Marketing management	Social networking, customer acquisition and retention, online sales platform, e-commerce model, sales skills, website topics and activities, data analysis
Comprehensive skills	Professional quality Interpersonal communication Office automation	Work attitude, executive ability, psychological quality, learning ability, thinking ability, language ability, team ability, management ability, office software, copy editing and writing

4. EMPIRICAL STUDIES

4.1 Analysis of the Overall Need for Talent in the Computer Industry

I statistically analyzed the collected recruitment information for computer science-related positions in terms of overall demand, demand for various positions, academic requirements, and salary levels. I used various graphical methods to display the results of all aspects of my analysis.

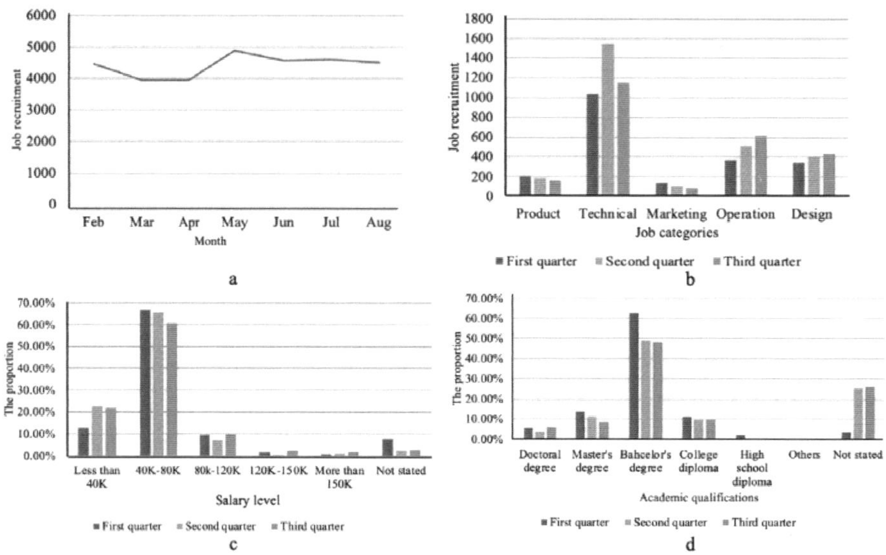

Figure 1. (a) Trend of total recruitment (b) Total comparison of job categories (c) Comparison of salary (d) Comparison of academic qualifications

I present the statistical trends found in the total amount of recruitment information in Figure 1(a). The period ranged from February to August 2021, spanning three financial quarters. The figure shows that during March to April, the demand for jobs slightly declined. When summer arrived, the market for computer jobs peaked compared to February through May. The market high endured over the next few months.

To clearly analyze my data, I divided my almost 12 months of data into four quarters. January to March is the first quarter; April to June is the second quarter; July to September is the third quarter; and October to December is the fourth quarter. I chose the median month of each quarter to represent its quarter. I classified recruitment positions into job categories, and I grouped the job categories into five categories: product, technology, marketing, design, and operation.

Figure 1(b) presents the statistics of the recruitment information data for the first three quarters of 2021. In terms of job categories, in the first quarter, technical jobs had the most significant market demand. In the second and third quarters, the number of job types changed significantly. The number of operation and design job postings gradually and steadily increased, while the number of product and marketing job postings slightly decreased. Commodity circulation channels in the computer industry are increasing so operations are critical to any computer-related enterprise and demand in this talent pool is relatively extraordinary. The demand for talent in marketing and production in computer-related industry weakened, especially in marketing.

Because business enterprises and organizations use different salary calculation methods when posting recruitment information, it was impossible for me to make a unified analysis. I adjusted all the salary postings to determine an annual salary for each posting. Figure 1(c) compares the salaries for the computer industry postings. The salary range with the most significant proportion of available jobs during the three quarters was the 40k to 80k per year salary range. The proportion of available jobs in the second and third quarters for this salary range progressively dropped, but they still surpassed 60% for those two quarters. The lowest paying jobs were in the less than 40k per year range and the fewest available jobs in that range were in the first quarter. An increase in talent demand indicates that the computer industry has increased its ability to pay competitive salaries, which, in turn, attracts more talent to the industry.

Figure 1(d) shows that the overall change in level of education was not significant over the three quarters for each educational requirement. The educational requirements for available positions mainly required a Bachelor's degree. The annual statistics showed that a Bachelor's degree was required for more than 40% of available jobs, followed by the Master's degree and college diploma, both required by approximately 10% of available jobs. The percentage of jobs requiring Doctoral degrees or only high school diplomas was not very high, and these educational requirements were polarized.

4.2 The Talent Skill Demand of Computer Industry

I divided the skills requirements into technical dimensions, business dimensions, and comprehensive dimensions. Using the skills dimensions of my dictionary, I determined eight first-level indicators, 30 second-level indicators, corresponding text information, and word frequency statistics which I listed in Table 2. In the table, "Q1", "Q2" and "Q3" represent the three quarters; "freq" is the short form of "frequency", the number of times that keywords appear in the text; and "Prop" is the short form of "Proportion", which represents the percentage of the total number of analyzed texts.

From an overall perspective, the top three first-level indicators in the first quarter were Website construction and maintenance (40.33%), Basic computer knowledge (24.66%), and Interpersonal communication (22.38%), followed by Office automation and Marketing management. The ranking of the first-level indicators in the second quarter did not change, and the overall ranking was the same. In the third quarter, the ranking of the top three indicators changed, but Website construction and maintenance still ranked first. However, there were apparent changes in Interpersonal communication, which accounted for 5.66% more than Basic computer knowledge in the total text proportion.

Table 2. Skill dimension frequency statistics

1st Level Skills indicators	2nd Level Skill indicators	Q1 freq	Prop	Q2 freq	Prop	Q3 freq	Prop
Basic computer knowledge		1337	24.66%	1822	34.17%	1622	25.83%
	The operating system	890	16.42%	1705	31.98%	1452	23.12%
Website construction and maintenance		2180	40.33%	2953	55.38%	2824	44.98%
	programming language	910	16.84%	1112	20.86%	949	15.11%
	Database application	810	14.99%	967	18.14%	887	14.13%
Interpersonal communication		1234	22.83%	1757	32.95%	1977	31.49%
	Language ability	735	13.60%	1297	24.32%	1524	24.27%

The second-level indicators show that the top three indices in the first quarter of the class varied. Website construction and maintenance focused on the mastery of programming languages and the use of databases, accounting for about 15% of the total text. The rankings show that programming ability was no longer a major skill requirement for Website construction and maintenance, and more attention was paid to the level of the website itself. As for Basic knowledge of computers, more attention was being paid to Operating system skills. For skills in Interpersonal communication, language ability was most required.

Table 3. Skills indicators and skills keywords

1st Level Skills indicators	The top skills keywords in different quarter	1st Level Skills indicators	The top skills keywords in different quarter
Basic computer knowledge	Linux, Linux, Linux	Sales	Walmart, Amazon, Facebook
Website construction and maintenance	JavaScript, C++, Web	Marketing management	Data Analysis, Activities performed, Activities performed
Search engine optimization	Google, Google, Code optimization	Interpersonal communication	Communication, Experiences, Experiences
Office automation	Office, Office, Word	Professional quality	Learning ability Learning ability Learning ability

According to the Basic computer knowledge index, knowledge of Linux, Windows, iOS, Android, TCP/IP and other computer and mobile operating systems and computer protocols should still be mastered. Table 3 shows that JavaScript, Java, and C++ were the skills mainly required in the first quarter, while C++ and Web technology ranked first in the second and third quarters. For other skill indicators, there was no significant difference in the rankings of specific skills keywords in the three quarters. Google, code optimization frequently appeared under Search engine optimization. Office automation focused on the operation of office software and the writing of schedule text. Sales focused on the familiarity and understanding of major social platforms and online shopping platforms. Marketing management focused on data analysis and activities performed. In terms of Interpersonal communication, organizations wanted more communication skills and experience. In terms of Professional quality, organizations focused on individuals' learning ability.

The higher the keywords of a certain (type) skill are, the more basic the skill demand is and the more frequently it is used. In Figure 2, skill keywords for five job categories in different quarters are shown, with three colors representing three quarters. Technical class for technical requirements on data, for SQL has been a high concern. The product category has high requirements for data analysis. Design class requires a full understanding of product requirements and skilled use of Photoshop. Operation requires innovative ability of product solutions and post-implementation analysis. Marketing candidates are required to have a positive attitude towards work and customers.

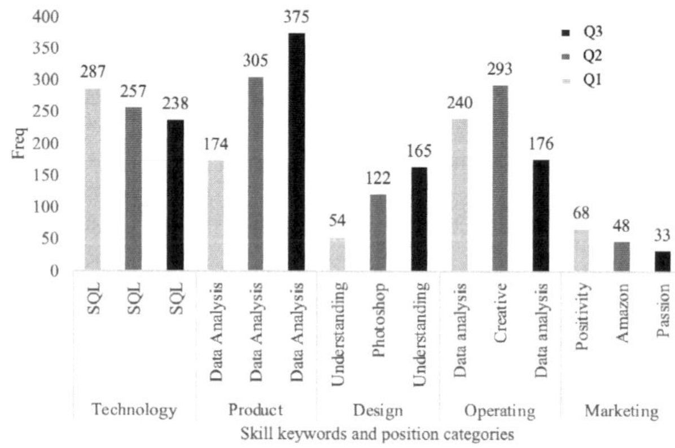

Figure 2. High-frequency skill words in position categories

Relevance in my study referred to the degree of correlation between documents consistent with the search criteria and the number of documents in the set of all documents that contained the specified skills dimensions or keywords. I computed the correlation using Equation 2.

Equation 2: $C= P_n/P_N=(n_s/n)/(N_s/N)=(n_s*N)/(n*N_s)$. Where C represents the correlation value. n is the frequency of a certain type of job post appearing in the recruitment information. N is the quantity of the total recruitment information data. P_n is the frequency of a specific type of skills keyword, S, appearing in certain types of recruitment information data. P_N is the frequency of a certain type of skills keyword appearing in the total recruitment information data. n_s is the frequency of a certain type of skills keyword, S, appearing in certain types of recruitment information data. N_s is the frequency of S in the total recruitment information data.

In addition, after data processing and analysis, I found that the correlation between each position category and the first-level skills index was generally consistent. Using the first quarter as an example, Table 4 shows the correlation between job categories and first-level skills in that quarter of 2021. Among them, Basic computer knowledge, Website Construction and maintenance, Sales and Search Engine optimization are most related to technical positions. Marketing Management, Professional Quality and Office Automation are more focused on operations. Interpersonal communication is most related to product positions.

Table 4. Relevance between position categories and skill indicators

1st Level Skill indicators	Relevance	1st Level Skill indicators	Relevance
Basic computer knowledge	Technical 3.6	Personal communication	Product 3.2
Website construction and maintenance	Technical 3.2	Professional quality	Operation 2.8
Sales	Technical 2.9	Search engine optimization	Technical 2.9
Marketing Management	Operation 3.2	Office automation	Operation 2.8

4.3 The Trends of Computer Industry Skills Demand

Because the amount of data gathered at each time step was essentially the same, I used the frequency as the observed value to facilitate analysis and calculation. I selected Programming languages, Database, Web development as related indicators using the frequency of the core skills of keywords as observations, including Java, JavaScript, C++, C#, Python, SQL, and CSS.

I used a test algorithm to observe the trend of the skill word itself. Finally, I computed the smoothing coefficient for each skills keyword after running a test algorithm for which I set the smoothing coefficient of all the skills keywords to be 0.8.

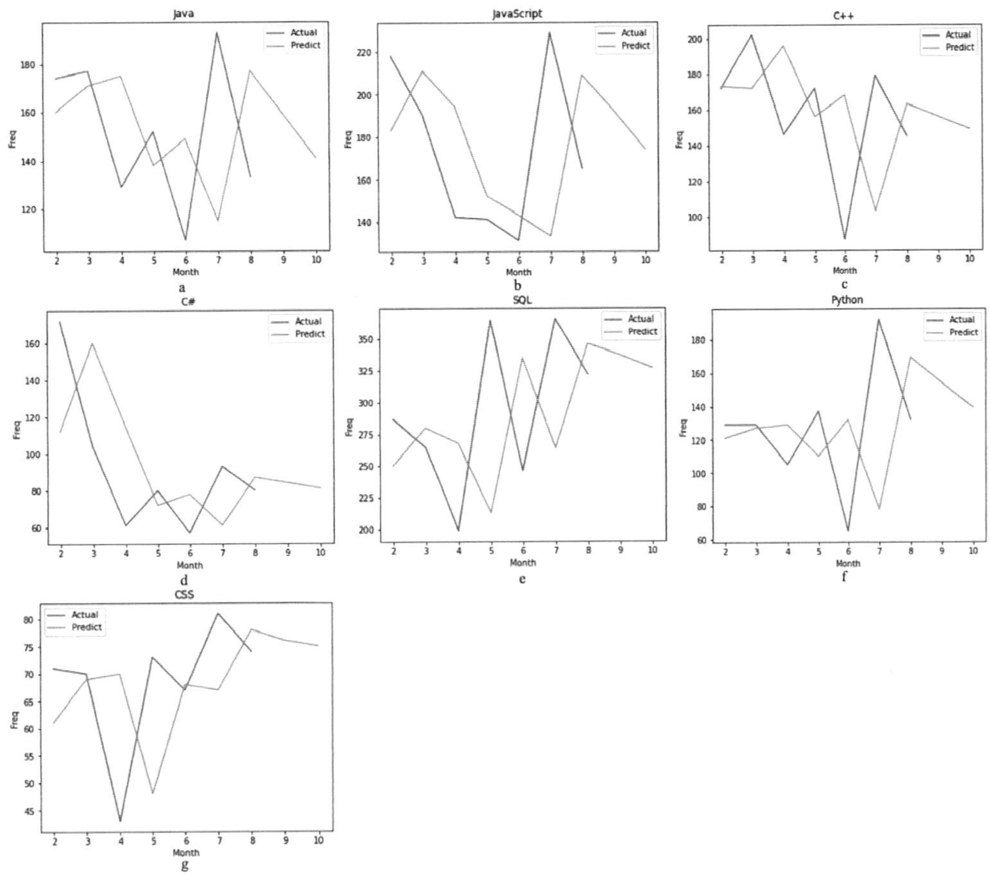

Figure 3. Actual (dark line) and predicted (light line) skills keyword for (a) "Java", (b) "JavaScript", (c) "C++",(d) "C#", (e) "SQL", (f) "Python", and (g) "CSS"

Figures 3(a) and (b) reveals a significant downward trend in spring for the skills keywords, Java and JavaScript. The figure shows a good fit of the predicted values to the observed values so I am confident that the algorithm can be used to predict the skills trend for the fourth quarter. Figures 3(c) and (d), show that the observed values of C++ and C# in April and June noticeably dropped. Moreover, the predicted value of C# sharply declined from the first quarter to the third quarter before stabilizing in the fourth quarter. The predicted results of skills keywords SQL and Python are shown in Figures 3(e) and (f). Both of these keywords had an overall upward trend, and the predicted values of the fourth quarter declined compared with the observed values of the third quarter. The figure also shows that the number of jobs requiring SQL and Python skills in the Canadian job market increased since the start of 2021. Because website development remains a popular profession, there is still high demand for this skill. Figure 3(g) for CSS shows that CSS had the same overall trend as the other keywords for which the observed values and predicted values increased. In the fourth quarter, the graph shows that CSS was predicted to decrease.

4.4 Suggestions for Training Industry Talent

From the perspective of businesses and other enterprise growth, I suggest that businesses and organizations develop their human resources continuously by making talent reserves, planning human resource needs in advance. Businesses should offer employees relevant business training with regards to the industry and general business background knowledge as it applies to operations of the organization. In addition, Business enterprises can also cooperate with colleges and universities to actively help orient training.

Regional governments can focus on policy. Regional governments can provide support in terms of capital, preferential terms, and talent introduction by formulating relevant policies. In addition, colleges and universities in these regions could create related professional and research institutions with regards to the demand for talent of computer-related industry.

Colleges and universities should pay more attention to the impact of such technological transformation on talent training and adjust their curriculum accordingly. I suggest that academic institutions address these higher level requirements. Practical experiences can be offered through classroom simulations and more cooperative training programs between institutions and businesses and organizations.

5. CONCLUSION AND FUTURE WORK

The purpose of my research was to analyze the characteristics of talent demand in the Canadian computer science industry and to forecast the future trends. I extracted keywords related to required skills from numerous recruitment information posts on three recruitment websites to construct a talent skills dictionary, and I analyzed the degree of correlation between skills and related job categories. Lastly, using a machine learning algorithm, I used timeseries analysis to analyze and forecast job demand trends with regards to my skills inventory of keywords. Combining my research results, the methods and technology of Big Data with emphasis on industry personnel training associated with business and organizational needs and the external environment factors, I confidently suggest improvements to talent training for the computer industry.

The following are some thoughts for future work:

There is a particular deviation between the actual results and expectations. In the future, I suggest in-depth research at longer time scales for the recruitment information data to further examine the need for computer science talent.

My time series analysis method is relatively simple and had few data variables, so the degree of confidence for the curve fitting was relatively poor. In the future, I hope to add more data and make more accurate predictions by using more complex time series methods, such as double exponential smoothing or triple exponential smoothing.

REFERENCES

Amudha, S., and Phil, M. 2017. *Web crawler for mining web data*. International Research Journal of Engineering and Technology, 3, 128-136.

Bekhradnia, B. 2007. *Demand for Higher Education to 2020 and beyond*. Oxford: Higher Education Policy Institute, Oxford, England.

Computing Technology Industry Association, 2020. CompTIA's IT Industry Outlook 2021. CompTIA, Downers Grove, USA. Retrieved from: https://www.comptia.org/content/ research/it-industry-trends-analysis

Feldman, R., and Dagan, I. 1995. Knowledge Discovery in Textual Databases (KDT). In *KDD*, Vol. 95, pp. 112-117.

Feldman R. et al. 1998. Text Mining at the Term Level[C]// Proceedings of the Second European Symposium on Principles of Data Mining and Knowledge Discovery. *Springer-Verlag*, pp. 65-73.

Hyndman, P. J, and Athanasopoulos, G. 2018. *Forecasting: Principles and practice*. OTexts.

Rijmenam, M. V. 2013. *A Short History of Big Data*. Data Floq. Retrieved from: https://datafloq.com/read/big-data-history/239

Vassakis, K., Petrakis, E., & Kopanakis, I. 2018. Big data analytics: applications, prospects, and challenges. In *Mobile Big Data*. Springer, Cham, pp. 3-20.

A FRAMEWORK FOR THE APPLICATION OF MACHINE LEARNING IN IS LITERATURE REVIEWS

Yusuf Bozkurt, Reiner Braun and Alexander Rossmann
Department of Computer Science, Reutlingen University, 72762 Reutlingen, Germany

ABSTRACT

The rapid development and growth of knowledge has resulted in a rich stream of literature on various topics. Information systems (IS) research is becoming increasingly extensive, complex, and heterogeneous. Therefore, a proper understanding and timely analysis of the existing body of knowledge are important to identify emerging topics and research gaps. Despite the advances of information technology in the context of big data, machine learning, and text mining, the implementation of systematic literature reviews (SLRs) is in most cases still a purely manual task. This might lead to serious shortcomings of SLRs in terms of quality and time. The outlined approach in this paper supports the process of SLRs with machine learning techniques. For this purpose, we develop a framework with embedded steps of text mining, cluster analysis, and network analysis to analyze and structure a large amount of research literature. Although the framework is presented using IS research as an example, it is not limited to the IS field but can also be applied to other research areas.

KEYWORDS

Systematic Literature Review, Machine Learning, Text Mining, Research Method

1. INTRODUCTION

The information systems (IS) research field is characterized by diversity, heterogeneity, and interdisciplinarity (Okoli, 2015; Tate et al., 2015). The IS research community originated in the 1960s and has proved its scientific orientation through solid research traditions (Paré et al., 2015). The rapid development and growth of existing knowledge has resulted in a rich stream of literature on various topics. IS research is becoming increasingly extensive, complex, and heterogeneous. Therefore, a proper understanding and timely analysis of the existing body of knowledge are important to identify emerging topics and research gaps (Bandara et al., 2011; Paré et al., 2015). IS researchers are often faced with the task of conducting a systematic literature review (SLR) of a domain, because the analysis of related works is the foundation of any scientific research process (Webster & Watson, 2002). High-quality literature should be systematically analyzed and synthesized to (1) provide a solid foundation for the research process, (2) contribute to IS knowledge, and (3) provide an agenda for the research domain. However, conducting a suitable SLR is not trivial, given the number of pitfalls to manage, such as the rapid growth of knowledge in the IS area (Bandara et al., 2011) and the heterogeneity and lack of consistency in metadata (Tate et al., 2015).

The interest in research methods with respect to SLRs in IS cannot be overlooked (Kitchenham & Charters, 2007; Levy & Ellis, 2006; Okoli, 2015; Webster & Watson, 2002). Leading journals often encourage authors to contribute to IS theory and methods (e.g., MISQ Theory and Review) (Paré et al., 2015). Furthermore, special issues such as the *CAIS Special Issue: The Literature Review in Information Systems* foster the development of corresponding methods. The intent of the current work is not to replicate the valuable prior work (Kitchenham & Charters, 2007; Okoli, 2015; Webster & Watson, 2002), and a list of all the different methods and approaches to SLRs is beyond its scope. On a meta level, a general process for SLR includes six steps: (1) formulating the problem, (2) conducting a literature search, (3) screening to include the relevant literature, (4) ensuring quality control, (5) extracting information, and (6) carrying out analysis and synthesis (Tate et al., 2015). Data analysis plays an important role in those steps. Therefore, Tate et al. (2015) note a relevant research gap in the area of SLRs: "We do not believe that discussion of the literature review in information systems reached saturation from this 'renaissance' of literature analysis methods publications. For example, the potential of 'big data'-type analytics using text-mining approaches in literature analysis remains relatively unexplored."(p. 108). Despite the advances of information technology in the context of big data, machine learning, and text mining, the implementation of SLRs in IS is in most cases still a purely manual task. This might lead to serious shortcomings in SLRs in terms of quality and time. Motivated by this challenge, we addressed the research question:

- *How can machine learning approaches be applied in SLRs to explore a broad research topic?*

To answer the research question, a framework was developed to support the SLR process with machine learning techniques. The framework contains steps for text mining, cluster analysis and network analysis to analyze and structure a large amount of text data. In this way, in an interdisciplinary field such as IS, insights are possible that are not immediately visible, the process of analyzing literature is accelerated and human bias in selecting and evaluating literature is counteracted.

A typical SLR is still characterized by a strong manual process (Bandara et al., 2011), but given the rapid development and growth in IS, this is becoming increasingly difficult. It is also important to conduct an effective literature review within a short time (Bandara et al., 2011; Tate et al., 2015). Therefore, the motivation of and justification for this study are due to four aspects: (1) the rapid growth of the literature volume, (2) the increasingly easy access to relevant articles, (3) the availability of work in electronic form, and (4) the transparent presentation of the developed method to support the IS community in the adoption and further development of machine learning and data analytics methods in SLRs. We contribute to the body of knowledge by addressing an important research method and extending it with machine learning techniques. Furthermore, we intend to provide a detailed description of the developed framework of a machine learning–supported literature review (ML-SLR) and an exemplary implementation. Although the approach is presented using IS research as an example, it is not limited to the IS field but can also be applied to other research areas.

We begin by presenting a collection of related work to investigate existing research using machine learning in SLRs. The selection of related work involves conventional methods and manual exclusion. The reason is that the scope of related work is quite narrow and the focus is on a limited area with a manageable amount of literature. Then, in section 3, we provide firstly an short overview of machine learning and text mining to familiarize the reader with some concepts. Subsequently, we describe the developed framework in its overall structure and explicate each phase. The framework is described in section 3 without referring to specific tools, as an exemplary implementation for the domain of smart city research with concrete tool and software suggestions are presented in the fourth section. Finally, the research concludes with a discussion and suggestions for further research.

2. RELATED WORK

The application of machine learning approaches in a literature review is not a completely novel approach. Current articles predominantly include the application of text mining and natural language processing in SLR. Therefore, we explored the existing literature to gain an understanding of the research structure and to clarify the position of the contribution of this work. For this purpose, we conducted an analysis on related works in the databases IEEE, ACM, EBSCOhost, and Web of Science. To obtain consistent results, each database was queried using the same search criteria. The starting point of the database search was the search string "text mining" OR "NLP" OR "natural language processing" AND "literature review" OR "literature analysis" queried on article titles. To ensure high quality of the sources, we considered only peer-reviewed articles by selecting article (journal)/proceedings as the document type. The results uncovered 82 articles from Web of Science, 62 articles from ACM, 23 articles from IEEE, and 10 articles from EBSCOhost. In total, the search delivered 177 articles. After excluding duplicates and articles that did not match the search criteria, the total number of valid articles were 69. A review of the titles and abstracts of these 69 articles indicated that 58 of 69 studies applied text mining as a technique. The review shows that text mining is common in the biomedical field e.g., to identify specific diseases, genes, drugs, and their relationships (Alshuwaier et al., 2017; Libbus & Rindflesch, 2002; Martin et al., 2004; Quan et al., 2014; Singhal et al., 2016).

Eleven of 69 papers are related on text mining systems and tools. For example, Phongwattana and Chan (2018) present a framework that uses text mining techniques to search for similar articles and to show the most relevant sentences of the identified works. This framework facilitates the search for suitable articles by using the whole abstract of an input article instead of searching with key words. Nuzzo et al. (2010) describe an automated method for analyzing scientific literature and extracting knowledge that consists of several tools and techniques. However, the approach is specifically adapted to biomedicine, in which special tools and databases support the analysis (e.g., Unified Medical Language System, Gene Extractor). The goals of it are to derive literature-based gene annotations and to identify correlations of diseases and genes. Mergel et al. (2015) address the methodology of performing a systematic literature analysis by using text mining but focus only on designing proper search strings by means of text mining. They present a method to optimize the search criteria by identifying additional relevant search terms in a research topic. The implemented tool for their approach extracts relevant search terms from selected articles by using text mining. IEEE Xplore is utilized as the database and provides meta-information and abstracts of the selected articles by the user. By selecting one article, further search terms are suggested based on article abstracts, and the researcher can build the search string in an iterative way (Mergel et al., 2015).

A gap remains with regard to the question of how machine learning can be embedded in the overall process of SLR. Especially there is little methodological work from this perspective within the IS community; most of the presented articles either use text mining procedures for their specific domain to identify relationships in the literature or deal with tools and systems for text mining. For example, Phongwattana and Chan (2018) state that their approach is well suited as a supplementary research tool; however, they do not discuss a methodological way or focus on text mining techniques for identifying suitable articles based on the article abstracts. Nuzzo et al. (2010) describe their text mining system as well as the method of knowledge generation using text mining, but they refer to the special field of biomedicine. Mergel et al. (2015) contribute to IS research by optimizing SLRs with text mining. They describe a method of iterative search string design; however, they do not discuss the details of implementation and only cover the task of search string building. The paper at hand contributes to IS research by supporting the whole process of conducting an SLR with machine learning approaches such as text mining and cluster analysis. It describes how machine learning and text mining can support an SLR, especially in fast-growing domains. An exemplary implementation in the field of smart cities provides ample details for a simple reconstruction of the process in other research domains. By maintaining the qualitative part of a traditional SLR, as described by several IS articles (e.g., (Kitchenham & Charters, 2007; Okoli, 2015; Webster & Watson, 2002)), our method can help in broad research fields such as smart cities ((Albino et al., 2015; Batty et al., 2012; Chourabi et al., 2012; Meijer & Bolívar, 2016)), and artificial intelligence ((Das et al., 2015; Nilsson, 1982; Peek et al., 2015)) to quickly establish a general understanding of the research topic without neglecting the qualitative and in-depth analysis of the most important articles.

3. APPROACH

3.1 Concepts

Machine learning deals with the extraction and analysis of patterns in data using concepts from statistics, text mining, and data mining (Das et al., 2015; Peek et al., 2015). Text mining refers to a collection of several computer-aided techniques, algorithms, and methods to extract implicit knowledge from unstructured text data. Text mining does not search for specific information, but rather aims to uncover patterns and relationships that human beings often cannot recognize because of the large amount of content. In contrast with data mining, the input data in text mining are unstructured in the form of documents, web pages, and so on (Gupta & Lehal, 2009; Hippner & Rentzmann, 2006; Hotho et al., 2005). A human-readable text is not usable for statistical procedures such as classification or clustering without computer-aided pre-processing (Hotho et al., 2005). For this reason, we define the process of analysis in four stages, which form the basis of the framework:

1. Data gathering: The building of source data set (in our case, text documents).
2. Text encoding: This step transforms text documents into a computable form. All words in the text document are extracted and represented as word vectors with a weighted value. The encoded text can be considered structured data.
3. Data mining: The structured data (text) is suitable for different data mining approaches.
4. Visualization: This step is not trivial; through interactive and proper visualization, humans can recognize patterns and relationships.

3.2 ML-SLR Framework

In general, the ML-SLR framework consists of two types of tasks, the human task and the machine task. In addition, artifacts are illustrated throughout the framework, which are either explicitly or implicitly produced after each task or serve as input for other tasks. The framework shows that the machine learning approach for conducting literature reviews is an iterative processing and the critical reflection by the researcher in some crucial tasks are necessary. The qualitative and critical mind of the researcher is supported by machines, but not replaced by them. The core of the framework is highlighted by the Machine Learning–Supported Phase (see Figure 1).

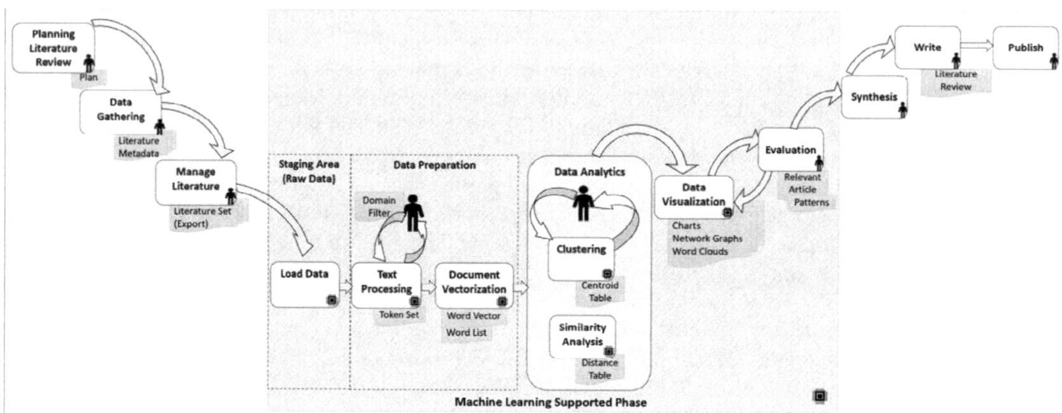

Figure 1. ML-SLR framework

The approach begins with the planning of the literature review – *Planning Literature Review*. The planning phase can be time-consuming, and we consider it one of the most important phases in the framework. It is important that fundamental considerations are made about the purpose and aim of the literature review. Answering some key questions can be helpful. For example, what is the purpose of the literature review? Who is the audience? Which research questions will the literature review answer? What is the search strategy (e.g., filters, databases), and how will the process be recorded? Here, the results form the artifact of this phase.

The *Data Gathering* task implements the defined search strategy. For this purpose, academic databases and search engines are queried. These databases allow a metadata export of the resulting articles as RIS, BibTex, or CSV files. The export data include title, author, journal, year of publication, abstract, and other information. In general, the goal is to extract as much information as possible, for potential use in data analysis. However, at least the abstract and the title of the article should be extracted, as the abstract is used for analyzing and the title for assigning. Analyzing abstracts is advantageous because these are usually written by the authors themselves and precisely summarize the core aspects of the article. Furthermore, as the word count is much lower than that of the full text, there is less "noise", which could falsify the analysis. The data gathering task results in several database exports in different formats.

The gathered data/literature is managed with a reference management software in the task *Manage Literature*. The use of such software is essential because it allows easy integration of the different database exports. Furthermore, duplicates in the data set can be easily identified and removed. After all database exports are integrated in the reference management software and all duplicates are removed, the entire library can be extracted as a CSV or XML file.

The first step in the *Machine Learning–Supported* phase is to import the literature set. The database should contain at least the abstracts and titles of articles. The imported raw data are loaded into the *Staging Area* of the analytics software – *Load Data*. The raw data must be transformed and prepared to apply analytical methods. These methods have their origin in the related discipline of data mining, in which structured data is analyzed. In text mining, however, the information is encoded in texts (in our case, article abstracts). Although humans are able to interpret and contextualize what they read, analytical methods cannot process this information, which is why we use the term unstructured data (Kaiser, 2009). Therefore, a data preparation phase is required to transform the abstract of each article into a computable structured form.

The *Data Preparation* phase consists of two tasks: *Text Processing* and *Document Vectorization* (text encoding). The *Text Processing* task involves splitting each document's text into single indexable elements. The ML-SLR framework segments the text on the word level. This operation is called "tokenization". With the extraction of words in single tokens, the complexity of subsequent analysis operations is reduced. On the one hand, this increases the quality of the analysis, and on the other hand, the whole process becomes more performant (Aggarwal & Zhai, 2012b; Weiss et al., 2010). For this purpose, the *Text Processing* task combines a set of operations for data preparation:

- Removal of stop words: Stop words in English are, for example, "a," "the," "this," "me," and "you" and are not necessary for the analysis. By filtering out these words, "background noise" in the data set is eliminated.
- Uniform spelling: Uniform spelling simplifies the analysis, which is why all tokens are converted to either lower- or uppercase letters.
- Filter tokens by length: An article abstract sometimes has a few tokens with only one letter. These either were tokenized incorrectly or are no longer meaningful. Therefore, a filter by token length (min. 2 letters) is recommended.
- Word stems: A word-stemming method can be used to reduce the complexity of the data set by returning the individual tokens to their basic form or to a uniform word stem (e.g., with the snowball-stemming algorithm). However, it has the disadvantage that the interpretability of the analysis results can be affected. Therefore, the necessity of word stemming should be examined for the respective application and research domain (Kaiser, 2009).
- Domain filters: Good data quality is the basis for any analysis. Therefore, a domain filter that removes certain irrelevant words is highly recommended. Especially in research articles, the abstracts often contain words such as "article" and "paper". To create such filters, the text mining process is first executed to determine the filter words from the resulting word list.
- N-grams: The complexity of the data set should be reduced, but in some cases, terms consist of two or more words and only make sense in combination. An example is "big data", which is a bigram (n = 2). N-gram algorithms are used to form such word combinations from single tokens. For example, a bigram algorithm combines two consecutive tokens and creates a new one containing both words. The use of n-grams should be considered individually, because it also generates irrelevant and meaningless combinations.

The *Text Processing* task creates a set of tokens for each article based on its abstract. The *Document Vectorization* task then transforms the data into an interpretable form and provides two artifacts, a word list and a document vector. The word list contains all tokens after the text processing and how often they occur. The document vector is created from the tokens of the word list and the loaded documents (articles). The tokens are represented in columns and the documents (e.g., with the title) in rows. Thus, each document becomes a vector through the use of a weighting method (e.g., term frequency–inverse document frequency) for the occurrence of a single token. Thus, the documents are presented in a structured form and can be analyzed with different data mining methods.

The analysis of texts can be divided into two basic procedures. The first is classification methods, in which a model is created by assigning (labeling) sample data sets (documents) to individual categories. This procedure is also called "supervised machine learning" (Aggarwal & Zhai, 2012a). The second procedure is clustering methods, in which similar data are clustered without a model or training data set. These methods do not require any pre-labeling by the researcher and are considered unsupervised machine learning (Feldman & Sanger, 2007). For our approach, we use unsupervised methods, because unknown structures in the data are to be determined without a target variable. The *Data Analytics* phase is structured as follows. Cluster algorithms group documents by their attributes and similarity values. This information is available in the vector space model, which has previously been built. For the determination of this similarity value, the cosine similarity has proved particularly suitable in the field of text mining (Li & Han, 2013). A good cluster result occurs if there is high thematic similarity of the documents within a cluster but dissimilarity to the other clusters. An important variable in clustering is the number of clusters to be generated (Hotho et al., 2005). Note that the number of clusters strongly depends on the preferred level of observation. For a high level of observation, in which the main topics of a research field should be highlighted, we recommend a low number of clusters. The number of clusters can always be increased to gain more detailed insights into the structure and sub-themes. In cluster analysis, the researcher should iteratively define several cluster sizes and evaluate the results, for which methods such as the elbow method can be helpful to determine the number of clusters. For each iteration, the centroid table of the cluster is stored. In addition to the assignment of single articles to clusters, the linking of single articles to each other (*Similarity Analysis*) is an important insight for a literature review. The output of the *Similarity Analysis* is a distance table, which shows the distance of each article to the remaining articles and can be used to create a network graph.

The artifacts created so far can be used for *Data Visualization*. For example, the word list can be used to create word clouds. The artifacts centroid table and distance table can be used to create network graphs.

The *Evaluation* phase goes hand in hand with the visualization. Various visualization options support the researcher in gleaning insights and recognizing patterns: Support points of each document and linkages to other documents help identify important articles for full text reading. Furthermore, visualizations on the clustering results highlight the research structure and key topics within the research domain. By adjusting the number of clusters, a drill-down and roll-up of the research structure can be realized, allowing a detailed or abstract view of the research domain.

In the *Synthesis* task, the researcher first evaluates and synthesizes all insights from the analyses and full text reading of the identified articles and then aggregates, organizes, and compares the extracted findings (Kitchenham & Charters, 2007; Okoli, 2015; Webster & Watson, 2002). The results of the synthesis flow seamlessly into the writing process.

The penultimate step of the ML-SLR framework is *Write*. As already described in the introduction section, writing the literature review in an accessible way is important, so that readers can follow all steps exactly. Also relevant is describing the steps and decisions taken and providing the protocol of the literature search and extraction. SLRs contribute greatly to the body of knowledge. For example, they can evolve into frequently cited works of literature because they provide a sound basis for other researchers to conduct their own research (Okoli, 2015; Paré et al., 2015; Webster & Watson, 2002). Therefore, the ML-SLR framework ends with the task *Publish*.

4. EXEMPLARY IMPLEMENTATION: SMART CITIES

In this paper, we demonstrate the ML-SLR framework using an exemplary implementation. The underlying research domain is smart cities, which are particularly suitable for the implementation because of its complex and heterogeneous structure and large number of publications. Given space limitations, we emphasize only the core of the ML-SLR framework in this example. A comprehensive description of the implementation is available on GitHub[1] to allow easy replication of the example.

4.1 Setup

We collected the data set for the example from four scientific databases: IEEE, EBSCO, ACM, and Web of Science. Only peer-reviewed articles with the terms "smart city" OR "smart cities" in the title and published in the 2009–2019 period were included in the search. Of the articles, 2264 came from IEEE, 453 from EBSCO, 325 from ACM, and 1828 from Web of Science. For the integration and management of the individual data exports, we used the reference management software Citavi 6 (Swiss Academic Software, 2021). After removing duplicates, we exported the entire library with 4219 articles in total as an Excel file. The exported

[1] https://github.com/yusufbzk/SLR-Text-Mining

data set was processed with RapidMiner according to the ML-SLR framework and visualized with Gephi. RapidMiner is a machine learning and data mining environment that is a suitable tool for the ML-SLR framework because of its text processing extensions (RapidMiner, 2021). For the visualization of interactive and complex graphs, we used the open source software Gephi (Gephi Consortium, 2021), with a focus on network analysis. The following subsections show the most important artifacts of the method. We explain how these can be interpreted and how they can support the SLR. Again, this is only an example, and derivations can differ from research domain to research domain.

4.2 Results of the Data Preparation and Text Mining Process

As input for the analysis in RapidMiner, we exported an Excel list from Citavi 6, which contains information about the article's author, title, year of publication, publishing journal or conference, the DOI number, and the abstract. As this information is to be combined with the other artifacts at a later time, we assigned each publication an ID number. A first indication of the subject areas appearing in the record comes from the frequently appearing words. Figure 2a), shows the created word cloud. A word cloud reflects the frequency of words and can serve as a first indication. That is, a word cloud gives an indication of the importance of the corresponding words and also how the topics can be divided into clusters. Therefore, the next step considers which words and topics may result when clustering is performed with the k-means algorithm.

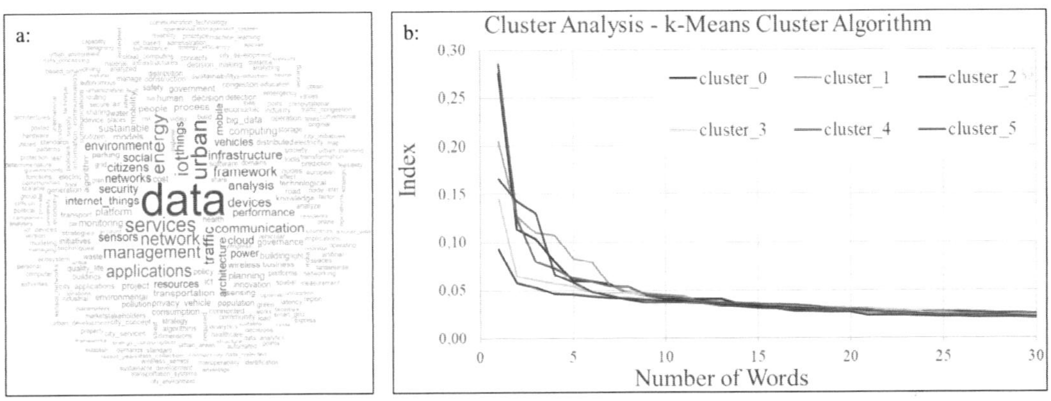

c:

Nr.	cluster_0		cluster_1		cluster_2		cluster_3		cluster_4		cluster_5	
1	iot	0.275	traffic	0.205	urban	0.093	data	0.146	energy	0.285	security	0.166
2	things	0.112	vehicles	0.126	social	0.058	network	0.065	power	0.125	services	0.142
3	internet_things	0.103	parking	0.109	governance	0.053	applications	0.061	consumption	0.080	privacy	0.130
4	devices	0.079	vehicle	0.107	sustainable	0.046	mobile	0.060	grid	0.073	citizens	0.066
5	waste	0.059	transportation	0.082	innovation	0.045	big_data	0.054	electric	0.062	data	0.059
6	data	0.059	road	0.078	citizens	0.044	cloud	0.048	electricity	0.059	city_services	0.048
7	applications	0.056	congestion	0.055	government	0.042	computing	0.047	energy_consumption	0.054	framework	0.044
8	iot_devices	0.046	mobility	0.048	economic	0.042	networks	0.047	buildings	0.054	architecture	0.040
9	services	0.044	car	0.045	initiatives	0.040	sensors	0.045	energy_efficiency	0.045	cyber	0.038
10	sensors	0.041	transport	0.044	analysis	0.040	sensing	0.043	building	0.044	infra_structure	0.037

Figure 2. a) Word cloud, b) centroid chart, c) centroid table with corresponding top 10 words

Figure 2c), shows the six clusters and the corresponding words in the clusters with their importance index. To evaluate which words and topics are still relevant for a cluster, displaying them graphically is helpful (see panel b). The index value of the words shows an exponential curve. As soon as the index value of the individual words in the clusters are resembling each other (in panel b at point 10), the individual topics and words can no longer be clearly assigned to the clusters. In the case described here, words with an index below 0.05 are no longer considered. Whether the classification of the clusters and the words is reasonable is now judged by the researcher.

4.3 Data Visualization and Evaluation

The last step of the implementation is to display the results in a network graph, which aids in visualizing the complex relationships. Figure 3 shows the network graph for the smart city area. Cluster 1 has two centers that are spatially separated from each other, cluster 4 has only one strong center that is close to cluster 2, and cluster 3 is strongly connected with all the other clusters. With regard to the individual topics in the clusters in Figure 2c), the following can be derived: the area mobility (cluster 1) has strong connections with the areas IoT and data (cluster 0), and the area data and big data (cluster 3) is connected with almost all the clusters.

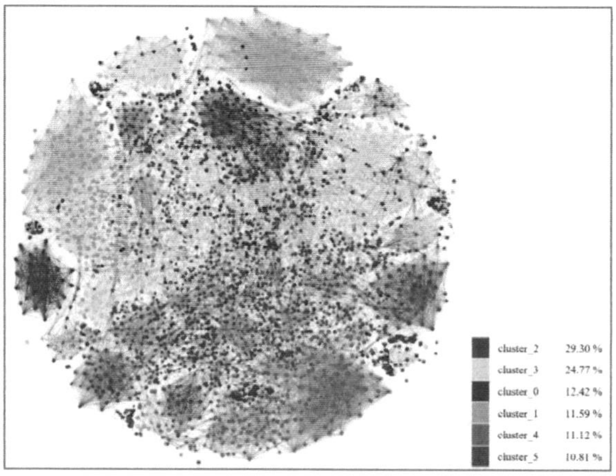

Figure 3. Network graph

5. DISCUSSION AND FURTHER RESEARCH

The main goal of this paper was to show a method for how machine learning can support SLR researches. Motivated by the heterogeneity of IS research and the increasing number of easily accessible literature streams in electronic form, we developed the ML-SLR framework. The framework is based on the insights of the established SLR methods in IS research and combines machine learning and text mining to facilitate analyses of literature, especially in extensive research domains. The framework begins with the planning phase of a literature review. This is an important phase because it is the fundamental basis of a literature review, in which the scope is defined, research databases are identified, and search criteria are determined. The results of a suitable analysis are based on its input, so the research team should pay special attention to this. The implementation of search criteria and the resultant collection of data from different research databases are not trivial steps. Dealing with research databases can be challenging, because different databases have different types of query syntax and generate different output data. The collected data can be created and exported relatively easily into a central library with a reference management software. We recommend to extract as much metadata about documents as possible, so that analysis possibilities are not limited from missing data. However, the minimum information to be collected is the abstract and title. This information is accessible to humans as text but cannot be processed in its raw form by machine learning techniques. Therefore, the first phase in the core of the framework is the transformation of the unstructured data (text) into structured data (vector space). This transformation requires the active involvement of the researcher, which means filtering out the domain-specific irrelevant words. In the context of data analytics, the clustering method and similarity analysis are used. The evaluation represents the last step in the core. During the evaluation phase, the researcher evaluates the results of the data visualization. Here, the structure of the research domain can be explored, networks and patterns can be revealed, and important articles can be identified. Furthermore, different visualizations based on different numbers of clusters allow different depths of analysis. It is important that all articles are clearly retrievable (e.g., with a unique ID and title assignment). This allows identifying important articles for full text reading. After this stage, the findings from the full text reading and insights of the data analysis of the entire library are integrated into a synthesis to write the final literature analysis. The framework is based on the combination of human knowledge and machine learning techniques. Thus, the critical view and creativity in writing are combined with the speed and ability of machine learning techniques to process large amounts of data.

The presented framework provides a solid basis to support the researcher in the preparation of an SLR. Individual researchers need to consider when this framework is suitable. For example, in the related work section we carried out the literature review manually using conventional approaches. The reason is that the scope for the related work is narrowly defined and the focus is on a limited area with a manageable number of articles. Therefore, this framework is particularly suitable for SLRs with following characteristics: (1) the research domain is interdisciplinary and its research streams are heterogeneous, (2) a large number of publications can be considered for analysis, and (3) the research streams cannot be estimated in advance. Finally, the outcome of such a literature analysis is the identification of the research structure, research streams, theories and concepts, trends, and the creation of a research agenda that highlights research gaps. Unsupervised methods can be used to perform data-driven analyses in unknown research domains with little manual effort. Here, the data can speak for themselves, and completely new aspects can emerge that would not have been known in advance. The framework is also relevant in rapidly growing areas, particularly in the IS domain, to help react quickly to trends. A large amount of data cannot be analyzed in a suitable time frame using conventional methods. As another contribution, the framework helps prevent human bias in the early phase of literature identification, thus avoiding manual exclusion based on title and abstract, which is inherent in conventional methods (Kitchenham & Charters, 2007; Okoli, 2015; Paré et al., 2015). Thus, no important information in the article or the article itself is filtered out as a result of human misinterpretation. Furthermore, titles do not fully reflect the precise content of articles, and as such, important information can be lost unless the researcher invests a great deal of time to read all of the abstracts in the selected literature. This time-consuming, and what can be an erroneous, process can be avoided by using our framework, which adds all the results of database queries into data analysis without human filtering. In this way, a large data set can be made accessible to the researcher.

As in any data analysis, data preparation plays an important role, as the analysis procedures are only as good as the data that go into the methods. Therefore, the data preparation should be individually adapted to each application domain. A limitation of this framework is that the researcher must interpret the formed clusters by him- or herself, whereas in conventional literature reviews, such clusters are derived from the theoretical knowledge. However, this limitation can be overcome by using a supervised method in the analysis that employs classification instead of clustering. This method helps build the model on the basis of established theory. A drawback, however, is that human bias can become a handicap when creating the training model. Thus, we recommend the validation of the tagging by a team of experts. In supervised machine learning, a given set of text documents is tagged by the user with classification examples that the algorithm should search for. The dataset tagged by the user constitutes the trained model. Subsequently, the trained model is used to evaluate new text documents according to the model (Carrizosa & Romero Morales, 2013; Cunningham et al., 2008; Liu et al., 2002). A supervised method can be applied in the presented framework in the data analytics phase. For this, the researcher needs to manually tag a given amount of articles into topics based on the abstract. Thereafter, the trained model is used to classify new articles.

Further research could extend the data analytics part of the framework by using a supervised technique. Analysis of full text instead of abstracts would also be a fruitful path for research. In this case, however, the data preparation phase of the documents needs to be more complex, because many factors can falsify the analysis, such as filler words and references, as can the related work section of an article. In the future, the planning phase could also be optimized by machine learning and text mining, with the search string creation approach by Mergel et al. (2015). According to them, one of the most challenging tasks in conducting a literature review is the proper selection of search terms of the search string. The affect of the search string on the output of a literature review is considerable, as it is one of the major input parameters and the starting point of a literature review. Using a weak search string can lead to irrelevant results or may even exclude relevant articles (Babar & Zhang, 2009; Dybå & Dingsøyr, 2008; Mergel et al., 2015). We will further evaluate the framework in the next step by conducting more systematic literature reviews. So far, two are currently under development in the research areas 1) data governance and 2) application of artificial intelligence in marketing. In addition, the framework will be iteratively improved and extended by feedback from other researchers.

REFERENCES

Aggarwal, C. C., & Zhai, C. (2012a). An Introduction to Text Mining. In C. C. Aggarwal & C. Zhai (Eds.), *Mining Text Data* (pp. 1–10). Springer US.

Aggarwal, C. C., & Zhai, C. (2012b). A Survey of Text Clustering Algorithms. In C. C. Aggarwal & C. Zhai (Eds.), *Mining Text Data* (pp. 77–128). Springer US.

Albino, V., Berardi, U., & Dangelico, R. M. (2015). Smart Cities: Definitions, Dimensions, Performance, and Initiatives. *Journal of Urban Technology*, *22*(1), 3–21.

Alshuwaier, F., Areshey, A., & Poon, J. (2017). A comparative study of the current technologies and approaches of relation extraction in biomedical literature using text mining. In *4th IEEE International Conference on Engineering Technologies and Applied Sciences (ICETAS).*

Babar, M. A., & Zhang, H. (2009). Systematic literature reviews in software engineering: Preliminary results from interviews with researchers. In *3rd International Symposium on Empirical Software Engineering and Measurement.*

Bandara, W., Miskon, S., & Fielt, E. (2011). A systematic, tool-supported method for conducting literature reviews in information systems. *Proceedings of the 19th European Conference on Information Systems (ECIS 2011).*

Batty, M., Axhausen, K. W., Giannotti, F., Pozdnoukhov, A., Bazzani, A., Wachowicz, M., Ouzounis, G., & Portugali, Y. (2012). Smart cities of the future. *The European Physical Journal Special Topics*, *214*(1), 481–518.

Carrizosa, E., & Romero Morales, D. (2013). Supervised classification and mathematical optimization. *Computers & Operations Research*, *40*(1), 150–165.

Chourabi, H., Nam, T., Walker, S., Gil-Garcia, J. R., Mellouli, S., Nahon, K., Pardo, T. A., & Scholl, H. J. (2012). Understanding Smart Cities: An Integrative Framework. In *45th Hawaii International Conference on System Sciences* (pp. 2289–2297). IEEE.

Cunningham, P., Cord, M., & Delany, S. J. (2008). Supervised Learning. In M. Cord & P. Cunningham (Eds.), *Cognitive Technologies. Machine Learning Techniques for Multimedia* (pp. 21–49). Springer Berlin Heidelberg.

Das, S., Dey, A., Pal, A., & Roy, N. (2015). Applications of Artificial Intelligence in Machine Learning: Review and Prospect. *International Journal of Computer Applications*, *115*(9), 31–41.

Dybå, T., & Dingsøyr, T. (2008). Strength of evidence in systematic reviews in software engineering. In D. Rombach, S. Elbaum, & J. Münch (Eds.), *Proceedings of the Second ACM-IEEE international symposium on Empirical software engineering and measurement* (p. 178). ACM Press.

Feldman, R., & Sanger, J. (2007). *The text mining handbook: Advanced approaches in analyzing unstructured data.* Cambridge University Press.

Gephi Consortium. (2021). *Gephi.*

Gupta, V., & Lehal, G. S. (2009). A Survey of Text Mining Techniques and Applications. *Journal of Emerging Technologies in Web Intelligence*, *1*(1).

Hippner, H., & Rentzmann, R. (2006). Text Mining. *Informatik-Spektrum*, *29*(4), 287–290.

Hotho, A., Nürnberger, A., & Paass, G. (2005). A Brief Survey of Text Mining. *LDV Forum - GLDV Journal for Computational Linguistics and Language Technology*, *20*, 19–62.

Kaiser, C. (2009). Opinion Mining im Web 2.0 — Konzept und Fallbeispiel. *HMD Praxis Der Wirtschaftsinformatik*, *46*(4), 90–99.

Kitchenham, B., & Charters, S. (2007). Guidelines for performing Systematic Literature Reviews in Software Engineering. *Technical Report No. EBSE-2007-01.*

Levy, Y., & Ellis, T. J. (2006). A Systems Approach to Conduct an Effective Literature Review in Support of Information Systems Research. *Informing Science: The International Journal of an Emerging Transdiscipline*, *9*, 181–212.

Li, B [Baoli], & Han, L. (2013). Distance Weighted Cosine Similarity Measure for Text Classification. In H. Yin, K. Tang, Y. Gao, F. Klawonn, M. Lee, T. Weise, . . . X. Yao (Eds.), *Lecture Notes in Computer Science. Intelligent Data Engineering and Automated Learning – IDEAL 2013* (Vol. 8206, pp. 611–618).

Libbus, B., & Rindflesch, T. (2002). NLP-based information extraction for managing the molecular biology literature. *Amia 2002 Symposium, Proceedings: Biomedical Informatics: One Discipline*, 445–449.

Liu, B., Lee, W. S., Yu, P. S., & Li, X. (2002). Partially supervised classification of text documents. In *ICML*.

Martin, E., Bremer, E., Guerin, M.-C., DeSesa, C., & Jouve, O. (2004). Analysis of protein/protein interactions through biomedical literature: Text mining of abstracts vs. text mining of full text articles. *Knowledge Discovery in Life Science Literature, Proceedings*, *3303*, 96–108.

Meijer, A., & Bolívar, M. P. R. (2016). Governing the smart city: a review of the literature on smart urban governance. *International Review of Administrative Sciences*, *82*(2), 392–408.

Mergel, G. D., Silveira, M. S., & da Silva, T. S. (2015). A method to support search string building in systematic literature reviews through visual text mining. In *Proceedings of the 30th Annual ACM Symposium on Applied Computing - SAC '15*.

Nilsson, N. J. (1982). *Principles of Artificial Intelligence* (1. Aufl.). Springer Berlin Heidelberg.

Nuzzo, A., Mulas, F., Gabetta, M., Arbustini, E., Zupan, B., Larizza, C., & Bellazzi, R. (2010). Text Mining approaches for Automated Literature Knowledge Extraction and Representation. *E-Health - for Continuity of Care, 160*, 954–958.

Okoli, C. (2015). A Guide to Conducting a Standalone Systematic Literature Review. *Communications of the Association for Information Systems*, *37*(1), Article 43, 879–910.

Paré, G., Trudel, M.-C., Jaana, M., & Kitsiou, S. (2015). Synthesizing information systems knowledge: A typology of literature reviews. *Information & Management*, *52*(2), 183–199.

Peek, N., Combi, C., Marin, R., & Bellazzi, R. (2015). Thirty years of artificial intelligence in medicine (AIME) conferences: A review of research themes. *Artificial Intelligence in Medicine*, *65*(1), 61–73.

Phongwattana, T., & Chan, J. H. (2018). A Combination of Text Mining Techniques for Relevant Literature Search and Extractive Summarization. In *Proceedings of the 2nd International Conference on Natural Language Processing and Information Retrieval - NLPIR 2018,* Bangkok, Thailand.

Quan, C., Wang, M., & Ren, F. (2014). An Unsupervised Text Mining Method for Relation Extraction from Biomedical Literature. *PloS One*, *9*(7).

RapidMiner. (2021). *RapidMiner Studio.*

Singhal, A., Simmons, M., & Lu, Z. (2016). Text mining for precision medicine: automating disease-mutation relationship extraction from biomedical literature. *Journal of the American Medical Informatics Association*, *23*(4), 766–772.

Swiss Academic Software. (2021). *Citavi.*

Tate, M., Furtmueller, E., Evermann, J., & Bandara, W. (2015). Introduction to the Special Issue: The Literature Review in Information Systems. *Communications of the Association for Information Systems*, *37*(1), 103–111.

Webster, R., & Watson, R. (2002). Analyzing the Past to Prepare for the Future: Writing a Literature Review. *MIS Quarterly*, *26*(2), 13–23.

Weiss, S. M., Indurkhya, N., & Zhang, T. (2010). *Fundamentals of predictive text mining. Texts in computer science.* Springer.

RETAIL SALES FORECASTING INFORMATION SYSTEMS: COMPARISON BETWEEN TRADITIONAL METHODS AND MACHINE LEARNING ALGORITHMS

Emerson Martins and Napoleão Verardi Galegale[1]
Centro Paula Souza – CPS, Brazil
[1]Prof. Dr.

ABSTRACT

Retail companies, as production systems, must use their resources efficiently and make strategic decisions to obtain growing and stable revenues, especially when market conditions are becoming more competitive and profit margins are increasingly pressured. Thus, sales forecasting is crucial to maintain competitiveness in the retail segment, but obtaining inaccurate forecasts can lead to stock shortages, causing delays in deliveries and generating customer dissatisfaction, as well as increasing inventory, increasing the cost of warehousing, forcing the "burn" of stock through promotional campaigns, directly affecting profitability. Forecasting the demand for products and services and adapting the supply chain by finding a balance has always been and will continue to be a challenge in the retail segment. This research aims to evaluate the main methods and identify the one with the greatest accuracy in sales prediction. Based on an integrative literature review (ILR), three main methods were evaluated: time series, artificial neural networks and machine learning algorithms. The results show that machine learning is more suitable in terms of accuracy, particularly when models contain exogenous and endogenous variables, in addition to allowing the identification of hidden patterns in demand that can be used to identify market trends. However, in markets with constant demands and few external interferences, its use is not justified because, for these cases, the use of time series is simpler and less costly.

KEYWORDS

Sales Forecast, Retail, Machine Learning, Time Series, Productive Systems

1. INTRODUCTION

In the last two decades, computing power has evolved considerably, in this context we can mention: large data storage, more robust processors, faster internet connection, among other examples. Problems that seemed to be extremely complex or costly to solve are now within our reach. New trends such as Big Data, Cybersecurity, Internet of Things (IoT) and blockchain have emerged, jointly exploiting the technological advances mentioned above. The IoT, which aims to use embedded systems, including sensors and actuators, together with the internet, to allow control and immediate access to information in real time (Atzori, 2010; Cecchinel, 2014), represents one of these challenges, as the report of "Juniper Research", informs that by 2024 we will have more than 83 billion devices and sensors connected (IoT). In addition, some of these devices will have the ability to generate significant amounts of data on the order of Zettabytes, information that can be valuable for a company's strategy, so sales forecasting cannot ignore these new trends; it must use it to support competitive advantage.

Currently, data processing through information systems to generate knowledge has become vital for decision makers, particularly in some important areas such as forecasting sales of retail products or services, in which external variables such as weather or global economy can affect people's consumption decisions (Krawczyk, 2016).

One of the recent and popular techniques aimed at tackling these new business challenges is Big Data Analytics (BDA). A precise definition of BDA is given in Hofmann (2018). In short, it is the alignment of Big Data and Machine Learning (ML) techniques to provide reliable insights for decision making. ML and Big Data benefit from each other as they can be coupled to create more complete models. Furthermore, the main purpose of the BDA is to transform information into useful knowledge.

Predictive analytics, in turn, encompasses methods that use information to create models and perform simulations that will provide insights into future events, allowing the most attentive executives to be able to predict strategic actions that improve their company's performance. By definition, the results obtained through these techniques are not 100% accurate, as no method can predict the future, so a good predictive analysis is one that provides the most accurate results in a reasonable time (Castilho *et al*, 2017).

One of the common uses of predictive analytics in business is sales forecasting – this point will be covered in section 3 of this paper – but there are also several other applications in domains such as: cost estimation, where (Loyer *et al*, 2016) applied techniques of ML to quickly estimate the cost of manufacturing aircraft engine components. In the performance evaluation, (Fan *et al*, 2013) used ML to estimate the performance of the supply chain based on the "5 Dimensional Balanced Scorecard" (5DBSC), in order to provide quick results and avoid biased performance evaluations by the managers.

The machine learning (ML) or machine learning approach can be described as the study of computer algorithms that automatically improve with experience. It is treated with an artificial intelligence (AI) subarea. Machine learning algorithms build a model based on sample data, known as "training data", in order to make predictions or decisions without being explicitly programmed to do so. Machine learning algorithms are used in a wide variety of applications, such as email filtering and computer vision, where it is difficult or impractical to develop conventional algorithms to perform the necessary tasks (Raschka *et al*, 2017).

Humans learn through experience, we use a process of trial and error to figure out what actions should be taken under certain circumstances. This allows us to make abstractions and build knowledge. ML is somewhat similar, it can be seen as algorithms that aim to improve a performance measure, automatically deriving their own rules and creating their own decision models based on certain information (Raschka *et al*, 2017) and Mitchell (1997).

In this context, the purpose of this paper is to provide an insight into the latest ML techniques applied to retail sales forecasting through an ILR. The question that guided the research can be posed as follows: Is ML more suitable than traditional methods of forecasting retail sales, in terms of accuracy, particularly when the models contain exogenous and endogenous variables?

2. RESEARCH METHODOLOGY

For this descriptive and qualitative research, an ILR was carried out on the use of ML to forecast sales in the retail segment. The PRISMA-P protocol was used, this protocol aims to support researchers to improve the reporting of systematic reviews and meta-analyses, filtering the number of publications with greater relevance to the research topic (Moher *et al*, 2015)

In the identification stage, a search was performed for publications in the Google Scholar, Microsoft Academic and Scopus databases, with the following search string: (("Sales Forecasting" OR "Sales Predictions" OR "Predictive") AND ("Machine Learning" OR "Algorithm" OR "Big Data Analytics") AND Retail"), in the period from 2015 to 08/2021. 1,022 publications were returned.

In the screening stage, 87 Books were removed, 159 publications classified as HTML and PDF, 13 Conference Papers and 7 publications classified as "Other", totaling 266 records excluded, resulting in 756 records selected for the next stage. The inclusion and exclusion criteria of the studies are presented in Table 1.

Table 1. Criteria for inclusion and exclusion of studies

Inclusion criteria
It helps to define what sales prediction is and the impact of exogenous and endogenous variables
Helps categorize types of ML algorithms
Presents accuracy metrics for evaluating ML algorithms
Exclusion Criteria
Duplicate paper
Other literatures, that is, they are not scientific papers (theses, books, dissertations, interviews, etc.)
Search outside the scope of interest

In the eligibility stage, 193 papers without an H-Index were excluded, 43 papers whose access is not public, 488 papers whose title and keywords are not related to the objective of this research. After exploratory analysis of the remaining 32 papers, 23 papers with low adherence to the research topic were discarded, as the content of the papers did not present metrics used to assess the performance of the algorithms presented. Thus, 9 publications were selected for qualitative analysis as shown in Table 2.

Table 2. Papers selected for this research

	Title	**Author**	**Year**
01	Machine learning methods for demand estimation	P Bajari, D Nekipelov, SP Ryan, M Yang	2015
02	A machine learning framework for customer purchase prediction in the non-contractual setting	A Martínez, C Schmuck, S Pereverzyev Jr	2020
03	Retail forecasting: Research and practice	R Fildes, S Ma, S Kolassa	2019
04	A deep learning approach for the prediction of retail store sales	Y Kaneko, K Yada	2017
05	Sales forecasting by combining clustering and machine-learning techniques for computer retailing	IF Chen, CJ Lu	2017
06	Intelligent Sales Prediction Using Machine Learning Techniques	S Cheriyan, S Ibrahim, S Mohanan, S Treesa	2018
07	Applying computational intelligence methods for predicting the sales of newly published books in a real editorial business management environment	Castillo, P.A., et al	2017
08	Sales-forecasting of retail stores using machine learning techniques	A Krishna, V Akhilesh, A Aich	2018
09	Comparison of different machine learning algorithms for multiple regression on black friday sales data	CSM Wu, P Patil, S Gunaseelan	2018

3. INTEGRATIVE LITERATURE REVIEW (ILR)

Traditional forecasting methods are based on time series, this means that they are applied under the assumption that past demand can statistically estimate future demand. Typically, these methods are easy to apply and perform well in markets where demand is mostly stable (Chopra *et al*, 2013). Unfortunately, we have many cases where this scenario cannot be applied, as demand often depends on exogenous factors that are not effectively represented by past values. For example, on-demand transport services such as UBER cannot estimate their demand just relying on time series, they must take into account other elements such as weather conditions, time of day, day of the week (Ke *et al*, 2017).

To satisfy this need, other types of forecasting, known as causal modeling, propose methods that include exogenous elements, such as macroeconomic variables, weather conditions, marketing strategies, etc. (CHOPRA *et al*, 2013). These techniques allow us to face the limits found in time series models. In this sense, ML itself could be considered as a causal modeling provider because it can deal with time series, categorical variables, fuzzy variables, text analysis, images and other elements.

ML has been applied to sales forecasting since 1980 through methods such as Artificial Neural Networks (ANN) (Hippert *et al*, 2001). Over the past two decades, these methods have yielded interesting results and demonstrated some potential, but several ANN search applications were not valid due to validation or implementation issues (Adya, *et al*, 1998). This problem was probably caused by the scarcity of data to effectively train ANNs, as this technique has a good generalizability, but it needs a lot of data, well distributed data and time for training. Previous limitations, such as limited storage capacity, low computing power and slow internet connections, could have influenced the reluctance to use ML in forecasting sales.

Nowadays, ML enjoys a good reputation, probably because most of the aforementioned restrictions have been overcome. Thanks to this, new applications were published leading to new trends and techniques. To identify these new trends and meet the objective of this research, a literature study was carried out, according to the steps described in section 2.

As a result, 9 publications presented in Table 2 were selected. For each study, the objective of the application, the type of resource found in the dataset, the method used for data pre-processing and the ML techniques used for sales prediction are presented. Some nomenclatures are used in this paper: (T) - Time series variables (past sales); (Ve) - Endogenous model variables (price, POS number, period of sale); (Vx) - Exogenous model variables (Weather, time of day, day of the week (weekend), spatial location, seasonality, unemployment rate, inflation rate, population size, average income).

In the paper (Bajari *et al*, 2015), 1,510,563 sales transactions were analyzed in a supermarket chain with 3,149 stock keeping units or SKUs (Stock Keeping Units), the data was collected through IRI Marketing Research through an academic license from the university. of Chicago. 25% of the data was used as a validation sample, 15% for validation and 60% for training. The RMSE root mean square prediction error metric was used to assess the accuracy of the methods used. As a result, the RF and SVM algorithms presented an accuracy of 65% and 15% respectively, while the traditional Linear Regression method presented 6% of precision.

(Martínez *et al*, 2020) highlights that one of the main challenges of retail is to differentiate customers who made a punctual purchase and do not intend to make new purchases, from customers who are more likely to make regular purchases but are "paused" between a purchase and other. It is accepted by business wisdom and research literature that it costs five to ten times more to acquire a new customer than it does to retain an existing customer (Daly, 2002; Bhattacharya, 1998). In this study, a data set with more than 10,000 customers and 200,000 purchase transactions was used, and the GTB method achieved the best performance, achieving 89% accuracy and 0.95 (AUC - Area Under The Receiver Operating Characteristic Curve) in predicting monthly purchases in the test dataset.

In (Fildes *et al*, 2019), the authors perform a benchmark through a literature review comparing the results of other researchers in various scenarios in the retail segment, confirming that time series models have been widely used to forecast aggregate retail sales, where Simple Exponential Smoothing and its extensions, together with ARIMA models, have been the most used time series models for sales forecasts, but due to dependence on limited data or use of inadequate evaluation metrics, such as sample adjustment, some researchers have found that standard time series models are sometimes inadequate to assess aggregate retail sales, identifying evidence of nonlinearity and volatility in the retail sales time series, for example (Alon *et al*, 2001; Chu & Zhang , 2003; Kuvulmaz, Usanmaz, & Engin, 2005; Zhang & Qi, 2005), they resorted to nonlinear models, especially artificial neural networks. The results indicate that traditional time series models with a stochastic trend, such as Simple Exponential Smoothing and ARIMA, performed well when macroeconomic conditions are relatively stable, however, when economic conditions are volatile (with rapid changes in economic conditions), Artificial neural network ANNs have been claimed to outperform linear methods (Alon *et al*, 2001). As a result, Clustering techniques and DT algorithms showed the best results for forecasting sales for new items with limited historical data. In another scenario, 2 mass brands were evaluated in two different retail stores, with a history of three years of daily sales in promotional products, the SVM and ANNs methods showed better results.

In the study (Kaneko and Yada, 2017), three-year data from a point-of-sale (POS) collected between 2002 and 2004 from a supermarket located in the Kanto region of Japan were used, in order to predict the sales volume of the next day, applying Deep Learning (DP) methods in comparison with the LGR logistic regression model. Sales data were grouped into three categories according to product attributes: Category 1 (62 attributes), Category 2 (569 attributes) and Category 3 (3,312 attributes). The three years of data were divided so that 80% was used for learning and 20% for verification. As a result, the DL was superior to the LGR obtaining an accuracy of 86%.

In (Chen and Lu, 2017), actual sales data from 124 points of sale between Jan-2005 and Sept-2009 of three large retailers with domain in computer products in the Taiwan region were grouped. Three products were considered for the sales history: Computers (PC), Notebooks (NB) and Liquid Crystal Displays (LCD). In the study, three clustering data clustering techniques were compared: SOM, GHSOM and K-Means, together with two ML algorithms: SVM and ELM. The data sets PCs, NBs and LCDs were subjected to six cluster-based prediction models and also in isolation using two machine learning techniques (single SVR) and (single ELM), that is, without using a clustering algorithm. The first 88 points of sale (71% of the sample) are used as a training sample, while the remaining 36 points of sale (29% of the sample) are used to forecast sales. Two evaluation criteria were used to measure sales performance: MAPE and RMSPE.

The experimental result demonstrated that of the 8 models created the combination of the GHSOM clustering with the ELM machine learning algorithm provided superior performance for all 3 selected products.

In (Cheriyan *et al*, 2018), it is highlighted that the precision in the sales forecast has a great impact on the business. Data mining techniques are very effective tools in extracting hidden knowledge from a huge dataset to increase prediction accuracy and efficiency. Organizations face serious challenges to identify a data mining technique and an effective presale strategy (Mathew *et al*, 2015), due to the exponential growth in the volume of data used in e-commerce transactions. Traditional forecasting methods are difficult to handle a large amount of Big Data data, in this context the Data Mining data mining technique becomes a strong ally in sales prediction. At the organizational level, sales forecasts are essential inputs to support decision making in various business areas, such as operations, marketing, sales, production, logistics, inventory, finance (cash flow). With almost 85,000 records, the initial database considered in this research was reduced after pre-processing due to redundant records as well as irrelevant information for analysis. The dataset used for this paper is based on a fashion store with three consecutive years (2015 to 2017) of sales data. In this paper, three ML algorithms were compared: GTB, DT and GLM, which showed 98%, 71% and 64% accuracy respectively.

(Castillo *et al*, 2017) mentions the problem of predicting sales for newly launched products on the market. For this study, sales data consisting of 6000 books from a Spanish publisher Trevenque Editorial S.L were collected, whose data were analyzed using the SOM classifier and two pre-processing techniques: Correlation-based feature selection and Relief for attribute estimation. This is a challenge for the industry, as printing a much larger number of volumes than those eventually sold will lead to losses, while printing an adequate number of copies will optimize the publisher's sales and profits. In addition, there are several difficulties inherent in forecasting new book sales, such as the limited amount of historical data or market variability (fads, seasonality) that make the task of predictive methods difficult. As a result, the DT and RF algorithms showed the highest precision and the best performance.

In the paper (Krishna *et al*, 2018), the precision of different algorithms in the dataset extracted from the website https://www.kaggle.com/ was compared, where AdaBoost and GTB presented RMSE of 1,350 and 1,088 respectively, thus GTB presented lower error rate, therefore better precision in the evaluated dataset.

In the paper (Wu *et al*, 2018), a dataset with 550,000 sales transactions is collected from a retail company to train supervised ML algorithm to predict the amount of customer purchases, enabling the creation of personalized offers according to their consumption profile. customers during the Black Friday period. In the research, it is highlighted that in ML algorithms, the data set used must be balanced, that is, all classes must contain the same number of samples, otherwise, the prediction or classification will be biased towards that category of data in which the data is skewed, meaning a good ML algorithm is useless without the proper data. The accuracy of the prediction model depends on the reliability of the data it is built on, however, real world data is often confusing and needs cleaning, to aid in this task there are pre-processing techniques. As a conclusion it is highlighted that complex models such as neural networks are overkill to deal with simple problems such as regression, in this way we can use simpler models together with pre-processing to obtain better results. In the applied ML methods, XGBoost which internally uses SR and RR presented the best precision with 2400 RMSE. It is evident that ML can be applied to forecast sales in a wide range of different types of products.

(Bajari *et al*, 2015; Fildes *et al*, 2019; Castillo *et al*, 2017) highlight that methods such as RF and DT provide an unparalleled level of interpretation, together with good accuracy and decreasing computation time.

Most studies include endogenous inputs and exogenous (Fildes *et al*, 2019; Castillo *et al*, 2017) in their models, which shows the good flexibility of ML to handle a wide range of inputs. Furthermore, (Castillo *et al*, 2017) addressed the problem of implementing sales forecasting in new products for which historical sales data is not available. For this, historical data from other products were used, along with endogenous variables, such as the number of weeks on sale and the retail price.

In (Cheriyan *et al*, 2018; Castillo *et al*, 2017; Krishna *et al*, 2018; Wu *et al*, 2018) data pre-processing techniques were effectively applied, which resulted in simpler models, lower computational cost and good precision. As we are in an era with a high volume of data being generated daily, this causes noisy and meaningless variables, so analysing the most relevant variables in real world applications is mandatory, this way we can differentiate whether a model will be useful or not.

3.1 Comparing Machine Learning and Traditional Forecasting Methods

Traditional models offer enormous advantages in terms of simplicity and accuracy, as they can forecast sales in a matter of seconds for multiple SKUs (Yu *et al*, 2011). However, they need to be designed by an expert who can tailor it to the company's needs. Also, do not include exogenous variables. ML models partially solve this problem because they can include other types of data, such as endogenous and exogenous variables, allowing a better representation of reality. Furthermore, ML techniques that are correctly implemented outperform most traditional forecasting methods (Yu *et al*, 2011). In order to assess whether this statement is valid in our study of the literature, the Table 3 mentions which were the traditional and ML models applied by the authors and which had better accuracy.

Table 3. Comparison of ML with traditional sales forecasting methods

Paper	Application	Data Set	Pre-processing technique	Statistical and/or classification methods	Evaluation metrics	ML	Model with better accuracy
01	Grocery, 6-year database – 3,149 SKU and 1,510,563 sales transactions	T, Ve	-	Linear Regression	RMSE	SR, FSR, LASSO, SVM, Bag, RF	RF, SVM
02	10,000 customers and 200,000 purchase transactions	T, Ve	-	-	Precision, AUC	GTB, LASSO, ELM	GTB
03	482 textile items with 52 weeks of sales history. 2 pasta brands from 2 different retail stores, with 3-year historical data with daily sales	T, Ve, Vx	-	Simple Exponential Smoothing, ARIMA ARIMA, ETS e HW	RMSE, MAPE, MdAPE	DT SVM, ANN	DT, SVM, ANN
04	Three-year data from a point-of-sale (POS) collected between 2002 and 2004 from a supermarket located in the Kanto region of Japan	T, Ve	-	Logistic Regression	Accuracy, Precision, Recall, F-measure, AUC	-	DL
05	Actual sales data from 124 points of sale from Jan-2005 to Sept-2009 of three large IT-domain retailers in Taiwan region	T, Ve	-	SOM, GHSOM, K-Means	MAPE, RMSPE	SVR, ELM	GHSOM + ELM
06	Actual sales data collected from a fashion store for three consecutive years (2015 to 2017)	T, Ve	outlier detection	-	Accuracy, Error Rate, Precision, Recall, Kappa	GLM, DT, GTB	GTB

07	Sales forecast for new books	T, Ve, Vx	Correlation-based feature selection, Relief for atribute estimation	Multiple Linear Regression	MAE, RMSE, RAE, RRSE	ELM, KNN, DT, ANN, RF, SVM	DT, RF
08	Kaggle dataset, with 8,523 entries	T, Ve	Outlier detection, including missing values	Multiple Regression, Polynomial Regression, Ridge Regression	RMSE	AdaBoost, LASSO, GTB	GTB
09	Dataset with 550,000 transactions in the Back Friday period	T, Ve	Transforming categorical data into numerical data	Logistic, Polynomial, Stepwise, Ridge, Lasso and Elastic Regression	RMSE	LR, MLK, DL, DT, Bagging, XGBoost	XGBoost

The fact that ML outperforms traditional models in the sales forecasting landscape does not necessarily mean that companies should change their forecasting tools. This leads us to consider an important question: when should companies invest in ML for sales forecasting?

Sales forecasting must be flexible and responsive, especially when it comes to short-term forecasting, which is needed in industries like retail. Forecast calculation should be agile as most companies have hundreds or even thousands of SKUs, all of which may need an immediate estimate.

Even though data pre-processing techniques can substantially reduce computing time, they are still complex and therefore costly to establish in a company, as they require skilled people with adequate equipment. This difficulty is especially present in small companies, where available resources are limited and employees rarely have advanced knowledge on the subject. In this case, if a company is positioned in a stable market and if historical demand is sufficient to achieve good sales forecast accuracy with traditional methods, this company should postpone the migration to ML techniques until it really identifies an added value in use them.

On the other hand, if a company sells products in a market subject to constant evolution, where it is mandatory to be at the forefront of trends for being competitive, ML models for sales forecasting will be a valuable asset. However, it is not an easy change, as companies must guarantee three fundamental aspects: data storage capacity, data processing capacity and employee qualification. Data storage is essential, as ML needs to deal with Big Data for good performance, and this requires large storage capacity, as well as data processing capacity can vary from simple models to more robust models (Zhou *et al*, 2017); therefore, the company must consider its objectives versus the resources it needs.

In short, a company should choose to use ML over traditional sales forecasting methods when its economic environment really requires a digital transformation, and when the company is able to muster the necessary resources to take on the challenge of projecting future sales.

4. CONCLUSION

Dealing with a high volume of data is one of the most common challenges posed by modern business trends. As data has become one of the most valuable resources, sales managers are eager to extract relevant information that will lead to a competitive advantage. This paper conducted a literature study to investigate the application of ML in sales forecasting as a method to achieve this advantage. Nine recent research papers that apply ML to sales forecasting were selected and analyzed to identify new trends. One of the findings was that ML extends the reach of sales prediction, as it is capable of dealing with complex variables. More precisely, ANN approaches have shown excellent performance when dealing with imprecise data such as exogenous variables, while DT and RF offer incredible interpretability. Furthermore, data pre-processing techniques have been proven to substantially reduce the complexity of models, allowing both good accuracy and reasonable computation time.

As the process of adapting a company to new technologies often comes with doubts raised by uncertainty, a comparison between ML and traditional forecasting methods was made with the aim of providing insights to managers who are willing to implement ML in their processes. The results of this study show that ML is more suitable than traditional forecasting methods in terms of accuracy, particularly when models contain both exogenous and endogenous variables. In addition, it allows the identification of hidden patterns in demand that can be used as a baseline to identify new market trends.

In the findings, it is evident that the absence of a reliable training base, that is, one that accurately reflects real-world transactions, affects the algorithm's efficiency, containing biases that make its usefulness unfeasible. Furthermore, it is found that in markets with constant demands and few external interferences, the use of ML is not justified, because for these cases the use of traditional methods through time series is simpler and less costly.

For further research, a similar study should be carried out on data pre-processing techniques, as they offer significant advantages in terms of computational cost reduction in the application of ML models. In addition, the processing cost and time for each method must be evaluated. Finally, addressing these new trends for small businesses is vital as they are numerous but often lack the financial means or experience to implement disruptive technologies.

ACKNOWLEDGEMENT

I first thank God, who allowed all the achievements in my life to materialize. Thanks to CPS, which gave me the knowledge I needed to complete this work. Thanks to my advisor for all the help and guidance. I thank my mother, wife and son for their understanding of my absence at various times.

REFERENCES

Adya, M. and Collopy, F., 1998 - *How effective are neural networks at forecasting and prediction? A review and evaluation*. - Journal of Forecasting.

Alon, I. et al, 2001 - *Forecasting aggregate retail sales: A comparison of artificial neural networks and traditional methods* - Journal of Retailing and Consumer Services.

Atzori, L. et al, 2010 - *The internet of things: A survey* - Computer Networks.

Bajari, P. et al, 2015 - *Machine learning methods for demand estimation* – American Economic Review

Bhattacharya, C. B., 1998 - *When customers are members: Customer retention in paid membership contexts* - Journal of the academy of marketing science.

Castillo, P.A. et al, 2017 - *Applying computational intelligence methods for predicting the sales of newly published books in a real editorial business management environment* – Knowledge-Based Systems

Cecchinel, C. et al, 2014 - *An architecture to support the collection of big data in the internet of things*. - IEEE World Congress on Services.

Chen, I-F. and Lu, C-J., 2017 - *Sales forecasting by combining clustering and machine-learning techniques for computer retailing* – Neural Computing and Applications

Cheriyan, S. et al, 2018 - *Intelligent Sales Prediction Using Machine Learning Techniques* – 2018 International Conference on Computing, Eletronics & Communications Engineering (iCCECE)

Chopra, S. and Meindl, P., 2013 - *Supply Chain Management* - Pearson Education, Inc.

Chu, C. W. and Zhang, G. P., 2003 - *A comparative study of linear and nonlinear models for aggregate retail sales forecasting* - International Journal of Production Economics.

Daly, J. L., 2002 - *Pricing for profitability: activity-based pricing for competitive advantage* – Vol. 11 - John Wiley & Sons.

Fan, X., et al, 2013 - *An evaluation model of supply chain performances using 5DBSC and LMBP neural network algorithm* - Journal of Bionic Engineering.

Fildes, R. et al, 2019 - *Retail forecasting: Research and practice* – International Journal of Forecasting

Hippert, H. S., et al, 2001 - *Neural networks for short-term load forecasting: a review and evaluation* - IEEE Transactions on Power Systems.

Hofmann, E. and Rutschmann, E., 2018 - *Big data analytics and demand forecasting in supply chains: a conceptual analysis* - International Journal of Logistics Management.

Juniper Research, 2020. Available in: https://www.juniperresearch.com/press/iot-connections-to-reach-83-bn-by-2024?ch=IOT%20CONNECTIONS%20TO%20GROW

Kaneko, Y. and Yada, K., 2017 - *A deep learning approach for the prediction of retail store sales* - 2016 IEEE 16th International Conference on Data Mining Workshops (ICDMW).

Ke, J., et al, 2017 - *Short-term forecasting of passenger demand under on-demand ride services: A spatio-temporal deep learning approach* - Transportation Research.

Krawczyk, B. 2016 - *Learning from imbalanced data open challenges and future directions* - Progress in Artificial Intelligence - Springer.

Krishna, A., et al, 2018 - *Sales-forecasting of retail stores using machine learning techniques* - 2018 3rd International Conference on Computational Systems and Information Technology for Sustainable Solutions (CSITSS)

Kuvulmaz, J., et al, 2005 - *Time-series forecasting by means of linear and nonlinear models* - In A. Gelbukh, A. DeAlbornoz, & H. TerashimaMarin (Eds.), MICAI 2005: Advances in artificial intelligence.

Loyer, J. L., et al, 2016 - *Comparison of machine learning methods applied to the estimation of manufacturing cost of jet engine components.* - International Journal of Production Economics.

Martínez, A., et al, 2020 - *A machine learning framework for customer purchase prediction in the non-contractual setting* – European Journal of Operational Research

Mathew, N. M. and Jomo, K., 2015 - *A Survey on the Clustering Algorithms in Sales Data Mining* - International Journal of Computer Applications Technology and Research.

Mayo, M., 2016 - *The data science puzzle, explained.* Available in: https://www.kdnuggets.com/2016/03/data-science-puzzle-explained.html/2

Mitchell, T. M., 1997 - *Machine Learning* - McGraw Hill.

Moher, D., et al, 2015 - *Preferred reporting items for systematic review and meta-analysis protocols* (PRISMA-P).

Raschka, S. and Mirjalili, V., 2017 - *Python Machine Learning, 2nd Ed.*- Packt Publishing, Birmingham.

Vahdani, B., et al, 2016 - *A high performing meta-heuristic for training support vector regression in performance forecasting of supply chain* - Neural Computing and Applications.

Wu, CSM., et al, 2018 - *Comparison of different machine learning algorithms for multiple regression on black friday sales data* - 2018 IEEE 9th International Conference on Software Engineering and Service Science (ICSESS)

Yu, Y., et al, 2011 - *An intelligent fast sales forecasting model for fashion products* - Expert Systems with Applications.

Zhang, G. P. and Qi, M., 2005 - *Neural network forecasting for seasonal and trend time series* - European Journal of Operational Research.

Zhou, L., et al, 2017 - Machine *learning on big data: Opportunities and challenges* – Neurocomputing.

DESIGNING A MEDICAL EXPERT SYSTEM BASED ON FUZZY LOGIC

Rustam Burnashev, Arslan Enikeev, Adelya Enikeeva and Ilyuza Fakhrtdinova
Institute of Computational Mathematics and Information Technologies, Kazan Federal University, Russia
Kremlyovskaya 35, Kazan, Russia

ABSTRACT

During the COVID-19 pandemic, humanity faced various health problems. One of the most common diseases is pneumonia. The life of every person depends on the correct and effective diagnosis of the disease. Currently, a large number of software applications with elements of artificial intelligence are being developed, which can reduce the time of patient care, improve the methodology and efficiency of disease diagnosis.
With our research, we strive to contribute to the development of such software applications, namely, to develop software tools with elements of fuzzy logic. To develop a decision-making system, scales and algorithms in order to assess we considered the prognosis of the severity of community-acquired pneumonia PORT(PSI), CURB/CRB-65 and SMART-COP/SMART-CO. To improve the quality of processing fuzzy production rules of knowledge base, the logic programming language Prolog was used. The created application is planned to be integrated into medical information systems.

KEYWORDS

Expert Systems, Fuzzy Logic, Rules, SWI-Prolog, Pneumonia

1. INTRODUCTION

Modern information and communication technologies are widely introduced and used in all spheres of society. Every year a person uses a large number of software applications with elements of artificial intelligence that functions on various computing devices (Gibadullin et al., 2020; Gibadullin et al., 2021).

One of such software applications is expert systems based on fuzzy logic (Zadeh, 1996; Altunin et al., 2000; Zadeh, 1983), which allow users to make decisions relying on facts and rules in the knowledge base in conditions of incomplete certainty.

The use of fuzzy logic is relevant in cases of incomplete certainty in course of diagnosing, since much in a person's life depends on making the right decision. For example, a doctor cannot always choose the right treatment and diagnosis of a disease, prescribe a medication plan, etc.

2. RELATED WORKS

To ensure effective healthcare, it is important to make a right decision on the diagnosis and to treat various diseases using modern technologies (Abbod et al., 2001; Boegl et al., 2004; Di Lascio et al., 2002; Park et al., 1996; Phuong et al., 2001).

Taking into account the findings of our previous research, we developed an integrated environment for building expert systems (System) created by using dynamically updated knowledge base (Zainullina et al., 2017; Burnashev et al., 2017). In the expert systems created, we performed data processing and search in the knowledge base using a logical inference mechanism. The functioning of the logical inference mechanism was carried out through the use of the SWI-Prolog environment, which was integrated into the System (Burnashev et al., 2019).

Currently, we have set a new research goal - the design of software tools using elements of fuzzy logic, which will form an adaptive decision-making system in the future.

The present study is devoted to the using of software applications in the medical field, namely, the design of software tools for creating expert systems based on fuzzy logic for the diagnosis of diseases associated with community-acquired pneumonia.

The duration of the course of the disease can be acute and prolonged.

- Prolonged pneumonia includes the course of the disease, which does not pass in a four-week period, despite administering timely antibacterial therapy.
- Prolonged pneumonia can occur as a secondary disease. In this case, aggravation is often possible.

Consequently, it is very difficult for specialists and experts of the subject area to determine the diagnosis, treatment and prevention. In reality, and in conditions of uncertainty, it is very difficult to make the right choice.

In this regard, it was decided to develop software tools for subsequent integration into a single adaptive decision-making system based on fuzzy logic.

3. PRELIMINARY

There are many methods for diagnosing pneumonia. Consequently, we considered classifying the severity of the course of a disease (Table 1.) and algorithms for assessing the prognosis of the severity of community-acquired pneumonia.

Classification by severity. Pneumonia is classified into the following types according to its severity: mild, medium, severe. There are special scales which determine the severity of the course of pneumonia. They estimate its severity and make prognosis of patients with community-acquired pneumonia (Rudnov et al., 2007).

We considered scales and algorithms for assessing the prognosis of the severity of community-acquired pneumonia PORT (PSI), CURB/CRB-65 and SMART POLICEMAN/SMART-CO to develop a decision-making system.

In our study, the CURB/CRB-65 scale and the corresponding algorithm for assessing the risk of an unfavorable prognosis and choosing a place of treatment for community-acquired pneumonia on the CURB-65 scale were used to develop fuzzy rules.

Symptoms and signs:

- Assessment of consciousness.
- Blood Urea Nitrogen > 7 mmol/L.
- Respiratory rate >= 30/min.
- Systolic blood pressure < 90 or diastolic BP <= 60 mmHg.
- Age >= 65.

Table 1. Assessment to determine the severity and place of treatment

0 – points	1-2 points	3-4 points
Outpatient treatment	Observation and evaluation in the hospital	Emergency hospitalization

4. MODEL AND IMPLEMENTATION

A linguistic model based on fuzzy logic with linguistic truth values was chosen as a decision-making model. The fuzzy systems development route includes the stages of algorithmic, architectural and circuit design.

The functioning scheme (Figure 1) includes:

- Module 1: User Interface.
- Module 2: Fuzzification of input variables;
- Module 3: Fuzzy Inference mechanism;
- Module 4: Defuzzification of output variables.

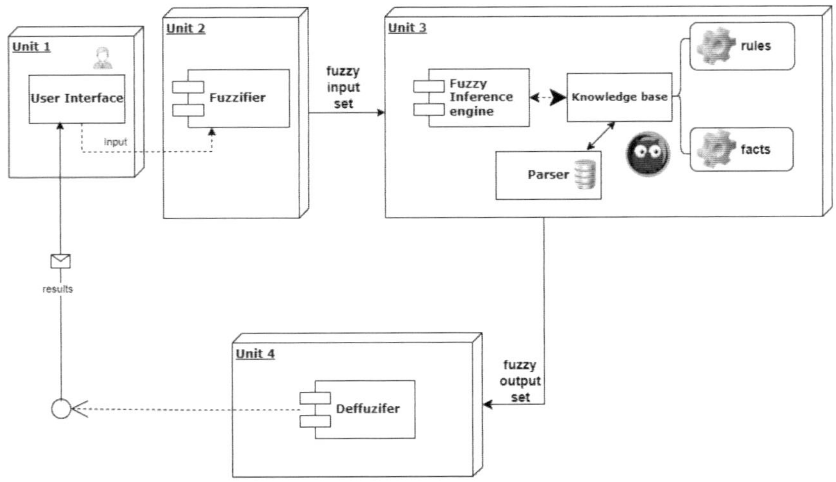

Figure 1. The scheme of functioning of the system based on fuzzy logic

At the algorithmic level of hierarchy design, the algorithm of the system functioning is described, linguistic variables, their membership functions, the mechanism of fuzzy logical inference and the corresponding methods of defuzzification are determined. At the first stage, the input and output interface of the fuzzy system is determined (inputs and outputs are specified).

The definition of linguistic variables includes: the definition of the universal set U (the domain of reasoning), the definition of the range of variation of the base variable, the definition of the values of linguistic variables (specifying the form of the membership function, setting reference points).

The model of a fuzzy system at the algorithmic level is given in the form of triples

$$(X, R, Y), \quad (1)$$

where X, Y - are the base sets on which inputs X_i and outputs Y_i are set, R is the fuzzy "input-output" correspondence.

The management strategy and the functioning of the system are described in the form of fuzzy production rules linking linguistic variables.

The description of fuzzy systems is carried out using graphical and textual tools integrated into the environment, and it includes a base of fuzzy rules and membership functions. At the same time, fuzzy inference mechanism is used.

The Patients table with the following fields was used as test data: Patient Id, age, blood pressure, respiratory rate, etc. Initialization of facts was performed in the SWI-Prolog software environment for importing facts into the Prolog knowledge base using the predicates specified in Table 2. The shell was developed using the XPCE library (Burnashev et al., 2020).

Each row is a separate row of the table, and the columns are separated by special delimiter characters (Burnashev et al., 2019). The SWI-Prolog inference mechanism was used to make queries to the knowledge base using introduced facts and fuzzy production rules. The following sequence of actions was chosen to determine the degree of affiliation and solve the task:

1. Creating a fact table in CSV format.
2. Importing a fact table from a CSV file into a fact database.
3. Working with the database of facts in SWI-Prolog.

The SWI-Prolog implementation includes predicates that simplify working with the file, the main ones are shown in Table 2:

Table 2. Properties of predicates in SWI-Prolog for working with a file

Name of the predicate	Description
csv_read_file(File, RowList, [separator(0';)])	Entering data from a CSV file File — the name of the file in a special format. rowList - a list of rows after importing. The name of the file from which the import will be performed is specified at the input of the function. A parameter that defines the separator between the fields is also set.
file(base1, csv, 'file.csv'). file(base1, base, 'file.pl').	Determining the file name by facts
:- dynamic(base1/n).	Definition of the fact base.
abolish(base1/n)	Updating facts
forall(member(row(N1, N2, .., N,_),RowList), assert(base1(N1,N2,..N))).	Generating a database from a list. Knowledge preprocessing is being performed. The assert predicate adds a fact to the base. The forall predicate for all alternatives (1 parameter) performs the action specified by the second parameter to find solutions.
file(base1, base, F), tell(F), forall(base1(N1,N2,..,N), (writeq(base1(N1,N2,..,N)), write('.'), nl)), told	Saving the database in an external file
file(base1, base, File), consult(File).	Loading and reading a database of facts from a file

5. EXPERIMENTAL ANALYSIS AND RESULTS

To develop fuzzy production rules in the knowledge base of the system based on fuzzy inference, the following stages were implemented:

- Stage 1. Formation of the rule bases of the fuzzy inference system;
- Stage 2. Fuzzification of input variables;
- Stage 3. Aggregation;
- Stage 4. Activation;
- Stage 5. Defuzzification.

Let's consider each of the stages:

Stage 1. Formation of the rule base of the fuzzy inference system.

The developed base of rules for determining the severity of the course and the place of treatment of pneumonia in the decision-making system is described by a system of conditional statements in terms of fuzzy and linguistic variables that establish a relationship between input and output parameters.

In the created system of fuzzy inference, the rules of fuzzy productions are used, in which the conditions and conclusions are formulated in terms of fuzzy linguistic statements.

Linguistic variables were formed based on the selected characteristics of pneumonia detection (Table 3, Table 4).

Table 3. Definition of linguistic variables for the construction of fuzzy production rules (part of the rules)

Criteria	Linguistic variable	Boundaries for setting the set function	Function	a, b
B	normal	> 100	s	[90, 110]
	low	< 100	z	[90, 110]
D	absent	< 1	z	[0, 2]
	traced	> 3	s	[2,5]
C	normal	< 6.4	z	[6, 6,8]
	high	> 6.8	s	[6.4, 7.2]
E	not_often	<= 22	z	[18, 26]
	often	> 23	s	[18, 28]
A	middle	< 55	z	[50, 60]
	older	> 57	s	[50, 64]

where,

Age (A); Blood Pressure (B); Blood Urea Nitrogen (C); Assessment of consciousness (D); Respiratory rate (E)

Table 4. Definition of linguistic variables for building knowledge bases

B	D	C	E	A	Result
normal	traced	normal	not_often	middle	1
normal	absent	normal	not_often	middle	0
normal	traced	high	not_often	middle	2
normal	absent	high	not_often	middle	1
low	traced	high	often	older	5
low	absent	high	often	older	4

At the initial stage of building and forming the knowledge base, membership functions were defined, which were implemented in the SWI-Prolog environment. A fragment of the program code is shown below:

```
b(X, "normal", R): - X>90, X<100, X1 is ((X-90)/20),
pow(X1, 2, X2), R is 2*X2.
b(X, "normal", R): - X>=100, X<110, X1 is ((110-X)/20),
pow(X1, 2, X2), R is 1-2*X2.
b(X, "low", R): - X>90, X<100, X1 is ((X-90)/20), pow(X1, 2, X2),
R is 1-2*X2.
b(X, "low", 1): - X=<90.
```

Stage 2. Fuzzification of input variables

The purpose of this stage is to establish a correspondence between the specific value of a separate input variable of the fuzzy inference system and the value of the membership function of the corresponding term of the input linguistic variable. At this stage, the degree of operation (truth) of each prerequisite of each rule for the given values of input variables of the form is determined:

$$\mu_{A_{i,j}}(x_i)(i,j) = 1,2 \quad (2)$$

A fragment of the program code combining the rules of fuzzification, aggregation is shown below:

```
truth_calculation(X1, X2, Xn, F_A1, F_A2, F_A3, F_AN, Y): -
      B(X1, F_A1, A1),D(X2, F_A2, A2),E(X3, F_A3, A3),…,
minimum_list([A1, A2, A3,.., An], Y).
rule_1(X1, X2, X3, X4, X5, Y, B): -
      computation_of_the_truth(X1,X2,X3,X4,X5,"normal","traced","normal",
      "not_often", "medium", Y), B is 1.
```

```
rule 2(X1,X2,X3,X4,X5,Y,B): -
      computation_of_the_truth(X1,X2,X3,X4,X5,"normal","none","normal",
      "not often,", "older than",Y), B is 0.
rule3(X1, X2, X3, X4, X5, Y, B): -
      computation_of_the_truth(X1, X2, X3, X4, X5, "normal", "tracked",
      "high", "not often", "adult", Y), B equals 2.
rule4(X1, X2, X3, X4, X5, Y, B): -
      computation_of_the_truth(X1, X2, X3, X4, X5, "normal", "none",
      "high", "not often," "older than", Y), B is 1.
```

Stage 3. Aggregation.

Aggregation is a procedure for determining the degree of truth of conditions for each of the fuzzy inference rules. Aggregation of the degrees of truth of the premises for each of the rules α_i:

$$\alpha_i = min\left\{\mu_{A_{i,j}} x_j, \mu_{A_i}(x_m)\right\} \tag{3}$$

In the knowledge base, rules were implemented to perform aggregation of degrees of truth of premises. Below is a fragment of the program code:

```
min(X,Y,X):-Y>X.
min(X,Y,Y):-X>=Y.
min_list([X],X).
min_list(S, X):-
      car(S,Y1),cdr(S,Y3),min_list(Y3,Y2),min(Y1,Y2,X).
truth_calculation(X1, X2, Xn, F_A1, F_A2, F_A3, F_An, Y):-
...
min_list([A1, A2, A3, A4, An], Y).
```

Stage 4. Activation

Activation or composition of conclusions in fuzzy rules The procedure for activating conclusions of fuzzy production rules includes in determining the modified membership functions of these conclusions for each i-th (i=1, ..., n) rule $\mu_{B_i}(y)$ based on performing a composite operation modified for fuzzy products between the aggregated value of the degrees of truth of the premises of this rule α_i determined at the previous stage and the corresponding membership function of its conclusion $\mu_{B_i}(y)$

For a simplified fuzzy inference algorithm, the activation stage is represented as:

$$y_i = c_i \tag{4}$$

In many systems, there is also an accumulation stage, but in our system it is absent due to clear values of output variables.

Stage 5. Defuzzification

The reduction to clarity includes in converting the fuzzy values of the found output variables into clear ones.

The created system uses the fuzzy mean method. Their values are calculated using a modified center of gravity method, namely the fuzzy mean method, as follows:

$$y = \frac{\sum_{i=1}^{n} \alpha_i c_i}{\sum_{i=1}^{n} \alpha_i} \tag{5}$$

where α_i is the aggregated degree of truth for all the prerequisites of the i-th rule; ci is the value of the output variable of the i-th rule $y_i = c_i$; n is the number of rules in the database.

A fragment of the program code for the defuzzification stage implemented in the SWI-Prolog environment is shown below:

```
fuzzy_otput(X1, X2, X3, X4, X5, Y):-
      rule1(X1, X2, X3, X4, X5, Y1, B1),
```

```
rule2(X1, X2, X3, X4, X5, Y2, B2),
rule3(X1, X2, X3, X4, X5, Y3, B3),
.........................................
rulen(Xn, Xn, Xn, Xn, Xn, Yn, Bn),
Y is (Y1*B1 + Y2*B2 + Y3*B3+Y4*B4+
+Yn*Bn)/(Y1 + Y2 + Y3+ Y4 +.....+Yn).
```

Graphical interface for testing knowledge bases. In scientific research, for the development of knowledge bases, most systems with elements of the logical inference mechanism use SWI-Prolog, which has been constantly developing since its creation (Burnashev et al., 2020). For the development of graphical shells of software systems, the distribution package includes tools that allow you to develop a graphical user interface. Such a tool as part of SWI-Prolog is the XPCE graphical shell.

Based on the knowledge of the subject area, a graphical interface was developed (Figure 2), which includes the following:

- Identification data (Surname, First Name);
- Age (A);
- Blood pressure (B);
- The level of urea nitrogen in the blood (C);
- Impaired consciousness (D);
- Respiratory rate (E);
- Severity rating level (Prognosis) (Result) and Saving the results in the database.

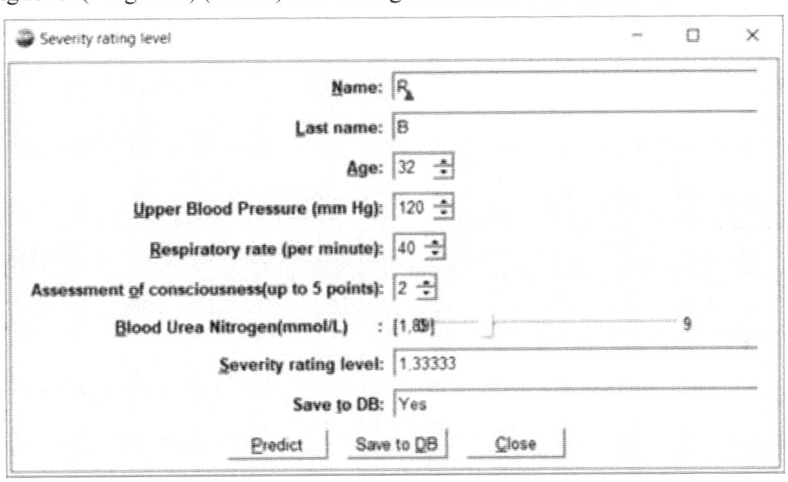

Figure 2. Interface for assessing the severity of pneumonia

The CURB/CRB-65 scale was used to create the graphical shell. Using the algorithm used, the degree of risk assessment of an unfavorable prognosis and the choice of a place of treatment for community-acquired pneumonia on the CURB-65 scale was determined.

The developed medical expert system based on fuzzy logic includes the following functions:

1. Description of the input and output interfaces of the fuzzy system.
2. Definition of the membership function for input and output data.
3. Setting fuzzy "input-output" correspondences.
4. Translation of the source description files into an internal representation.
5. Choosing a strategy for fuzzy inference and defuzzification.
6. Performing fuzzy inference and graphical representation of simulation results.

The following fuzzy methods and operations are implemented in the knowledge base using the SWI-Prolog environment:

- simplified fuzzy inference method (Mori & Sone, 1998);
- fuzzy values: min operation (Godo et al., 1991);
- for single-point sets, a variation of the center of gravity method (Van Broekhoven & De Baets, 2006) is used.

6. CONCLUSION

The proposed system is a software tool based on fuzzy logic. The system was implemented in the Prolog language of the SWI-Prolog environment using the XPCE library. The developed software tools can function on all operating systems, thereby ensuring cross-platform compatibility.

We plan further development of software tools and subsequent integration into a single adaptive system with the use of genetic algorithms in medical information systems.

ACKNOWLEDGEMENT

This paper has been supported by the Kazan Federal University Strategic Academic Leadership Program (PRIORITY-2030).

REFERENCES

Abbod, M.F., von Keyserlingk, D.G., Linkens, D.A. and Mahfouf, M., 2001. Survey of utilisation of fuzzy technology in medicine and healthcare. *Fuzzy Sets and Systems*, *120*(2), pp.331-349.

Altunin, A.E. and Semuhin, M.V., 2000. Modeli i algoritmy prinjatija reshenij v nechetkih uslovijah. *Tjumen': Izdatel'stvo Tjumenskogo gosudarstvennogo universiteta*.

Boegl, K., Adlassnig, K.P., Hayashi, Y., Rothenfluh, T.E. and Leitich, H., 2004. Knowledge acquisition in the fuzzy knowledge representation framework of a medical consultation system. *Artificial intelligence in medicine*, *30*(1), pp.1-26.

Burnashev, R. A., Yalkaev, N. S., Enikeev, A. I., Georgiev, V. O., 2017. Data Structuring and Data Processing for the Information Intellectual Applications. *Journal of Fundamental and Applied Sciences*, Vol. 9(1S), pp 1403-1416.

Burnashev, R.A., Enikeev, I.A. and Enikeev, A.I., 2020. Design and Implementation of Integrated Development Environment for Building Rule-Based Expert Systems. *In 2020 International Multi-Conference on Industrial Engineering and Modern Technologies (FarEastCon)* (pp. 1-4). IEEE.

Burnashev, R.A., Gabdrahmanov, R.G., Amer, I.F., Vakhitov, G.Z. and Enikeev, A.I., 2019. Research on the Development of Expert Systems Using Artificial Intelligence. In International Conference on Information Systems Architecture and Technology (pp. 233-242). Springer, Cham.

Di Lascio, L., Gisolfi, A., Albunia, A., Galardi, G. and Meschi, F., 2002. A fuzzy-based methodology for the analysis of diabetic neuropathy. *Fuzzy sets and systems*, *129*(2), pp.203-228.

Gibadullin, R.F. and Marushkai, N.S., 2021. Development of Predictive CNN Based Model for Vital Signs Alerts. In *2021 International Conference on Industrial Engineering, Applications and Manufacturing (ICIEAM)* (pp. 404-409). IEEE.

Gibadullin, R.F. and Zakirov, R.R., 2020. Mobile Application for Neural Network Analysis of Human Functional State. In *International Russian Automation Conference* (pp. 745-755). Springer, Cham.

Godo, L., Jacas, J. and Valverde, L., 1991. Fuzzy values in fuzzy logic. *International Journal of Intelligent Systems*, *6*(2), pp.199-212.

Mori, H., & Sone, Y., 1998. A simplified fuzzy inference method with tabu search for short-term load forecasting in power systems. In *Proceedings of the 37th IEEE Conference on Decision and Control (Cat. No. 98CH36171)* (Vol. 4, pp. 4240-4245). IEEE.

Park, K.S., Chae, Y.M. and Park, M., 1996. Developing a knowledge-based system to automate the diagnosis of allergic rhinitis. *International Journal of Biomedical Soft Computing and Human Sciences: the official journal of the Biomedical Fuzzy Systems Association*, *2*(1), pp.9-18.

Rudnov, V.A., Fesenko, A.A. and Drozd, A.V., 2007. A comparative analysis of diagnostic values of prognostic scales in patients with communityacquired pneumonia admitted to ICU. *Klinicheskaya mikrobiologiya i antimikrobnaya khimioterapiya*, *4*(9), pp.330-336.

Van Broekhoven, E., & De Baets, B., 2006. Fast and accurate center of gravity defuzzification of fuzzy system outputs defined on trapezoidal fuzzy partitions. *Fuzzy sets and systems*, *157*(7), pp.904-918.

Zadeh, L.A., 1983. The role of fuzzy logic in the management of uncertainty in expert systems. *Fuzzy sets and systems*, *11*(1-3), pp.199-227.

Zadeh, L.A., 1996. Fuzzy sets. In *Fuzzy sets, fuzzy logic, and fuzzy systems: selected papers by Lotfi A Zadeh* (pp. 394-432).

Zainullina, A.R., Larionov, G.V. and Burnashev, R.A., 2017. DEVELOPMENT OF THE PROTOTYPE EXPERT SYSTEM" DATA BASE RECOMMENDER". *Journal of Fundamental and Applied Sciences*, 9, pp.1417-1429.

INFORMATION SYSTEMS RESEARCH: DETERMINING THE CORRECT RESEARCH PARADIGM FOR A SPECIFIC RESEARCH PROBLEM

Lizani Botha and Estelle Taylor
North-West University, Potchefstroom Campus, South Africa

ABSTRACT

A researcher should understand the research philosophy or the principles of the research paradigm that he/she chooses and should show that the research philosophy is suited to the research problem being addressed. Students and early career researchers find this difficult. The aim of this paper is to describe research terminology, as well as aspects that should be taken into account when choosing a research paradigm for a specific problem. Terminology such as information systems research, quantitative research, qualitative research, mixed methods research, methodology, research method and research paradigm are discussed. Four research paradigms are also investigated including positivistic, interpretivist, critical theory, and design science research. Each of these research paradigms are discussed and compared according to their ontology, epistemology, and methodology. How would one determine which research paradigm is suitable to a study? This is a question that many researchers struggle with and an example of how to determine the appropriate research paradigm is discussed. The conclusion is that knowledge of the different paradigms and their ontological and epistemological assumptions is necessary to choose the research paradigm for a specific research problem. The definitions, comparisons and example applied in this paper may provide guidance to researchers new to the field of research.

KEYWORDS

Information Systems Research, Research Concepts, Research Paradigms

1. INTRODUCTION

One of the requirements of research is that the researcher should understand the research philosophy or the principles of the research paradigm that he/she chooses, and the researcher should show that the research philosophy is suited to the research problem being addressed. It is important that research be guided by a paradigm. Yet, Kivunja and Ahmed (2017) write that many higher degree students, as well as researchers early in their career, find it very hard to understand research concepts such as research paradigms. Queiros et al. (2017) refer to "several difficulties in choosing the most appropriate research methodology and methods best suited to a given study". Furthermore, Makombe (2017) states that many researchers early in their research career, do not mention the research paradigm guiding their research, or that they often do not use research terminology in the correct way. Even experienced researchers often use the terms research paradigm, research method and research design in a confusing manner, and this leads to confusion to students and other less experienced researchers (Makombe, 2017). Ragab and Arisha (2018) write that researchers need a good understanding of the different research methodologies to be able to identify the methods suited to a specific the research question, but that many find this challenging. The aim of this paper is to describe research terminology, as well as aspects that should be taken into account when choosing a research paradigm for a specific problem. In Section 2, information system research is discussed, followed by important research terminology in Section 3. In Section 4 different research paradigms are described, and in Section 5 an example is given of the application of these descriptions. The conclusion is given in Section 6.

2. INFORMATION SYSTEMS RESEARCH

Research done in information systems is usually applied research. Theory, frequently from other disciplines, such as economics, computer science and social sciences, is applied to solve problems that can be found at the intersection of information technology and organisations (Peffers *et al.*, 2006:84). Information systems research can serve two purposes: improve practice and/or contribute to research done in the field (Loebbecke *et al.*, 2007:1). The term information systems research is explained by defining information systems and research separately. Information systems involve "a variety of information technologies, such as computers, software, databases, communication systems, the Internet, mobile devices and much more" that allows various actors, in different organisational or social contexts, to perform specific tasks (Boell & Cecez-Keemanovic, 2015:4959; Orlikowski & Barley, 2001:146). The term research is defined as an organised investigation, that includes steps such as development, testing and evaluation and that contributes to generalisable knowledge (Ahmad, 2016:1; Mackenzie & Knipe, 2006:194). Research is also sometimes defined as creating new knowledge, using an appropriate process, to the satisfaction of the user(s) of the research (Oates, 2006:6). From the definitions for the term research, it can be concluded that a process should exist which guides the researcher to develop and share new knowledge. The basic principle of research includes the gathering of data, information, and observations to advance not only the researcher's knowledge but also the audience to which the research is presented. For this paper, the term research is defined as a process followed by a researcher to produce new knowledge and present the knowledge to an appropriate audience, whether the knowledge is gained by testing and assessing results or by designing and developing an artefact or prototype.

Next, research terminology considered important is discussed.

3. RESEARCH TERMINOLOGY

Burrell and Morgan (1979:1) argue that social science can be conceptualised in terms of four sets of assumptions which relate to methodology, ontology, epistemology and human nature. The term research methodology can be defined as a way to systematically solve the research problem (Kothari, 2004:8). The term methodology and the term research method should not be confused, as methods are the specific techniques and procedures used for the collection and analysis of data (Scotland, 2012:9; Wahyuni, 2012:72). Wahyuni (2012:72) indicates the difference between the term research methodology and the term research method as follows: a research method is a practical application of doing research whereas a research methodology is the theoretical and ideological foundation of a research method. Research methodology is defined as the "strategy or plan of action which lies behind the choice and use of particular methods" (Scotland, 2012:9). Thus, research methodology is concerned with the why data is collected, what type of data is collected, from where and how the data collection and data analysis take place (Scotland, 2012:9).

Methodology can also be defined as "a model for undertaking a research process in the context" of a paradigm (Wahyuni, 2012:70) or as "a branch of knowledge that deals with the general principles or axioms of the generation of new knowledge and the rationale and philosophical assumptions that underlie any natural or human science study" (McGregor & Murnane, 2010:420). "A methodology provides a piece of research with its philosophy, the values and assumptions which drive the rationale for the investigation, as well as the standards that will be utilised" to interpret the gathered information and to attempt to draw conclusions (Almalki, 2016:290). Methodology is concerned with why, what, from where and how data collection and analysis happen (Scotland, 2012:9). Philosophical assumptions (ontology and epistemology) are used to help the researcher develop new knowledge. For this paper, the term methodology is defined as follows: Methodology utilises the philosophical assumptions of a research paradigm to drive a study or investigation, which will contribute to new shareable knowledge.

Research methods are the instruments or tools that the researcher uses while administering any form of inquiry or investigation (Almalki, 2016:290). The definition for a research method that is used in this paper is as follows: A research method is any procedure or tool used during research to gather and analyse data. Research methods used by a researcher can be used to identify the methodology, epistemology and ontology of a chosen research paradigm (Myers, 1997:241; Scotland, 2012:10).

In table 1 some of the most important research concepts are summarized. Table 1 depicts the research term, the definition used in this paper, the author(s) who contributed to the definition that has been defined, the terminology associated with the term, as well as an example of the term.

Table 1. Summary of research terminology

Research term	The definition used in this paper	Author(s) contributed to the definition	Terminology associated with the term	Example
Research	A process followed by a researcher to produce new knowledge and present the knowledge to an appropriate audience, whether the knowledge is gained by testing and assessing results or by designing and developing an artefact or prototype.	Boell & Cecez-Keemanovic (2015:4959); Orlikowski & Barley (2001:146); Ahmad (2016:1); Mackenzie & Knipe (2006:194); Oates (2006:6); Kothari (2004:2)	(All terms listed in this table can be associated and linked to the term research.)	Quantitative research, qualitative research, mixed methods research etc.
Quantitative research	Quantitative research is concerned with gathering quantitative data which is data, or evidence that is based on numbers.	Myers (1997); Oates (2006)	Quantitative data	Surveys, laboratory experiments, mathematical modelling, etc.
Qualitative research	Qualitative research is concerned with gathering qualitative data, which consist of all non-numeric data, for example, words, images, sounds, etc. Qualitative research methods are designed to help researchers understand people and the social and cultural contexts in which they live.	Creswell (2014); Myers (1997); Oates (2006)	Qualitative data	Action research, case study research, ethnography, etc.
Mixed methods research	The class of research where the researcher mixes or combines quantitative and qualitative research techniques, methods, approaches, concepts, or language into a single study	Halcomb & Hickman (2015:41)	Blended research, multi-methods research, mixed research, etc.	Examples from quantitative and qualitative research as above can be used.
Methodology	The methodology utilises the philosophical assumptions of a research paradigm to drive a study or investigation which will lead to the development of new shareable knowledge.	Wahyuni (2012:70); McGregor & Murnane (2010:420); Scotland (2012:9)	-	Survey, case study, action research, etc.
Research method	A research method is any procedure or tool used during research to gather and analyse data.	Almalki (2016:290); Myers, (1997:241); Scotland (2012:10)	-	Questionnaires, experiments, interviews, etc.

4. CLASSIFICATION SCHEME AND RESEARCH PARADIGMS

Different classification schemes exist to identify research paradigms used in information systems research. Researchers classify certain research paradigms together and then use the classification to identify the research paradigm that is most suited to their research (Friedrich *et al.*, 2017:1113). Guba and Lincoln (1994:108) classify four paradigms that can be used in qualitative research: "positivism, post-positivism, interpretivism and critical theory". However, Klein and Myers (1999:68) suggest that only three paradigms should be used as a classification, which includes positivism, interpretivism and critical theory. This same classification scheme is suggested by Orlikowski and Baroudi (1990:4). In recent years, design science research has gained acceptance and greater recognition as an appropriate information systems research paradigm (Ayanso *et al.*, 2011:1; Dinter & Krawatzeck, 2015:1; Vaishnavi *et al.*, 2017:6). Vaishnavi *et al.* (2017:1) discuss design science research as a fourth possible paradigm, along with positivism, interpretivism and critical theory. Van der Merwe *et al.* (2020:2) also discuss design science research as a fourth paradigm that can be used in information systems research and developed guidelines to assist researchers with design science research.

The term paradigm is defined by Smyth and Morris (2007:424) as a rational framework that represents a person's beliefs, perspectives, and ideas. Oates (2006:13) defines the term paradigm as "a pattern or shared way of thinking". Willis (2007:8) defines a paradigm as "a comprehensive belief system, world view, or framework that guides research and practice in a field". Chalmers (1999:108) lists five components of a paradigm: a paradigm includes theoretical assumptions, as well as explicitly stated laws; a standard way of applying the stated laws to a diversity of situations and environments; instrumental techniques that allow a researcher to bring the laws of the paradigm to stand in the real world; to guide work within the paradigm general metaphysical principles are used; and general methodological prescriptions that guide the researcher on how to conduct research within the paradigm. For this paper, the term research paradigm will be defined using the definitions described above, as well as the five components of a paradigm by Chalmers (1999:108). The term research paradigm will be defined as a pattern or framework, consisting of philosophical assumptions and metaphysical principles that are used to guide a researcher while conducting research.

Ontology is concerned with the nature and existence of reality, and various ontological positions reflect different prescriptions of what is real (Willis, 2007:9). Scotland (2012:9) defines ontology as being concerned with what constitutes reality. When choosing a research paradigm, a researcher needs to take a position regarding his/her perception of how things really are and how things really work (Scotland, 2012:9).

The term epistemology was derived from the Greek word *epistêmê* which means knowledge (Krauss, 2005:758). Epistemology is concerned with what we can know about reality, however, this reality is defined, and how we can know it (Willis, 2007:10). Scotland (2012:9) defines epistemology to be concerned with the nature and forms of knowledge, for example how knowledge can be created, acquired, and communicated. To summarise, ontology is concerned with how the world or reality is perceived, while epistemology is concerned with how a researcher and the participants of a study have come to know this world or reality (Krauss, 2005:758). As discussed in Section 3 the methodology of a research paradigm is concerned with the best approach for a researcher to learn whatever he/she believes can be learned.

The classification scheme that will be used throughout this paper is the suggested scheme by Van der Merwe et al. (2020:6), including positivism, interpretivism, critical research and design science research. Next, the philosophical assumptions of the listed research paradigms are discussed.

4.1 Positivist Research Paradigm

The positivist research paradigm is also known as the scientific method and rose to prominence during the Enlightenment (1600-1800) (McGregor & Murnane, 2010:421; Scotland, 2012:11). The term positivism was propagated by seventeenth-century French philosopher, Auguste Comte, in the 19th century when he sought to apply the scientific paradigm, which originated by studying the natural world in relation to the social world (Hjørland, 2005:132; Scotland, 2012:11; Willis, 2007:12). The methodology of the scientific method encompasses the empirical methodology, meaning data is derived from experimentation and observation (McGregor & Murnane, 2010:421). Oates (2006:283) is of meaning, that the scientific method is based on two fundamental assumptions: first, that a researcher can objectively investigate the world we live in, and second, that the world we know is ordered and consistent and should not be considered as random. By choosing the positivist research paradigm, a researcher chooses to separate himself/herself from the world being studied, while researchers in other paradigms acknowledge that participation in the real world serves as a way of understanding and expressing its emergent properties and features (Krauss, 2005:760).

4.1.1 Philosophical Assumptions and Beliefs of Positivism

A researcher choosing to use a positivist research paradigm should consider the following philosophical assumptions and beliefs:

Ontology: Researchers making use of this paradigm assume an objective physical and social world that exists independent of humans, and the nature of which can be relatively unproblematically comprehended, characterised and measured (Orlikowski & Baroudi, 1990:9; Scotland, 2012:10). The ontological assumption is one of realism. Realism is the view that objects have an existence independent of the researcher, while the researcher conducts research objectively (Scotland, 2012:10).

Epistemology: The researcher and the subject being investigated are assumed to be independent entities. The researcher should be capable of studying the object without being influenced by the object or influencing it. A variety of strategies exists which can be followed when influence in either direction is recognised or even suspected (Guba & Lincoln, 1994:110; Orlikowski & Baroudi, 1990:12). If the prescribed procedures are rigorously followed, values and biases that the researcher has will not influence the outcomes. The findings are claimed as "true" if the findings can be repeated and the same results are produced (Guba & Lincoln, 1994:110). The epistemological assumption of positivism is objectivism (Scotland, 2012:10).

Methodology: By stating questions and/or hypotheses in propositional form and subject to empirical testing, the researcher follows an experimental methodology (Guba & Lincoln, 1994:110; McGregor & Murnane, 2010:421). The conditions in which the research takes place should be carefully controlled to prevent outcomes from being improperly influenced.

4.2 Interpretive Research Paradigm

Orlikowski and Baroudi (1990:5) state "that interpretive studies assume that people create and identify their own subjective and intersubjective meanings while interacting with the world around them". Interpretive researchers attempt to comprehend a particular singularity or phenomena by interacting with and attempting to relate to the study's participants (Orlikowski & Baroudi, 1990:5).

4.2.1 Philosophical Assumptions and Beliefs of Interpretivism

Ontology: The interpretive research paradigm "emphasises the importance of subjective meanings and social-political, as well as symbolic action in the processes through which humans construct and reconstruct their reality" (Orlikowski & Baroudi, 1990:13). In interpretivism, multiple mental constructs form the realities that exist in a world and these mental constructs are influenced and based on the social and experientially environments of the people who hold these constructs (Travis, 1999). Interpretive research in information systems accepts that the social world, whether it is social relations, organisations, division of labour, etc., are not "given" (Orlikowski & Baroudi, 1990:14).

Epistemology: The interaction between the researcher and the participant is used as a basis for the research findings of an interpretive study. The interpretive researcher's work is subjective, and the research is based on a recognised bias and consideration of particular ethical issues (Travis, 1999).

Methodology: The hermeneutic approach is used to elicit and refine individual constructions. This means that the researcher aims to generate one or more social construction whilst comparing individual constructions. In interpretive research, the researcher also has the objective to generate a common understanding (Travis, 1999).

Creswell (2014:9) summarises the philosophical assumptions of interpretivism as human beings constructing meanings as they engage with the world they are interpreting. Humans engage with their world and make sense of it based on historical and/or social perspectives. Interpretive research attempts to understand a phenomenon through the meanings constructed by humans (Klein & Myers, 2001:220).

4.3 Critical Theory Research Paradigm

According to researchers that use the critical theory research paradigm, social reality and the society we live in have objective features that lean toward influencing a person's experiences and their view or perception of the world (Oates, 2006:296). Critical theory is characterised by Brooke (2002:49) as "a form of historical materialism which is influenced by issues, such as class, ethnicity and gender". A critical theory researcher follows the approach that the participant's or subject's outlook and mindset might be controlled by another participant or subject, which possesses more power and therefore needs to be studied and brought under attention (Brooke, 2002:49). The philosophical assumptions and beliefs of critical theory are discussed next.

4.3.1 Philosophical Assumptions and Beliefs of Critical Theory

Ontology: The reality is shaped by social, political, cultural, economic, ethnic and gender values which is crystallised over time, this is also known as historical realism. Guba and Lincoln (1994:110) argue that there is a virtual or historical reality and that the structures used in the critical theory research paradigm are regarded "real" for all real-world reasons.

Epistemology: An assumption is made that the researcher and the participant or situation being studied are interactively connected, with the values and beliefs of the researcher certainly influencing the study. The findings of critical theory research are therefore value-mediated (Guba & Lincoln, 1994:110).

Methodology: A dialogue between the researcher and the participants or subjects being studied is required, enforcing the transactional nature of the inquiry. The dialogue must be dialectical in such a way that ignorance and misapprehensions can be transformed (Guba & Lincoln, 1994:110). The methodology for critical theory is known to be dialogical and dialectical.

4.4 Design Science Research

According to Vaishnavi *et al.* (2017:1), design science research is a lens or a set of synthetic and analytical techniques and perspectives that complements positivistic, interpretive and critical theory philosophical assumptions when performing research in information systems. Even though design science research complements the research paradigms discussed in this section, the philosophical assumptions of design science research are not derivable from any of these research paradigms. The end products of using design science research are either constructs, methods, models, instantiations or a combination thereof in the form of an artefact. The artefact provides a real-world outcome and not an overall description of the world. The design science research process involves the search for a relevant problem, the design and construction of an IT artefact, and its *ex-ante* and *ex-post* evaluation. An important goal in design science research is to search for and solve practically relevant real-world problems. The philosophical assumptions and beliefs of design science research are discussed next.

4.4.1 Philosophical Assumptions and Beliefs of Design Science Research

As the research moves through the design science research cycle, the ontological and epistemological assumptions of design science research evolve (Vaishnavi *et al.*, 2017:25). The ontological assumption that design science researchers follow states that multiple, contextually situated alternative world states exist (Vaishnavi *et al.*, 2017:25). The epistemological assumption includes that the design science researcher knows that a piece of information is factual and knows further what that information means through the process of development (Vaishnavi *et al.*, 2017:25). Design science research aims to construct socio-technical artefacts that intend to solve organisational problems (Dinter & Krawatzeck, 2015:1). A design theory is the desired form of knowledge contribution from a design science research project (Vaishnavi *et al.*, 2017:17). Artefacts, such as constructs, models, frameworks, etc. are constituents of a design theory but do not constitute a design theory by themselves (Vaishnavi *et al.*, 2017:17).

4.5 Summary and Comparison of Research Paradigms and Approaches

Table 2 shows a comparison of the various research paradigms discussed in the preceding sections. This summary is compiled by the researcher, based on literature reviewed.

Table 2. Comparison of research paradigms discussed

	Positivism	***Interpretivism***	***Critical Theory***	***Design science research***
Ontology (What is reality?)	Reality is perceived as real but understandable, naïve realism.	Local and localized created realities, relativism.	Historical realism, social, political, cultural, economic, ethnic, and gender values all influence how reality is perceived.	Multiple, contextually situated alternative world states exist.
Epistemo-logy (How does a person know reality?)	The findings are true, regardless of whether they are dualistic or objectivist.	Findings are formed, whether transactional or subjectivist.	Findings are value reconciled, whether transactional or subjectivist.	Knows that a piece of information is factual and knows further what that information means through the process of development.

Methodology (How can a person find out about reality?)	Experimental – questions and hypotheses are stated in propositional form and subjected to empirical testing.	Hermeneutical or dialectical.	Dialogical or dialectical	Developmental
Axiology	The researcher is independent of the study and the values that the researcher has do not influence the research being done.	The researcher forms part of the research and the values of the researcher are bound to the research.	The critical researcher can't keep his/her values, perspectives, emotions, etc. from influencing the research study.	The researcher tries to bring improvement and find understanding in the chosen research environment.
Reason for doing research	To discover laws that are generalisable and govern the universe	To understand and describe human nature	To destroy myths and empower people to change society radically	Artefacts to attain goals, serve a human purpose and solve organisational problems
Research outcomes	Hypotheses, theorem proofs, laws, techniques and methods and application of a model	Models, frameworks, new concepts, insights or theories, as well as new applications	Emancipatory models and frameworks, concepts, insights or theories, as well as a changed organisation or system	Artefact, models, frameworks, constructs
Type of research	Mainly quantitative research	Quantitative and/or qualitative, but qualitative research is preferred.	Quantitative and/or qualitative, but qualitative research is preferred.	Quantitative and/or qualitative research
Research methods	Experiments (laboratory, field or natural) surveys, case studies, action research and design and creation	Ethnography, case studies, action research and design and creation	Action research and design and creation	Controlled experiments, case studies, field studies, experiments, etc.
Data collection techniques	Questionnaires and interviews	Interviews, observations, questionnaires, documents and field notes	Surveys, case studies, field notes and ethnographies	Case studies, field notes, questionnaires, interviews, etc.
Data analysis techniques	Computer-aided analysis techniques and statistical techniques, as well as graphs, charts and tables.	Techniques for computer-assisted analysis and coding.	Techniques for computer-assisted analysis and coding.	Statistical-, dynamic analysis techniques, testing etc.

5. EXAMPLE AS APPLICATION

In this section, the suitability of each paradigm for a specific research problem is discussed. Two research problem examples are used as an application for this paper. The first research problem is the best practices that can be used for brewing a cup of coffee for a software developer. This research problem can include different variables for example: the temperature of the water, the quality of the coffee and if it is instant coffee or freshly grinded coffee beans, the number of cups a software developer drinks daily, if milk is added or not, etc.

In the example given when a researcher decides to study the phenomenon of how to identify an approach for brewing a cup of coffee for a software developer, the researcher can choose one of the four research paradigms discussed in this paper. A researcher should always determine if the ontological and epistemological assumptions are suitable for a study.

For example, if the researcher chooses to apply a positivistic research paradigm to guide him/her during the research and to try and find the best approach the researcher will typically try and find a generalisation or pattern. If the research is done over a period of 10 work days the researcher will identify a population of software developers. The researcher can then use surveys as a research method to gather quantitative data and analyse the data to try and find patterns and generalisations. The researcher can also use experiments and each day try a different approach when making coffee for a group of software developers, whilst using the different variables listed and mapping it to certain parts of the research. The findings and solution to the research problem if using the positivistic research paradigm will conclude to: Filter coffee is the preferred approach when serving software developers coffee. They find it easily accessible and enjoy the fact that the filter coffee machine keeps the coffee hot. They also find that this approach is time-saving as only one person has to place the filtered coffee in the coffee machine, add water and turn it on and it can server 8 to 10 cups of coffee depending on the litres of water the coffee machine can be filled up with. From the data that was analysed it found the 58% of the participants prefer milk in their coffee.

If the researcher chooses to use interpretive research as research paradigm the variables used in the study will not only be concerned with factors that influence the coffee but also factors that influence the software developer whilst drinking the coffee. The researcher can for example present different types of coffee each morning and then interview each of the identified software developers after they had their cup of coffee taking into consideration the schedule and workload of the software developer as well and how the coffee influenced the software developer. The findings and the solution to the research problem will contain a human behaviour element, for example software developers with a busy schedule prefer a cup of instant coffee but on days that the workload is less they prefer to use a coffee machine that freshly grinds the beans and froths the milk producing a cappuccino.

When using critical theory as research paradigm for this example the researcher will typically challenge power and authority structure that may control a person or a specific situation. A critical theory researcher also tries to eliminate situations, objects or other people that are responsible for domination and alienation. For example, the researcher will try and challenge the research problem as to why there are only focused on the approaches used to make coffee and not tea and if the software developers are being forced to only drink coffee by management of the company. The critical theory researcher will typically then take action by speaking to management and trying to get more options for the software developers who might be seen as the oppressed if only having the option of coffee at work. The findings of the study will for example be: Only filter coffee was being served by management when the study started and after various discussions with management the software developers now have the following options of which they can choose: instant coffee, filter coffee, green tea and loose-leaf black tea.

Lastly a researcher can choose to apply design science research to a study. In the example that has been used a researcher choosing design science research will try and firstly gain any knowledge regarding the research problem. For example, if the researcher finds that the software developers prefer cappuccino made by a coffee machine but that it is time consuming to make by adding in coffee beans and milk into the milk frother the researcher will try and develop an artefact which can assist in solving this problem. The artefact might go through a few iterations, in this example the researcher might have three iterations of the built artefact. The first iteration the coffee bean packet and milk can be placed on a shelf right at the top of the coffee machine and at the correct angles and strings can be attached which a software developer can then pull to pour the coffee beans and the milk. After this iteration the researcher will find that the software developer still needed to get up from his/her desk and press the button for a cappuccino. In the second iteration the researcher will make adjustments to his/her artefact adding another string which is attached to a poking device which can press the button for cappuccino. Hence through each iteration the design of the artefact is improved and new knowledge is gained. As a result, to the research problem the researcher using design science research would have built a fully functioning artefact that addresses almost every area of the research problem from placing a clean cup via a conveyer belt for the next cup of coffee on the coffee machine to even determining the strength of the coffee by providing different roast options of coffee beans for the software developer.

An example of how the researcher can determine which research paradigm is best suited to an information system study follow. In this example the research problem is as follow: Determine the most suited data model approach an organisation can choose from for a data warehouse that will improve business intelligence. The research plan is to firstly do a pilot study using a test data set and then use three different companies' data to identify the best suited data model based on characteristics such as business rules, data characteristics, current software environment, etc. During the development of different data models for the different data sets the researcher plans to build a framework consisting of guidelines which can assist in choosing a data modelling approach.

The positivistic research paradigm is not suited for this study, as neither the ontological nor epistemological assumptions of positivism are suitable for this example. Not only one single objective reality is taken into consideration. The research is dependent on the social and physical realities of each participant and the reality in which a data set of a company is used. As the researcher is involved in the development of the pilot study and each data model, as well as the framework, this contrasts the epistemological and axiological assumptions of positivism.

The interpretive research paradigm's qualities and characteristics correspond to the research methods connected with the paradigm. This ensures that the participant's environment or setting is objectively observed, while also ensuring that the researcher's own beliefs, paradigms, and experiences have no influence on the research. Although there are many critics of the interpretivist research paradigm, arguments such as confirmability, dependability, trustworthiness, and transferability can be easily justified if a researcher can explain every stage of the study process (Oates, 2006:294). Interpretivism is not suited for this study. The goal of this study is the creation of a framework and not understanding a specific phenomenon. The knowledge generated when using interpretivism focuses on the perceptions of the participants. Even though the researcher is interested in these perceptions, other areas of knowledge, such as reviewed literature are also considered important.

Critical theory research challenges power and authority structures that may control a person or a specific situation. By going beyond the understanding of a situation, a critical theory researcher focuses mainly on the dissatisfactions and conflicts in the current setting or society (Oates, 2006:296). A critical theory researcher also tries to eliminate situations, objects or other people that are responsible for domination and alienation. This study does not focus on challenging power structures, disapprovals and conflicts in the current society or eliminating objects or elements of domination. Therefore, the critical theory research paradigm is also not suited to this study.

After evaluation of positivism, interpretivism, critical theory and design science research, design science research was chosen as the research paradigm for this study. Design science research is chosen as the research paradigm for this study as it focuses on the creation and evaluation of innovative information technology artefacts that enable organisations to address important information-related tasks (Hevner *et al.*, 2004:98). The researcher develops an artefact (framework) to help solve a real-world problem within an organisation. Both the ontological and epistemological assumptions of design science research are the most suitable for this study.

6. CONCLUSION

The aim of this paper is to describe the most important aspects that should be taken into account when choosing a research paradigm for a specific problem. The introduction was given in Section 1. In Section 2, information system research was discussed, and important terminology was explained in Section 3. In Section 4 different research paradigms were described, and in Section 5 an example was given of how these can be applied to choosing a paradigm for a specific research problem. The conclusion is that knowledge of the different paradigms and their ontological and epistemological assumptions is necessary to choose the research paradigm for a specific research problem. The definitions, comparisons and example in this paper may provide guidance to researchers new to the field of research.

REFERENCES

Ahmad, S. S. 2016. Research And Its Importance. *The Ophthalmology Open Journal,* 1:1-2.

Almalki, S. 2016. Integrating Quantitative And Qualitative Data In Mixed Method Research – Challenges And Benefits. *Journal Of Education And Learning,* 5:288-296.

Ayanso, A., Lertwachara, K. & Vachon, F. 2011. *Design And Behavioral Science Research In Premier IS Journals: Evidence From Database Management Research* [Online]. Available: Https://Digitalcommons.Calpoly.Edu/Cgi/Viewcontent.Cgi?Referer=Https://Www.Google.Com/&Httpsredir=1&Article=1014&Context=Mgmt_Fac [Accessed 15 May 2019].

Boell, S. K. & Cecez-Keemanovic, D. 2015. What Is An Information System? *Hawaii International Conference On System Sciences.* Hawaii.

Brooke, C. 2002. What Does It Mean To Be 'Critical' In IS Research? *Journal Of Information Technology,* 17:49-57.

Burrell, G. & Morgan, G. 1979. *Sociological Paradigms And Organisational Analysis*, Heinemann Educational Books.

Chalmers, A. F. 1999. *What Is This Thing Called Science?,* Indianapolis, Hackett Publishing Company, Inc.

Creswell, J. W. 2014. *Research Design – Qualitative, Quantitative And Mixed Methods Approaches,* United States Of America, Sage Publications.

Dinter, B. & Krawatzeck, R. 2015. Towards A Configurative Publication Schema For Design Science Research *Thirty Sixth International Conference On Information Systems.* Forth Worth, Texas.

Friedrich, T., Schlauderer, S., Weidinger, J. & Raab, M. On The Research Paradigms And Research Methods Employed In The BISE Journal – A Ten-Year Update Internationalen Tagung Wirtschaftsinformatik 2017 St. Gallen, Switzerland. 1111-1125.

Guba, E. G. & Lincoln, Y. S. 1994. *Handbook Of Qualitative Research,* London, Sage.

Hevner, A. R., March, S. T., Park, J. & Ram, S. 2004. Design Science In Information Systems Research. *MIS Quarterly,* 28:75-105.

Hjørland, B. 2005. Empiricism, Rationalism And Positivism In Library And Information Science. *Journal Of Documentation,* 61:130-155.

Klein, H. K. & Myers, M. D. 1999. A Set Of Principles For Conducting And Evaluating Interpretive Field Studies In Information Systems. *MIS Quarterly,* 23:67-94.

Klein, H. K. & Myers, M. D. 2001. A Classification Scheme For Interpretive Research In IS 219-240.

Kothari, C. R. 2004. *Research Methodology – Methods & Techniques,* New Delhi, New Age International (P) Ltd, Publishers.

Krauss, S. E. 2005. Research Paradigms And Meaning Making: A Primer. *The Qualitative Report,* 10:758-770.

Loebbecke, C., Berthod, O. & Huyskens, C. 2007. Research Importance In The Information Systems Field: A Citation Analysis. *Twenty-Eight International Conference On Information Systems.* Montreal.

Mackenzie, N. & Knipe, S. 2006. Research Dilemmas: Paradigms, Methods And Methodology. *Issues In Educational Research,* 16:193-205.

Mcgregor, S. L. T. & Murnane, J. A. 2010. Paradigm, Methodology And Method: Intellectual Integrity In Consumer Scholarship. *International Journal Of Consumer Studies,* 34:419-427.

Myers, M. D. 1997. Qualitative Research In Information Systems. *MISQ Discovery,* 21:241-258.

Oates, B. J. 2006. *Researching Information Systems And Computing,* United Kingdom, Sage Publications.

Orlikowski, W. J. & Barley, S. R. 2001. Technology And Institutions: What Can Research On Information Technology And Research On Organizations Learn From Each Other? *MIS Quarterly,* 25:145-165.

Orlikowski, W. J. & Baroudi, J. J. 1990. *Studying Information Technology In Organizations: Research Approaches And Assumptions* [Online]. Available: Https://Ssrn.Com/Abstract=1289076 [Accessed 10 February 2019].

Peffers, K., Tuunanen, T., Gengler, C. E., Rossi, M., Hui, W., Virtanen, V. & Bragge, J. 2006. The Design Science Research Process: A Model For Producing And Presenting Information Systems Research. *DESRIST.* Claremont, California.

Scotland, J. 2012. Exploring The Philosophical Underpinning Of Research: Relating Ontology And Epistemology To The Methodology And Methods Of The Scientific, Interpretive, And Critical Research Paradigms. *English Language Teaching,* 5:9-16.

Smyth, H. J. & Morris, P. W. G. 2007. An Epistemological Evaluation Of Research Into Projects And Their Management: Methodological Issues. *International Journal Of Project Management,* 25:423-436.

Travis, J. 1999. *Exploring The Constructs Of Evaluative Criteria For Interpretivist Research* [Online]. Available: Http://Citeseerx.Ist.Psu.Edu/Viewdoc/Download?Doi=10.1.1.4.1994&Rep=Rep1&Type=Pdf [Accessed 17 December 2018].

Vaishnavi, V. K., Kuechler, W. L. & Petter, S. 2017. *Design Science Research In Information Systems* [Online]. Available: Http://Www.Desrist.Org/Design-Research-In-Information-Systems/ [Accessed 26 February 2019].

Van Der Merwe, A., Gerber, A. & Smuts, H. 2020. Guidelines For Conducting Design Science Research In Information Systems. *Communications In Computer And Information Science,* 1136:1-16.

Wahyuni, D. 2012. The Research Design Maze: Understanding Paradigms, Cases, Methods And Methodologies. *Journal Of Applied Management Accounting Research.* , 10:69-80.

Willis, J. W. 2007. *Foundations Of Qualitative Research,* United States Of America, Sage Publications.

EVALUATING THE PERFORMANCE OF A CARE PROCESS BASED ON SIMULATION: MATERNITY CASE

Thouraya Menyaoui[1,2], Nesrine Missaoui[1,2] and Sonia Ayachi Ghannouchi[1,3]
[1]RIADI Laboratory, ENSI, University of Manouba, Tunisia
[2]Higher Institute of Computer Science and Communication Technique of Sousse, University of Sousse, Tunisia
[3]Higher Institute of Management of Sousse, University of Sousse, Tunisia

ABSTRACT

Whatever the context, modeling is defined as the first step in a decision support project (Kowalsky, (2006)). More precisely modelling in hospitals, born from the needs arising from the increasing complexity of hospital services, is a discipline that aims to be able to model hospital systems taking into account the many factors entering the online accounts for their actual behaviors simulation. It is also of interest when used to model random patient flows.
The work presented in this article addresses the problem of minimizing the time cycle of a patient's journey through the maternity ward of Farhat Hached Sousse Hospital with the aim of improving the perfection of this service. More precisely, we take the case of the outpatient consultations of this service. Indeed, the evaluation of the performance of a real system consists of a modeling step, to move from the system to the model in order to better identify the problems encountered and a step of analyzing the performance of the model thus obtained.
For modelling, we opted for a modelling of the care process by adopting Bonita 6.5.2 software and for performance analysis; we chose simulation to test the scenarios resulting from the change of some parameters, using Bonita Simulation 6.5.2 software. The results obtained indicate that patients spend a significant amount of time waiting for an appointment and for registration.
We have thus brought ideas to help those in charge of the Maternity Department of the Farhat Hached Sousse hospital to determine and rank in an order of importance the improvement actions that allow the minimization of the duration of the cycle of care.

KEYWORDS

BPM, Business Process Modeling, Simulation, Performance Evaluation, Maternity Unit

1. INTRODUCTION

Nowadays, with the increasing use of technology and communication techniques, the situation of patients within the care process model has been transformed from a "spectator" to an "active" actor who contributes to the improvement of the workflow of activities within a process.

We will focus specifically on the flow of patients' for the maternity process because we noticed several difficulties related to the execution and organization of activities, such as the increase of patient wait time, weak anticipation of the patient care process, the lack of good control upstream and downstream of the patient's journey and the multitude of stakeholders.

Hospital performance depends on optimizing quality, cost and time (Minvielle, 1996). Simulation is becoming a standard tool for studying the organization and management of hospital systems, with a view to improving their operation and reducing costs. The purpose of this research is to study and evaluate the performance of a business process based on the simulation technique. Simulation visualizes and evaluates conceptual models about observed process behavior and helps in analysis, forecasting and decision support (Shull et al. 2008). Simulation has become an increasingly used tool in health systems, It is about a technique allowing stakeholders to experiment with representing models of real systems (Robinson et al. 2004).

To do so, we have first presented a lifecycle of business process management in which we have included the simulation technique in order to improve the performance of the process. Then, the proposed lifecycle was evaluated through its application for the real world process of patient treatment within the maternity service. We have considered a number of simulation parameters such as patient wait time, execution time of the process and resource availability in order to minimize patient waiting time, improve the patient treatment process and reduce execution time of the process.

The remainder of this paper is organized as follows: section 2 gives an overview of simulation approaches for BP modeling proposed in literature. In section 3, a new lifecycle for BPM based on the simulation technique is introduced where we have identified in each phase of the lifecycle its corresponding simulation step(s). Section 4 presents the implementation of our proposed model into an example describing patient treatment in maternity service. The conclusion in section 5 gives a summary of the presented work and deals with implications for further research.

2. RELATED WORK

Business process modeling and simulation is a new quantitative approach to model, analyze, and improve the efficiency and effectiveness of business processes in a structured manner (Safari, 2016)

Many research studies have been interested by the idea of associating simulation with business process modeling, to optimize the performance of the process.

Indeed, Van Der Aalst et al. (2010) proposed an improved version of traditional simulation approach. They identified in their work a list of problems encountered during simulation. These problems are related to decision problems, organizational problems and others related to the use of historical artifacts and data as well as resource management issues. The authors' work focuses on resource management issues where they have proposed a new simulation approach that takes into consideration the availability of resources defined in the workflow system. The approach was defined by the CPN and YAWL tools and tested to demonstrate its feasibility. These experiences showed the positive effect of resource management on the behavior of a business process. However, the work focused only on managing the simulation resources and did not consider other parameters of simulation such as process status, event logs, historical data, etc.

Bartlomiej et al. (2015) have demonstrated in their work that the execution of various scenarios of a process requires a simulation model that is digitized and fed by real process data reflecting the different operations executed in an organization. They defined an "As-Is simulation" model based on historical data that truly reflects the behavior of the process. This model was defined from a study, developed in a telecommunication company, and constructed with basic data, observations, staff knowledge and experiences.The proposed model consists of three steps: data collection step from the executed instances, followed by the processing and data analysis step using "process mining" technique, and a process-based optimization step. However, the proposed model does not take into consideration the parameters of human resources management and the waiting activities (time to complete). Also, the generated instances only show a specific period of process execution.

Another area of research is presented by the work of Olegas et al. (2016), who considered that traditional approaches for implementing and simulating a BP do not cover the real needs of the company, which are rapidly evolving. According to the authors, the simulation tools presented in literature are only useful for static processes that determine which activities will be performed and in which sequence. Thus, the approach proposed by the authors focuses on presenting the dynamicity of a business process while defining a list of concepts (requirements) presenting a dynamic business process (DBP). To define them, a modeling and simulation approach has been defined. It is based on changing the rules of executing a BP (conditions), the sequence of executing instances, and the context of the system (environment). Based on the proposed approach, a reference architecture and a prototype with a simulation tool for DBP were developed.

We were inspired by these approaches in order to define our own simulation approach in that we simultaneously take into account availability of resources, historical data and dynamicity of business process. We apply it to a real process example corresponding to the sequence flow of activities in the maternity service.

3. PROPOSED SOLUTION

This section presents our proposed approach. The goal of our work is to combine the two concepts of Business Process Management (BPM) and simulation and propose an advanced BPM model that improves process performance while being based on the simulation technique.

The implementation of simulation generally goes through four macro stages, according to (Ricordel et al, 2000), which are Analysis that represent the description of the type of problem and its field of application. Then Modelling that is a structured representation by using a declarative model or relying on specific languages such as (UML, MERISE, Petri nets, etc.). After that Computer implementation that defined by the construction of a functional solution to the problem, by coding the solution with a particular programming languages).And finally Simulation which is the use of the implemented model to deal with concrete problems.

Several models have been proposed to describe the BPM lifecycle, the model proposed by (Gillot, 2008) was chosen since the structure of the model has the same structure as the chosen simulation process model which facilitates the sharing and use of data and information within a process: First Modelling phase that supports an approach using a graphical modelling notation generally based on the adoption of the Business Process Modeling Notation (BPMN) standard (OMG, 2011). Second the Implementation phase in which the created process is transformed and enriched in order to be executed by a process engine.). After that Execution phase that represents the operational phase where the BPM solution is implemented. Finally Analysis and optimization phase, This phase is used to monitor the operational execution of business processes and measure performance.

While applying this approach in the healthcare field, the objective of our work is to improve the performance of a maternity department. More precisely, we deal with the modeling and the execution of the healthcare process in this maternity department by applying a BPM approach in a first place and secondly we focus of the simulation and the optimization of patient flows.

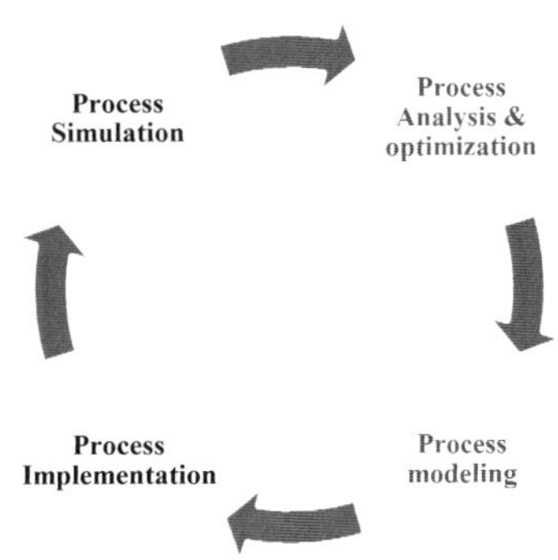

Figure 1. Proposed model for process simulation

As presented in figure 1, the four steps of our approach are the following: Process modeling, process implementation, process simulation and process analysis & optimization. For each of these steps, we indicate below the way in which it is applied.

- Process modeling: collect information by consulting the involved actors for modelling the process.
- Process implementation: Apply a process-oriented modeling method for implementing the process.
- Process Simulation: Proceed by process simulation, analyze the simulation results and detect problems encountered during the execution of the process
- Process analysis and optimization: Analyze and measure the performance of the executed process.

4. PRACTICAL APPLICATION

In order for a business process to be managed it has to be modeled in the first place (Pereira et al. 2019). So to evaluate the feasibility of our proposed model, we have chosen to work on an example of a health care process since this domain requires to continuously improving the performance of its processes in order to improve the quality of their services and satisfy their patients' needs.

For this, we took the healthcare process within the maternity unit where we visited the outpatient department and interviewed the service team (doctors, nurses) as well as patients. Following the visit and based on the answers of the interviewees, we modelled the care process and we found that the department suffers from several problems.

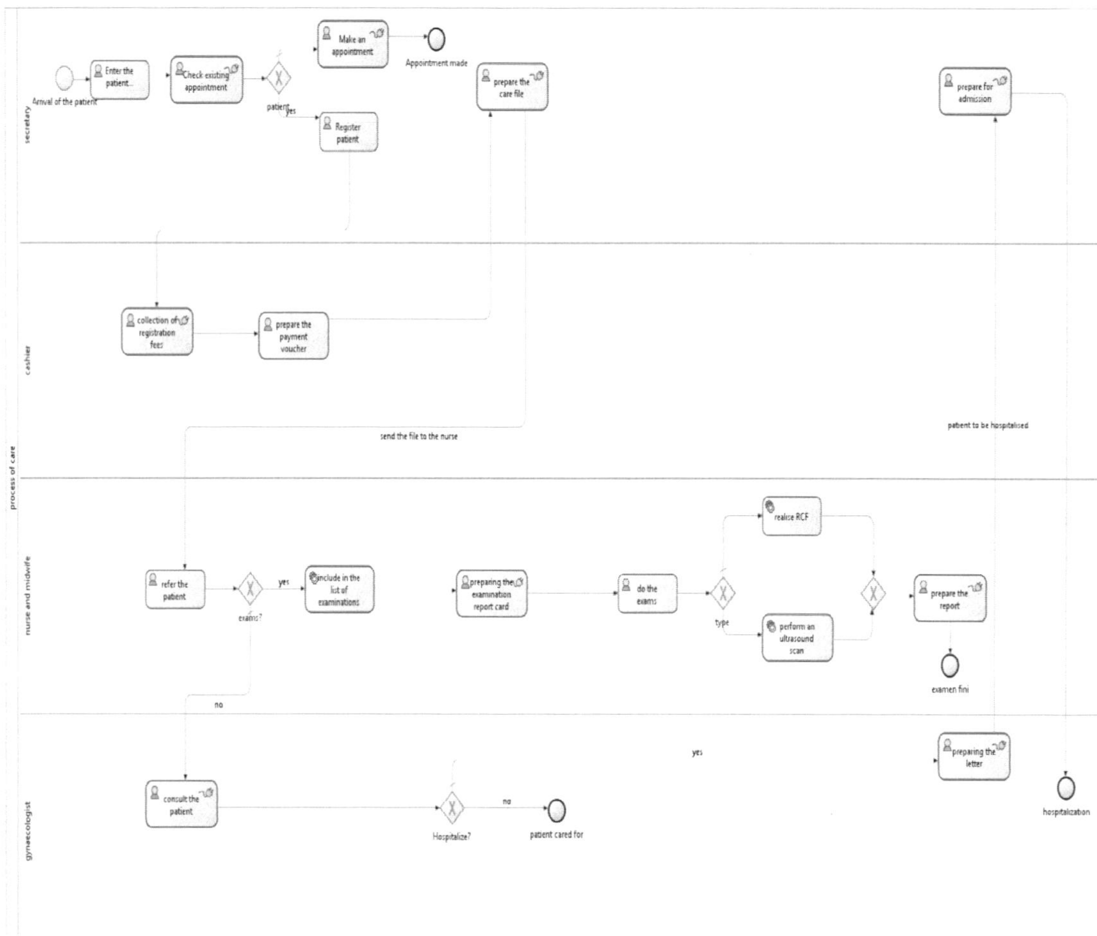

Figure 2. BPMN Process of care in the maternity unit

The modelled process is presented in figure 2, it is a BPMN model which describes in details the path through which a patient passes from his/her arrival until he/she leaves the maternity unit.
The main problems from which suffers this process are presented below:

- Patient dissatisfaction for especially appointment dates
- Huge waiting time in the lines
- Clutter of the department
- Inadequate number of medical and paramedical personnel compared to the needs of patients.

Hence, the necessity to improve the quality of services by always seeking to put in place an approach that allows:

- Satisfying patients by meeting their needs
- Reducing waiting time
- Reducing, as much as possible, the clutter of the service

Thus, we propose improvements in the sequence flow within the department in order to improve the execution of the process and make it more efficient while based on the simulation technique. In fact, simulation can be used to predict the effects of process improvement actions (Pourbafrani et al. 2020).

In order to have concrete observations, we will focus on simulating the tasks achieved by the secretary, specifically activities and gateways presented in the secretary Lane.

Appointment and registration tasks are the most important tasks in our analysis, as the waiting time for these two activities is greater than that of other activities, which leads to problems of poor organization and clutter in the secretary's box.

Thus, for simulation parameters, we have included information regarding execution time of an activity, the minimum threshold (minimum time) and the maximum threshold (estimated time) for the period of the simulation.

For the activity of making appointment, according to the study of the data collected, we included the following data:

- Running time: 7 hours and 30 minutes.
- Estimated time (minimum execution time): 5 hours.
- Maximum time: 10hours.

For the task of registering patients, we have:

- Running time: 11 hours and 30 minutes.
- Estimated time (minimum running time): 8 hours and 30 minutes.
- Maximum time: 17 hours and 30 minutes.

In addition, for the gateway "patient", we defined the following probabilities: 70% cases of patients with appointment and 30% cases of patients without appointment.

The simulation was be launched in a period ranging from 08/01/2018 to 17/05/2018 with 100 process instances.

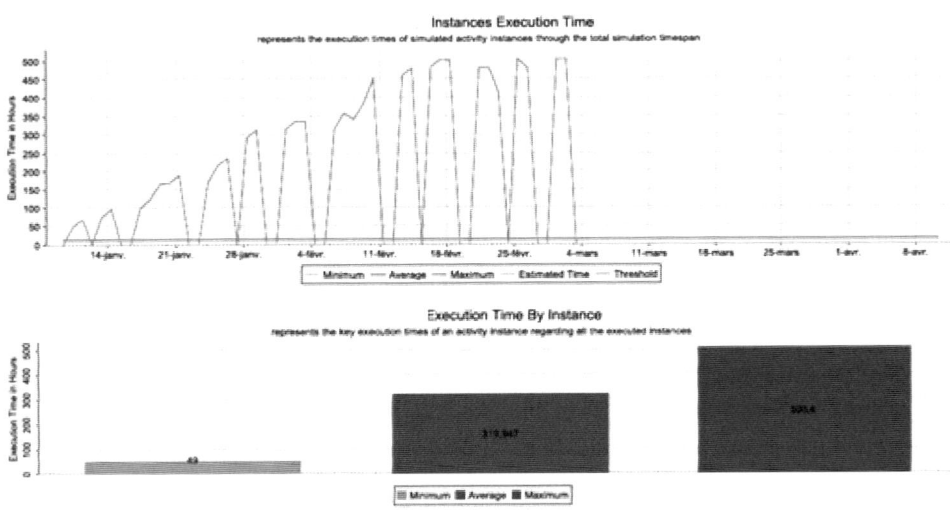

Figure 3. Result of the simulation for fixing appointment task

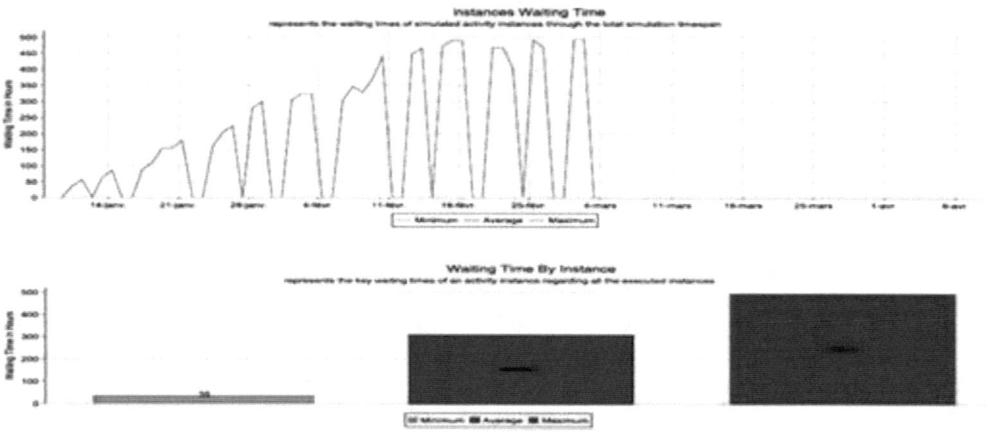

Figure 4. Fix an appointment: Waiting time for an instance

Figure 3 presents the results of simulating the task "Fix appointment" where we noticed that, throughout the simulation period, the average execution time exceeds the minimum time and takes the value of 5 hours of execution compared to the 49 minutes of execution for the minimum time. Also, for the curve showing the waiting time of an instance as presented in Figure 4, the average time is close to the maximum: 3 hours of waiting time compared to 5 hours for the maximum time.

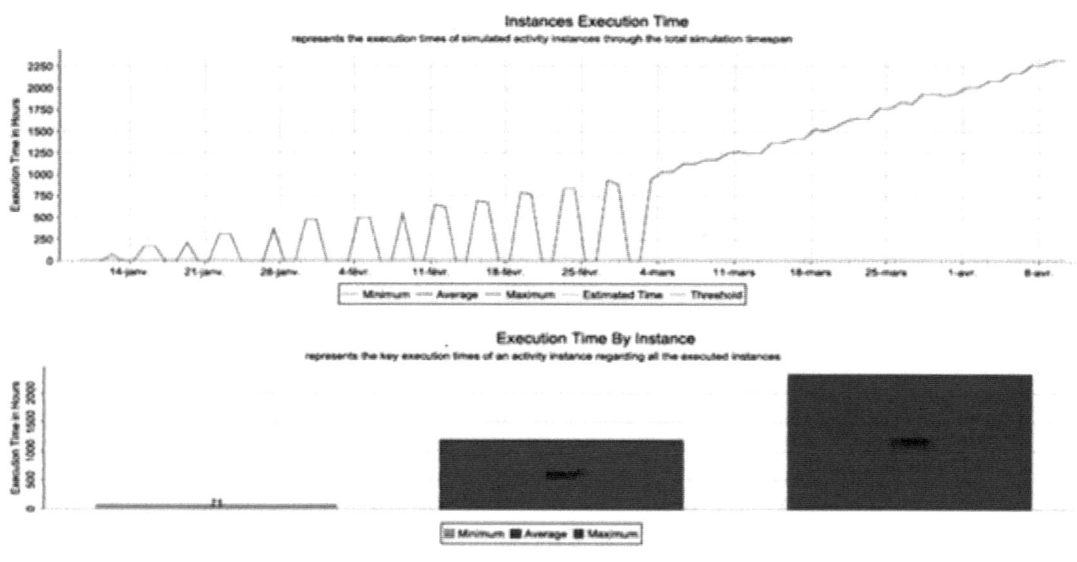

Figure 5. Simulation results for the patient registration task

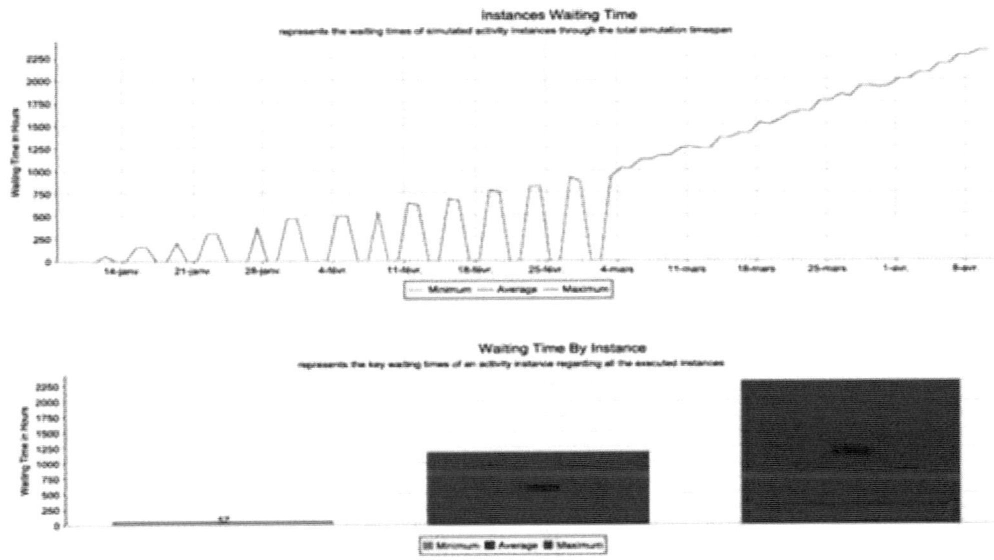

Figure 6. Fix an appointment: Waiting time for an instance

For the registration activity, as presented in Figure 5, we found that throughout the simulation period, the average running time exceeds the minimum time and takes the value of 22 hours of execution compared to 71 minutes of execution for the minimum time. Also, for the curve showing the waiting time of an instance as presented in Figure 6, the average time is close to the maximum time: 11 hours of waiting time compared to 23 hours for the maximum time.

These results are due to the overload of work for this activity since each box registers at least 40 patients a day. This leads to patient dissatisfaction and work overload which has an impact on the performance of the process, especially for the activities of consultation and payment of registration fees.

Thus, to improve the performance of the process and specifically the execution of the two activities: "Fix an appointment" and "Register," we propose to:

- Increase the number of reception desks.
- Increase the number of human resources carrying out these activities.
- Separate the registration desk from the appointment-fixing desk,
- Add boxes for consultation as well as exam rooms.

These improvements can affect the performance of the care process by reducing the time it takes to complete all the activities and increasing the quality of services provided to patients and therefore meeting the needs and expectations of patients.

5. CONCLUSION AND FUTURE WORKS

The presented work deals with the concepts of BPM (Business Process Management) and simulation. It aims at developing an improved BPM model integrating simulation steps with the BPM phases in order to improve the performance of business processes. The proposed model was evaluated based on a practical example describing the process of patient treatment within a maternity department.

This area of research is very broad and remains very topical, in which there are always new approaches proposed and various ideas for future work. Among these ideas, we will consider the following:

- A study of patient satisfaction following the actual application at the maternity service of proposed solutions such as the addition of a consultation room and a reception desk.

- The separation of the registration desk from the outpatient department of the maternity ward to make it only dedicated to the corresponding patients. Other patients interested in further consultations should then go to different queues. A new study (modeling and performance analysis) can then be conducted to assess the improvements that will be achieved.
- An expansion of our study to no longer be limited to appointment-making and registration activities, but a consideration of all the activities of our maternity care process.
- The simulation should be repeated after implementing the proposed actions to ensure that the proposition is suitable.

REFERENCES

Bartlomiej et al. (2015) Bartlomiej Gzwin, Bartosz Marankowski: *How close to reality is the « as-is » Business Process Simulation Model*

Gillot, (2008) Gillot , J.-N., *The Complete Guide to Business Process Management: Business Process Transformation or a Way of Aligning the Strategic Objectives of the Company and the Information System Through the Processes*. Edition Lulu.com.

Kowalsky (2006) Y. Kowalsk,i, *Aide à la décision par l'analyse sémantique et la simulation des interactions dans l'organicube, modèle qualitatif général d'audit pour les entreprises*. Université de Fribourg, Suisse.

Luís et al. (2019) Luís Pereira, J., & Paulo Freitas, A. *Towards a characterization of BPM tools simulation support:the case of BPMN process models*. International Journal for Quality Research, 13(4).

Minvielle, (1996) Etienne Minvielle, *the organization of work at the hospital, manage the singularity on a large scale*.

Olegas et al. (2016) Olegas Vasilecas, Diana Kalibatienne, DejanLavbic: *Rule and context based dynamic business process modelling and simulation*.

OMG, (2011) OMG O. M. (2011, January) *Business Process Model and Notation (BPMN) Version 2.0*. Récupéré sur http://www.omg.org/spec/BPMN/2.0/PDF.

Pourbafrani et al. (2020) Pourbafrani, M., van Zelst, S. J., & van der Aalst, W. M. (2020, June). Supporting automatic system dynamics model generation for simulation in the context of process mining. *In International Conference on Business Information Systems* (pp. 249-263). Springer, Cham.

Ricordel et al. (2000) Ricordel , P.M. et Demazeau, Y. , From Analysis to deployment: A Multi-Agent Platform Survey. *Proceedings of 1st International Workshop on Enginnering Societies in the Agents World (ESAW)*, ECAI'2000, A. Oinici R. Tolksdorf, and F. Zambonelli, (Eds.), Berlin, Germany, Springler Verlag pp. 93-105

Robinson et al. (2004) Robinson S, Nance RE, Paul RJ, Pidd M and Taylor SJE, *Simulation Model Reuse: Definitions, Benefits and Obstacles. Simulation Modelling: Practice and Theory*.

Safari (2016) Arsalan Safari, *An Effective Practical Approach for Business Process Modeling and Simulation in Service Industries*.

Shull et al. (2008) Shull F, Singer J, Sjøberg DI. *Guide to advanced empirical software engineering*: Springer.

Van Der Aalst et al. (2010) W.M.P. Van Der Aalst, J. Nakatumba, A. Rozinat, and N. Russell: *Business Process Simulation: How to get it right*.

DATA-DRIVEN TRANSFORMATION JOURNEY THROUGH DATA DEMOCRACY: A CASE STUDY OF A SWEDISH BANK

Irsa Amerian and Fisnik Dalipi
Department of Informatics, Linnaeus University, Växjö, 351 95, Sweden

ABSTRACT

Nowadays, data has emerged as a resource of prime importance, and an insightful use of it in a data-centric workforce can provide continuous competitive advantage. In their journey of becoming data-driven, many organizations invest in underlying resources and adjust business models accordingly. In the academic literature, the importance of becoming data-driven and utilizing the data analytics tools in achieving the transformation vision has been widely discussed and explored. Nevertheless, when it comes to data democracy and opening the data within organizations, there is still a noticeable gap. The significance of this paper relies on the relevance of empowering organizations toward creating the right instruction on how to achieve data democracy in their data-driven transformation path. By focusing on a case study, this work reveals, among others, the correlation between the benefits from empowering different players of the organization with the needed data knowledge, and the acceleration of the digital transformation journey.

KEYWORDS

Digital Transformation, Data Democracy, Data Analytics, Citizen Data Scientist, Data-Driven Decision Making

1. INTRODUCTION

In the age of digital transformation, many businesses are evolving at an increasingly rapid rate, and the main catalyst for such evolution is advancing technology, with data as a key focal point. What makes data so powerful is that it can be used for a nearly infinite number of purposes across a multitude of industries, such as finance, healthcare, engineering, etc. From a business standpoint, this involves an organization using tools, technologies, and processes to extract data and ultimately improve business objectives and decision making. In addition, because of the increasing competition between organizations, being data-driven has become more important than ever for an organization's survival. As also evidenced in the state-of-the-art literature, companies that employ a data-driven approach are more successful in contrast to those with a decision-making process being mostly based on "gut-feeling" (Berndtsson et al., 2020; Storm & Borgman, 2020).

In their efforts to become more data-driven, successful companies have steadily invested in Big Data and AI initiatives (Rean, 2021). However, this is not a trivial process as companies are still struggling to derive value from these investments and to become this reality, such as legacy data environments, skill sets, and culture. Other factors such as data transparency, democracy and governance also play an indispensable and critical role towards enabling, supporting, and sustaining the data-driven ecosystem in organizations.

Big Data analytics, which is also coined as a management revolution by (McAffe et al., 2012), can especially be utilized to simplify the path in achieving the requirements that an organization needs in this challenging transformation journey. However, an organizational change is a prerequisite for harnessing the valuable benefits from investment made in data and analytics (Rean, 2021). Thus, organizations should consider appropriate strategies to bridge cultural resistance and motivate or persuade the employees to adapt into a data-driven mindset (Halper & Stodder, 2021). In this perspective, data democracy is among the factors that have an important impact on the data-driven business transformation of an organization. As described by (Halper & Stodder, 2021), data democracy describes the efforts in making data available, spreading, and popularizing and even crowdsourcing the data and as a result diminishing the cost related to not having data available to those who might need it. By practicing the democratization of data, organizations can capacitate their employees across various levels of organization and inspire a sense of shared responsibility and duty, factors that can result in highly appreciated competitive advantages (Matisoff, 2021).

The significance of this paper relies on the importance of empowering organizations in creating the right instruction on how to achieve data democracy in their data driven transformation journey. By focusing on a case study, the paper aims to justify the importance and role of data democracy in becoming a data-driven organization. Furthermore, it intends to provide an extra investigation on the role of data analytics tools in achieving data democracy.

The following research questions guide this study:

1. *How to improve data-driven decision making in an organization through practicing data democracy?*
2. *How can data analytics tools help non-technical employees to contribute to improving data-driven decision making?*

The rest of the paper is structured as follows: the next section provides background information and lists some of the important related works in the field. Section 3 describes the methodology being used in the study. Findings and analysis are given in section 4, whereas section 5 outlines discussions in relation to the state-of-the-art. Section 6 concludes this paper.

2. BACKGROUND AND RELATED WORK

Nowadays becoming data-driven represents the ultimate goal of many organizations. According to (Andersson, 2015), true data-driven organization is a data democracy which has a great number of stakeholders who are vested in data, data quality, and the best use of data to make informed decisions and to exploit data for sustained competitive advantage.

While the significance of becoming data-driven and the relevance for using data analytics tools in achieving transformative vision have been widely discussed, when it comes to data democracy within organizations, there is a noticeable gap in the existing literature. And as highlighted by (Awashi & George, 2020), while open government data (OGD) has widely gained acceptance and has been more thoroughly explored, we lack the same enthusiasm within organizations, except very few. As far as the banking industry is concerned, all enquiries on the field of opening the data provide results about open banking. As elaborated by (Awashi & George, 2020), open banking entails sharing the banking data with application programming interfaces (APIs) with other actors in the financial market.

Traditionally, the banking industry has been strictly controlled and heavily regulated. Consequently, this has forced these organizations to be extremely careful when it comes to the availability of customer data, limiting the access to even non-sensitive data to only a small group of employees. However, such scenarios can produce frustrations due to the trouble in the communication of data-driven insights or because of the long days in producing reports by the overworked data analysts (Cornelissen, 2018). And one of the solutions for avoiding such intricacies is the democratization of data, which has its core principles in recent related movements like data philanthropy and open data (Schlagwein et al., 2017). The main aim of data democracy is to assist employees towards faster and easier access to data and to benefit from the business insight without the interference of external parties (Marr, 2016).

It is worth mentioning that data democracy does not simply emerge from placing datasets in an open shared drive, nor when the data seekers have very limited technical skills (Cornelissen, 2018). Therefore, there is a need for some assisting tools which would enable employees to extract the necessary insight from data. Since the volume of data generated nowadays is growing exponentially, organizations need various data analytics tools to handle the large volume of unstructured data and make it more understandable even for non-technical employees.

Three pillars that constitute data democracy are *share data*, *share data skill*, and *share data responsibility* (Awashi & George, 2020). Share data refers to the data analytics tools which in many organizations are handled by the data science team, and as (Cornelissen, 2018) suggests, all employees must have equal access to such tools. Sharing data skills refers to sharing the skills required for using these tools to extract patterns from the data. Equipping more non-technical team members with basic analytical skills will result in improved outcomes from the organization as a whole and eventually would create a shared sense of data responsibility. The distribution of the data science skills across various departments of the company leads to turning employees into a citizen data scientist of the organization (Bullard, 2016).

Although the importance of data analytics tools in banking sector has been studied in the existing literature (Delgosha et al., 2020; Chen, Chiang & Storey, 2012; Simonson & Jain, 2014; Kumar & Garg, 2018, Leo et al., 2019), this area is mostly mentioned regarding how an organization can become a data-driven, and not on how it can achieve data democracy. On the other hand, the role of the non-technical employees in the path of becoming data-driven has not gained the needed attention to help organizations in using their full potential. These gaps in the literature have motivated our study to focus on investigation regarding the importance of data democracy in a data-driven journey of an organization, and the role that data analytics tools could play in simplifying the path to attaining data democracy.

3. METHODOLOGY

This study is based on a case study of a Swedish bank and was aimed to collect qualitative data through online semi-structured interviews and explore secondary data from available documentation in the bank. Figure 1 provides a presentation of the different stages of the research design.

Figure 1. Research design stages

3.1 Data Collection

To perform this study both primary and secondary data has been gathered. The secondary data is collected through reviewing of the existing published literature and the internal and external documentation of the bank and the primary data is gathered via 10 in-depth digital face to face interviews with the bank's staff. Since the first author of this study is employed by the selected bank and has deeper insights about the organization, a *purposive sampling* technique was used to recruit the interview participants (Onwuegbuzie & Collins, 2007). The type of the interviewing selected in this study is the semi-structured interview, where probing was also applied in order to obtain more meaningful responses and to discover hidden issues.

Table 1. Interview participants in the study

#	Position of interviewee	Date of interview	Duration
1	Quantitative analyst	24.03.2021	25 minutes
2	Data scientist	26.03.2021	40 minutes
3	Data project manager	26.03.2021	30 minutes
4	Data scientist	01.04.2021	45 minutes
5	Product owner of a data analytics tool	06.04.2021	45 minutes
6	Manager of customer insight analytics	08.04.2021	30 minutes
7	Advanced customer analyst	12.04.2021	40 minutes
8	Customer insight analyst	16.04.2021	35 minutes
9	Deputy head of Group Information Office	19.04.2021	30 minutes
10	Data Management team member	22.04.2021	30 minutes

The digital face to face interviews were conducted with all the bank's employees through MS Teams. The interviews focused on discovering the overall viewpoint of the organization concerning the importance of data democracy in becoming a data driven bank, along with the role that the data analytics tools play in this transformation journey. The data collected through the interviews helped to achieve an understanding about these concepts from different perspectives and to gain a deeper insight compared to what was provided through the bank's internal and external documentation on these topics.

The key criterion for choosing the interviewees was their knowledge on the data driven transformation journey happening inside the bank. As shown in Table 1, the respondents were selected from two groups of employees; the data specialists who directly work with data and data analytics tools, and managers and decision makers who are aware about the organization's strategies on taking use of data and data analytics tools, but do not necessarily work directly with the data.

In this study, ethical issues were addressed based on criteria discussed by (Creswell & Creswell, 2017). Prior to conducting the interviews, the information consent regarding the method of performing and recording the interviews and how long the author intends to keep the recorded files were communicated through email to the interviewees. The informed consent also emphasized that the results of this study will solely be used for scientific purposes. Moreover, the same information was provided again at the beginning of each interview to make sure they understood the terms and to give them the opportunity to ask their remaining questions. Finally, to make sure that no data that can harm the organization is included in this study, all material gathered from the organization was sent to the designated supervisor in the organization who decided upon which information can or cannot be shared externally.

3.2 Data Analysis

In analyzing the collected data in this research, the general steps in an inductive research approach presented by (Saunders, Lewis & Thornhill, 2009) are followed. First the most relevant information is extracted from the data collected through interviews. The main themes/codes are identified, and the data is reduced to access the most relevant parts.

After retrieving and organizing the data, the process of interpretation is started. The identified themes are matched with the secondary data and finally, through establishing relationships between the collected data and research questions the conclusions are verified.

4. FINDINGS AND ANALYSIS

As also shown in Figure 2, the data gathered through internal and external documentation along with the data gathered via interviews are presented in three main themes, i.e., data-driven organization, openness of data, and data-analytics and decision making. It is worth mentioning that secondary data collected through documentation is very limited due to sensitivity and confidentiality.

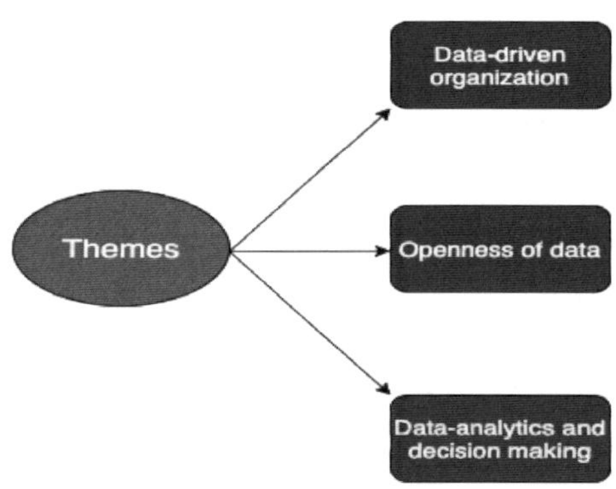

Figure 2. Presentation of the main themes

When it comes to the first theme, the thematic analysis yielded findings that the organization has since long ago aimed and invested resources to become a data-driven bank to achieve its primary goal of delivering world class service to its customers. Also, according to interviews the main vision communicated with the employees is to be data-driven in the business processes and the decision. However, as they mostly believe, there is still a long way ahead for this vision to be truly data driven. As the data analyst mention:

"Although the data specialists create data-driven decision-making foundations, the implementation on the business side of the bank is not yet successful enough [...]"

In general, three patterns or sub-themes are characterizing the data-driven concept: impact of data-skilled employees (data specialists), impact of non-data-skilled employees, and citizen data scientists. Based on the performed interviews, what data specialists can contribute to helping the organization become data-driven can be grouped into four major categories: showing the importance of data-driven decision making, setting up the guidelines for an overarching data governance system, using their data expertise in different levels from creating reports to the high-end solutions, and providing help and training to the other parts of the organization. But being a large organization with a long history, although positive in many aspects, has created difficulties in having an overarching data governance. Different groups and departments have used data in different ways and now the duty stands on the data specialists' shoulders to solve this issue by setting the structures of working with data, clarifying the definition of being data-driven and working towards having all the organization on the same boat. On this issue, one data specialist claims:

"... the mission of the data specialists is to work more with analysis and data modelling and less with data administration."

In contrast to the role of data specialists, the impact of non-data-skilled employees on accelerating the data-driven transformation is not completely straightforward. Even though the awareness for embracing data-driven mindset across the organization is high, still several aspects need to be enhanced. This encompasses communication, training, cooperation, and data governance. The notion "data-driven" is vague for many employees and it should be further communicated and explained to gain an implicit understanding. Moreover, motivation and support are needed to involve the employees in various training activities and cooperate with data specialists. The role of data in the organization should also be properly articulated by having one common data governance/management.

Another important aspect that was observed from the interviews is the role that non-data-skilled employees can play while putting in action their domain knowledge to be combined with knowledge and expertise of data-skilled employees. This would result in creating *citizen data scientists*, which would further simplify the data-driven transformation path. Once non-data technical employees get access to the data and work together with their data technical peers, the common trust in data will increase in all parts of the organizations. One interviewee is in favour of this by claiming:

"... You get the most value out of the data when you have these two, domain knowledge and some experts that can work with data."

One of the main strategies taken by the bank in order to move toward becoming data-driven, is to open up the data outside the local systems. Through this openness, a larger group of employees can have access to data and gain insight from it. When it comes to the question that if opening the access to data for the non-technical employees can benefit the bank in its journey of becoming data-driven, the respondents, with only one exception, agree with the statement. On the other hand, it should be mentioned that the respondents altogether agree that all data cannot be shared with everyone within the bank. Sharing up the data even shares the responsibility of taking care of the risk and security issues related to data. As one of the interviewees explained:

"Opening up the data puts a major responsibility on the data users on understanding the possibilities and risks."

Regarding the third theme, findings from interviews indicated that the general sentiment towards data analytics tools was positive and the promotion along with the utilization of data analytical tools should involve everyone. The outcome generated by cutting-edge visualization tools creates new analytical possibilities and for non-technical employees such tools increase the chances to engage in reading, understanding, or even creating analytical reports/outputs. Nevertheless, to some extent, mistaken beliefs still prevailed among employees that these analytical tools are meant to be used primarily by the staff with data analytics expertise.

5. DISCUSSION

Based on the findings of this study, turning into a data-driven organization, although achievable, is not an easy task and requires several fundamental changes. However, once all actors took their responsibilities and followed the guidelines, the result of this transformation is promising, the organization will become smarter and can make smarter decisions and gain smarter results.

Both the findings of the current research and the study (Hagen and Hess, 2020) have substantiated the strong connectivity between the benefits of empowering different actors of the organization with the needed data knowledge and the speeding up of the data-driven transformation journey. Based on (Hagen and Hess, 2020), turning into a data-driven organization requires substantial transformations among various components and the attention should be assigned to the different actors of the organization and on their collaboration and interrelation. And as stated in the findings of our study, the employees based on their knowledge level of data, contribute to this journey in different levels.

Additionally, the organizations can be successful in the path of becoming data driven when they invest on the reusable capabilities of its employees by discovering the data science skills across various departments and turning employees into citizen data scientists of the organization (Woddie, 2018).

By having access to the needed data, the employees can extract new insights they need for the daily work, improve their way of working and enhance the innovation and efficiency of their performance (Kaivo-oja et al., 2015). The findings of the study demonstrate the positive outcomes of opening up the data access to the internal stakeholders of the organization, a process which also relates to data democracy.

Data democracy produces significant positive outcomes for the employees, the organization as a whole and consequently for its customers and clients. This as a result will bring higher motivation and involvement in the organization in making sense of the data, in higher contribution in collecting the accurate data and consequently in generating operational excellence and higher profitability. And, according to (Court, 2015), through practicing data democracy the organization can ensure effective data use and empower employees to make data-driven decision making. In his study (Anderson, 2015), the author believes that opening the access to data can empower employees to achieve a sense of shared responsibility and duty towards data. As the respondents of the interview stated, this shared responsibility will result in a higher sense of duty in taking care of the risks and security issues related to the data, and even into higher motivation in collecting high quality data by the non-data technical employees.

The state of the art indicates that for a company to realize the true value of analytics, the data-driven decision making should be squeezed deeper in the organizational culture through increasing the number of people involved in the decision-making processes or improving the collaboration possibilities between the actors in such processes (Hagen and Hess, 2020; Ruijer, Grimmelikkhuijsen & Meijer, 2017). In our case, the organization in the process of becoming data driven tries to provide the analytics tools not only to the data specialists but even to the non-data technical employees. By providing support, training, and collaboration possibilities between the two groups of employees, the organization attempts to enable the second group to extract the insight from the data, independent from the help of the data scientists.

When talking about what type of the analytics tools suitable to be shared between the non-data technical employees, both state of the art and the finding of this study illustrate that the visualization tools are the most popular and helpful type of data analytics used for this purpose. As (Halper & Stodder, 2021) emphasized, the core idea is to empower these employees to perform more advanced analysis without relying on data specialists' assistance.

6. CONCLUSION AND FUTURE WORK

In today's data-driven environment, data analytics has significantly changed business operations. Thus, managers increasingly are considering data as an important driver of innovation and as a crucial source of value creation and competitive advantage. With digital transformation efforts underway at many organizations, including the bank in this study, businesses are gathering more data than ever before. This process provides them with many opportunities and challenges in achieving data democracy at different organizational levels.

The findings from this study associated with the first research question highlight the strong connection between the benefits from empowering different actors of the organization with the needed data knowledge and the acceleration of the data-driven transformation journey. Once organizations have devised proper strategies to open and democratize the access to the data internally, this empowers a larger number of internal stakeholders to gain insight from data and base their decision makings on facts rather than feelings.

Furthermore, as another finding of this study indicates, an organization can succeed in the path of becoming data-driven when they invest in the reusable capabilities of its employees by discovering the data analytics skills across various departments and turning their domain experts into citizen data scientists of the

organization. And by offering the needed support, training, and collaboration possibilities, it should be attempted to enable the second group to extract the insight from the data more independently.

The current study provides an outline on the possibilities that data democracy provides for improving data-driven decision making between different groups of the employees. The conclusions originate from one company (bank) and thus they should not be generalized. As a future work, it can be interesting to perform longitudinal research and investigate the real outcomes over a longer period of time, and to extend the research to other banks or even other organizational fields.

This study divides the employees of an organization into two groups, data technical employees such as data scientists, data engineers and data analysts and the non-data technical employees which involves all employees who do not directly work with data. The empirical findings discovered a third group, the citizen data scientists who are in between the other two. It can be very useful for both academic and business world to gain a deeper understanding of how an organization can employ, produce and train more of such data-interested-domain-specialists. Therefore, performing research that focuses on this group of employees would add significant value in the field.

ACKNOWLEDGEMENT

The authors would like to thank the interview participants for their generous participation to make this work possible.

REFERENCES

Anderson, C., 2015. *Creating a Data-Driven Organization.* O'Reilly Media, USA.

Awasthi, P., and George, J.J., 2020. A case or Data Democratization. *Proceedings of 23rd Americas Conference on Information Systems*. Texas A&M University, virtual conference. AIS eLibrary.

Bean, R. 2021. Why is it so hard to become a data-driven company? *Harvard Business Review*. Available at https://hbr.org/2021/02/why-is-it-so-hard-to-become-a-data-drivencompany, last accessed 2021/10/09.

Berndtsson, M., Lennerholt, C., Svahn, T. and Larsson, P. 2020. Organizations' Attempts to Become Data-Driven. *International Journal of Business Intelligence Research (IJBIR)* 11(1), pp.1-21.

Bullard, B., 2016 Style and statistics: the art of retail analytics. *John Wiley &Sons*, USA.

Chen, H., Chiang, R. H., Storey, V. C., 2012. Business intelligence and analytics: From big data to big impact, *MIS Quarterly* 36 (4), pp.1165-1188. Management Information Systems Research Center.

Cornelissen, J., 2018. The democratization of data science. *Harvard Business Review*. Available at: https://hbr.org/2018/the-democratization-of-data-science, last accessed 2021/09/06.

Court, D., 2015. Getting big impact from big data. *McKinsey Quarterly,* 1(1), pp.52-60. McKinsey & Co. Inc.

Creswell, J.W., Creswell, I.D., 2017. Research Design (5th edition). *Sage Publishing*.

Delgosha, M.S., Hajiheydari, N. and Fahimi, S.M., 2020. Elucidation of big data analytics in banking: a four-stage Delphi study. *Journal of Enterprise Information Management*. https://doi.org/10.1108/JEIM-03-2019-0097, Emerald Publishing Limited.

Hagen, J.A. and Hess, T., 2020. Linking Big Data and Business: Design Parameters of Data-Driven Organizations. *Proceedings of 23rd Americas Conference on Inormation Systems*. Texas A&M University, virtual conference. AIS eLibrary.

Halper, F. and Stodder, D. What it takes to be data-driven: Technologies and Best Practices for Becoming a Smarter Organization. Transforming Data with Intelligence Best Practices. Available at https://tdwi.org/research, last accessed 2021/10/05.

Kaivo-oja J., Virtanen P., Jalonen H., Stenvall J., 2015. The Effects of the Internet of Things and Big Data to Organizations and Their Knowledge Management Practices. In: Uden L., Heričko M., Ting IH. (eds) Knowledge Management in Organizations. KMO. *Lecture Notes in Business Information Processing*, vol 224. Springer, Cham. https://doi.org/10.1007/978-3-319-21009-4_38.

Kumar, V. and Garg, M.L., 2018. Predictive analytics: a review of trends and techniques. *Int. J. Comput. Appl* 182(1), pp.31-37. Foundation of Computer Science.

Leo, M., Sharma, S. and Maddulety, K., 2019. Machine learning in banking risk management: A literature review. Risks 7(1), p.29. MDPI.

Marr, B., 2016. Big data in practice: how 45 successful companies used big data analytics to deliver extraordinary results. *John Wiley & Sons*, USA.

Matisoff, E. Why Data Democratization Is Crucial to Your Business [Online]. Available at: https://www.adobe.com/br/insights/data-democratization-is-crucial-to-yourbusiness, last accessed 2021/10/04.

McAfee, A., Brynjolfsson, E., Davenport, T.H., Patil, DJ., and Barton, D., 2012. Big data: the management revolution. *Harvard Business Review 90(10),* pp. 60-68. Harvard Business School Publishing.

Onwuegbuzie, A.J., Collins, K.M.T., 2007. A typology of mixed methods sampling designs in social science research. *Qualitative Report* 12(2). pp. 281-316. Nova Southeastern University School of Social and Systematic Studies.

Saunders, M., Lewis P. & Thornhill, A., 2009. Research Methods for Business Students (5th ed). *Harlow: Prentice Hall.*

Schlagwein, D., Conboy, K., Feller, J., Leimeister, J. M., and Morgan, L., 2017. 'Openness' with and without Information Technology: A Framework and a Brief History," *Journal of Information Technology* (32:4), pp. 297–305. Sage Publications.

Simonson, E. and Jain, A., 2014. Analytics in Banking Conquering the Challenges Posed by Data Integration, Technology Infrastructure, and Right Talent to Operationalize Analytics in Banking. *An Everest Group Report. Everest Global.*

Storm, M., and Borgman, H., 2020. Understanding challenges and success factors in creating a data-driven culture. *In Proceedings of the 53rd Hawaii International Conference on System Sciences (HICSS)*, pp. 5399-5408, Maui, Hawaii, IEEE.

Ruijer, E., Grimmelikhuijsen, S. and Meijer, A., 2017. Open data for democracy: Developing a theoretical framework for open data use. *Government Information Quarterly*, 34(1), pp.45-52. Elsevier.

Woodie, A.: Empowering Citizen Data Science. Available at: https://www.datanami.com/2018/08/13/empowering-citizen-data-science, last accessed 2021/08/29.

NEW INSIGHT OF DATA MINING-BASED FRAUD DETECTION IN FINANCIAL IT-SYSTEMS

Salah Baïna and Ayoub Rihi
Alqualsadi, Rabat IT Center, ENSIAS, Mohammed V University in Rabat, Morocco

ABSTRACT

Nowadays, money exchanges are oriented to be more digitized in order to reduce personal contacts and maintain safety from the pandemic covid-19.
The most important aspect of any financial institute is to be secure and protected from any suspicious action that can harm the security system and be ready for any type of fraud that can happen such as money laundering, internet frauds, credit card frauds or any other financial fraud. In this paper we present a state of the art of the newest and the most efficient strategies that help financial institutes to be well secure, more reliable, starting from a state of the art of existing ML algorithms used and ending by a benchmark of those algorithms.

KEYWORDS

Financial Fraud, Fraud Detection, Machine Learning, Money Laundering, Internet Fraud, Credit Cards Fraud

1. INTRODUCTION

Recently the financial domain got an upsurge in data incoming, especially with the confinement protocol against "covid-19" that transforms all kinds of money exchanges into virtual transactions, which makes a serious challenge for banks to control the amount of actions done by clients especially those who are related to internet transactions.

Financial institutes, like banks and insurances are more likely to face those frauds, and are responsible for any fraud that can happen, in addition traditional rules of fraud detection are no longer capable of detecting the massive data of incoming transactions effectively, on the other hand the fraudsters doesn't stop to innovate new ways to steal and falsify client accounts and make frauds in a unexpected way, which explain the presence of a lot of published articles in this domain by the years to maintain the fraud changes, but in those recent years and fortunately with the appear of machine learning techniques the process of detecting frauds become more developed and automated by the fact that ML models can easily process a huge number of transactions whether in batch or in real time processing.

This paper reviewed the literature, describing the use of data mining algorithms including statistical test, regression analysis, Neural Network, decision tree, Bayesian network etc, for financial accounting fraud detection and making a benchmark helping the community of financial institutes to better decide the best algorithm performing for the exact fraud problem depending on data used, preferences etc. The advantage of data-mining techniques is the ability to use a large amount of complex data to characterize some financial phenomena that are difficult to be found by traditional methods. The drawbacks of traditional methods of detecting fraud that are based just on learning how a normal individual behaves and then find patterns that differ from this behavior, in contrary of data mining algorithms including statistical test, regression analysis, Neural Network, decision tree, Bayesian network etc are perfect for solving this case of problem regarding of the results assessed proved by evaluation metrics such as accuracy, precision, recall etc. The paper present a systematic literature review of relevant paper tackling the fraud problem and presume a comparison between different machine learning algorithms and ending with the use-case of every algorithm in the fraud detection depending on the experiments cited in different articles (Deng & Ruan 2019; Khedmati, Erfani, & GhasemiGol 2020; Lima n.d.; Lopez-Rojas & Axelsson 2016; X. Zhang, Han, Xu, & Wang 2019) and the type of fraud in question. Different types of fraud exist such as Bank Impersonation, loan frauds, Money Laundering, tax evasion, Credit card fraud, Embezzlement and more. In this article we are interested only in electronic frauds, including for example money laundering which is the process of making large amounts of money generated by a criminal activity such as terrorist funding or drug trafficking, appears to have come from a legitimate source. And the term "launders" is to make it look clean, also loan fraud as the most important service of most banks, it is about lending money for significant, but necessary items like a car, student loan or home and in exchange for future repayment of the loan value or principal amount. All the banks are trying to figure out effective business strategies to persuade customers to apply their loans. However, there are some customers which behave negatively after their applications are approved. and other electronic frauds can be mentioned in the next sections.

2. LITERATURE REVIEW

With the maturity of technologies used to detect frauds and the use of machine learning and deep learning algorithms many research paper has been published categorized between quantitative papers which present new models used in fraud detection giving concrete results and quality assessment of the model, and qualitative research paper which are generally specialized to give a compromising comparative between some researches done in fraud detection, we cite Z. Zhang, Zhou, Zhang, Wang, and Wang (2018) which proposes a fraud detection model based on the convolutional neural network in the field of online transactions, which constructs an input feature sequencing layer that implements the reorganization of raw transaction features to form different convolutional patterns. The overall structure of the model is divided into two parts: the model training part and the transaction detection part, and also the training part of the model is divided into feature sequencing layer and the CNN and the author of this papers prove that this algorithm over-perform both the traditional CNN and the BP Neural Network by considering three evaluation metrics which are accuracy, precision and recall. in the same field Lima (n.d.) explain the Auto encoders as a algorithm that compare the input data with the output data(comparison between coded and decoded data) and apply a correction mechanism (i.e. Gradient descend) is activated until a minimum error is reached. other researcher used also the auto encoder algorithm (semi adversarial auto-encoder) to omit noisy features and get efficient low dimension features then apply the auto-encoder network algorithm to update the fraud blacklist Deng and Ruan (2019).Otherwise Askari and Hussain (2020) which is a recent paper presume that Most of the works are using data mining, neural networks, SVM and decision tree based techniques. Several other approaches in terms of machine learning (ML) have been implemented, a mixture of naive Bayes and decision tree algorithm was recommended by Khedmati et al. (2020) which focused on the construction of the achievement of Naive Bayesian (NB) classifier and ID3 algorithm and also propose one class classifier as a new method that train the classifier based on only non-fraud samples using support vector data description (SVDD) in order to reduce the number of samples and select those that keep the shape of data. Askari and Hussain (2020) develop a new mathematical solution for E-transactional fraud detection using intuitionistic fuzzy logic. In this work the new concept of intuitionistic fuzzy logic with the C4.5 decision tree is used to develop the new mathematical solution for e-transactional fraud detection.

Other researches focus on creating frameworks that deal with fraud and anomaly detection problems. Pang, Shen, and Hengel (2019) present an end-to-end framework learning of anomaly scores by neural deviation learning and also contribute to a novel method namely deviation networks (DevNet 2) to perform data-efficient and effective learning of the anomaly scores.X. Zhang et al. (2019) present a framework named HOBA (homogeneity-oriented behavior analysis) starting with a comparative study to assess the effectiveness of the proposed framework. This framework is based on deep learning methods, including convolutional networks, deep belief networks and deep auto-encoders using a real-life dataset from one of the largest commercial banks in China. Lopez-Rojas (n.d.) presents an interesting contribution using RetSim which is an agent-based simulator of a shoe store based on the transactional data of one of the largest retail shoe sellers in Sweden. The aim of RetSim is the generation of synthetic data that can be used for fraud detection research. Statistical and a Social Network Analysis (SNA) of relations between staff and customers was used to develop and calibrate the model. and apply the same simulator to detect frauds. Moreover a framework named DEAL(Deep Ensemble Algorithm) was proposed by Arya and G (2020) transactions in real credit card data streams. Besides quantitative analysis research, [1309.3944] A Review of Financial Accounting Fraud Detection based on Data Mining Techniques (n.d.) reviewed the literature describing use of data mining algorithms including statistical test, regression analysis, Neural Network, decision tree, Bayesian network etc for financial accounting fraud detection and common classification techniques include neural networks, the Na¨ive Bayes technique, decision trees and support vector machines. Such classification tasks are used in the detection of credit card, healthcare and automobile insurance, and corporate fraud and suggests that using only financial statements data may not be sufficient for detection of fraud. otherwise Lopez-Rojas and Axelsson (2016) argue that many of the fraud detection methods are based on learning how a normal individual behaves and then find patterns that differ from this behavior also Eneji, Eneeji, Udie, Eyong, and Chimdike (2019) work reviewed two of such technologies. The use of artificial neural network and geographic information system (GIS) and gives out the result in the form of a map. In the map, the regions where threats are predicated by the network are indicated.

3. FRAUD DETECTION

Fraud detection has been one of the major problems for most firms, especially those in the financial sector. This affects negatively an organization's bottom line, its reputation and dissuade future prospects and current customers alike to transact with it.Machine learning comes to save the situation and propose a variety of algorithms to sight fraud and setting up automated data science processes with deep learning algorithms, in order to greatly reduce the risk of their exposure to most of such frauds.

In banking, fraud covers a variety of types like using stolen credit cards, forging checks, misleading accounting practices, etc. In insurance, 25% of claims contain some form of fraud, resulting in approximately 10% of insurance payout dollars.With all the different methods of fraud, finding it becomes harder still.

We gather the most common types of bank fraud include:

- **Bank Impersonation:** one or a lot of people act as a financial organization, usually by putting in faux corporations, or making websites, in order to lure folks into depositing funds.
- **Stolen Checks:** fraudsters might get jobs that offer access to mail, like the post workplace, mailbox stores, a tax authority, or company payroll company. Once stealing checks, they open a checking account mistreatment of a false name, and deposit the checks.
- **Forgery:** forgery happens once someone alters a check by changing the name or another info on the face. altering the number of the check, like adding a zero to the tip of the variety, will flip a 20$ check up on a 200$ check, putting more cash into the forger's pocket. Forging in order to cash or deposit a check also falls under this category.
- **Fraudulent loans:** an individual who takes out a loan, knowing that he will immediately file bankruptcy, has committed bank fraud. The same is true if the borrower uses a false identity in order to become approved for a loan, or forges information on a loan application.
- **Internet Fraud:** as it relates to bank fraud, internet fraud occurs when someone creates a website for the purpose of posing as a bank or other financial institution, to fraudulently obtain money deposited by other people.
- **Money laundering:** Money laundering is the process of making large amounts of money generated by a criminal activity, such as drug trafficking or terrorist funding, appear to have come from a legitimate source.

3.1 Challenges of Fraud Detection

During the implementation of the fraud detection model many challenges reveals that we must take in consideration during the model definition and which are specific to the fraud problem such as:

- Class imbalance for exp: (100,000:non fraud vs 1:fraud), means that the fraudulent transactions are very scarce.
- Assigning fraud labels from historical data.
- Fraud is ambiguous.

- Not all features available in real-time.
- Most machine learning sees transactions atomically.

4. COMPARATIVE ANALYSIS AND BENCHMARKING

In this can be presented into three categories:

- Quantitative results which present all research papers with a concrete contribution approved by the quality assessment results.
- Qualitative results: present all state of the art or benchmarking papers that presume a set of quantitative/qualitative papers into one article. We gathered the most prominent state of the art in order to ensure the best analysis of the problem and came up with a useful chart that clarifies the recent successful algorithms used in this field.
- We extract three interesting frameworks applied in the anomaly detection field and we make a comparison in such a way that helps the community to better take advantage of those frameworks.

4.1 Quantitative Analysis

In this research paper we try to reduce as max as possible the recent solutions of fraud detection and gather all the results assessed by essential metrics like Accuracy/ Recall/ Precision/ F1-score.

Table 1. Result of recent relevant model in fraud detection domain

		Metrics			
Article	Model	Accuracy	Recall	Precision	F1-score
Z. Zhang et al. (2018)	CNN Based on Feature Sequencing	98.5%	94%	91%	0.92
Z. Zhang et al. (2018)	Convolutional Neural Network	89%	89%	64%	0.74
	BP Neural Network	79%	60%	55%	0.59
Khedmati et al. (2020)	Support Vector Data Description	97.75%	85.57%	91.94%	0.8864
	SVM	94.60%	75.50%	84.41%	0.7971
Deng and Ruan (2019)	FraudJudger	98.5%	92.3%	90%	0.91
	Linear Discriminant Analysis (LDA)	94.6%	NA	NA	NA
	Random Forest	93%	NA	NA	NA
	AdaBoost	97.5%	NA	NA	NA
Askari and Hussain (2020)	Intuitionistic fuzzy logic based decision tree	98%	NA	81%	0.86

4.2 Qualitative Analysis

In the financial domain, the authors in Table 2, show that the technical data mining and logistic models, neural networks, Bayesian networks, and decision trees have been extensively applied to provide solutions to the problems of fraud detection and classification. From the study of hundreds of articles on fraud in the financial system. Below table presents a summary of the survey.

Table 2. Survey of the model used for fraud detection problem in financial domain

Article	Year	NN	NB	BBN	DT	Heuristic	RM	LR	KNN
[1309.3944] A Review of Financial Accounting Fraud Detection based on Data Mining Techniques(n.d.)	2019	X	X	X	X	X	X		
Eneji et al.	2019	X							
Sadgali et al.	2019	X	X		X			X	X
Lopez-Rojas and Axelsson	2016	X	X				X		

4.3 Frameworks Based Fraud Detection

In this section we propose three famous framework of fraud detection and there results depending on the data used Table 3:

Table 3. Quality assessment of Fraud detection frameworks

			Metrics			
Article	Framework name	Data Description	Accuracy	Recall	Precision	F1-score
Arya and G (2020)	DEAL	Fraud transactions in real credit card data stream ➔ number of instances: 284,807 ➔ Fraudulent: 492 ➔ Legitimate: 284,315	99.81%	98.01%	71.22%	0.824
X. Zhang et al. (2019)	HOBA	real-world dataset from one of the largest commercial banks in China ➔ number of instances: 61,735 ➔ Fraudulent: 2042 ➔ Legitimate: 59693	98.25%	51.96%	62.60%	0.568
Pang et al. (2019)	DevNet	nine publicly available real-world data sets are used	88.32%	NA	NA	NA

5. CONTRIBUTION

To avoid those problems we propose in this article a new transformation of data that helps machine learning models get better insight about the data and thus be able to generalize.

The use of this transformation has two interesting effects. The first one is for enlarging the data so a deep learning algorithm will be preferable since a deep learning algorithm requires a large dataset. The second reason is to avoid all the challenges we already mentioned in the previous section. This transformation is inspired by the fact that most machine learning algorithms treat transactions atomically which mean that a transaction is complete or not so they don't get enough information about sequences of events, even the correlation and the dependency across many features. For that reason, we think that transforming raw data into images using some patterns is a very good solution to tackle the two problems at the same time.

We start our transformation by making a correlation matrix which is calculated as below:

$$R_{jk} = \frac{S_{jk}}{S_j S_K} = \frac{\sum_{i=1}^{n} \quad (x_{ij} - \underline{x_j})(x_{ik} - \underline{x_k})}{\sqrt{\sum_{i=1}^{n} \quad (x_{ij} - \underline{x_j})^2 (x_{ik} - \underline{x_k})^2}}$$

We choose the top 8 correlated features for every feature in the dataset, and we replace every value of the dataset by a kernel of 3*3 and we fill the center of the kernel with the origin value. The other cells of the kernel will be filled in a clockwise manner by the values of the top 8 correlated features that we are working on, starting from the top center of the kernel. and so one until we get a $(RowData_x * 3, RowData_x * 3)$ as a new shape at the end of the transformation. the below figure give the exact formulation of the transformation in each specific cell:

5.1 Experiment Results

The following images represent the output of our transformation. It contains 9 transactions including to frauds,the patterns of the images show clearly the differences between legitim transactions and fraudulent ones just by seeing the image we can retrive where the fraud is located.

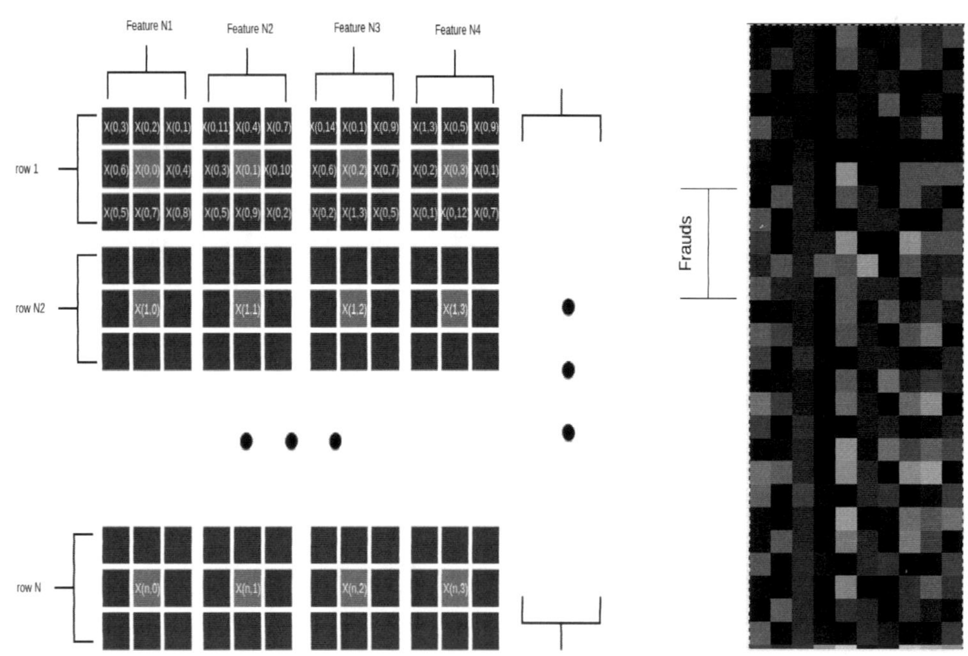

Figure 1. Quality assessment of Fraud detection framework

6. DISCUSSION

This paper presents a brief vision of models used to detect frauds in the financial domain and gives a clear idea of the choice of the model that should be done, depending on the metrics assessment and the existing data type and characteristics to detect anomalies. Our paper presumes all the existing research done for fraud detection in the financial domain into one paper within three categories which we took ad-vantages from each category and present it in such a way that helps the community to better make the decision. from the first category of papers we observe the domination of Neural Network models such as Convolutional Neural network, BP Neural Networkwhich gives a clear idea that Neural Network Models in most of time can perform very good on this use case, but as we all know the fact that NN models needs to be feeded by a large dataset to give similar performance which is not present on all the cases.otherwise the other model also can be an alternative solution for those who wants to start by a medium data volume or maybe less. The other categories offer other aspects of proposed solutions like how much such an algorithm is cited in the majority of articlethat treat this problem more specifically.

7. CONCLUSION

The problem of fraud can be curtailed. It will however take time, money, and a combined effort on the part of many researchers. We see in this paper how fraud problems can cause dramatic damage and even destroy the baseline of a bank structure since clients are money in the banking industry. Many researches tackle this problem and still developing their solutions, because fraud is not a static problem, it develop by the development of other fields like marketing and trading, and by the augmentation of competitively between banks, thus it is important to be aware of the most recent contributions done in the other domains related to fraud, so that rules can be changed regularly and continuously over the time. We believe that there is a lot of work to do in the future by making a framework for fraud challenges that makes both prevention and detection of frauds and in real time processing.

REFERENCES

[1309.3944] A Review of Financial Accounting Fraud Detection based on Data Mining Techniques [WWW Document], n.d. URL https://arxiv.org/abs/1309.3944 (accessed 12.5.19).

Arya, M., G, H.S., 2020. DEAL – 'Deep Ensemble ALgorithm' Framework for Credit Card Fraud Detection in Real-Time Data Stream with Google TensorFlow. Smart Science 8, 71–83. https://doi.org/10.1080/23080477.2020.1783491

Askari, S.Md.S., Hussain, Md.A., 2020. IFDTC4.5: Intuitionistic fuzzy logic based decision tree for E-transactional fraud detection. Journal of Information Security and Applications 52, 102469. https://doi.org/10.1016/j.jisa.2020.102469

Deng, R., Ruan, N., 2019. FraudJudger: Real-World Data Oriented Fraud Detection on Digital Payment Platforms. arXiv:1909.02398 [cs].

Eneji, D., Eneeji, S., Udie, M., Eyong, W., Chimdike, K., 2019. A Study of Electronic Banking Fraud, Fraud Detection and Control 4, 4.

Hoffmann, A.O.I., Birnbrich, C., 2012. The impact of fraud prevention on bank-customer relationships: An empirical investigation in retail banking. Intl Jnl of Bank Marketing 30, 390–407. https://doi.org/10.1108/02652321211247435

Khedmati, M., Erfani, M., GhasemiGol, M., 2020. Applying support vector data description for fraud detection. arXiv:2006.00618 [cs].

Lima, S., n.d. Deep learning for fraud detection in the banking industry. Fraud detection in the Banking industry.

Lopez-Rojas, E.A., n.d. Applying Simulation to the Problem of Detecting Financial Fraud 202.

Lopez-Rojas, E.A., Axelsson, S., 2016. A review of computer simulation for fraud detection research in financial datasets, in: 2016 Future Technologies Conference (FTC). Presented at the 2016 Future Technologies Conference (FTC), pp. 932–935. https://doi.org/10.1109/FTC.2016.7821715

Lopez-Rojas, E.A., Elmir, A., Axelsson, S., 2016. PAYSIM: A FINANCIAL MOBILE MONEY SIMULATOR FOR FRAUD DETECTION.

Pang, G., Shen, C., Hengel, A. van den, 2019. Deep Anomaly Detection with Deviation Networks. arXiv:1911.08623 [cs, stat].

Paula, E.L., Ladeira, M., Carvalho, R.N., Marzagão, T., 2016. Deep Learning Anomaly Detection as Support Fraud Investigation in Brazilian Exports and Anti-Money Laundering, in: 2016 15th IEEE International Conference on Machine Learning and Applications (ICMLA). Presented at the 2016 15th IEEE International Conference on Machine Learning and Applications (ICMLA), pp. 954–960. https://doi.org/10.1109/ICMLA.2016.0172

Sadgali, I., Sael, N., Benabbou, F., 2019. Performance of machine learning techniques in the detection of financial frauds. Procedia Computer Science, The Second International Conference on Intelligent Computing in Data Sciences, ICDS2018 148, 45–54. https://doi.org/10.1016/j.procs.2019.01.007

Zhang, X., Han, Y., Xu, W., Wang, Q., 2019. HOBA: A novel feature engineering methodology for credit card fraud detection with a deep learning architecture. Information Sciences. https://doi.org/10.1016/j.ins.2019.05.023

Zhang, Z., Zhou, X., Zhang, X., Wang, L., Wang, P., 2018. A Model Based on Convolutional Neural Network for Online Transaction Fraud Detection. Security and Communication Networks 2018, 1–9. https://doi.org/10.1155/2018/5680264

USING DESIGN SCIENCE RESEARCH AS PARADIGM FOR INFORMATION SYSTEM RESEARCH: AN APPLICATION

Lizani Botha and Estelle Taylor
North-West University, Potchefstroom Campus, South Africa

ABSTRACT

Design science research (DSR) is a research paradigm with great potential in information systems (IS) research, but it may be challenging for researchers wanting to apply this relatively new approach, to choose and then apply a methodology to a specific problem. The aim of this paper is to describe an example of how the design science research paradigm, as well as a design science research framework, can be applied to a specific research problem. The ontological and epistemological assumptions of design science research, as well as different perspectives of design science research are discussed. The design science research framework, guidelines established by authors known for their contribution in design science research can offer researchers the opportunity to easily utilize this research paradigm in their research. A study investigating data modelling approaches in data warehouse is used as an example of the application of design science research. This example should provide students and researchers early in their research career with one example of how to apply all of these to do design science research.

KEYWORDS

Design Science Research Paradigm, Guidelines, Frameworks

1. INTRODUCTION

Design science research (DSR) is a research paradigm with great potential in information systems (IS) research, as it brings both practical relevance (via artifacts) and scientific rigor (via the formulation of design theories) to IS research (Baskerville et al. (2018). Venable et al. (2017) refer to Design Science Research (DSR) as a popular new research approach and paradigm, for which several research methodologies have been developed, and they mention that one of the challenges facing researchers wanting to apply this new approach, is the choice of research methodology. They write: "*Like the cooking example, if you are trying to do Design Science Research, it is a good idea to have some guidelines or a cookbook. As a new design science researcher, you face a choice of DSR "cookbooks" and methodologies*". Students or researchers early in their career, are faced with first identifying a research problem, then choosing a research paradigm, then choosing a methodology, and then applying that methodology to a specific problem.

The aim of this paper is to describe how the design science research paradigm, as well as the design science research framework of Vaishnavi and Kuechler (2007:27), can be applied to a specific research problem.

In Section 2 the assumptions of design science research are described. In Section 3 a possible application is explained, followed by a conclusion in Section 4.

2. DESIGN SCIENCE RESEARCH

Design science research involves "a rigorous process to design artefacts which are intended to solve observed problems, to make research contributions, to evaluate the designs and to communicate the results to appropriate audiences" (Hevner *et al.*, 2004:82; Peffers *et al.*, 2006:50). The ontological assumption of design science research indicates that multiple, contextually situated realities exist (Vaishnavi *et al.*, 2017:25). The epistemological assumption of design science research indicates that knowledge can only be gained with the creation of artefacts (March & Smith, 1995:253). The purpose of the artefact is to serve human needs within a specified environment (March & Smith, 1995:253). Different definitions of design science research, as well as the research process models followed by several researchers, are discussed in Table 1. The table is a summary, based on research done by Vaishnavi *et al.* (2017:21). The researchers identified in Table 1 were chosen by Vaishnavi *et al.* (2017:21), based on the contribution to design science research knowledge and published articles.

Table 1. Different perspectives on design science research

	Takeda et al. (1990)	***March & Smith (1995)***	***Hevner et al. (2004)***	***Peffers et al. (2006)***	***Vaishnavi & Kuechler (2007)***
Design science research definition	Takeda *et al.* did not refer to the term design science research, but rather to the term design process. The term design process is defined as a mapping from the function space to the attribute space, both of which are defined over the entity concept set (Vaishnavi *et al.*, 2017:4).	Design science is concerned with devising artefacts to attain goals and serve a human purpose (March & Smith, 1995:253).	Design science creates and evaluates IT artefacts intended to solve identified organisation problems (Hevner *et al.*, 2004:77).	Design science research creates and evaluates any designed object with an embedded solution to an understood research problem (Peffers *et al.*, 2006:86).	Design science research is a "lens" or set of synthetic and analytical techniques and perspectives (complementing positivist, interpretive, and critical perspectives) for performing research in IS (Vaishnavi & Kuechler, 2007:10).
Design science research process model steps	Enumeration of problems, suggestion, development, evaluation to confirm the solution and decision on a solution to be adopted (Vaishnavi *et al.*, 2017:11).	March and Smith (1995:254) argue that design science includes two major steps: build and evaluate.	Identify business needs (through people, organisational strategies, current technology infrastructure, etc.), develop/build, justify/evaluate while adding to the current knowledge base (Hevner *et al.*, 2004:80).	Problem identification and motivation, the definition of the objectives for a solution, design and development, demonstration, evaluation, and communication (Peffers *et al.*, 2006:89).	Adapted from Takeda et al. (1990). Awareness of problem, suggestion, development, evaluation and conclusion (Vaishnavi & Kuechler, 2007:45).

The following characteristics of design science research are identified by both Vaishnavi *et al.* (2017:13); Weber (2012:3):

- Design science research defines a problem solution and stems from the engineering discipline.
- The end products of using design science research are either constructs, methods, models, instantiations or a combination thereof in the form of an artefact. The artefact provides a real-world outcome and not an overall description of the world.

Gregory (2010:9) discusses the following additional characteristics of design science research:

- The primary focus in a design science research project is mostly on the design science research part as opposed to generating new knowledge.
- The design science research process involves the search for a relevant problem, the design and construction of an IT artefact, and its *ex-ante* and *ex-post* evaluation.
- An important goal in design science research is to search and solve practically relevant real-world problems.
- Design science research is a general research approach that can be used in combination with different research methods.
- The outcome of design science research and the problem solution are mostly an individual or local solution and the results cannot be readily generalised to other environments or settings.

To summarise, design science research is a lens or a set of synthetic and analytical techniques and perspectives that complement positivistic, interpretive and critical theory philosophical assumptions when performing research in information systems. There are three design science research cycles in any design research project: the relevance cycle, the design cycle, and the rigor cycle (Hevner & Chatterjee, 2010:16).

The relevance cycle connects the design science efforts to the application context. People, organisational, and technical systems interact to achieve specific goals in the application context or environment. The requirements are described as inputs in the application context, as well as acceptance criteria for evaluation. An important question that needs to be answered is: Does the design artefact improve the environment and how can this improvement be measured? At the end of the design science research cycle, the output and results must be returned into the application context for evaluation (Hevner & Chatterjee, 2010:17). By returning the results and evaluation taking place, the researcher can determine if additional iterations of the relevance cycle are needed. The requirements might also change when the results from the design science activities are applied in the application domain. By applying the relevance cycle in this study, the researcher can determine the requirements, problems and opportunities.

The second cycle is known as the design cycle and iterates between the core activities of building and evaluating the design artefacts and processes of the study (Hevner & Chatterjee, 2010:17). Requirements are updated until a satisfying design is reached, and a balance should be found between the time spent building and evaluating the artefact's evolving design (Hevner & Chatterjee, 2010:19). The artefact should be rigorously and thoroughly tested before it is released in the application context.

The third cycle is known as the rigor cycle and draws from a vast knowledge base of scientific theories and engineering methods (Hevner & Chatterjee, 2010:17).

It is important for a researcher following design science to continuously research and reference the knowledge base in order to ensure that the designs produced are contributing to the research field (Hevner & Chatterjee, 2010:18). Definitive research contributions are essential when presenting the research to both an academic and technical audience (Hevner & Chatterjee, 2010:18).

The end products of using design science research are either constructs, methods, models, instantiations or a combination thereof in the form of an artefact. The artefact provides a real-world outcome and not an overall description of the world. The design science research process involves the search for a relevant problem, the design and construction of an IT artefact, and its *ex-ante* and *ex-post* evaluation. An important goal in design science research is to search for and solve practically relevant real-world problems.

3. APPLICATION TO A SPECIFIC RESEARCH PROBLEM

In this section an example is used in which design science research was applied to a problem in the field of Information Systems. The research problem that will be used as an example is: Organisations are faced with difficult choices when attempting to implement a data warehouse and choosing data modelling approaches that will benefit their business intelligence the most. What aspects or factors should be considered when selecting an appropriate data modelling approach in a data warehouse? The main research objective of this example is the creation of a framework that guides the selection of a suitable and feasible data model for a data warehouse that has a direct impact on the business intelligence system. This framework should consider characteristics, such as business information needs, data parameters, enterprise size, business processes, current data architecture, as well as data strategy.

To identify a solution for the research problem and to achieve the main research objective sub-objectives were set and are listed below:

SO1: Research, investigate and compare literature regarding data warehouses, as well as data modelling techniques, for example, dimensional modelling, data vault modelling, relational models, and hierarchical models.

SO2: Identify characteristics of data sets and data models which can influence a business intelligence system.

SO3: Investigate and compare current technologies being used to design, develop and implement data warehouses and data models.

SO4: Survey to determine the end user's needs and current dependency on information.

SO5: Design and develop data models for three data warehouses, each with unique data, by identifying the best-suited data model, based on the knowledge gained in SO1 to SO4.

SO6: Evaluate the data models by gaining feedback from end-users to ensure that the expectations of their data needs have been met and that mature decision making has been made possible.

SO7: Create a framework by establishing guidelines that can be used in the selection of data models for a data warehouse that can improve business intelligence.

SO8: Draw a conclusion on which data models have the most impact on business intelligence.

Design science research is used in both the theoretical and empirical parts of the study used as an example. The theoretical study included reviewing literature and gaining knowledge with regard to the research problem, whilst the empirical part of the study included the development of data models for data warehouses, as well as a framework which can then be used by an organisation as a guide when choosing a data model approach. These data models and the framework can be described as artefacts and because the application domain of these artefacts is organisational systems, the researcher made use of design science research cycles and guidelines as developed by Hevner *et al.* (2004:83). These guidelines assist the researcher in conducting and evaluating good design science research. In Table 2, the seven guidelines of design science research are given, as well as a description of each guideline according to Hevner *et al.* (2004:83). A brief description of how the guideline is applied in this study is also given.

Table 2. Design science research guidelines according to Hevner *et al.* (2004:83) and application to study used as example

Guideline	***Description***	***Application to the study used as an example***
Guideline 1: Design as an artefact	Design science research must produce a viable artefact in the form of a construct, a model, a method, or an instantiation.	A framework is produced during this study by using design science research. This framework can be implemented in other research projects, as well as the information technology industry.
Guideline 2: Problem relevance	The objective of design science research is to develop technology-based solutions to important and relevant business problems.	The artefact is a proposed solution to assist a business or organisation when selecting a data modelling approach that will be beneficial to business intelligence.
Guideline 3: Design evaluation	The utility, quality, and efficacy of a design artefact must be rigorously demonstrated via well-executed evaluation methods.	The usefulness and effectiveness of the artefact are demonstrated to chosen audiences, whereafter the design of the artefact is revisited and refined. The researcher uses descriptive design evaluation methods, by using information from the knowledge base, e.g., literature reviews, to build an argument for the artefact's utility. Detailed scenarios can also be constructed around the artefact to demonstrate the utility of the artefact.
Guideline 4: Research contributions	A clear and verifiable contribution should be made to areas of artefact design, foundations and methodologies of design, then only is design science research considered to be effective.	This study contributes to the fields of not only information system design science research, but also knowledge of business intelligence, data warehouses, data vaults, etc.
Guideline 5: Research rigor	In both the production and evaluation of the design object, design science research relies on the use of rigorous techniques.	To characterize the stated and constructed artefact, mathematical formalism is employed; rigor is also assessed in terms of the artefact's applicability and generalisability.
Guideline 6: Design as a search process	The search for an effective artefact necessitates the use of readily available tools to achieve desired goals while	Using feedback from technology-oriented, user-oriented and management-oriented audiences the design of the artefact and

	adhering to established laws in the issue context.	development of the framework is constantly revisited to determine the most suitable data modelling approach while business parameters, rules and processes are considered.
Guideline 7: Communication of research	Design science research must be presented effectively to both technology-oriented and management-oriented audiences.	The results of the study are communicated to technology- and management-oriented audiences through related articles, and demonstrations of the artefact.

For the study used as example, the seven guidelines of design science research (Table 2) were used, as well as a checklist of eight questions were used during the study to assess progress. This checklist with eight questions for design science research has been formulated by Hevner and Chatterjee (2010:20). The questions are stated in Table 3 (column 1) and answers to the questions are provided in column 2. In column 3, the DSR guideline (from Table 2) is referenced that can assist in answering the question in column 1 of Table 3.

Table 3. Checklist for design science research

Questions as by Hevner and Chatterjee (2010:20)	***Answer***	***DSR guideline that can accompany question***
1. What is the research question (design requirements)?	The research question for this study is: What aspects or factors should be considered when selecting an appropriate data modelling approach in data warehouses?	Guideline 2
2. What is the artefact? How is the artefact represented?	The artefact is data models for three different data sets. From each iteration, a framework is built to aid in developing a business intelligence system with the best-suited data modelling approach.	Guideline 1
3. What design processes will be used to build the artefact?	The design science research framework and the three design science cycles are used to build the artefact. The researcher also makes use of surveys/questionnaires to determine if all the requirements were met after a specific data model was chosen.	Guidelines 3 & 6
4. How are the artefact and design processes grounded by the knowledge base? What, if any, theories support the artefact design and the design process?	Before the development of the artefact can be done, the knowledge base is established through literature reviews. The design and development of the artefact are based on knowledge built up during the literature reviews.	Guidelines 3 & 6
5. What evaluations are performed during the internal design cycles? What design improvements are identified during each design cycle?	The research is evaluated from two perspectives, *ex ante* and *ex post* evaluation.	Guidelines 3 & 5
6. How is the artefact introduced into the application environment and how is it field tested? What metrics are used to demonstrate artefact utility and improvement over previous artefacts?	A pilot study is done in the study to determine a base foundation for choosing a data model that will be best suited to the business intelligence requirements of an organisation whereafter iterations of the three design science cycles are done. The application environments of the same companies that produce the data are used.	Guideline 6
7. What new knowledge is added to the knowledge base and in what form (e.g., peer-reviewed literature, meta-artefacts, new theory, new method)?	A framework is added as new knowledge to the knowledge base. This framework is based on iterative cycles and results from questionnaires.	Guidelines 4 & 7
8. Has the research question been satisfactorily addressed?	This question can only be answered during the conclusion of the study.	Guideline 5

The questions listed in Table 3 (column 1) ensures that a researcher, no matter the level of experience, is able to identify the research problem, determine how the knowledge that is gained during the study will contribute to the development of the artefact, as well as how the artefact will be evaluated to ensure that a solution for the problem domain has been found. An important part of design science research is to continuously test and evaluate not only the design theories but also the applicability, the understandability and the application of the artefact in practice (Hevner & Chatterjee, 2010:221). The seven guidelines as listed in Table 2 by Hevner *et al.* (2004:83) combined with the eight questions for design science research by Hevner and Chatterjee (2010:20) is a great guide to assist a researcher who is considering design science research as a research paradigm.

If a researcher is of the opinion that the guidelines and questions assisted in identifying if design science research is the suitable research paradigm but lacks a process of starting with the actual research process then the design science research framework by Vaishnavi and Kuechler (2007:27) can be implemented (illustrated in Figure 1).

This framework includes five steps; the first step is the awareness of a problem. The main goal of the design science research framework is to identify the problem and to define it (Hevner & Chatterjee, 2010:26). As an example, the researcher can then make use of Question 1 from Table 2. The second step is to identify a preliminary suggestion(s) or solution for the problem identified in the first step of the framework. This can be done by answering Question 2 and Question 3 from Table 2. The suggestion(s) or solution(s) is based on existing theory or knowledge or developed by using a suitable research methodology (Hevner & Chatterjee, 2010:26). The third step involves the actual development. This is a creative stage and the design is further refined and an actual artefact is produced. By answering Question 4 from Table 2 a researcher can ensure that the development of the artefact is based on knowledge gained during the first two steps of the design science research framework. When the development of the artefact is completed, the fourth step is to evaluate the artefact according to the functional specification. Question 5 and Question 6 (Table 2) can contribute to ensure robust and rigorous evaluation of the artefact. The fifth and final step is to terminate the project and conclude (Hevner & Chatterjee, 2010:27). By answering Question 7 and Question 8 (Table 2) a researcher is then able to confirm if the study was a success and if the research problem was solved.

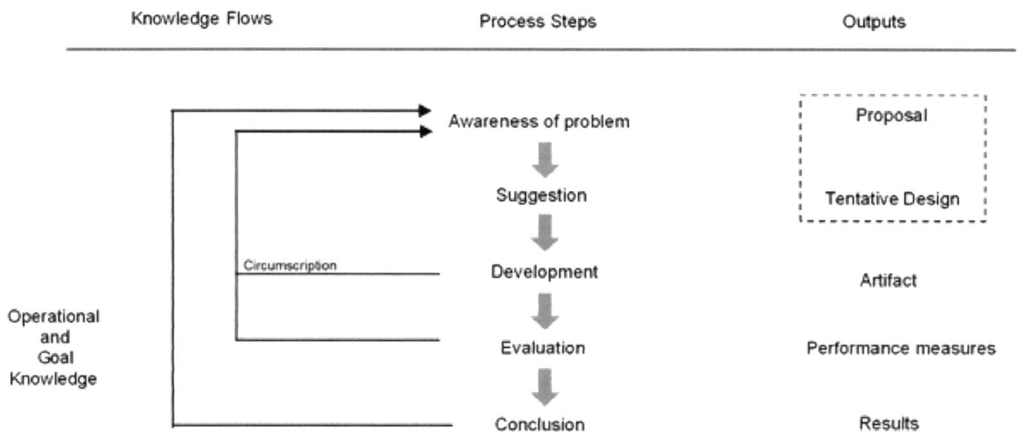

Figure 1. Design science research framework (Vaishnavi & Kuechler, 2007:27)

A researcher can also combine the design science research framework by Vaishnavi and Kuechler (2007) with the design science research cycles by Hevner and Chatterjee (2010). Based on the design science research framework by Vaishnavi and Kuechler (2007), the example study divides the five steps (Figure 1) into three phases which is based on the three design science cycles by Hevner and Chatterjee (2010): relevance-, design- and rigor cycle (as discussed in Section 2). The term phase is used in this example as a researcher can then utilise project management skills to set project milestones within a phase and ensure the scope of a phase is managed and completed before the next phase is started.

Figure 2 depicts the five steps, as well as how the five steps are divided into the three phases. The first two process steps (awareness of the problem and suggestion) of the design science research framework are combined into one phase, as are the last two process steps (evaluation and conclusion) of the framework.

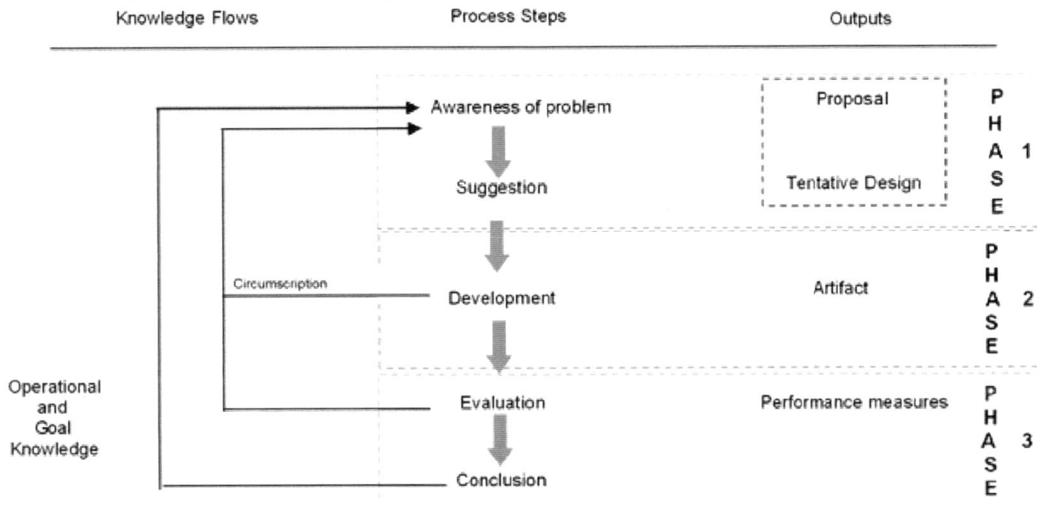

Figure 2. Phase division of this study according to the design science research framework

The objectives set for a research project can then be divided into the different phases and executed through a process step. The three phases, as well as the sub-objectives (highlighted earlier in this section) that are addressed in each phase are discussed next.

Phase 1: Awareness of problem and suggestion

The sub-objectives that can be considered for this phase and which can assist the researcher with understanding the problem area and enable the researcher to form a suggestion or solution for the identified problem are:

SO1: Research, investigate and compare literature regarding data warehouses, as well as data modelling techniques, for example, dimensional modelling, data vault modelling, relational models, and hierarchical models.

SO2: Identify characteristics of data sets and data models which can influence a business intelligence system.

SO4: Survey to determine the end user's needs and current dependency on information.

In phase 1, the problem is identified and defined. Based on existing knowledge and theory of the problem area, a suggestion or problem solution is formed. The problem being addressed in the study used as an example is which data model will be best suited for a data set being worked with to develop a business intelligence system. Only after the background research has been done can the researcher start with the development of a suggestion or problem solution.

Phase 2: Development

For phase 2 the following sub-objectives are identified:

SO3: Investigate and compare current technologies being used to design, develop and implement data warehouses and data models.

SO5: Design and develop data models for three data warehouses, each with unique data, by identifying the best-suited data model, based on the knowledge gained in SO1 to SO4.

SO6: Evaluate the data models by gaining feedback from end-users to ensure that the expectations of their data needs have been met and that mature decision making has been made possible.

Based on the knowledge gained in phase 1, the researcher will be able to start the design and development of the artefact in phase 2. Research methods such as questionnaires are used to strengthen the suggestion/problem-solution formed in phase 1 and to gain more information regarding the data set and data models that are developed in this example study. Phase 2 and phase 3 will be iterations for each data set used in the example. For example, phase 2 will be applied for the pilot study from which the knowledge and information gained will be used to start the creation of the framework (artefact in this example). Phases 2 will then be applied to the scenario and data set of Company A and the framework will then be elaborated on, based on knowledge and information gained from this iteration. This will be followed by applying phase 2 on Company B's and Company C's data set and elaborating the framework.

The last phase includes the evaluation of the results and the conclusion of this research. This is discussed next.

Phase 3: Evaluation and conclusion

The results evaluation and concluding the study are phase 3. The following sub-objectives are of importance for this phase:

SO7: Create a framework by establishing guidelines that can be used in the selection of data models for a data warehouse that can improve business intelligence.

SO8: Draw a conclusion on which data models have the most impact on business intelligence.

For this study, the researcher needs to evaluate the use of the developed data models to determine if the data model used increases the knowledge that the end user can gather from the data set. With every iteration of development, more knowledge is gained and this can be used to develop a framework which the organisation can use to choose a data model which will provide sustainable business intelligence. After each iteration of phase 2, the knowledge and information gained from the iteration are used to build and elaborate the framework.

4. CONCLUSION

The aim of this paper is to describe how the design science research paradigm, as well as the design science research framework of Vaishnavi and Kuechler (2007:27), can be applied to a specific research problem.

In Section 2 the assumptions of design science research were described. In Section 3 a possible application was explained, followed by a conclusion in Section 4.

Venable et al. (2017) mention 6 possible methodologies that can be followed when doing design science research. In this example one of these, namely the DSR Process Model (DSRPM) of Vaishnavi and Kuechler (Vaishnavi & Kuechler, 2004, 2007, 2015), is applied to a specific problem. These 5 steps are used in combination with 3 phases of research, as well as the 7 guidelines of Hevner *et al.* (2004:83) and a checklist for design science research (Hevner and Chatterjee (2010). By leveraging off and combining different frameworks and guidelines from authors known for their research in design science research a researcher will be able to apply design science research successfully to a study in information system research.

This example should provide students and researchers early in their research career with one example of how to do design science research.

REFERENCES

Baskerville, R., Baiyere, A., Gregor, S., Hevner, A., & Rossi, M. 2018. Design science research contributions: Finding a balance between artifact and theory. Journal of the Association for Information Systems, 19(5), 3.

Dinter, B. & Krawatzeck, R. 2015. Towards a Configurative Publication Schema for Design Science Research *Thirty Sixth International Conference on Information Systems.* Forth Worth, Texas.

Gregory, R. W. 2010. Design Science Research And The Grounded Theory Method: Characteristics, Differences, and Complementary Uses. *18th European Conference On Information Systems.* Pretoria, South Africa.

Hevner, A. & Chatterjee, S. 2010. *Design Research In Information Systems,* New York, Springer.

Hevner, A. R., March, S. T., Park, J. & Ram, S. 2004. Design Science In Information Systems Research. *MIS Quarterly,* 28:75-105.

March, S. T. & Smith, G. F. 1995. Design And Natural Science Research On Information Technology *Decision Support Systems,* 15:251-266.

Peffers, K., Tuunanen, T., Gengler, C. E., Rossi, M., Hui, W., Virtanen, V. & Bragge, J. 2006. The Design Science Research Process: A Model For Producing And Presenting Information Systems Research. *DESRIST.* Claremont, California.

Takeda, H., Veerkamp, P., Tomiyama, T. & Yoshikawa, H. 1990. Modeling Design Processes. *AI Magazine.*

Vaishnavi, V. K. & Kuechler, W. L. 2007. *Design Science Research Methods And Patterns,* Boca Raton, New York, Auerbach Publications.

Vaishnavi, V. K., Kuechler, W. L. & Petter, S. 2017. *Design Science Research In Information Systems* [Online]. Available: Http://Www.Desrist.Org/Design-Research-In-Information-Systems/ [Accessed 26 February 2019].

Venable, J. R., Pries-Heje, J., & Baskerville, R. L. 2017. Choosing A Design Science Research Methodology.

Weber, S. 2012. Comparing Key Characteristics Of Design Science Research As An Approach And Paradigm. *16th Pacific Asia Conference On Information Systems.* Ho Chi Minh City, Vietnam.

MATURITY AND QUALITY LEVELS IN THE USE OF INTEROPERABLE INFORMATION SYSTEMS FOR ECONOMIC REACTIVATION OF TOURISM-HOSPITALITY-GASTRONOMY SECTOR POST-PANDEMIC. CASE STUDY: ECUADOR

Rubi Rojas, Manuel Tupia and Mariuxi Bruzza
Department of Engineering, Pontificia Universidad Católica del Perú
Avenida Universitaria 1801 San Miguel, Lima, Perú

ABSTRACT

As a result of the global pandemic of COVID 19, many socio-economic sectors have been affected, the most affected being the tourism, hospitality, and gastronomy industries, which are closely related. As part of the reactivation activities proposed by different governments around the world, in addition to financial support, technological solutions have been determined for these sectors in such a way that responsible public entities have had the need to propose interoperability solutions that help increase the number of customers in these three sectors as the restrictions have been decreasing in terms of attendance at hotels, restaurants and several tourist centers. This paper presents the current state of maturity in the application of interoperable information systems by public institutions responsible in Ecuador, as well as a preliminary approach to a model for evaluation of this type of IT solutions.

KEYWORDS

Interoperability, Information System, Tourism, Hospitality, Post-Pandemic, Economic Recovery

1. INTRODUCTION

One of the economic sectors that has suffered greatest impact during COVID-19 pandemic is tourism, since as indicated by the World Tourism Organization (2020), the almost total confinement imposed in response to the pandemic reduced in May the number of international tourists by 98% compared to 2019. According to a study conducted by the UN, it makes clear the importance of restarting tourism "as soon as it is safe to do so". In particular, the current COVID-19 crisis has caused a significant drop-in tourism activity in Latin America, where this activity is a key generator of foreign exchange, income and employment, representing around 10% of the region's total GDP (United Nations, 2020).

Also, since process of digitization of technological solutions that enable the reactivation in form of digital services has been accelerated by the global health crisis as mentioned (Agudelo et al., 2020), organizations must provide both high levels of quality in electronic service (Villarejo & Sanchez, 2004) and maturity levels appropriate to specific contexts (MinTIC et al., 2019). It becomes necessary to have tools to assess performance of an organization in terms of quality and maturity of IT solutions it offers, especially at public administration. Maturity refers to the capacity of institutions to provide such services, while quality defines the adjustment of processes to what is expected of them (ISACA, 2015).

In this scenario, it becomes important to establish e-government solutions for the reactivation process of different economic sectors. While e-government has been defined as the digital interaction between the central government, local governments, and citizens through the implementation of e-government; interoperability is the ability of two or more systems to exchange and use information to provide services to citizens (G2C), businesses (G2B) and other governments (G2G) (Bruzza, 2020). The importance of these concepts lies in the fact that the absence or inadequate use of interoperability could generate inefficiencies in the management of organizational resources (Gallaher et al., n.d.). Especially when several institutions related to sectors such as tourism, hospitality and gastronomy are required to work together in the implementation of reactivation solutions with open data and interoperability (exchange of information and services).

It is in this context that present research is developed. The content of which will be presented as follows: in section 2, the problem will be shown with an orientation towards the case study developed in Ecuador; in section 3, the measurement of maturity carried out in a group of Ecuadorian state institutions related to the problematic sectors of tourism, hospitality and gastronomy is presented following the principles presented by (Turban et al, 2002); in section 4, the preliminary model for the evaluation of the maturity and quality of interoperable information systems solutions proposed by the authors is presented; finally, section 5 presents the conclusions and future works.

2. PROBLEMATIC

Our research focuses on the review of the maturity and quality factors that any information system that has interoperability characteristics focused on the reactivation of the tourism sector and related sectors. For this purpose, a list of public institutions in Ecuador, responsible for both the regulation of these sectors and the post-pandemic reactivation by COVID-19 was established as a case study.

Currently, most relevant models used to measure maturity are CMMI, EIF, EIMM, IMM, among others. However, in some cases those models applied to certain interoperable solutions are not appropriate, as mentioned in (Akatkin et al. 2016), since they do not consider the organizational aspects of interoperability. It is necessary to understand that a model is a way to describe a set of components and their relationship to describe a process, in this case, assessment as mentioned in (ISACA, 2015); while a framework of good practices can be adopted as a reference for any of the activities performed by an organization.

In turn, for quality measurement, periodic surveys about e-government solutions to users are used, as well as models such as ODIN, WebQual4.0, E-GovQual, among others (Purwandari et al., 2019). Although in some cases important criteria such as the size of the organization, number of citizen users and available resources are left aside (Peters et al., 2004), or the total population is not considered within the surveys conducted (Akatkin et al., 2016). This results in the use of unsuitable models to measure the quality of interoperable e-government solutions in tourism. The following table shows the problem tree identified from the state-of-the-art review of the problem:

Table 1. Problem tree

Causes	Central problem	Effects
Absence of a model or standard to measure th quality and maturity of e-government solutior in a comprehensive and simultaneous manner	**Inadequate assessment of the quality and maturity of interoperable e-government solutions in tourism institutions**	Existing e-government solutions oriented for tourism institutions do not meet minimum quality criteria and have low maturity levels
Absence of interoperable tourism-oriented e-government solutions.		Existing e-government solutions oriented for tourism institutions do not follow good practices about quality and maturity.
Inadequate application of internationally accepted best practices for maturity and qualit in tourism-oriented interoperable e-governme solutions.		Low levels of satisfaction (from citizen – G2C, or private enterprise – G2B) about existing e-governm services related with tourism.

2.1 State-of-Art Review

The review of the state of the art indicates that within e-government solutions based on information systems in tourism-related sectors, no models or standards are applied to measure maturity or quality.

This indicates poor quality management, which is the set of paths by which quality is achieved and allows each of these problems to contribute to the low user satisfaction with existing e-government tourism services, in addition to revealing that there are e-government solutions that apparently do not meet basic quality criteria.

Another problem identified is the small number and complexity of interoperable solutions in Latin America, which means that few public institutions work collaboratively sharing information and generating joint procedures for their citizen users (open data). In Brazil, Mexico and Uruguay, the number of interoperable procedures that citizens can initiate is around 62% of the total number of procedures allowed, while in the rest of the region it does not even reach 50%; this figure is much lower than the European Union average (81%) with peaks of 95%. In general, Latin America has low levels of interoperability maturity (Roseth et al., 2018).

Roseth states that even if it is an interoperable e-government solution, this is no guarantee of usability for a citizen. Such is the case of Paraguay, which, despite having a single business window called the Unified System for Opening and Closing Businesses (SUACE), fails to adequately simplify its procedures, since just to open a business, the entrepreneur must go through 14 steps, submit 11 different documents, hire third parties, and wait approximately 60 days to complete the entire process.

Even the perception of insecurity is considered, which suggests that, in most cases, either security is not a concern, or that any concern about security affects the decision to carry out a procedure through one channel or another. This is how low confidence is generated in the information provided by tourism services on the part of users (Kim et al., 2020).

Finally, the review has shown a gap, where it can be observed that there is no comprehensive model to measure these two concepts quality and maturity, in conjunction with interoperable e-government solutions for tourism institutions. Therefore, this thesis project will develop a model to measure maturity and quality in an integral and simultaneous way, following international standards, frameworks, and models, and as a case study, these measurements will be performed in public institutions that manage tourism in Ecuador.

2.2 Selected Problem

As a summary, it is established that the selected central problem that will be developed throughout this work is the inadequate evaluation of the quality and maturity of interoperable e-government solutions in tourism institutions.

3. CASE OF STUDY: ECUADOR

Present section shows the evaluation of all public institutions in Ecuador involved in the management and reactivation process after the COVID-19 pandemic in the tourism and related sectors (hospitality and gastronomic)

3.1 Theoretical Framework

Turban (2002) mentions six stages that public institutions may go through as they develop interoperable e-government solutions, being these stages:

- Stage 1: Information Dissemination / Publication.
- Stage 2: Two-way Official Transactions
- Stage 3: Multipurpose portals
- Stage 4: Portal Customization
- Stage 5: Bundling of common services
- Status 6: Full Integration and (Digital) Business Transformation

The more complex the technology used (e.g., interoperable information systems that by their very nature are complex) and the more advanced the digital transformation process within the public institution, the higher level of maturity of these organizations. This is illustrated in Figure 1:

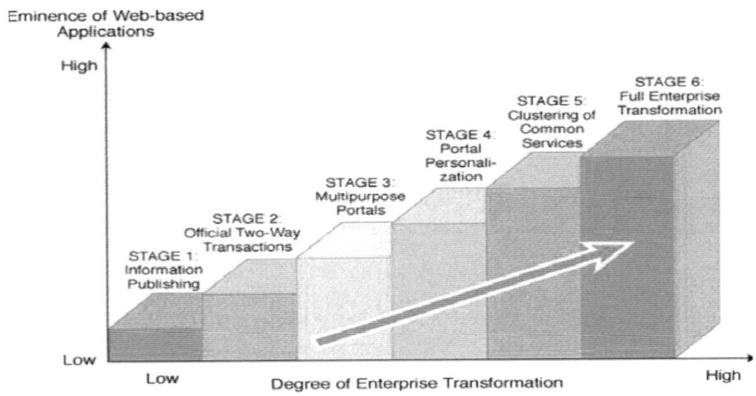

Figure 1. Eminence of interoperability web-based applications according (Turban et al, 2002)

Turban approach has been the basis for more modern frameworks and models covering the maturity of e-government services in general, usability and accessibility to such services among other aspects included in the works of (Días, Bruzza and Tupia, 2019) and (Salas, Tupia and Bruzza, 2021). Obviously, Turban has been based on the maturity levels proposed at the time by CMMI, which can be seen today oriented to IT services in (Kawashita, Baptista and Soares, 2020).

3.2 Information Gathered for Case Study

For the case study, the web portals of each Ecuadorian entity related to the tourism sector and responsible for the economic reactivation process have been identified, developing interoperable information systems.

Then, it is classified by assigning a stage of Turban's taxonomy, adequately justifying this choice. This can be seen in table 2:

Table 2. State of maturity of Ecuadorian state institutions responsible for the tourism, hospitality, and gastronomy sectors according to (Turban, et al 2002)

Nº	Web	Stage	Explanation
1	macco.ec	1	Web portal offers information about services available: museum opening hours and various events. Beyond that and a newsletter, website does not offer any other kind of information. Although the site has the appropriate digital certificates, it does not offer monetary transactions. Then it is not a multipurpose portal and does not offer customization.
2	www.turismo.gob.ec	2	The web page corresponds to the Ministry of Tourism of Ecuador, and contains information about: 1. Information about covid 2. Holidays 3. Accountability of the Ministry 4. Training 5. Single point-of-sale: this option is linked to other pages that provide citizens with the possibility of carrying out a wide variety of online procedures. 6. It also offers a virtual assistant that works by analyzing basic terms to give general information about the pandemic and travel recommendations (no AI chatbot).
3	mintur.turismo.gob.ec	1	The web page is a system that links different modules of the platform of the Ministry of Tourism of Ecuador; however, all the links except the first one does not work (for December 2020). On the other hand, there is an intranet that must be registered to access. It could easily not even be considered in status 1.
4	cayambeturismo.gob.ec	1	The website offers detailed information about the different tourist services offered, specifying routes, schedules and information about the place, as well as an option of

			recommendations to know what can be done. However, it does not offer monetary transactions, such as the purchase of a tourist package or renting the service of a tour guide, so this website does not achieve the status 2, besides being only an information website and not multipurpose.
5	www.ambiente.gob.ec/	2	The website of the Ministry of Environment and Water in general shows a lot of information on *Transparency, Programs/Services, Library and News sections*. In the *Links and Government* sections it usually takes you to different government websites in general. In the *Ministry* section there are also parts that only have information, and the *Intranet* section shows Document Management Systems *Quipux*, which is private for employees-only.
6	www.quito-turismo.gob.ec	1	The website presents detailed information on procedures and formalities. In addition, each step is explained in detail, including situations that may arise during the process. There is no mention of the need to use digital signatures. In addition, in the case of other services, by going to Services > Tourism Quality (https://www.quito-turismo.gob.ec/calidad-turistica/) it also allows downloading forms in pdf format for the application to the *Distintivo Q program*, as well as the user's guide. In addition, it presents the contact options for further information.
7	areasprotegidas.ambiente.gob.ec	1	The website has information related to the National System of Protected Areas of Ecuador (SNAP). The most outstanding feature of this portal is the large amount of information focused on providing recommendations for visiting natural areas in this country. In addition, it has a wide variety of informative and legal documentation on natural areas and the actions to be taken for their protection by the Government.
8	tpm.ec	2	The website offers 4 types of online services: outbound import cargo, direct customs clearance, national fishing, and export, which allow the user to upload information about the products to be imported or exported and the transport (driver and vehicle) in charge of the operation. Stage 2 is assigned because the web page allows for two-way transactions, since after uploading all the information required by the service, a QR code is provided, which is presented at the port to ship or pick up the products.
9	www.orellanaturismo.gob.ec	1	The website offers information about the services offered, as well as recommendations, videos of the places and promotions. Information offered is divided into various sectors such as: adventure, nature, culture, and relaxation. These are also included in blogs where they publish additional information about the destinations and the cultures they represent. It also allows to add personal data to be able to quote accommodations. We have found links to other services such as: training, advisory and consulting services but they are not currently in operation
10	sancristobalgalapagos.gob.ec	1	The page is purely informative. The information provided corresponds to tourist attractions in the Galapagos region, where they provide information on climate, activities, tours, food, etc.
11	www.patrimoniocultural.gob.ec	1	The website shows information about Ecuador's cultural heritage in the form of maps and photographs. It has a menu with different categories where you can find services, FAQ, social networks, etc. It does not have a virtual payment platform, but it has many links to pages related to its purposes.
12	ciudadalfaro.gob.ec	2	The web page shows a series of different sections that specify what the Civic Center is made up of. On the one hand, it presents services, elements and spaces related to its activities. In addition, it provides redirection links to entities associated or related to the Civic Center “Ciudad Alfaro” such as -

			governmental links, national public procurement service, foreign travel requests, Quipux document management
13	www.hojas-jaboncillo.gob.ec/	1	The page shows diverse information about the "*Hojas Jaboncillos*" such as: -Location, aerial connectivity, terrestrial connectivity. -Maps of the patrimonies of the place, such as forests, basins, topography, vegetation, wells, surrounding communities, among others. -Offer of services of the place: tourist guide, gastronomy, beach tour. It also offers links to the governmental portal of Ecuador where services are provided for citizen procedures, for example: -Covid19 vaccination passport. -Free software for signing and validating electronic documents.
14	www.gob.ec/mintur/tramites/actualizacion-datos-registro-turismo-alojamiento	3	The website shows a wide variety of services to be performed online. When accessing each service, it shows a description, to whom it is addressed, what is needed to carry out the procedure, forms and annexes, how to carry out the procedure, cost of the procedure, opening hours and contact information for citizen services. It also includes a search engine for quick access to services and a menu showing the number of services distributed in 20 categories. Likewise, it complies with stage 2 since the procedures can be carried out online. There are 4 steps to complete the procedures: applicant data, procedure data, signature and voucher. In addition, it complies with stage 3, since it is possible to pay for some procedures online, it should be noted that payment is provided through other entities, where an identification number must be consulted on platforms such as COSEDE to make this payment.
15	www.yakumuseoagua.gob.ec	1	The website of Yaku (Water Museum) of Ecuador is in state 1 of e-government, which is the dissemination and publication of information, given that: -Provides public information about the museum -Displays maps showing how to get there
16	www.museociudadquito.gob.ec	1	The entity's website belongs to State 1 as it provides information about the services provided by the museum as well as the museum itself.
17	captur.com	1	The website of the Pichincha Chamber of Tourism belongs to the s1, although there is a membership form, which is in a very basic state, and there is no payment method for membership. On the other hand, this page presents informative services, such as the benefits offered to members, some videos about CAPTUR - EGEDA benefits and CAPTUR - SOPROFON benefits, among others.
18	turismo.ruminahui.gob.ec	1	The website presents *Rumiñahui* as a tourist destination and shows all the information about the Ecuadorian canton and what places can be visited if we decide to travel to this place, even has a service to make a panoramic view tour of these sites, but it does so in an extensive and merely informative way. Although the portal includes a form to contact those in charge of the tourism department of *Rumiñahui*, it does not allow us to make any transaction.
19	www.museos.culturaypatrimonio.gob.ec	1	The consulted website of the National Museum Network belongs to stage 1, since it shows public information about museums in Ecuador, such as contact numbers, address, and opening hours of each one, as well as additional information. Specifically, it belongs to this state because it has sections where certain queries can be made (which, by the very nature of the website, are related to museum information). For example, it shows a "Digital Catalog of Cultural Assets",

			where citizens can enter certain data, through filters, and obtain a list of results.
20	guayaquilturismoep.gob.ec	1	The website of the Municipal Public Company of Tourism, Civic Promotion and International Relations of Guayaquil belongs to stage 1, since it consists of a static page, with general information of the Company, a list of services that redirects to external pages along with publications and events and a static transparency portal.
21	turismo.gadsantacruz.gob.ec	1	Website pertaining to Santa Cruz Island in the Galapagos group of islands. In this website we find mainly static information (text and images) about the mentioned place and details like location, climate, fauna, flora, etc. There is also information on how to get to Santa Cruz considering prices. All this information is available to the user in the main view and in the different tabs.

4. PRELIMINARY MODEL FOR MEASURING MATURITY AND QUALITY OF E-GOVERNMENT SERVICES BASED ON INTEROPERABLE INFORMATION SYSTEMS

The proposed component model is based on the COBIT 2019 structure (ISACA, 2018): it is divided into domains directly related to the strategic dimensions of the balance scorecard (BSC) tool. Obviously, adaptations have been made to replace the commercial and customer dimensions and replace them with organizational and technical dimensions oriented to provide citizen services on behalf of state enterprises.

Then, each domain has two elements associated with it:

- Objectives to be achieved: these objectives relate to what the public entity must achieve in terms of interoperability, open data, data governance, and quality and maturity good practices. These objectives are presented on table 3 and have been finalized. The objectives are both organizational and technical in nature because is necessary a combination of structural aspects within the public organization (which can lead to digital transformation projects) and IT aspects that must be covered to provide interoperable e-government services, whether for tourism sector or in general, for all sectors affected by pandemic.

Table 3. Business and IT objectives

Perspective from Balance Scorecard	Business objectives and IT objectives
Client	**1. Guarantee the integrity and confidentiality of public information.** **2. Achieve high levels of citizen confidence in the security of data.** **3. Guarantee access to quality and relevant information for the citizen.** **4. Simplify the citizen experience in the use of e-government services.** **5. Achieve high levels of citizen trustworthiness in e-government services.** **6. Ensure the capacity, continuity, and availability of e-government services.**
Internal	**7. Promote transparency and accountability to stakeholders and relevant entities.** **8. Ensure timely and inclusive electronic access to e-government services.** **9. Ensure consistent delivery of value of e-government services (efficiency in resource allocation).** **10. Assess and manage the risks involved in the delivery of e-government services.** **11. Comply with laws and regulations related to e-government** **12. Comply with laws and regulations related to IT technologies and services.** **13. Optimize costs in the delivery of e-government services to the citizen**
Technical	**14. Ensuring information security** **15. Achieve a comprehensive and integrated vision of e-government services.** **16. Simplify the administrative activity of e-government services.** **17. Maximize the added value of e-government services.** **18. To ensure the optimization of resources allocated to IT solutions related to e-government services.** **19. Comply with internal policies related to quality, security, capacity, and scope of delivery of e-government services.**

Improvement and innovation	**20. Optimize the management of information involved in the delivery of e-government services.** **21. Ensure data sharing among state institutions (open data).** **22. To procure the use of open standards and applications to reduce IS development.** **23. Establish mechanisms for continuous improvement of the quality of e-government services. 24.** **24. Optimize the design of e-government services.** **25. Ensure the flexibility and scalability of e-government services.**

- Processes to execute through which, precisely, the public institution will achieve above objectives. The relation between objective and process is 1:1. What do these processes contain or represent? All the activities that must be conducted to achieve the objectives described above. These activities are based on internationally accepted good practices of governance and management of IT and e-government services. Details of the proposed processes can be seen below, in Figure 2.
- Finally, last component is an implementation guide that is being designed for those responsible for e-government can apply the entire model, establish the metrics and indicators for each process and proceed to measure these results in such a way that they can self-assess the state of quality and maturity of their interoperability solutions. This gives them independence so that e-government managers, quality specialists and even internal auditors can make the evaluations deem appropriate. Even during the implementation of interoperable solution construction projects. For example, in the preliminary study phases (business case) or in the evaluation process of the IT suppliers that could take charge of the construction of the solution itself.

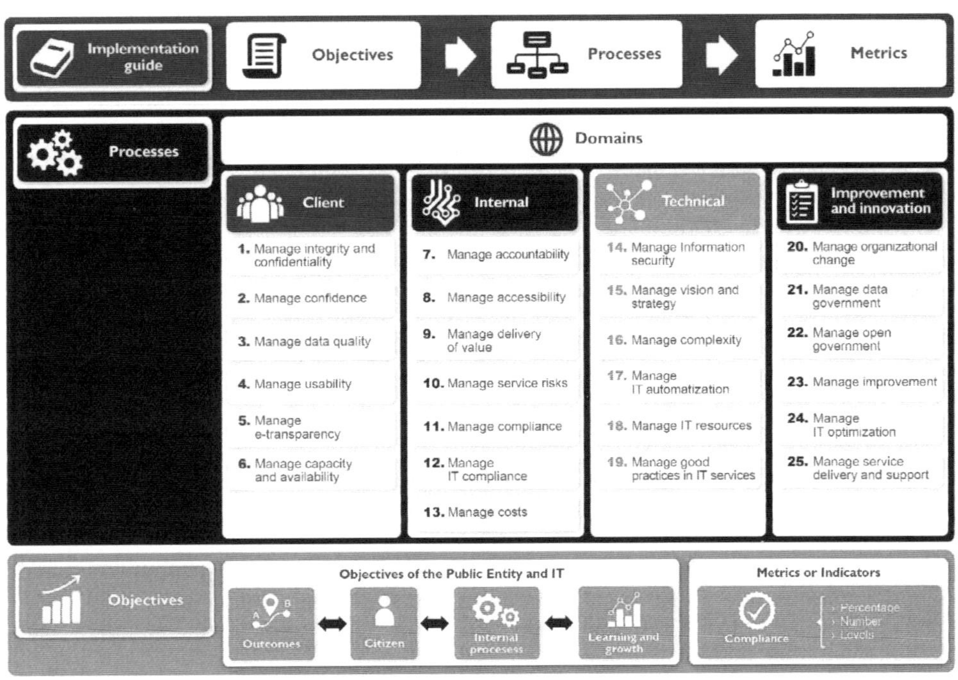

Figure 2. Core model components

5. CONCLUSION

Clearly, it can be concluded that the level of development of interoperable information systems is on average at the initial stage, which means that the economic reactivation process for the sector may be at risk. On the other hand, it has been identified that most of the interoperable solutions only involve the participation of 2 different public entities (except for one case), which reduces the complexity and scope of the services.

In terms of the model, the objectives in question will then be converted into IT management processes based on best practices such as COBIT 2019, ITIL V4, VeriSM, among others. Then, each process will have assigned maturity metrics to be achieved by way of a service level agreement. Finally, each interoperable solution will have a set of indicators that will allow validating its quality in the provision of services to the citizen. In summary, maturity will be measured at the level of the public entity and quality at the level of the information systems development life cycle and the perception of value given by the citizen plus usability and accessibility considerations such as those seen in (Dioses, Tupia and Bruzza, 2021).

Proposed future works consist of finishing the model with the metrics and indicators mentioned above, developing the guide for the improvement of interoperable services for a sample of public institutions related to economic reactivation, and extending its scope to any economic sector that requires e-government services in addition to financing for such reactivation. The next case studies will be in Ecuador (expanding the solutions base) and Peru.

REFERENCES

Agudelo, M. et al, 2020. *Las oportunidades de la digitalización en América Latina frente al Covid-19. Agenda Digital Para América Latina y el Caribe 2020-2022*. Santiago de Chile, Chile, pp. 5-25.

Akatkin, Y. et al, 2016. Towards the digital government in Russia: integrative approach. *Proceedings of the International Conference on Electronic Governance and Open Society: Challenges in Eurasia*, St. Petersburg, Russia, pp. 41-48.

Bruzza, M., (2020). *Diseño de un modelo para la implementación de gobierno electrónico en instituciones estatales*. Tesis doctoral, Pontificia Universidad Católica del Perú, Lima, Perú.

Dias, G. P., Bruzza, M. and Tupia, M., 2019. Local E-Government Sophistication in Ecuador: The Case of the Manabí Province. *Proceedings of the International Conference on eDemocracy & eGovernment (ICEDEG)*, Quito, Ecuador, pp. 24–26.

Dioses, L., Tupia, M. and Bruzza, M., 2021. State-of-art for Accessibility Measurement in Electronic Government Services for People with Visual Disabilities. *Proceedings of Iberian Conference on Information Systems and Technologies (CISTI)*, Chaves, Portugal, pp. 23–26.

Gallaher, M. P., et al., 2004. *Cost Analysis of Inadequate Interoperability in the U.S. Capital Facilities Industry*. National Institute of Standards and Technology, Maryland, USA.

ISACA, 2015. *ISACA Interactive Glossary & Term Translations*. ISACA Publishing, Illinois, USA.

ISACA. 2018. *COBIT 2019 Framework: Introduction and Methodology*. ISACA Publishing, Illinois, USA.

Kawashita, S, Baptista, A. and Soares, D. 2020. E-government maturity models: more of the same? *Proceedings of Seventh International Conference on eDemocracy & eGovernment (ICEDEG)*, Buenos Aires, Argentina, pp. 58-66.

Kim, M., Hall, C. M. and Kim, D. K., 2020. Why do investors participate in tourism incentive crowdfunding? The effects of attribution and trust on willingness to fund. *Journal of Travel & Tourism Marketing*, Vol. 37, No. 2, pp. 141–154.

MinTIC, iNNpulsa Colombia, IDOM, and Tecnalia Colombia, 2019. Modelo de madurez para la transformación digital. MinTic, *Dirección de Transformación Digital*.

OMT. 2020. El impacto de la COVID-19 en el turismo mundial queda patente en los datos de la OMT sobre el coste de las parálisis. *Comunicado de Prensa*, Vol. 34.

ONU Habitat. 2020. Tecnologías digitales y la pandemia de COVID-19. *Ciudades y Gobiernos Unidos*, Vol. 17.

Peters, R. M., Janssen, M. and van Engers, T. M. 2004. Measuring e-government impact. *Proceedings of the 6th international conference*, Delft, The Netherlands, pp. 480-489.

Purwandari, B., et al. 2019. Strategies to improve quality of data dissemination website: a case study of the Central Bureau of Statistics. *Proceedings of IADIS International Conference Information Systems,* Utrech, The Netherlands, pp. 155-162.

Roseth, B., et al., 2018. *El fin del trámite eterno: Ciudadanos, burocracia y gobierno digital*. Inter-American Development Bank, New York, USA.

Salas, L., Tupia, M. and Bruzza, M., 2021. A Measurement Maturity Model in the Use of Spatial Data Applied to e-Government. *Proceedings Iberian Conference on Information Systems and Technologies (CISTI)*, Chaves, Portugal, pp. 1-8.

Turban, E., et al, 2002. *Electronic commerce 2002: A managerial perspective*. Pearson Education, New Jersey, USA.

Villarejo, Á., and Sánchez, M., 2004. La calidad de servicio electrónico: un análisis de los efectos moderadores del comportamiento de uso de la web. *In Cuadernos de Economía y Dirección de La Empresa*, Vol. 21, pp. 121–152.

CHALLENGES AND MITIGATION STRATEGIES IN THE USE OF THE SEMI-STRUCTURED INTERVIEW TECHNIQUE

Tiko Iyamu and Maria Mutudi
Department of Information Technology, Cape Peninsula University of Technology, South Africa

ABSTRACT

Despite the growing popularity of the semi-structured interview technique, there remain challenges that threaten the richness of the data that it is used to collect. As consistently revealed in literature, although efforts have been made to address some of the challenges, they persist. Some of the challenges manifest from various environmental and cultural factors, which make them unique. Hence it is essential to continue work in the area, in enhancing the technique and fortifying data collection. This paper reports on the challenges experienced by a researcher (postgraduate student) during data collection using the semi-structured interview technique. In gathering the experience, the storytelling approach was employed and the interpretivist approach was followed in the analysis. This study helps to gain better understanding about some of the challenges that are encountered, and the implications of practice in the use of the technique. From the analysis, this paper proposes how the challenges can be explicitly addressed in the process of collecting data using semi-structured, especially in an environment where there are language and cultural differences.

KEYWORDS

Data Collection, Case Study, Semi-Structured Interview

1. INTRODUCTION

Increasing, many postgraduates are applying the semi-structured interview technique in collecting data. Some of the rationale for selecting the technique are because it allows conversation between the interviewer and interviewees, which helps to gain deeper understanding of what, why, and how things happen (Yin, 2018). Subsequently, realities, interaction and relationship between actors are better understood. This contribute to why the technique has been employed in many different studies, such as in business (Scuotto, Ferraris & Bresciani, 2016) and health (Bearman, 2019). Despite the growing popularity, many students continue to encounter challenges, which sometimes threaten the data collection processes.

This study examines the challenges experienced by an IS researcher when collecting qualitative data using the semi-structured interview technique. Even though the technique was most appropriate for the research, many challenges were experienced, which threatened the richness of the data. Apparently, this type of challenge is not peculiar to the student (or research), as many of aspiring scholars (postgraduates) have at one point or the other experienced similar challenges. This is despite intensive preparation prior to conducting the research, particularly about an environment, concepts, themes, and models (Jebreen, 2012). Although there are benefits for using the semi-structured interview technique, it comes with many challenges as well, which can be mitigated using very precise wordings. Some of the challenges are discussion of sensitive information, and potentially confusing terminologies that are often used by individuals or groups.

The objective of this paper was to explicitly provide mitigation against the challenges encountered by a researcher during data collection. The intention is to provide collegial answers to questions others often have as they experience similar difficulties. Even though this paper concerns young scholars from almost all disciplines, it does lean more towards IS research, primarily because the research being reported was conducted in IS field. Although the challenges revealed in the paper are contextual, researchers in other disciplines can also experience them.

2. REVIEW OF RELATED LITERATURE

The review began with case study primarily because the semi-structured interview is often associated with the approach. A case study is profound and comprehensive for studying phenomena, which makes it preferable in many IS studies. Yin (2018) states that the focus of a case study is on current situations within its occurring environment. According to Wohlin and Aurum (2015), the case study approach is most suitable for qualitative empirical type of research because it allows the researcher to get a deeper understanding of contemporary complex phenomena. This is mainly because, the researcher seeks answers to questions such as why and how (Yin, 2018). This involves direct interactions with the participants to get in-depth knowledge about and an understanding of the phenomenon within its natural setting (Bygstad & Munkvold, 2016).

Increasingly, the case study approach and the semi-structure technique are employed in IS research (Stokes and Urquhart, 2013). Many postgraduate students employ these approach and technique even though they continue to experience challenges with them in practices. As a result, study, such as Myers and Newman (2007) has in the past highlighted and tried to address some of the challenges. Recker (2012) explains that one of the challenges involves data collection skills, specifically in the areas of interviewing participants in a case study research. According to Avison and Pries-Heje (2005), interaction with both organisations and their employees (potential interviewees) can be challenging.

The semi-structured interview is a well-documented technique that is used to gather qualitative data by engaging in an in-depth discussion or conversation with participants about the phenomenon being studied. The technique is common in IS research, which could be due to its flexibility, and allowing the ability to probe responses for clarifications, to gain better understanding of why and how things happens (Marshall, Brereton & Kitchenham, 2015). However, scholars such as Adams (2010) and Irvine, Drew and Sainsbury (2013) asserted that the flexibility of semi-structured interview can serve as a benefit, and a challenge at the same time. Some of the challenges that have been highlighted in literature include relationship, letting the participant guide the interview, and maintaining the same level of attention from beginning to the end of the interview (Irvine et al., 2013; Adams, 2010).

Probationship is arguably one of the greatest benefits, and most challenging aspect, which many aspiring researchers encounter in using the semi-structured interviews. Iyamu (2018, pp. 2261-2262) defines the term 'Probationship' as "an act to prove or test a scenario through subsequent interrogation and instant inquiring into subject matter". This involves making the most of the unexpected responses from the participants and instantaneously seek clarification or ask follow-up questions (Yin, 2018). This is a challenge especially for postgraduate students, novices or aspiring researchers, mainly because experience is required in order to know when and how to probe without deviating from the original topic or question about the study.

3. OVERVIEW OF ORIGINAL RESEARCH

This section contextualises the research, whose challenges are being addressed in this study. The research was conducted by a researcher at CPUT. It reveals critical challenges during data collection. In the research, the case study approach and semi-structured interview technique were employed, primarily because the researcher wanted to have direct interactions with the participants, to get an in-depth understanding of the current system in Angola, a phenomenon being studied. Explicably, because IS solutions do not exist separately from human influence and interaction. The researcher employed the case study approach and semi-structured technique as explained by Yin (2018).

The research aimed at developing an information system framework, which could be used to validate individuals' physical addresses against identity documents in the Republic of Angola. The aim was split into two objectives as follows: (i) identify and examine factors of deficiencies in the current system that cause wrong or inconsistent physical addresses to be printed on identity documents of individuals; and (ii) examine both technical and non-technical factors that can improve the current system. Based on the objectives, the qualitative methods, case study approach, and the semi-structured interview technique were employed in the study. Figure 1 shows the research actions and steps that were undertaken towards achieving the objectives of the study. The justifications for selecting the approaches, methods, and technique are discussed herewith.

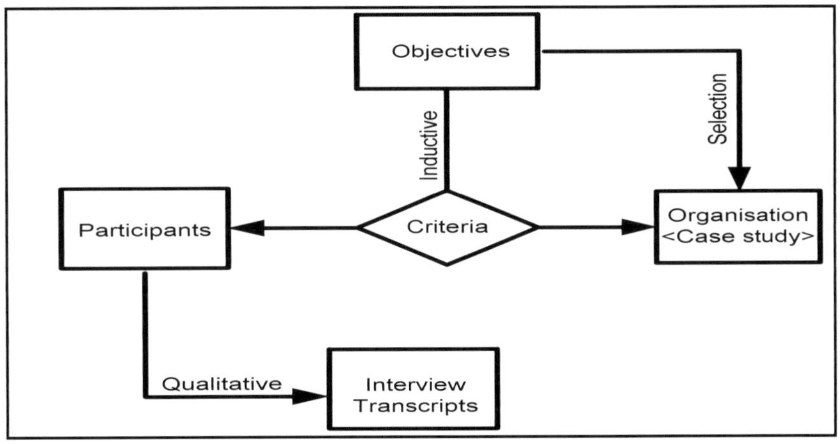

Figure 1. The study design

As shown in Figure 1, based on the objectives of the research, which was develop a framework (theory), the inductive approach was selected (Gray, 2013). This is mainly because the approach implies generating a theory from the data that was collected and analysed. This means that the framework was developed based on the data collected in a specific context (Republic of Angola). Also based on the objectives, the case study approach was selected (Creswell & Poth, 2017). According to the researcher, this was to ensure logical flow and practical influence. Research design should be logically linked to other approaches and methods including the data collection techniques that are applied in a study. The methodology which the researcher applied in the study is discussed in the remainder of this section. This includes criteria used in selecting participants, interview guidelines followed in the data collection, and the approach that guided the data analysis.

3.1 Methodology of Original Research

The methodology applied by the researcher is presented in this section. It was a qualitative research in which the case study approach was adopted, owing to some of its rationale: it enables (1) empirical examination of a phenomenon within its real-life context (Yin, 2018; Godwin & Potvin, 2017); and (2) in-depth examining of a case or cases in their natural settings (Wohlin & Aurum, 2015). Initially, two government Ministries in Angolan were selected as cases in the study. However, during fieldwork, it was realized that only one Ministry meets the criteria as set in the research: "at least a year of experience with the system", to ensure a full understanding. A pseudonym name, "Ministry of Homeland" was assigned to the Ministry due to ethical considerations.

The Ministry of Homeland (MoHL) directly focuses on the identification systems and physical addresses in terms of capturing data and issuing of IDs. The case selection was strictly based on the objectives of the study which were: (i) to identify and examine the factors of deficiencies in the current system whereby wrong, duplicate, inaccurate or inconsistent physical addresses are printed on identity documents of individuals and (ii) to examine both technical and non-technical factors that can improve the current system. Also based on the objectives, criterial for selecting participants, and questions that were used in collecting data were formulated.

3.2 Criteria for Selection Participants

To gather data that were related to the study, and at the same time ensure that the data was rich, towards achieving the objectives of the study, the researcher (student) created three criteria, which were used to select the participants: (1) participants must come from both IT and non-IT units of the organisation that is used as a case in the study; (2) each participant must have spent a minimum of one year working in the organisation (MoHL); and (3) community members who have ID must have changed address after obtaining the ID.

Based on the criteria, the technical and non-technical personnel were selected to participate in the study. in the study, technical personnel were referred to as the IT specialists who were responsible for enabling and supporting the government's systems. Non-technical personnel refer to the people who make use of the systems, to provide services to the community. The selection of the participants was based on their experience with the system, which was a minimum of one year, as this was considered long enough to have a good understanding of the system's functions, from both IT and users' perspectives. The community members who have changed physical addresses at least more than once were also selected to participate in the study. Community members were the ones who receive the services from the governmental institution.

3.3 Interview Guidelines

The Semi-structured interview technique was used in the collection of data. This was primarily because of its flexibility (Iyamu, 2018), allows for interview guidelines and the possibility to ask question, and get clarification when necessary (Marshall et al., 2015). The interview guidelines were formulated based on the two research questions: (i) What are the factors of deficiencies in the current system, which allows incorrect or inconsistent physical addresses of individuals to be printed on citizens' identity documents? (ii) What are the technical and non-technical factors that can improve the current system?

The two research questions were broken down into questions that enabled the researcher to elicit information, which led to answering the research questions. The questions were articulated as simple as possible to make it clear for the participants. Three interview guidelines were developed for the three groups of participants (i.e., IT specialists, non-IT personnel working in the organisation, and community members). This was because each of the groups would be speaking about the subject from different perspectives. The community members would be speaking from service recipient perspective. The IT specialists would be focusing on the technical aspect of the system, while the non-technical personnel would have experienced about how the system works from a non-technical viewpoint. All the interview guidelines were developed in English and then translated into Portuguese; participants' spoken language. A total of 16 people were interviewed at the point of saturation. This is a point where no new information was forthcoming.

3.4 Analysis of the Data

The student employed the duality of structure from structuration theory, as a lens in conducting data analysis. The rationale was that the duality of structure helps to gain an understanding of how information systems and information technology (IS/IT) enable and constrain the interaction that happen between agents (technical and non-technical), while at the same time the agents create the IS/IT artefacts. The primary focuses of the data analysis were on four main areas about the issuance of IDs in the country. Firstly, it reviews the relationship that existed between agents. Secondly, it examines the interactions that happen between agents and agencies, which were people-to-people; technology-to-technology; and people-to-technology. Thirdly, it tries to understand the rules, regulations, and resources (such as IT systems and solutions) that existed and used for various actions. Finally, through its modalities (interpretive scheme, facility, and norm), it assesses how rules, regulations, and resources were applied by the various agents (people).

From the thesis, the study finds (1) Validation of requirements; (2) Automated regulation; (3) Effect of urbanization; (4) Authenticity of proof of address; (5) Human interaction; (6) System interaction; and (7) System verification as the factors, which influence issuance of IDs in Angola. These factors were considered critical in that they constrain, and at the same time enable the efficiency and deficiencies in the current computer system. The factors were viewed from both technical and non-technical perspectives.

Despite the successful completion of the research, there were challenges, which could have derailed or disrupted the entire research primarily because data was centre to it. In the process of data collection, some of the critical challenges were: (1) the use of multiple languages, Portuguese and English; (2) cultural differences; (3) access to participants; and (4) translation from Portuguese to the English language.

4. METHODOLOGY (OF CURRENT RESEARCH)

This section should not be read with section 3, to avoid confusion. Section 3 provides detail account about the student's study where challenges were encountered, which led to this study. This section focuses on this study. The challenges that were revealed from the student's research were deemed worth a case to be studied further. This is purposely to mitigate against the challenges, particularly to assist postgraduates and aspiring researchers in avoiding the same pitfalls, or to be better prepared in similar circumstances. Two methods were employed in putting the data together: materials directly related to the study and storytelling (getting the student to tell her story as it happened).

4.1 Data Collection

The materials (documentations) that were used in the study by the postgraduate student were gathered, which included: (1) the research proposal that outlined the research problem, aim, objectives, questions, and methodology; (2) the interview guidelines that were used in collecting data; (3) the data that was collected from the participants; and (4) the research code of conduct that guided the student's engagement with the participants in her research. In the analysis, the subjective approach was applied from the interpretivist (Goldkuhl, 2012) perspective, to examine the materials.

In addition to the materials, the student narrated her experience through storytelling, to explicitly share the processes and events involved in collecting data. The storytelling method was employed to elicit information from the postgraduate student (Rasmussen, 2008), to tell her story as it happened in the process of collecting data. The method has been applied in IS research for over three decades (Cawkell, 1986), as well as various other fields (Madni, 2015). The student shared her experience. She was made to repeat the story three times on different days within a week. This was to ensure consistency in the story of her experience, and it had to stop when no contradictions were detected.

4.2 Trustworthiness of Data

The trustworthiness is essential and necessarily for qualitative research (Shufutinsky, 2020), to increase the richness of data (and its sources) used in this study. Stoffelen (2019) argues that triangulation of data in qualitative is purposely to improve the credibility and trustworthiness of the study. Our aim was to improve the quality of data and research and contribute to the level of insightfulness and transparency. In doing so, we engaged with the student in a rigorous manner by requesting confirmations of the documents and to tell the story as it happened during data collection process.

The researcher was requested to validate and confirm the existing materials that were collected. This included those that were in English and Portuguese languages. The student returned the documents with affirmation, and without changes. From the first story told by the student, notes were made, following the guidelines suggested by Silverman (2020). In the second round of telling the story, the notes were used for trustworthiness. This process was repeated three times, and there was consistency from the 'horse's mouth'.

4.3 Approach to Analysis

From the perspective of the interpretivist approach, the hermeneutics circle method was applied in the analysis of the data gathered from storytelling and existing materials. The hermeneutic method is a concept of gaining an understanding of data or system bit by bit (Shaw, Grainger & Achuthan, 2017). Young (2018) explains that the method draws an understanding based on subjective meanings. The hermeneutic circle enables iterative interrogative of data (Wohlin & Aurum, 2015), including the examining of individuals' experiences (Galehbakhtiari, 2015). It is therefore often used to conduct analysis on complex relationship between stakeholders (Shaw et al., 2017). The method was used to analyse the data, purposely to gain a deeper understanding of followings:

i. The interaction that happens between the postgraduate student and those who participated in her study.
ii. The ethical considerations that guided the research and culture practiced by the participants in the research.
iii. Translative power of the participants which the employ in describing and explaining some of the technologies' solutions and terms.

The documentations gathered were read repeatedly. Points that could be associated with any of the bullets stated above were highlighted and extracted. Those points were subjectively interpreted in relation to the objective of the study. Like the documentation approach, the recorded story was repeated played, and points were jointed. Points from both documentations and the recorded story were aligned, to ensure that there were no contradictions or disjoints. Collaboratively, factors that influence the student's challenges during data collection using semi-structured interview technique were revealed.

5. ANALYSIS (OF CURRENT RESEARCH)

Some of the challenges that were encountered by the student are not uncommon. What is essentially significant is how the challenges can be addressed. This helps to avoid the challenges from influencing and reshaping outcome of research, towards failure to achieve the aim and objectives of a research.

Despite two fundamental accounts, challenges occurred. Firstly, despite the intensity of prepared, the student, like many postgraduates and aspiring researchers encountered the challenges in the process of data collection. Secondly, even though criteria were set and used in the selection of the participants, there were challenges. As shown in Figure 2, there were five main challenges in the process of data collection using the semi-structured interview technique: (1) selection of cases; (2) the impact of linguistic; (3) cultural differences; (4) access to participants; and (5) translation from Portuguese to English. These factors are discussed below and should be read with Figure 2 in order to gain better understanding of how they are a challenging force in a process of data collection.

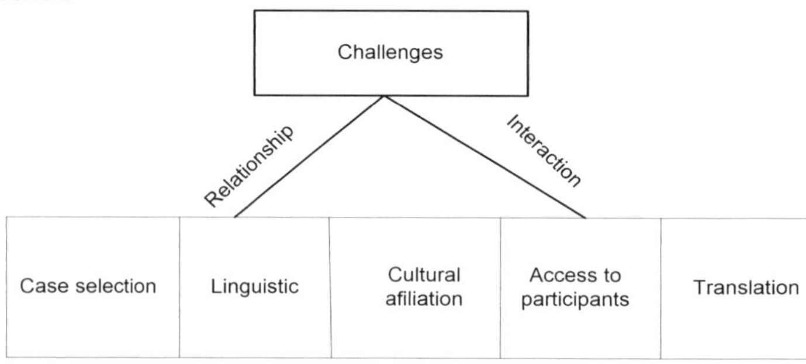

Figure 2. Challenging factors

For better clarity, the format of the discussion is that the overview of the challenge is first presented, followed by the actual challenge, and concluded with mitigation to the challenge.

5.1 Selection of Cases

Initially, two Ministries within the Angolan government were selected as cases for the study, because they were understood to be responsible for citizens' IDs and custodian of the physical address database system. One of the Ministries was quick to grant request, and the other Ministry initially declined the request, to participate in the study. The rationale for the decline was a proclamation that was based on an understanding of the study. The Directors that had the authority to grant or decline the request questioned why the student needed to engage the Ministry in the study. The Directors' view was that the objective of the study is most appropriate for a different Ministry. This was a way of diplomatically declining the request to participate in the study. However, the student persisted with her request, only to realise that her approach did not sit well with the authority, who saw the persuasion as aggressive.

Eventually the appropriate Ministry was selected, which helped to resolve the problem of confusion. In addition, an opportunity for further explanation was very helpful in that the notion of the student aggression was clarified. This entails 'speaking the language' that the representatives of the organisation understood, such as the manner of approach (not too formal, and tone that accords respect to an African elder). The manner of speaking was influenced by cultural affiliation and environmental context. If the Ministry had insisted a non-participative, it would have had serious implication for the study, because it means changes to the objectives, and development of new proposal. Ultimately, the period of the research had be extended, which would have been prohibitive for the student.

5.2 The Impact of Linguistic on Data Gathering

The student's place of birth is Angola, a Portuguese former colony. She was enrolled in a South African (a commonwealth country, English as an official language) university for a postgraduate program. The student is fluent in both Portuguese and English languages. The research focuses on the student's home country, meaning that data had to be collected from Angola. As already established, the semi-structured interview was employed as a technique. In the process, the student faced many challenges when trying to ask questions in Portuguese while thinking in English. This was because whatever is clear in English was not necessarily clear or straightforward in attempts to express it in Portuguese, especially when direct translation was involved. As a result, during the first set of interviews, the participants had difficulties in understanding what was being asked. This challenge was despite the practice before the commencement of the data collection process.

The solution to this challenge was to rephrase the questions every time the participants did not understand the question. Some participants were not shy to say so when they did not understand the questions. Some of the participants gave responses to every question including those they did not seem to understand. Through the answers, it was possible to realise that these participants did not understand the question and therefore the student had to quickly think on how to rephrase the question. The student's fluency in both, English and Portuguese, made her realise the depth of linguistic challenges and the impact it has on data collection. Thus, the student realised that the effect would have been worst if the service of an interpreter was sought. Also, many of the interviews took longer than anticipated, this come to show and confirm that duration of interview should not be anticipated from the student's perspective.

5.3 Cultural Affiliation

In Africa, cultural affiliation is considered very important, and influences activities and events in almost all walks of life. Thus, it is critical to gain an understanding of an environment that relates to social systems and involves humans in conducting studies. In terms of the community members, one of the challenges was to make them understand the objective of the study and culture. Most of the participants live in Luanda, the capital city of the country. However, the participants were originally from other provinces, where people are more conservative and uphold their culture in the strongest terms. To this group of participants, referring to an older person as "you" is considered disrespectful and offensive, which the student often forgets because she has lived outside of the country for many years. As a result, some of the participants hesitated in responding to questions.

The approach was to have a conversation about the topic before conducting the interviews. This was to allow the participants' flexibility and the convenience of asking any question or seeking clarification that they deem necessary and useful. Regarding the culture, the student had to refer to some participants as father, brother or sister, to avoid referring to them as "you", which would had been considered offensive or disrespectful. For cultural and traditional purposes, an understanding of the environment in which a study is conducted is critical. This is because of the crucial role an environment plays in influencing the content of the data. Culture underpins the behaviour and character of many rural duellers in certain events, actions and communication, in many African countries (Iyamu, 2018). Babbie (2007) describes environmental culture as respondents' responsibilities, which include protection of confidentiality, right to participate in a study, or not to do so.

5.4 Access to Participants

To ensure credibility and integrity, it was critical to adhere to research ethics' code of conduct as set out by the university (CPUT), as well as the policy of the organisation where data was being collected. Therefore, it was essential to get official permission to gain access to both technical and non-technical employees of the organisation, for interview purposes. In the process, the organisation sent the student back and forth several times before granting permission to conduct interviews with its employees. This was mainly because the requirements were consistently changed. Moreover, it was not easy to get access to or permission from individuals. Even though some of them had accepted to be interviewed, it was not easy to schedule a time with them for the interview. Also, some of them had specific venues where they wanted to meet for the interview. In addition, some participants were selective on the questions that they preferred and wanted to respond to. Even when some of the questions were rephrased, some of the participants still chose not to respond.

There was a need of being persistent in terms of requesting permission, otherwise the student would not have been able to collect data from the country. When it came to time limit, the student had to submit to the participants' time limit and tried to focus on responses that were related to the study. In selecting organisations as cases in a study, postgraduate students and aspiring researchers need to understand that access is required at both an organisational and individual levels. Hence it is essential to formulate a set of criteria that can be used at the various levels, to avoid confusion, approach most appropriate organisations and persons, and reduce bias. The criteria must be aligned with the aim and objectives of the study.

5.5 Translation between Two Languages

The interviews were conducted in Portuguese, and tape recorded. This meant that the transcript (voice) had to be transcribed into text (manuscript). In the process, some of the interviews were transcribed in Portuguese, and thereafter, translated to English language. Many of the interviews were transcribed directly to English language, as the student was fluent in both languages.

There were certain inevitable challenges in the process of translating the transcripts from Portuguese to English language. On the one hand, the researcher was enrolled in a South African university where English is the official language. This means that all documents related to the study, including the thesis, must be written in English language. On the other hand, data were being collected in Portuguese, the official language of Angola. There were some challenges in translating the interviews into English because some participants used colloquial terms, 'slang' (terms or words that were not in the Portuguese language dictionary). These types of words were very difficult to translate to English language. The challenge got worse when the people from whom assistance was sought associated various interpretation and meaning with the 'slang' words.

To address this challenge, the researcher had to solicit explanations from those who were familiar with the unfamiliar words and sentences (slang and other colloquial terms). The assistance was sought to translate the terms to meaning rather than to interpret word-by-word. Where the interpreters gave different interpretations of a 'slang or colloquial' word, the prevalent meaning was adopted. The observation and experience are that it is best for the interviewer to transcribe the interviews by him/herself. For example, only the interviewer can express unfamiliar words in the way and way the interviewees put them.

6. CONCLUSION

This paper reveals crucial challenges that are consistently experienced by aspiring researchers in the process of data collection, particularly, where cultural affiliation and linguistics differences are stand points. The proposed mitigation in this paper are intended to be of benefit to postgraduates and aspiring researchers in that: (1) whilst having conversation during data collection, the researcher can learn about the culture of the environment, which might be crucial and necessary for future purpose; (2) linguistically, the use of certain terms reduce tension between interviewer and interviewees, and crucially make associating means to things easier; and (3) being sensitive to interviewee's preference can improve interaction towards obtaining richness data.

Thus, the paper contributes from both practical and theoretical viewpoints. Practically, the findings point to pitfalls that should be taken into cognisance in using the semi-structured interview technique. The paper highlights crucial areas that can influence data richness, which many aspiring researchers across disciplines would have ordinarily taken for granted. Theoretically, the paper can be used as material in preparing postgraduate researchers in using the semi-structured technique for data collection. Additionally, the paper adds to existing literature in the areas of data collection and research.

Despite the outcome from this, and other works, there is more room for further studies in the areas of data collection. This includes how postgraduates' preparedness can be measured in order to reduce challenges, in the use of techniques for qualitative data collection in environments that are influenced by different unique factors.

REFERENCES

Adams, E. (2010). The joys and challenges of semi-structured interviewing. *Community Practitioner*, *83*(7), pp. 18-21.

Avison, D. & Pries-Heje, J. (Eds.). (200)5. *Research in information systems: A handbook for research supervisors and their students*. Boston, MA: Gulf Professional Publishing.

Babbie, E. (2007). The practice of social research. Belmont: Thomson.

Bearman, M. (2019). Eliciting rich data: A practical approach to writing semi-structured interview schedules. *Focus on Health Professional Education: A Multi-disciplinary Journal*, *20*(3), 1-11.

Bygstad B. & Munkvold B.E. (2016). Exploring the Role of Informants in Interpretive Case Study Research in IS. In: Willcocks L.P., Sauer C., Lacity M.C. (eds.) *Enacting Research Methods in Information Systems*. Switzerland: Palgrave Macmillan Cham: 84-115.

Cawkell, A.E. (1986). The real information society: Present situation and some forecasts. Journal of Information Science, 12(3), 87-95.

Creswell, J.W. & Poth, C.N. (2017). *Qualitative Inquiry and Research Design: Choosing Among Five Approaches*. 4th ed. Thousand Oaks*:* Sage publication.

Galehbakhtiari, S. (2015). A hermeneutic phenomenological study of online community participation: Applications of Fuzzy Cognitive Maps. *Computers in Human Behavior*, 48, 637-643.

Goldkuhl, G. (2012). Pragmatism vs interpretivism in qualitative information systems research. *European journal of information systems*, *21*(2), 135-146.

Godwin, A. & Potvin, G. (2017). Pushing and pulling Sara: A case study of the contrasting influences of high school and university experiences on engineering agency, identity, and participation. *Journal of Research in Science Teaching*, 54(4), 439–462.

Gray, D.E. (2013). *Doing Research in the Real World.* 3rd ed. Seaman. J. (ed.) Los Angeles: Sage Publications.

Irvine, A., Drew, P. & Sainsbury, R. (2013). Am I not answering your questions properly? 'Clarification, adequacy and responsiveness in semi-structured telephone and face-to-face interviews. *Qualitative Research*, *13*(1), 87-106.

Iyamu, T. (2013). Underpinning theories: order-of-use in information systems research. *Journal of Systems and Information Technology*, *15*(3), 224-238.

Iyamu, T. (2018). Collecting qualitative data for information systems studies: The reality in practice. *Education and Information Technologies*, 23(5), 2249-2264.

Jebreen, I. (2012). Using inductive approach as research strategy in requirements engineering. *International Journal of Computer and Information Technology*, *1*(2), 162-173.

Madni, A. M. (2015). Expanding stakeholder participation in upfront system engineering through storytelling in virtual worlds. *Systems Engineering*, *18*(1), 16-27.

Marshall, C., Brereton, P. & Kitchenham, B. (2015). Tools to support systematic reviews in software engineering: A cross-domain survey using semi-structured interviews. In *Proceedings of the 19th International Conference on Evaluation and Assessment in Software Engineering.* Nanjing: ACM, 26.

Myers, M. D., & Newman, M. (2007). The qualitative interview in IS research: Examining the craft. *Information and Organization*, 17(1), 2–26.

Rasmussen, L. (2008). The narrative aspect of scenario building-how story telling may give people a memory of the future. In Gill S. (Ed), Cognition, Communication and Interaction (pp. 174- 194). London: Springer.

Recker, J. (2012). *Scientific research in information systems: a beginner's guide*. London: Springer Science & Business Media.

Scuotto, V., Ferraris, A. & Bresciani, S. (2016). Internet of Things: Applications and challenges in smart cities: a case study of IBM smart city projects. *Business Process Management Journal*, *22*(2), 357-367.

Shaw, D.R., Grainger, A. & Achuthan, K. (2017). Multi-level port resilience planning in the UK: How can information sharing be made easier?. *Technological Forecasting and Social Change*, 121, 126-138

Shufutinsky, A. (2020). Employing use of self for transparency, rigor, trustworthiness, and credibility in qualitative organizational research methods. *OD Practitioner*, *52*(1), 50-58.

Silverman, D. (2020). Interpreting qualitative data: Methods for analyzing talk, text, and interaction (6th Edition), SAGE Publication.

Stoffelen, A. (2019). Disentangling the tourism sector's fragmentation: a hands-on coding/post-coding guide for interview and policy document analysis in tourism. *Current Issues in Tourism*, *22*(18), 2197-2210.

Stokes, P., & Urquhart, C. (2013). Qualitative interpretative categorisation for efficient data analysis in a mixed methods information behaviour study. Information Research, 18(1), 1–17.

Wohlin, C. & Aurum, A. (2015). Towards a decision- -making structure for selecting a research design in empirical software engineering. *Empirical Software Engineering*, 20(6), 1427–1455.

Yin, R.K. (2018). *Case study research and applications: Design and methods*. 6th ed. California, CA: Sage publications.

Young, A.G. (2018). Using ICT for social good: Cultural identity restoration through emancipatory pedagogy. *Information Systems Journal*, 28(2), 340-358.

DIGITAL PLATFORMS FOR THE CREATIVES TOWARDS A TAXONOMY

Pinelopi Stavrianidi and Anastasia Constantelou
University of the Aegean
Department of Financial and Management Engineering
Kountouriotou 41, 82100 Chios, Greece

ABSTRACT

The Creative sector is among the less examined sectors in terms of participation in the Digital Platform (DP) revolution. DPs provide platform-mediated labour to creative micro-entrepreneurs, offering them more than new selling opportunities. The proposed research is the first part of an on-going research effort which seeks to investigate the role of digital platforms in re-shaping the micro-entrepreneurial activities of the creative people (artists, makers, crafters). Etsy is the leading and most well-known among these platforms but there are other equally interesting internet-enabled platforms that operate at a regional, national or international level. As a first step, we identify various types of digital platforms designed to meet the needs of the creatives. By collecting information through their websites and by analyzing their content, scope and structure we aim to classify digital platforms for the creatives using theoretical constructs derived from the business model literature. To this end, we seek to shed light on the variety of configurations, mechanisms and applications through which these platforms operate, thus contributing to the discussion on the role of digital platforms for the creatives from a methodological and empirical point of view.

KEYWORDS

Taxonomy, Digital Platforms, Creative and Cultural Sectors

1. INTRODUCTION

Since the development and spread of the Internet and the establishment of Digital Platforms (DPs), dramatic changes have taken place in the creative and cultural industries. DPs provide platform-mediated labour to creative micro-entrepreneurs, offering them more than new selling opportunities. Creative people found new ways to exhibit their art, meet each other, collaborate, find suppliers, and achieve sales to a new, highly developed audience spread across the world. The proposed research is the first part of an on-going research effort which seeks to investigate the role of digital platforms in re-shaping the micro-entrepreneurial activities of the creative people (artists, makers, crafters). Etsy is the leading and most well-known among these platforms but there are other equally interesting internet-enabled platforms that operate at a regional, national or international level.

This paper aims to address the following overarching research questions:

- Which are the most widely known digital platforms used by the creatives?
- How can they be classified, and which criteria can be used for their taxonomy?

As a foundation for research on a novel phenomenon, we started by identifying the most popular digital platforms for the creators, and then we developed a taxonomy for their classification, applying Nickerson et al.'s (2013) step-by-step procedure to develop a taxonomy of platforms for the creatives. We first identify important design dimensions and characteristics of DPs from the literature. Then we use these dimensions to analyze ten DP cases in order to provide the empirical insights that define the final dimensions of the proposed taxonomy. We provide a basis for theorizing in this domain that may lead to archetypes of DPs for the creatives and we propose ideas for further research.

2. THEORETICAL BACKGROUND

2.1 The Creative and Cultural Industries (CCIs)

There are various definitions for the "Creative and Cultural" Industries in the literature, some of which are presented below:

–"Creative" industries" are those industries which use culture as an input and have a cultural dimension, although their outputs are mainly functional" (European Commission, 2010)

–"creative industries" are an umbrella term for those industries based on individual creativity, skill and talent and have the potential to create wealth and jobs through developing intellectual property (UK Department of Culture, 1998)

David Throsby (2008) proposed *the concentric circles model* to define CCIs. His model is based initially on the proposition that cultural goods and services give rise to two distinguishable types of value: economic and cultural. The assert of the model is that the cultural value, or cultural content, of the goods and services produced gives the cultural industries their most distinguishing characteristic. The model consists of four concentric circles to classify the industries that produce cultural goods and services. The categories and the main industries they contain are: Core creative arts (literature, music, performing arts, visual arts), Other core cultural industries (film, museums, galleries, libraries, photography), Wider cultural industries (heritage services, publishing and print media, sound recording, television and radio, video and computer games) and Related industries (advertising, architecture, design, fashion). Figure 1 presents Throsby's model.

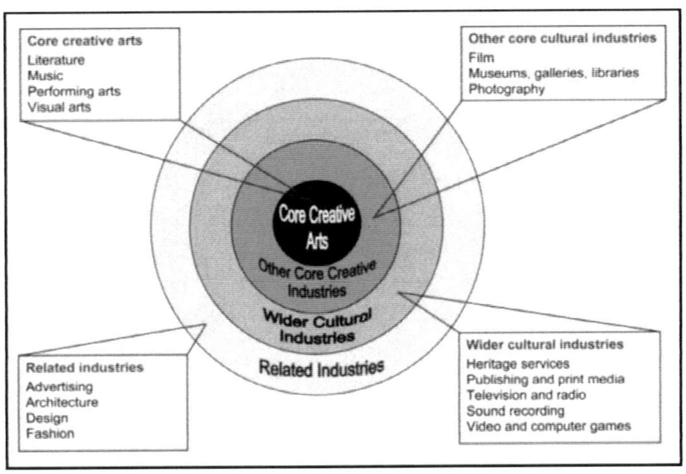

Figure 1. The concentric circles model David Throsby (2008)

2.2 Digital Platforms and Creative Entrepreneurship

Digital platforms have been rising rapidly causing significant changes and bringing a great potential for the economies and societies around the world. DPs have been defined as digital infrastructures that enable two or more user groups to interact, such as customers, advertisers, service providers, producers, suppliers, and allow them to perform various tasks (Srnicek, 2017; Cusumano et.al., 2019; de Reuveret et.al., 2018; Gawer, 2009).

Entrepreneurs in the creative sector are individuals equipped with entrepreneurial and resourceful mindsets which enable them to transform primary or intermediary inputs into creative outputs with market potential. According to Howkins (2002, p.29), "*creative entrepreneurs use creativity to unlock the wealth that lies within themselves*". In Europe, more than 80% of enterprises in the creative industries are very small or 'micro-enterprises' (employing fewer than 10 people). Almost 60% of these 'micro-enterprises' consist of very small micro-businesses with only 1 to 3 employees (HKU, 2010). There is a very high number of freelancers and sole proprietors who do not necessarily perceive themselves as entrepreneurs. The sector is characterized by *atypical* forms of employment and *precarious* working conditions involving flexibility, mobility, project work, voluntary or very low-paid activities (Benhamou, 2003). Digital platforms have provided platform-mediated work to these micro-entrepreneurs and offer them more than new selling opportunities.

2.3 Taxonomy Development Methods

UNCTAD Digital Economy Report of 2019 *–Annex II Summary of literature review on taxonomies used for classifying digital platforms* provides a non-exhaustive list of taxonomies of digital platforms found in the literature but there was not special interest in DPs for the creatives. Nickerson et al. *(2013)* method for taxonomy development has been very popular among Information Systems (IS) researchers, such as Prat et al. (2015), Blaschke et.al. (2019), Staub et.al. (2021) Van De Ven et.al. (2021). Nickerson's method is based on an iterative design scheme that uses pre-defined meta-characteristics and follows either an inductive (bottom up or empirical-to-conceptual) or a deductive (top-down or conceptual-to-empirical) procedure (or both) until ending conditions set by the researchers are met, which prove that the newly developed taxonomy is adequate and useful.

3. METHODOLOGY

3.1 Method Employed to Identify DP for the Creatives

In this section we describe the methodology that we followed to build a database of 100 selected Digital Platforms for the Creatives. We list these selected platforms in Table 1.

Table 1. List of Digital Platforms for the Creatives

1x	Cargoh	Fashion Cloud	Made it	Stylehub
3DTotal	CGSociety	Fiverr	MasterClass	TikTok
500px	Craftito	Flickr	Muzli Inspiration	The Dots
99designs	Cratejoy	Folksy	Numonday	The Museum Platform
Adobe Portfolio	CreativeLive	Freelancer	Odissa	Toftiaxa
Aerende	Dance umbrella	Gopillar	Pedddle	Tumblr
Amazon handmade	DancePlug	Graphicriver	PhotoBlog	Udemy
Amazon music	Dancio	Handartisan	Pinterest	Uncommongoods
Architonic	Deviantart	Houzz	PlatformE	Unity
Artblr	Domestica	Icraft gifts	Red Bubble	Ustrendy
Artfinder	Dreamy	Indiecart	Ruby Lane	Uxcel
Artfire	Dribbble	IndieMade	Saatchiart	Vimeo
Artstation	eBay	Instagram	Shopify	Virink
ArtsThread	Eclectic Artisans	Intelistyle	Skillshare	VSCO
ASOS Marketplace	Ecwid	Jamjar	SmugMug	Wix
Association of Illustrators	Ello.co	Juniqe	Songtradr	Workana
Aviarto	Etsy	Kosmimax	Spotify	Xeirotexnes
Behance	Exclusera	Learntodance	Squarespace	Yotpo
Big Cartel	EyeEm	LinkedIn	Steller	Zatista
Bonanza	Facebook	Lovel	Storenvy	Zibbet

To identify platforms of interest we conducted desk research: first we had to insure that the selected platforms for our data base had to relate to and/or include the widest possible range of creative works, for this reason we used the concentric circles model by including creators from all the four layers/circles.

We started a Google search using the following keywords/phrases:

"best social media platforms for creators"
"witch platforms architects use"
"freelancing platforms for creators"
"top platforms to sell fashion online"
"best platforms for makers"
"best social media platforms for artists"
"best portfolio platforms for designers"
"platforms like Flickr"
"platforms like Etsy"
"best places to sell handmade crafts"
"platforms for dance/music/museums"
"platforms like Domestica"

Using the above keywords/phrases we aimed to identify the most popular platforms promoted on the web. Lastly, to ensure the relevance of the empirical cases, other criteria were applied to the sample of platforms that resulted from the desk research. First criterion was that DPs should have an English version. Second, DPs should be in operation and not in the construction phase. Third, we included platforms with local, national, European and/or global geographical scope. Fourth, the success of the platform (based on the number of users) was examined, platforms with few users were excluded

3.2 Taxonomy Development Process

In this section, we describe the step-by-step procedure that we apply for our taxonomy development. We followed Nickerson et al.'s (2013) well-structured method for taxonomy development that has been frequently used in IS research. Meta-characteristics of the taxonomy are defined first. Next, the satisfactory conditions suggested by Nickerson et al. (2013) were employed. Then, the selection of the approach and the conceptualization of Dimensions and Characteristics where indentified. After every design iteration, the ending conditions were checked. The process stopped when most ending conditions were met. The taxonomy was indicatively tested in 10 selected DP cases from our database.

3.2.1 Definition of Meta-characteristics and Determination of Satisfactory Conditions

Meta-characteristics function as overarching characteristics of the object of interest (Nickerson et al., 2013). We chose key building blocks of the **Business Model Canvas (BMC)** framework originally proposed by Osterwalder (2005) as the meta-characteristics that will guide us in the choice of design dimensions during the taxonomy development process. To accept that the taxonomy meets our satisfactory conditions we must ensure that all our dimensions can be matched with one of the key building blocks of the BMC and that they are mutually exclusive and collectively exhaustive. Also, our final taxonomy must be robust, concise and extendible.

3.3 Selection of Approach

Nickerson et al. (2013) provide two different approaches, the empirical-to-conceptual (E2C) and the conceptual-to-empirical (C2E). We started with a conceptual-to-empirical approach where we sought to compare the concepts derived from the literature with information from the empirical cases. We continued with a round of empirical-to-conceptual procedure by empirically examining a number of Digital Platforms for the Creatives, which helped us to add additional dimensions to the taxonomy.

3.4 Conceptualization of Dimensions and Characteristics

In this study we are developing a taxonomy of DPs from a multi-stakeholder perspective on business models. The digital platforms that interest us are those for the creatives so we consider Digital Platforms for the Creatives-DPFC as digital systems where products or services are traded as an economic good that connects consumers, businesses and creators in creative and cultural industries. As an input to our taxonomy development process, we use literature on DPs and business models to identify the dimensions and characteristics to classify DPFC.

We structure the dimensions according to business model framework and we use five of its categories, i.e. value proposition, key partners, customer segments, customer relationship, revenue stream.

4. TAXONOMY DEVELOPMENT OF DIGITAL PLATFORMS FOR THE CREATIVES

Our final taxonomy of Digital Platforms for the Creatives based on the methodology we described above, consist of five categories, 11 dimensions and 35 characteristics and is presented in Table 2.

Table 2. Dimension and characteristics of DPs for the Creatives

CATEGORY	DIMENSIONS	CHARACTERISTICS				
Value Proposition	Key value proposition	Branding	Networking	Ease of use		
	Interaction type	Exchange	Marketing	Knowledg e/Educatio n	Makers' Tools	Combination of Services
	Data analytics tools	Yes	No			
	Security	High	Low			
Key Partners	Creators' origin	Local	European	Global		
	Target audience	Specific	Non-Specific			
Costumer Segments	Target costumer	Creators	Businesses	Consumers		
Costumers Relationship	Costumers' relationship	Transactional	Self service	Automated service	Communities	
	Specification control	High	Medium	Low		
	Accessibility	Open access	Direct access	Indirect access		
Revenue Stream	Key revenue stream	Listing fee	Sales fee	Subscriptio ns	Advertisin g	Combination of revenue streams

4.1 Description of Dimensions and Characteristics

In the Table 3 that follows we describe and analyze each dimension and its characteristics.

Table 3. The dimensions and characteristics description of digital platforms for the creatives

CATEGORY	DIMENSIONS	CHARACTERISTICS
Value Proposition	Key value proposition	The main benefit that the platform delivers to the participants. For some DPs Branding is the best benefit that ensure quality and of goods and services for the participants (Amazon), other DPs offer very large network (Facebook), and some are very ease to use (Houzz)
	Interaction type	Refers to the type of primary interaction among participants offered by the platform. Typical interaction types include: Exchange of products or services (Etsy), Marketing by advertising, portfolio browsing or website promotion (Theaoi), Knowledge/Education through online learning courses (Udemy), Makers' Tools by offering online tools (Unity), or Combination of Services (Deviantart)
	Data analytics tools	Refers to whether platform offers data analytics tools to participants or not

	Security	Refers to the level of security (of payments, copyrights, sensitive personal/financial information) that a platform can ensure for participants
Key Partners	Creators' origin	Refers to the origin of the creators that participate in the platform. For example, some platforms prefer/or are selected only by local creators, others by creators with European or international origin.
	Target audience	Refers to whether the audience of the platform belongs to and/or prefers creators from a specific field/are or from several
Costumer Segments	Target costumer	Refers to where the platform mostly directs its services: consumers, businesses, or peers
Costumers Relationship	Costumers' relationship	Refers to the type of relationship the platform establishes and maintains with participants
	Specification control	Refers to how strong is the platform's control over the final product specifications. For example *Amazon Handmade* allows only real handmade products to be sold through the platform. *Flickr* gives exact specifications about the size of uploaded photos
	Accessibility	Refers to the granting of access to the platform to its participants, whether its unobstructed access devoid of permissions (open access), or unobstructed access by permission (direct access), or obstructed access permission that needs approval (indirect access)
Revenue Stream	Key revenue stream	Refers to the platform's primary source of revenue.

We have embarked on an extensive testing of the usefulness of this taxonomy by analyzing a sample of different DPs that creators use. A typical example of this testing is presented in Table 4. Further testing of the sample platforms collected is on-going with the aim to reach specific archetypes of platforms used by the creatives.

Table 4. Taxonomy testing example

PLATFORM		**AMAZON HANDMADE**
Value Proposition	Key value proposition	Branding
	Interaction type	Combination of services
	Data analytics tools	Yes
	Security	High
Key Partners	Creators origin	Global
	Target audience	Specific
Costumer Segments	Target costumer	Creators
Costumers Relationship	Costumers' relationship	Automated services
	Specification control	High
	Accessibility	Direct Access
Revenue Stream	Key revenue stream	Combination of revenue streams

5. DISCUSSION AND CONCLUSION

This study has two key scientific contributions. First, we offer a first attempt to identify and collect digital platforms that meet the needs of creators and practitioners involved in CCIs, and to build a database that contains these platforms so that we can refer to them in future research. To better understand and analyze Digital Platforms for the Creatives and to contribute to further research we attempted to develop a first taxonomy pf DPs for the Creatives from a business model perspective. Following the approach of Nickerson et al. (2003) for taxonomy development our approach distinguishes 11 dimensions upon which we can build the taxonomy.

For future research the taxonomy can be tested to additional platforms from our database in order to identify the fundamental dimensions, which will then lead to a few model archetypes that we can propose for the categorization of these platforms.

DPs for the creatives contribute dynamically to the development and well being of the creative and cultural sectors. The use of those platforms helps creators to increase their audience, their financial prospects, and opens new opportunities for the development of their entrepreneurship. For the businesses and consumers, those DPs give them the endless choices, transaction safety and quality guarantees. We will continue the research in this domain, and we hope more researchers will accompany us in the future.

REFERENCES

Benhamou, F., 2003. Artists' labourmarkets. In: R. Towse (ed.): *A handbook of cultural economics*. Cheltenham, UK: E. Elgar.

Blaschke, M., Haki, K., Aier, S., Winter, R., 2019. Taxonomy of Digital Platforms: A Platform Architecture Perspective, *14th International Conference on Wirtschaftsinformatik, February 24-27, Siegen, Germany, pp. 572-586.*

Cusumano, M. A., Gawer, A., & Yoffie, D. B., 2019. *The business of platforms: Strategy in the age of digital competition, innovation, and power,* New York: Harper Business.

DCMS, 1998. *The Creative Industries Mapping Document*. UK Department of Culture, London.

De Reuver, M., Sørensen, C., & Basole, R. C., 2018. The digital platform: A research agenda. *Journal of Information Technology*, 33(2), 124–135.

European Commission, 2010. *Green paper –Unlocking the potential of cultural and creative industries*, Communication COM (2010) 183.

Gawer, A. (Ed.), 2009. *Platforms, markets and innovation*, Edward Elgar Publishing, Cheltenham.

HKU, 2010. *The Entrepreneurial Dimension of the Cultural and Creative Industries*. Hogeschoolvorde Kunsten Utrecht, Utrecht.

Howkins, J., 2002. *How people make money from ideas*, Penguin Books, London, UK.

Luckman, S. and J. Andrew, 2020. *Craftspeople and Designer Makers in the Contemporary Creative Economy*, Creative Working Lives, pp. 149-172

Luckman, S., 2015. *Craft and the Creative Economy*, Palgrave Macmillan, London, UK.

Nickerson, R. C., Varshney U. and Muntermann, J. 2013. A method for taxonomy development and its application in information systems. *European Journal of Information Systems* 22 (3), 336–359.

Osterwalder, A. Pigneur, Y. and Tucci, C.L., 2005. Clarifying Business Models: Origins, present and future of the concept. *Communications of the Assoc. of Information Systems*, Vol. 15

Prat, N. et al, 2015. A Taxonomy of Evaluation Methods for Information Systems Artifacts. *Journal of Management Information Systems*, Vol.32, Issue 3

RICHES-Renewal, Innovation and Change: Heritage and European Society, Deliverable 5.1 The Use of Craft Skills in New Contexts, 2015. Project funded under the 7thEuropean Framework Programme, Grant Agreement no. 612789.

Srnicek, N., 2017. *Platform Capitalism*. Polity Press, Cambridge, UK, Malden, USA.

Staub, N., Haki K, Aier S, Winter R., Taxonomy of Digital Platforms: A Business Model Perspective. *Proceedings of the 54th Hawaii International Conference on System Sciences | 2021, pp. 6163-6172.*

Throsby, D., 2008. The concentric circles model of the cultural industries. *Cultural Trends,* Vol.17, No. 3, pp.147-164.

Van de Ven, M. Abbas, A. E. Kwee, Z. & de Reuver, M., Creating a Taxonomy of Business Models for Data Marketplaces, *34th Bled E-conference Digital Support from Crisis to Progrecive Change, pp. 310-322.*

CLOSENESS ANALYSIS OF STUDENTS' WORD-USAGE LOCATED IN A HIGH-DIMENSIONAL SPACE

Toshiro Minami and Yoko Ohura
Kyushu Institute of Information Sciences
6-3-1 Saifu, Dazaifu, Fukuoka 818-0117 Japan

ABSTRACT

As a part of our studies in investigating the relations between university students' performances and their attitudes to learning, we propose a new method of representing word-usage profiles of students by embedding the word-usage vectors into a high-dimensional Euclidean space in this paper. The original source of data are the answer texts of students for a term-end evaluation questionnaire in a university class. By analyzing the relations in a couple of layouts of the word-vectors that are supposed to represent a kind of attitudes of students, we intend to find some kinds of relations between word-usages and academic achievements of students. The major achievements of this paper include (1) to investigate the relations of students' word-usages themselves as well as (2) to develop new methods that clarify the differences of students in terms of their viewpoint in comparison with their achievements through these layouts.

KEYWORDS

Educational Data Mining (EDM), Natural Language Processing (NLP), Word-Usage Analysis, Graph Drawing, Simplicial Complex, High-Dimensional Euclidean Space

1. INTRODUCTION

Our major concern in our studies in the field of educational data mining (EDM) (Ames et al., 1988)(Ames, 1992)(Romero et al., 2007)(Silva et al., 2017) is to have more appropriate image about the students who attend our classes in universities. Based on the image for students' learning attitudes, we are able to teach/guide/advise them more appropriately and motivate them for better learning. According to our observation as professor in some universities in Japan, quite a lot of students are not sufficiently motivated in learning and their attitudes to learning need to be improved in order to have more effective achievements as outcome.

It is often pointed out that many university professors lack teaching skills, probably including eagerness in education. We admit that this fact is true in one side. At the same time, it is true that students need to be more motivated in learning in another side. As a part of educational skill by professors, we are interested in understanding why such a number of students lack motivation toward learning. In order to understand more about students in their motivation, attitude, curiosity, interest range, etc. for learning, we have been conducting a series of study in analyzing data that can be obtained in our own experiences in teaching at classrooms; E.g. (Minami et al., 2017)(Minami et al., 2020)(Minami et al., 2022).

Our approach is different from many studies in the field of EDM, where quite a lot of studies use the target data which are obtained systematically or automatically from, for example, learning management systems (LMSs) so that the amount of data is big enough to be able to analyze them with the methods for big data (BD). For example, (Romero et al., 2008) gave a comparative study of data mining algorithms for classifying students using data from e-learning system and its major concern is to predict the student's outcome. In our approach, on the other hand, we aim to deal with student's psychological tendency in learning, such as eagerness, diligence, seriousness. Another feature is that we intend to deal with small data (SD) obtained in our everyday classes rather than to deal with a huge amount of big data (BD) (Faraway et al., 2018)(Kitchin et al., 2015).

As a part of studies in our approach to small data analysis, we have been investigating retrospective evaluation texts of students by looking-back the course at a term-end class; E.g., (Minami et al., 2014)(Minami et al., 2015)(Minami et al., 2015a)(Minami et al., 2017) (Minami et al., 2022). As a result, we found that the students who have broader viewpoints in learning tend to have better achievements than those who have narrower viewpoints in learning. In other words, the students who are able to locate the new knowledge in their knowledge network what they have already learned are tend to be able to get better achievements, or the term-end examination for evaluating what they have learned in the course.

We have also studied in analyzing class data with the seat occupation data in the classroom and we found that a student's seat positions in a classroom relate to their outcomes (Minami et al., 2018). In this paper, we deal with text data of the same course as was used in the papers (Ohura et al., 2018) (Minami et al., 2017). By combining results obtained in analysis of both types of data, we can understand more about students on their viewpoints and their styles of study.

The rest of this paper is organized as follows: In Section 2, we describe the outline of the target data to be analyzed in this paper. In Section 3, we conduct the data analysis. First, we show how the data are processed from the original text data that are obtained as answer to a looking-back questionnaire to the word vectors, where each vector is considered to represent the corresponding student in her word-usage profile. Then, the distances between word-usage profile data are calculated and used for layout the relationship of students. We discuss the relations between the location of students in layout and their achievement in learning. Finally in Section 4, we conclude our discussions in this paper and prospect our future plans.

2. DATA

The data used in this paper came from a course in 2009 named "Exercise for Information Retrieval" in a junior (2-year) college (Minami et al., 2022). The students who were attending the class are in their second year and are going to graduate. The number of registered students was 35. The course was compulsory in order to get certificate for librarian. Thus, the students of this course were generally more motivated than other courses.

The major aim of the course was to let students become expert information searchers so that they had knowledge on information retrieval, and had skills in finding appropriate search engine sites and search keywords by understanding the aim and the background of the retrieval. The course consists of 15 lectures.

The term-end examination of the course consisted of 3 questions. The aim of these questions was to evaluate the skills on information retrieval, including the skills for planning and summarizing. These skills are supposed to have learned and trained in the course, through their exercises in the classes and while they do homework. We consider the score of term-end examination as a measure for student's academic performance/achievement.

We also asked the students to evaluate themselves. The evaluation consisted of 12 questions; half of which are for evaluating the course, such as (Q1) What do you have learned in the course? Do you think they are useful? (Q2) What are the good points of the lectures? (Q3) What are the bad points that should be corrected? (Q4) Score the course as a whole, with the numbers from 0 to 100. The rests are evaluating students themselves: (Q6) What are the good points of the student herself regarding learning attitudes and efforts in learning during the course period? (Q7) What are the bad points that should be corrected of the student herself? (Q11) Score the student herself by considering her efforts and attitude in the course with the numbers from 0 to 100.

The amount of data used in this paper is very small. Therefore, it is impossible to extract useful information which is applicable in other classes. Our main aim of analysis of these small data is to find not only candidate findings that may be able to extend to other cases, but also to develop new analysis methods as many as possible as the first step to data analysis of lecture data we use. Then, we would apply the methods found in the first step to the data obtained from other classes. The methods are supposed to be evaluated according to their applicability to other classes, usefulness of the extracted information for lecturers in advising students.

3. ANALYSIS

In this section, we conduct analysis of the data which are described in Section 2. What we intend to do is to layout the closeness between a student and another student, and between a student and a group of students according to their word-usage profiles.

3.1 Outline of the Data Processing

Figure 1 shows the outline of the data processing in this paper. The process starts with the texts obtained as the answer to the questionnaire described in Section 2. They are converted to the corresponding word list using MeCab (MeCab). MeCab is a well-known morphological analyzer for Japanese texts. As the words in a sentence are not separated by spaces unlike in English, we need to use a morphological analyzer in order to deal with a word as a unit for processing. We are able to obtain the list of words with their part-of-speech (POS) information as the output by MeCab.

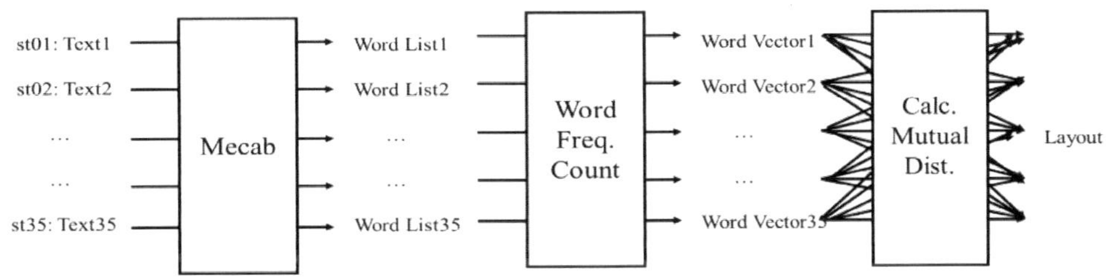

Figure 1. Processing Data from Answer Texts to Layout

Then we count the number of occurrences, or frequency, of each word and create a word vector from the word list. A word vector consists of the corresponding frequencies of the words. Lastly, we calculate the mutual distances, and similarities, between word vectors. We consider the word vector the representation of the word-usage profile of the corresponding student in this paper. Thus, the distance between two word-vectors is considered to be the distance of the two students in terms of their word-usage profiles. Cosine similarities between vectors are popularly used in order to measure the amount of closeness, which is not only easy to recognize intuitively, but also easy to calculate; by using inner product of vectors, i.e., component-wise product and summing them up.

However, we do not use cosine similarity directly for the index of closeness between students. As we can easily estimate that the usage of words would not be very different among students; frequently used words might be used frequently by all students and small number of words might be used differently by students to students. Thus, we use sine distance because its values are more different than cosine similarities for small angles. Also, sine distance can be calculated by using cosine similarities and easy to calculate as well.

In this section, we use two methods for drawing which show the layout how the students are close each other. The methods are (1) drawing layout by using graph drawing algorithm and (2) drawing layout by projecting into 2-dimensional plane after arranging the targets into a high-dimensional Euclidean space.

3.2 Calculating Distances between Students/Groups

We describe how to define the groups of students and how to represent word-usage. We also show how the distances are calculated in detail in this subsection. Let S be the set of students and W be the set of words. Let ans(s) be the text which is obtained as the answer to the questionnaire by the student s. Then ans(s) is of the form $w_1w_2...w_k$, where the number of the words $k=|ans(s)|$ is determined by the student s.

We get the word-list $w^*=[(w_1,pos(w_1)), (w_2,pos(w_2),...,(w_k,pos(w_k))]$ as the output of MeCab by giving ans(s) as input, where pos(w) is the part-of-speech (POS) of the word w. In this paper, however, we omit the pos part in the word list. Thus, we consider $w^*=[w_1,w_2,...,w_k]$. We denote the i-th element of the list w^* by $w^*[i]$; thus, $w^*[i]=w_i$.

Next, we count the frequency of words in a word list. The word vector $w^\#$ of w^* is defined as follows:

$$w^\# = [freq(w_1,w^*), freq(w_2,w^*),freq(w_3,w^*),...,freq(w_n,w^*)]$$

where n is the number of words in W ($n=|W|$) and $W=\{w_1, w_{2,...,} w_n\}$, and $freq(w,w^*)$ is the number of occurrences of the word w in the word list w^*; thus, $freq(w,w^*)=|\{i \mid w^*[i]=w, 1\leq i\leq k\}|$.

Now, we define the sine distance between two students using the corresponding word-vectors. Let $w^\#_1$ and $w^\#_2$ be the word vectors of student s1 and s2, respectively. Firstly, we adjust the lengths of the vectors to 1. Since the number of words used by a student varies a lot from student to student. Some students answer with a lot of words, whereas some students answer very shortly. In order to compare the word-usage profiles of

students, we have to adjust the length of the word vectors so that the component values represent some kind of ratios of words used by the student. Now, we define $w_i^{\#\prime}$ for i=1, 2 by: $w_i^{\#\prime} = w_i^{\#} / ||w_i^{\#}||$,
where $||w_i^{\#}||$ is the length, or norm, of $w_i^{\#}$, where norm is defined by $||w^{\#}|| = \sqrt{\sum_{j\in\{1,\ldots,|w^{\#}|\}} w^{\#}[j]^2}$, i.e., the length in the Euclidean space. Then, we define the cosine similarity of two vectors $w_1^{\#\prime}$ and $w_2^{\#\prime}$ by: CosSim($w_1^{\#\prime}$, $w_2^{\#\prime}$) = $w_1^{\#\prime} \cdot w_2^{\#\prime}$, where $\cdot$ denotes the inner product $\sum_{j=1}^{|w_1^{\#}|} w_1^{\#\prime}[j] w_2^{\#\prime}[j]$. Sine distance is defined by: SinDis($w_1^{\#\prime}$, $w_2^{\#\prime}$) = $\sqrt{1 - \mathrm{CosSim}(w_1^{\#\prime}, w_2^{\#\prime})^2}$ and distance of students by: d(s1, s2) = SinDis($w_1^{\#\prime}$, $w_2^{\#\prime}$).

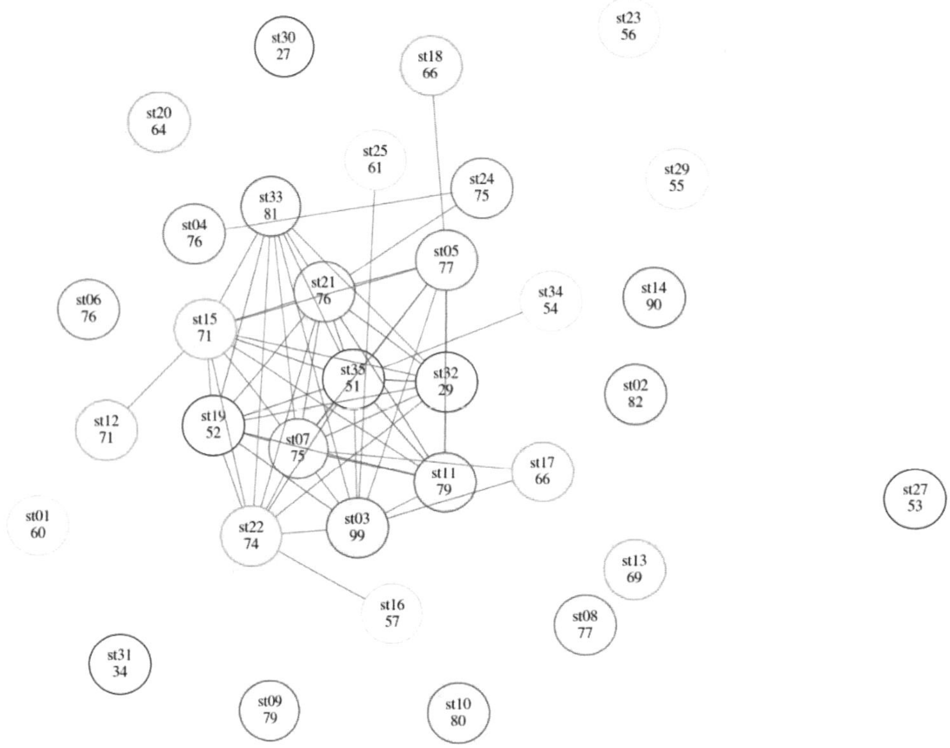

Figure 2. Layout of Students using graph drawing method by spring model

Figure 2 shows the layout of students using distances in this definition between students drawn by a graph drawing algorithm. A circle represents a student and the upper label shows the student's name, or ID, and the lower label shows the achievement score, i.e., the examination score, of the student. The color of the circle shows the group of the student based on the achievement score so that it becomes easy to see which group she belongs to. The edges that connect two students show that the distances between the students that the edge connects has higher closeness, i.e., small distance, than other pairs of students. As we observe Figure 2, we cannot say that students having similar achievement scores are close each other in their word-usages in general. On the other hand, some groups seem to be more separated than other groups in the graph. We would like to investigate more about the relationship between achievement scores and word-usages in the following sections.

3.3 Group-based Analysis using Graph Drawing Algorithm

As we have observed that the achievement scores and word-usages have little correlations in student to student, we divide the students into groups according to the achievements and see if the groups have some kinds of difference in word-usages. Firstly, we show the outline of grouping of students in this subsection. Table 1 shows outline of grouping. Students are divided into 5 groups, namely G1 to G5, according to their achievement scores so that each group contains 7 students. The achievement scores range from 79 to 99 and the mean score is 84.1 for G1, for example.

Table 1. Outline of Grouping

Group	Coloring	Number of Students	Minimum Score	Mean Score	Maximum Score
G1	Red	7	79	84.1	99
G2	Purple	7	75	75.9	78
G3	Green	7	64	68.6	74
G4	Light Blue	7	54	58.1	63
G5	Black	7	27	40.6	53

The word vectors of a group are calculated by just adding up all the number of word occurrences of the member of the group and the distances from a group to another group and a student are calculated in the same way as in calculating between students as has been described.

Figure 3 shows the layout of groups using the graph drawing method by spring model as was used in Figure 2. The edge labels show the distances between the groups. As we can see in Figure 3, the maximum distance value is 0.33 between G4 and G5, whereas the minimum distance value is 0.21 between G1 and G3. The mean value of a group to other 4 groups of G1 to G5 are 0.25, 0.27, 0.26, 0.31, and 0.30, respectively. Thus, roughly speaking, G1 is the group which is the mostly close to other groups, and the distances increase in the order of G3, G2, G5, and G4. Possibly, G1 is located in the center of the groups because of this property. Another interesting fact is that G3, the middle group in terms of achievement score, is the one closest to G1.

Next, we would like to arrange students by using the distances of a student to these 5 groups. We also use the spring algorithm by fixing the layout of the groups as in Figure 3. Figure 4 shows the results. We have to point out that the length parameter for the strength of spring is given by using the cosine similarity value because the length should be larger as the distance becomes smaller. Further, we multiply the similarity value by 8 for emphasis so that the groups and the students are located not too-close each other and well-separated.

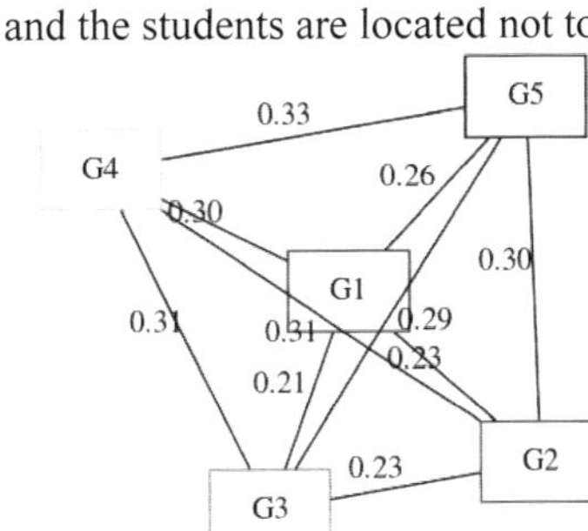

Figure 3. Graph-drawing of groups G1 to G5 using sprint algorithm with distance

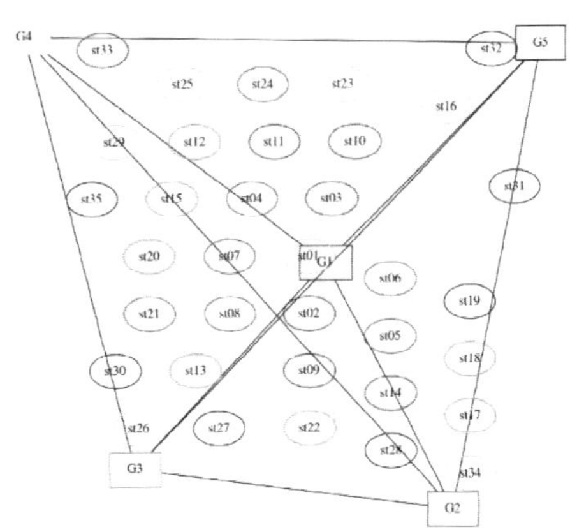

Figure 4. Graph-drawing of groups G1 to G5 using sprint algorithm with distance

As we can see, the students in G1 are located somewhere near G1 except st33. For G2, the students are located rather away from G2 in the central area of the graph, near G1. Among them, st24 is far away from G2 and is located in-between G4 and G5. For G3, the students are located relatively wide areas in the graph. 2 of them are close to G2, 3 of them are in-between G4 and G1, and the rest 3 are located relatively close to G3. For G4, the students are scattered in all areas of the graph. Among 7 students, 4 of them are located in the area in-between G4 and G5 and 3 others are located close to G1, G2 and G3 separated. For G5, students are also located separately in a wide area; st32 is located next to G5, st31 and st19 is in-between G5 and G2, st28 is very close to G2, st27 and st30 are close to G3, and st35 is located in-between G3 and G4.

3.4 Group-based Analysis by Embedding to Simplicial Complex in Euclidean Space

In this subsection, we propose a different approach to locate groups and students according to the distance data. As the graph drawing methods are supposed to arrange objects in 2-dimensional plane, 2 objects that have big distance may be located close to each other because of their distances to other objects. Thus, we cannot say that the two objects drawn close to each other are actually close to each other in terms of the distance value. Because of this, the observations from Figure 4, which are found in the previous subsection may be wrong, and thus we have to confirm them in different methods.

In the new approach, we realize the arrangement of objects (groups and students) so that their distances are preserved by embedding them into a high-dimensional Euclidean space as a simplicial complex (Tancer, 2011). As we cannot recognize how the objects are located in such a high-dimensional space, we project them into a 2-dimensional plane for visualization. Then, if we want to confirm the closely located two objects in the projected plane are actually close each other in the high-dimensional space, we can change the plane for projection so that we can see in a different angle and check if the two objects are still close to each other.

3.4.1 Simplicial Complex

Let X be the set of objects. We call K a simplicial complex of X if: (i) for any member x in K is a subset of X, and (ii) for any member x in K, any non-empty subset of x is also a member of K. We call a member of K a face of K and define the dimension of a face x by dim(x)=|x|-1. We call a face x as a vertex if dim(x)=0; i.e., a vertex is a face of K having only one element, i.e., x={v}. We identify {v} and v and deal with v as a vertex.

Our image for a simplicial complex with n-dimension is a kind of extended triangle. For example, the face {v1, v2} is a line segment that connects the vertices v1 and v2 which has dimension 1, and the face {v1, v2, v3} is a triangle having v1, v2, and v3 as its vertices and {v1, v2}, {v2, v3}, and {v3, v1} are its sides. The triangle's dimension is 2, which is easy to recognize because the triangles are embedded in a plane, which is 2-dimensional. We call the simplicial complex which consists of all subsets of objects complete and denote by K(O). Complete simplicial complex is the maximum simplicial complex of all. In this paper, we take the set of groups as O and deal with complete simplicial complex for O in the following sections.

3.4.2 Embedding a Simplicial Complex in a High-dimensional Euclidean Space

Let R be the set of real numbers and let d: O×O→R be the distance function which satisfies the following conditions: For any o_1, o_2, and o_3 in O, (i) d(o_1, o_2)≥0, (ii) d(o_1, o_2)=0 if and only if o_1=o_2, (iii) d(o_1, o_2)=d(o_2, o_1), and (iv) d(o_1, o_2)+d(o_2, o_3) ≥d(o_1, o_3). Note that the sine distance for the groups G={G1, G2,..., G5} satisfies these conditions. We denote d for the sine distance for G in the following discussions.

3.4.3 Layout of Groups and Students in a Euclidean Space and their Projected Image

We can embed the simplicial complex K(G) in R^4 by assigning coordinates to each group in G. We denote cor(Gi) for the coordinate assigned to Gi in R^4, and d_{ij} for d(Gi, Gj) for the groups Gi and Gj in G. Then, Cor(Gi) is determined step by step as:

(i) cor(G1)= (0, 0, 0, 0)

(ii) cor(G2)= (d_{12}, 0, 0, 0)

(iii) cor(G3)=(x, y, 0, 0), where x and y are determined by solving the equations

  a. d(cor(G1), cor(G3))= d_{13}, or x^2+y^2=${d_{13}}^2$ and

  b. d(cor(G2), cor(G3))= d_{23}, or $(x- d_{12})^2$+y^2=${d_{23}}^2$.

(iv) cor(G4)=(x, y, z, 0) such that x, y, and z satisfy the equations d(cor(Gi), cor(G4))= d_{i4} for i=1, 2, and 3.

(v) cor(G4)=(x, y, z, v) such that x, y, z, and v satisfy the equations d(cor(Gi), cor(G5))= d_{i4} for i=1, 2, 3, and 4.

As the result, we have the following coordinate assignment for the groups in G. (i) cor(G1)=(0, 0, 0, 0), (ii) cor(G2)=(0.23, 0, 0, 0), (iii) cor(G3)=(0.09, 0.19, 0, 0), (iv) cor(G4)=(0.11, 0.04, 0.28, 0), and (v) cor(G5)=(0.06, 0.04, 0.06, 0.24).

We may identify a group name and its coordinate.

We use weighted average for locating the students in R^4. Let s be a student and d(s,Gi) be the distance between s and group Gi for i=1, 2,…, 5, which we denote d_i for brevity. Let $d_i'=\frac{d_i}{\sum_{j=1}^{5} d_j}$.

In order to calculate the weighted average location for s, we have to define the weight w_i for Gi (i=1 to 5) so that $w_i \geq 0$ and sum(w_i)=1. Then we can define cor(s)=$\sum_{i=1}^{5} w_i \times Gi$.

Unfortunately, distance and weight relate inversely; weight increases as distance decreases, and vice versa. We define weight = $-log(distance)$ for inversing their values by considering that distance has a positive value with maximum of 1. Thus, the weight ranges from 0 to infinity.

Further, we use the emphasized weight by powering emphasis factor $(-log(distance))^{emph}$ so that the students are well-distributed. In our case we decided to use emph=16 after we tried several values.

Lastly, we have to decide how to visualize the layout in R^4. We choose the projection to a 2-dimensional plane. The plane is the one spanned by a pair of given 2 vectors in R^4 so that it contains the origin (0, 0, 0, 0).

Let v_1 and v_2 be vectors in R^4. We make an orthogonal coordinate system by giving two unit-vectors u_1 and u_2 as follows: $u_1 = v_1/\|v_1\|$, and $u_2 = u_2'/\|u_2'\|$ where $u_2' = v_2 - (v_2 \cdot u_1)\, u_1$ (Note that the dot operator ($\cdot$) is the inner product). Note that u_1 and u_2 are unit vectors by definition and they are orthogonal because their inner product is 0.

By using u_1 and u_2, the x- and y-coordinates on the projected plane of a vector v in R^4 is given by: (x,y) of v = (v$\cdot u_1$, v$\cdot u_2$).

Figure 5 (left) shows the projected layout of the groups and students by giving v_1=G2–G1 and v_2=G3–G1. Note that G1, G2, and G3 here are coordinates in R^4 and G2–G1 and G3–G1 are the vectors of cor(G2)–cor(G1) and cor(G3)–cor(G1), respectively. Figure 5 (right) shows the projected layout by giving v_1=G3–G1 and v_2=G5–G1.

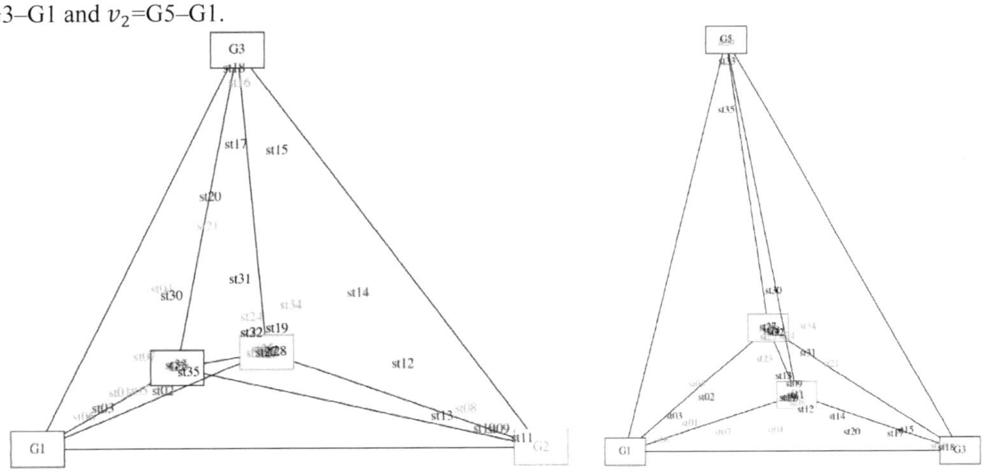

Figure 5. Layout projected on the plane spanned by G1-G2 and G1-G3 vectors (left) and Layout projected on the plane spanned by G1-G3 and G1-G5 vectors (right)

As we can see that st11 locates very close to G2 in both figures, we may be able to recognize st11 and G2 are located very close to each other in R^4. Similarly, st18 locates very close to G3.

4. CONCLUDING REMARKS

In this paper, we have investigated the relation between word-usage of a student and her academic achievement. The source data are obtained as the answer text to a term-end questionnaire. Distances were calculated from the word-usage vector. We considered the distance as the distance between a student and another student and the distance between a student and a group of students. The distances were drawn in two methods; (1) using graph-drawing algorithm and (2) projecting the layout in a high-dimensional Euclidean space into a 2-dimensional plane. Since the layouts of the students and groups of students are essentially high-dimensional, we cannot say the closeness of two objects just by looking in a visualized layout. We have to confirm by combining other method(s). In the second method we were able to change the plane for projection and see the relation in more precisely.

The topics to be investigated in the future include: (i) to explore further on the relation between the students' achievements and their viewpoints that appear in their answer text, (ii) to apply the proposed method to other data, including the one we used for seat position analysis such as (Minami et al., 2018), (iii) to digitize more educational data we have in our lectures and what we can find in these data, and so on.

ACKNOWLEDGEMENT

This work was supported in part by JSPS KAKENHI Grant Number JP17K00502.

REFERENCES

Ames, C. and Archer, J., 1988. Achievement Goals in the Classroom: Students' Learning Strategies and Motivation Processes. *Journal of Educational Psychology*. 80, 3, pp. 260-267.

Ames, C., 1992. Classrooms: Goals, Structures, and Student Motivation. *Journal of Educational Psychology*. 84, 3, pp. 261-271.

Faraway, J. and Augustin, N., 2018. When small data beats big data. *Statistics&Probability Letters*.

Kitchin, R. and Lauriault, T. P., 2015. Small data in the era of big data. *GeoJournal 80*, pp. 463-475.

MeCab: Yet Another Part-of-Speech and Morphological Analyzer. Available from https://taku910.github.io/mecab/ [2022.1.27]. (in Japanese)

Minami, T. and Ohura, Y., 2014. A Correlation Analysis of Student's Attitude and Outcome of Lectures Investigation of Keywords in Class-Evaluation Questionnaire. *Proceedings of Advanced Science and Technology Letters (ASTL)*, Vol.73 (FGCN 2014). pp. 11-16.

Minami, T. and Ohura, Y., 2015. Towards Improving Students' Attitudes to Lectures and Getting Higher Grades--With Analyzing the Usage of Keywords in Class-Evaluation Questionnaire--. *Proceedings of The Seventh International Conference on Information, Process, and Knowledge Management (eKNOW 2015)*. pp. 78-83.

Minami, T. and Ohura, Y., 2015a. How Student's Attitude Influences on Learning Achievement? --An Analysis of Attitude Representing Words Appearing in Looking-Back Evaluation Texts. *International Journal of Database Theory and Application (IJDTA)*, Science & Engineering Research Support Society (SERSC). 8, 2. pp. 129-144.

Minami, T. Ohura, Y. and Baba, K., 2017. A Characterization of Student's Viewpoint to Learning and its Application to Learning Assistance Framework. *Proceedings of the 9th International Conference on Computer Supported Education (CSEDU 2017) vol. 1: A2E*, SciTePress. pp. 619-630.

Minami, T. and Ohura, Y., 2018. A Correlation Analysis of Seat Positions between Students. *Proceedings of The Tenth International Conference on Advances in Databases, Knowledge, and Data Applications (DBKDA 2018)*. IARIA.

Minami, T. and Ohura, Y., 2020. How Different Are Full and Short Papers in Word-Usage?. *International Journal of Machine Learning and Computing (IJMLC)*, vol. 10, no. 1.

Minami, T. and Ohura, Y., 2022. A Characterization of Word-Usage of Students Using Part-of-Speech Information. Proceedings of The 5th International Conference on Information and Computer Technologies (ICICT 2022), New York. (to be published)

Ohura, Y. and Minami, T., 2018. On Characteristic Words Extraction by Text Mining and their Relationship with Level of Comprehension of Students, *Abstracts of the 46th Annual Meeting of the Behaviometric Society (supple)*, pp. 114-117. (in Japanese)

Romero, C. and Ventura, S., 2007. Educational data mining: A survey from 1995 to 2005. *Expert Systems with Applications*. 33, 1, pp. 135-146.

Romero, C. Ventura, S. Espejo, P. G. and Hervás, C., 2008. Data mining algorithms to classify students. *Proceedings of the 1st International Conference on Educational Data Mining (EDM 2008)*. pp. 8-17.

Silva, C., and Fonseca, J., 2017. Educational Data Mining: a literature review. *Track2 – Artificial Intelligence in Education, Distributed Artificial Intelligence in education (DAIED) and Web-based AIED systems*.

Tancer, M., 2011. Topological and Geometrical Combinatorics. *Charles University in Prague*. Doctoral Thesis.

THE INFLUENCE OF NATIONAL CULTURE DIMENSIONS ON AGILE IMPLEMENTATIONS IN THE SOUTH AFRICAN SOFTWARE DEVELOPMENT CONTEXT

Kirwin B. Matthews and Maureen C. Tanner
University of Cape Town, South Africa

ABSTRACT

Culture influences how agile frameworks are implemented, and agility is said to be suitable in contexts where flexibility and spontaneity are emphasized. While past studies have investigated the influence of national culture on Agile implementations in Western and Eastern contexts, studies focusing on a South African software development context is limited. Furthermore, few studies have focused on the effect of cultural differences within software engineering in general. The purpose of this study is to describe how national culture influences Agile practices within the South African software development context. The study was interpretive and was executed using a qualitative, semi- structured interview research strategy directed at Agile practitioners in South African software development teams. The thematic analysis technique was used to analyze the data. Seven propositions have been formulated to highlight how national culture dimensions influence Agile practices. The findings reveal that various national culture dimensions influence the decision-making process, the degree of sprint interruptions, participation in Agile ceremonies, adherence to policies and prescribed Agile practices, how teams reach agreement, approaches to process improvement and sprint planning.

KEYWORDS

Agile Software Development, National Culture, Agile Practices, South Africa

1. INTRODUCTION

Agile frameworks are underpinned by values and principles which are described in the Agile Manifesto for successful software implementations (http://agilemanifesto.org/). The Agile values emphasize collaboration and interaction to mitigate issues which often hamper the success of software projects (Joseph et al., 2016). Since agility is like a mindset or culture, it is imperative to have an environment that characterizes and supports the Agile software development process (Sidky et al. 2007). This is particularly important given that culture plays a role in how Agile frameworks are utilized and implemented (Sutharshan, 2013). For instance, the Agile culture requires the active involvement of team members and is said to be suitable where there is a flat structure (low power distance). Moreover, flexibility and spontaneity are emphasized (Siakas & Siakas, 2007). Cultures from Anglo countries, where Agile methodologies originate from, and Nordic countries, are closest aligned to Agile values (Palokangas, 2013). Since Agile values are based on Western culture, there is a need to investigate their suitability for contexts that demonstrate different values (Zhao, 2015). This is supported by recent concerns from Agile practitioners regarding whether it was possible to implement Agile practices with all nationalities and cultures (Gregory et al., 2016).

Zhao (2015) studied the impact of culture, namely Chinese and Swedish, on the implementation of Scrum, a type of Agile methodology. Their findings concluded that national culture influences Scrum implementations, in terms of how Scrum roles, ceremonies, and artifacts are utilized. Zhao (2015) proposed conducting their study in a different country context to China (Eastern culture) and Sweden (Western culture) to further explore how aspects of national culture might impact Agile implementations. This study has been conducted in response to this recommendation. Indeed, South Africa offers an interesting context of study, due to its heterogeneous cultural grouping (Mnkandla, 2013). While studies have been conducted to investigate the influence of national culture on Agile implementations in Western and Eastern country contexts, there is no research that explores the influence of national culture and the implementation of Agile methodologies in the

South African software development context. Furthermore, few studies have focused on the effect of cultural differences within software engineering in general (Darwish & Henryson, 2019).

According to Hofstede's culture classification, South Africa is identified as having high power distance, individualism, masculinity, and indulgence as well as low uncertainty avoidance and long-term orientation (Hofstede, 2013). For instance, South Africans enjoy clearly defined roles and therefore do not like to be called team members (Tanner & Noruwana, 2012). Moreover, South African culture is different to Western or Eastern culture in that it is less homogenous (Ward et al., 2015) and the introduction of different cultures in a team can be problematic for Agile implementations. Even though there is evidence in practice of Agile methods recently being incorporated in African countries, there is a lingering question about how its core values, with roots in western attitudes and behaviors, relates to non-western cultures (Jukich, 2018).

In response to the above-mentioned research problems, the purpose of this study is to describe how national culture dimensions influences Agile implementations within the South African software development context. This paper specifically reports on the findings related to the influence on Agile practices. The research question has been formulated as follows: How does national culture dimensions influence Agile practices within the South African software development context? This study contributes to Agile software development literature through 7 propositions articulating the influence of various cultural dimensions on Agile practices in South African software development teams. The findings are also relevant to other non-South African teams that demonstrate similar cultural traits.

The paper is organized as follows. Following on from the introduction, a review of literature is presented in relation to the research problem regarding national culture suited for Agile software development. The conceptual framework employed for this study is then described, followed by an overview of the methodology employed for the study. The findings are then described and discussed considering the extent literature to articulate the research contributions. The paper is then concluded.

2. LITERATURE REVIEW

2.1 Defining Culture and National Culture

Culture is composed of traits and characters peculiar to a group of people which makes them unique from other societies (Aziza, 2001). These traits include language, dress code, music, work, arts, religion, dancing and more. It also entails social norms, taboos, and values (Idang, 2015). Since culture is a broad term, in this research we will narrow the concept of culture to values and practices that people acquire by living in different countries i.e., national culture (Hofstede et al., 2010).

There are several frameworks used for studying national culture. Some examples include Hofstede (2013) and Hampton-Turner (1990). National cultures are a segment of the "mental software" we acquired during the first ten years of our lives and hold most of our basic values (Minkov & Hofstede, 2011, p. 14). This study focuses on the Hofstede and Globe national culture frameworks as data is available for South Africa pertaining to these frameworks. Moreover, other studies (e.g., Zhao (2015); Sutharshan (2013), Palokangas (2013)) have successfully employed these frameworks in the context of Agile software development. The frameworks are discussed in the Theoretical Framework section.

2.2 The South African Social Context

South Africa, which is also known as the "rainbow nation," has a culture that is one of the most multifaceted and diverse in the world (Tanner, 2009). It consists of 60.1 million people of which 30.8 million (51,1%) are female and 29.4 million (48,9%) are male (http://www.statssa.gov.za/, 2021). There are four distinct population groups namely, Black African, Colored, Indian/Asian, and White (South Africa. Statistics South Africa, 2016). In Southern Africa, among the traditional Nguni people which includes the Zulu, Xhosa, Ndebele, and Swazi people, there exists a common way of life known as 'Ubuntu' (Metz & Gaie, 2010). Ubuntu means humanity and the term can loosely translated as "I am because we are" (West, 2014). The core values of Ubuntu are summarized as respect for the dignity of others, group solidarity, teamwork, service to others, and the spirit of harmony and interdependence (i.e., 'each one of us needs all of us') (Mbigi, 2007). The fifth dimension, the spirit of harmony and interdependence, was labelled as the spirit of Ubuntu. Wanasika et al. (2011) posit the philosophy of Ubuntu encompasses human existence and social relations. Wanasika et al. (2011) then argues, that while there are views of collectivism being associated with current relationships, Ubuntu is grounded in history and includes the present and future obligations to individuals as well. Another example of the collectivism in Ubuntu is that there is no phrase or concept of "Agree to disagree," therefore a consensus must be reached on mutual understanding and agreement regarding a matter through socialization (Nussbaum, 2003). which is associated with modern society and the related practices embedded in education.

2.3 Agility and its Value System

Agile frameworks are based on values and principles defined in the Agile Manifesto. From a cultural point of view, Agile frameworks call for minimal hierarchy, and favor self-organization, equity, empowerment, commitment, responsibility, participation, learning and continuous improvement, consensus, respect, compromises, trust, honesty, openness, and communication (Iivari & Iivari, 2011).

According to the Manifesto, agility values individuals and interactions over processes and tools, working software over comprehensive documentation, customer collaboration over contract negotiation, and responding to change over following a prescribed plan. The Agile Manifesto also formulates twelve principles that guide the nature of Agile frameworks (Misra et al., 2012).

2.4 Scrum and its Value System

Scrum is one of the frameworks that falls within the Agile umbrella. The Scrum framework provides the flexibility to control and manage requirements and the development process by allowing software to be developed in small chunks in multiple iterations (Hayat et al., 2019). The life cycle of the Scrum framework includes planning, staging, development, and release (Sutherland, 2005). The Scrum values relate to Courage, Focus, Commitment, Respect and Openness and encourage management and team members to take responsibility instead of blame shifting (Neelima, & Saile, 2013). Schwaber and Sutherland (2017) suggest that Scrum teams need to become proficient in living the Scrum values to successfully use Scrum. The framework consists of three aspects namely roles, processes, and artifacts (Cervone, 2011), and are briefly summarized in Table 1.

Table 1. Description of Scrum aspects

Scrum Aspects	Description
Artifacts – Product backlog	The product backlog is a prioritized list of tasks that contains the product requirements (Girot, 2013). The purpose of the product backlog is to keep track of all work that must be done as well as bug fixes (Tanner, 2013).
Artifacts – Sprint backlog	The sprint backlog contains a subset of requirements derived from the product backlog that can be completed during a sprint (Girot, 2013).
Artifacts – Burndown chart	The burndown chart shows a holistic view of how the project is progressing and allows for an assessment of the rate at which items are completed (Neelima, & Saile, 2013).
Artifacts – Task board	The task board is used to track the status of all tasks pertaining to user stories (Tanner, 2013; Cervone, 2011).
Roles – Product Owner	The Product Owner is responsible for providing requirements and maintaining the product backlog (Schwaber & Sutherland, 2017).
Roles – Scrum Master	The Scrum Master is responsible for enacting the Scrum values and practices, and to remove impediments (Cervone, 2011).
Roles – Scrum team members	Scrum team members are responsible for achieving the project goals. The characteristics of the Scrum team are: self-organizing; cross-functional; no titles for Developers; does not recognize sub-teams; and there may be individuals who have specialized skills, but the responsibility lies with the team (Schwaber & Sutherland, 2017).
Processes – Sprint	A Sprint that is an event time-boxed to a month or less, where a useable, and potentially a releasable product is created (Schwaber & Sutherland, 2017).

Processes – Sprint planning	At the beginning of a Sprint, a Sprint Planning meeting is held where the Product Owner will communicate which components, or features identified in the backlog, are to be prioritized into the next Sprint and which features can be developed in other Sprints (Neelima, & Saile, 2013).
Processes – Daily Scrum	The daily Scrum is a fifteen-minute time-boxed event held every day between the Scrum Master and the team members (Schwaber & Sutherland, 2017).
Processes – Sprint review	The sprint review is held at the end of sprint to inspect the increment (i.e., demonstration to Product Owner) and to adjust the product backlog if necessary (Schwaber & Sutherland, 2017).
Processes – Sprint retrospective	During the sprint retrospective, the team reviews its past processes and creates a plan to improve during the next Sprint (Schwaber & Sutherland, 2017).

2.5 Influence of National culture on Agile implementations

Past studies have found that national culture can impact Scrum implementations. According to literature, Power distance influences Agile roles in relation to leadership qualities, responsibilities, and decision-making power (Zhao, 2015). For instance, Sutharshan and Maj (2011) found that in cultures with low power distance, employees are not afraid to challenge authority and leaders are not autocratic or paternalistic. Instead, a consultative style of decision-making and participative management style prevails. In individualist countries, team members emphasize the importance of personal responsibility pertaining to the quality of tasks completed (Zhao, 2015).

In relation to Scrum practices, teams with a higher uncertainty avoidance index demonstrate more rigorous planning practices, and use tried and tested tools instead of being open to risk-taking (Darwish & Henryson, 2019). Uncertainty avoidance plays a role in certain software practices, such as requirements being specified upfront, test-first programming, and making early design decisions (Darwish & Henryson, 2019). The use of burndown charts and limitations on sprint interruptions are also more prevalent in cultures with a high degree of uncertainty avoidance (Zhao, 2015).

3. THEORETICAL FRAMEWORK

This study employed the Hofstede and GLOBE project national culture dimensions to inform its theoretical framework. Hanges and Dickson (2004) compared the national culture dimensions of Hofstede to the GLOBE project national culture dimensions. Their findings indicate similarities between Hofstede's and GLOBE's power distance dimension. Hofstede's and GLOBE's uncertainty avoidance dimension are also similar. Hofstede's and GLOBE's individualism and collectivism dimensions share similarities, but GLOBE further classifies collectivism as institutional collectivism and in-group collectivism. Lastly, Hofstede's masculinity dimension is like GLOBE's societal assertiveness' scale. Venaik, Zhu and Brewer (2013) mention that Hofstede long-term orientation dimension and GLOBE future orientation dimension capture various aspects of time orientation of societies. Hofstede's long-term orientation focuses on the past (tradition) versus future (thrift) aspect of societies, while GLOBE future orientation dimension captures the present versus future (planning) practices of societies. The GLOBE future orientation dimension also reflects societal aspirations and preferences for planning. Although criticisms regarding the inconsistency for Hofstede uncertainty avoidance and masculinity national culture dimensions exist (Minkov & Kaasa, 2021), the study provides findings for both extremes of these dimensions in the context of South African Agile software development teams.

Table 2. Description of Hofstede and GLOBE National Culture Dimensions

National Culture Dimensions	Description
Power distance - (Hofstede, GLOBE)	Power distance is the extent to which people with less power expect and accept that the decision-making power is distributed unequally (Hofstede, 2013; House et al., 1999).
Individualism & Collectivism – (Hofstede, GLOBE)	Individualism is the acceptance that people in a nation have learnt to act as individuals, whereas collectivism is where people act as a member of a group. The Individualism dimension of national culture is classified from collectivist to individualist (Hofstede, 2011).
Uncertainty avoidance - (Hofstede, GLOBE)	Uncertainty avoidance refers to whether people in a nation prefer structured over unstructured conditions which is classified from relatively flexible to extremely rigid (Hofstede, 2013).
Masculinity / Assertiveness – (Hofstede, GLOBE)	Masculinity is the degree to which masculine values prevail over feminine values. Masculine values include assertiveness performance, success, and competition, and is classified in a range from tender to tough. Feminine values include warm personal relationships, modesty, quality of life, service, and caring for the weak (Hofstede, 2013). Assertiveness refers to the extent to which individuals in organizations or societies are assertive, confrontational, and aggressive in social relationships (House et al., 1999).
Long-term orientation (Hofstede)	Long-term orientation is "the fostering of virtues oriented toward future rewards, in particular, perseverance and thrift" (Hofstede as cited by Zhao, 2015, p. 17). This refers to a nation's time orientation and is characterized by "patience, perseverance, respects for older, tradition and ancestors, obedience sense and the duty towards the larger good" (Zhao, 2015, p. 18).
Future orientation - (GLOBE)	Future orientation refers to the extent to which individuals in organizations or societies engage in future-oriented activities such as planning, investing in the future, and delayed gratification (House et al., 1999).
Indulgence – (Hofstede)	In an indulgent culture it is deemed good to be free. Acting on impulses of what one wants to do is viewed as a good thing. In a restrained culture, the general sense is that life is hard, and that duty, not freedom, is the normal state of being (Hofstede, 2013).

4. METHODOLOGY

The section describes the research methodology followed for this study. The study employed a subjectivist and qualitative stance. The questions in the study were "how" questions in that the researcher wanted to describe how national culture dimensions impact on Agile practices in the South African context. The data that emerged was descriptive meaning that the data was reported in words instead of numbers (Creswell, 2003). This paper was written from an interpretivist paradigm perspective. The research question was answered using a deductive research approach, using a framework which informed the coding process (Braun & Clarke, 2006).

Data was collected using qualitative semi-structured interviews. Initial interview questions aimed to set the context for the rest of the interview. The national culture dimension questions required the participant to expound on the responses given in relation to the culture dimension and the influence it exerted on the Agile practices. The researcher probed into unexplored themes that arose or asked the participant to clarify where the researcher felt more information could be retrieved regarding the context. A cross-sectional timeframe was chosen. No previous data was used, and no data was collected after write-up of analysis. The data was collected over about a six-month period from December 2020 to May 2021.

Purposive sampling was used in this study. Within purposive sampling, judgmental sampling was specifically used as the researcher targeted participants who could provide the relevant information to meet the objectives of the study (Etikan & Bala, 2017). The target population was Agile practitioners within the software development context. Interviews were held with participants from various roles within the Agile methodology as well as management to get a different perspective which was often a more holistic view than the responses from a team member. Participants were asked about all the various practices and ceremonies within the Scrum framework. Furthermore, the researcher also targeted participants from a wide range of cultural groups in South Africa. Twenty-six semi-structured interviews were conducted with various project team members and stakeholders such as the Scrum team, Product Owner, Scrum Master, management, end-users, and customers across different teams and companies in South Africa. The interviews were held via digital video communication platforms such as Google Meet, Microsoft Teams, and Zoom. All interviews were transcribed. The participants' demographics are shown in Table 3.

Table 3. Respondents' Demographics

Person	Role	Race	Years of experience in role	Team Size
P1	Scrum Master	Black	5 yrs.	16-25
P2	Agile Coach	White	8 yrs.	7
P3	Scrum Master	White	1 year	9-13
P4	Agile Coach	White	3 yrs.	12
P5	Product Owner	White	3 yrs.	4-7
P6	Technical Product Manager	White	5 yrs.	4-11
P7	Credit Analyst	Black	8 yrs.	12
P8	Agile Coach	Black	2 yrs.	13
P9	Scrum Master	White	2 yrs.	6
P10	Product Owner	Coloured	1 year	8
P11	Scrum Master	White	5 yrs.	8-9
P12	Agile Project Manager	Coloured	1 year	12
P13	Project Manager	Coloured	5 yrs.	6
P14	Application Support Specialist	Coloured	1 year	20
P15	Solutions Architect	White	8 yrs.	8-9
P16	Agile Coach	White	1 year	~14
P17	Scrum Master	White	6 yrs.	15
P18	Agile Coach	Indian	5 yrs.	7
P19	Agile Coach	White	1 year	7
P20	Head Of Application Development	White	4 yrs.	5-10
P21	Agile Coach	White	5 yrs.	~10
P22	Product Manager	White	1 year	6
P23	Scrum Master	Coloured	5 yrs.	6
P24	Centre of Excellence Manager	Indian	6 yrs.	6-9
P25	Business Analyst	Coloured	2 yrs.	6-7
P26	Agile Coach	White	1 year at organization 9 yrs. in role	3 teams of ~ 5 people

Each participant answered the questions in line with their Agile implementation context and the events experienced within the teams they were part of or managed. Participants were involved in projects in various phases of the software development life cycle. Some were part of mature Agile teams while other teams were involved in newly formed teams. Some participants changed companies and were too new to answer questions for the team they were in at that point in time and referred to the previous team or organization they were part of since they had more experience to refer to for those teams. The researcher then focused on that selected team as the context for the interview. Most of the interview responses were based on the current context of the team within their team formation stage and software development life cycle. However, some respondents also provided data looking retrospectively and gave insight into how the team dynamics, processes, and artifacts changed over time. These responses were noted in the data analysis and the discussion sections.

The data was analyzed using thematic analysis. Analysis and data collection were conducted concurrently. In thematic analysis, responses are used to identify, analyze, and report patterns or themes within the data (Braun & Clarke, 2006). By way of example, the researcher coded the responses in a qualitative data analysis tool called NVivo. Themes were identified within the data for each question and reported on in the data analysis and discussion chapters. The collected data was organized and described in rich detail and various aspects of the research topic was interpreted. Thematic analysis entails the following phases: familiarizing yourself with your data, generating initial code, searching for themes, reviewing themes, defining, naming themes, and producing the report (Braun & Clarke, 2006).

This study made use of the following verification strategies: selecting the appropriate sample (Morse et al., 2002), comparing cases to seek out similarities and differences across companies to ensure different perspectives are represented, using 'rich' and 'thick' verbatim quotes from participants (Noble & Smith, 2015), consulting multiple data sources such as suggested links to concepts and other resources (Buchan et al., 2017), and reflexivity, where the researcher made notes of questions to change after each interview (Noble & Smith, 2015).

5. FINDINGS & DISCUSSION

This section is organized as follows. For each dimension, the empirical results are first presented including relevant quotes. Theoretical propositions are then formulated, and the findings are then compared to literature.

5.1 Power Distance and Agile Practices

In South African Agile teams, the decision-making process is influenced by the degree of power distance prevailing in the team. For instance, in smaller South African Agile teams with a flatter organizational structure, power distance is low and decision-making power is more equal among team members. Furthermore, these South African Agile teams implement various mechanisms (e.g., voting) to support a more democratic decision-making process to reach consensus: *"when it comes to making decisions, it would be a team discussion; we would explain why it is beneficial for the team, get their feedback; and then they would normally agree and be game to try it out"* (P23). In contrast, larger South African teams are more hierarchical, and the final decision is sometimes made by the Team Leader, or even management: *"The teams that I work with are still operating in an environment where senior management make decisions that often override the team regarding delivery timelines and attention to building in quality"* (P24).

In South Africa, power distance also influences the number of interruptions experienced by the Agile teams as well as the team's ability to decide on the scope of the sprint. In instances where high power distance prevails, Agile teams face numerous interruptions by management to change the scope of the sprint. In those instances, teams are less in control of the scope of the sprint: *"In pure scrum, [interruptions] is not allowed. But I think that when the team is under fire then it is necessary for having the conversation and drawing attention to new tasks that may be assigned"* (P20). During the sprint planning meetings, the scope is often decided by empowered individuals, with less input and consensus from the team. In contrast, in South African Agile teams with low power distance, the sprint scope could only be changed by team, and they could agree on the sprint scope through consensus. Furthermore, changes could be actioned by anyone, provided that the reason was valid. In line with the above findings, the following proposition is formulated: ***Proposition 1: In South African Agile teams, power distance influences the decision-making process and the degree of interruptions experienced by the teams during the sprint***

According to the findings, it can be posited that greater agility is achieved in South African teams with low power distance as this promotes self-organized teams. Indeed, Agile principle 11 states that self-organized teams achieve the best architectures, requirements and designs (https://agilemanifesto.org). The findings concur with literature whereby low power distance promotes shared understanding, discussion and consensus (Zhao, 2015). The principle of self-organized teams (Schwaber & Sutherland, 2017) is also supported when teams face minimal interruptions during the sprint, and when they can agree on the sprint scope democratically. Past studies have also found that in cultures with high power distance, interferences are often experienced and deemed acceptable (Zhao, 2015).

5.2 Individualism / Collectivism and Agile Practices

In South African Agile teams, the degree of individualism / collectivism influences the members' degree of participation in Agile ceremonies. In individualist teams, members do not actively participate in ceremonies. For instance, these members are only expected to provide feedback on their specific work items during daily stand-ups: *"With artifacts, there is an expectation to be involved overall for the team. Generally, there is a bit of a barrier to that and separation; for example, you would do what is in your lane instead of everyone working together on something. They were looking at who was accountable for something"* (P4). In contrast, in South African Agile teams with collectivist traits, members prepare for and participate in all meetings, whilst collectively providing input on all items on the agenda: *"We do a Sprint review which forms part of our planning. In terms of artifacts, reviews, and planning there is a collective responsibility. There is never an instance where one person runs the sprint planning. As we unpack stories, developers give their input. The expectation is that everyone in the team has to contribute to the sprint reviews, planning and artifacts"* (P23). However, in both individualist and collectivist teams, the degree of participation is mitigated by the team members' role. For instance, during sprint planning meeting 2, Business Analysts and Quality Assurance Testers might not have much to contribute as the meeting focuses on technical design tasks. In line with the above findings, the following proposition is formulated: ***Proposition 2: In South African Agile teams, the participation of team members in Agile ceremonies is influenced by the degree of individualism / collectivism manifested in the team.***

Based on the findings, it can be inferred that South African teams with collectivist traits are better able to adhere to the Agile value pertaining to collaboration. None of the past literature that was reviewed provided insights into the influence of individualism and collectivism on participation in Agile ceremonies. Past studies only mentioned that individualist teams require workshops and group social events to increase group cohesiveness (Brockmann & Thaumüller, 2009). The study therefore provides new insights into the role of individualism / collectivism in a team's ability to achieve agility.

5.3 Uncertainty Avoidance and Agile Practices

The study found that uncertainty avoidance influences the extent to which teams are comfortable with uncertainty and ambiguity during the sprints. South African Agile teams from larger companies typically demonstrate high uncertainty avoidance. Hence, they tend to strictly follow due procedures: *"They have become less tolerant of unorthodox methods and instead trying to become more team-orientated"* (P4). Smaller Agile teams, where low uncertainty avoidance is demonstrated, are flexible and less strict on adherence to policies. There might also be no documented policy and instead a standard way of working is commonly accepted in team: *"We aren't strict with regards to policies, procedures and Scrum processes, because I think you can lose agility as this is all about change and adapting"* (P23).

South African Agile teams with low uncertainty avoidance are also flexible and experiment with the sprint duration to suit their business practices. Intellectual autonomy prevails and team members are also encouraged to pursue their own ideas. Curiosity and creativity are valued, and the team is supported to experiment with Agile frameworks. In teams from larger companies, intellectual autonomy is also encouraged in theory, but not well implemented in practice. In line with the above findings, the following proposition is formulated: ***Proposition 3: In South African Agile teams, the degree of uncertainty avoidance influences the extent to which teams adhere to policies and prescribed Agile practices.***

South African teams with low uncertainty avoidance are more inclined to adapt their business processes and are therefore better adhering to the principle of empiricism of which transparency, inspection and adaptation are pillars (Schwaber & Sutherland, 2017). The findings concur with literature whereby teams with a higher uncertainty avoidance index use tried and tested tools instead of being open to risk-taking (Darwish & Henryson, 2019). Moreover, while past studies indicate that such teams tend to minimize risks (Darwish & Henryson, 2019), the findings from this study further reveal that this is achieved through strict adherence to policies and procedures.

5.4 Masculinity / Assertiveness and Agile Practices

According to the findings, masculinity / assertiveness influences Agile practices relative to how teams reach agreement, resolve conflict and the degree to which team members speak up during meetings. For instance, in South African Agile teams demonstrating low levels of masculinity, a democratic process is used to reach consensus. During this democratic process, each team member can provide input: *"To ensure consensus I use planning poker in order to get different perspectives of the complexity, uncertainty, risk and effort associated with the work to be committed to in the sprint. It also provides us with the final velocity score so that the team can agree on the commitment for the sprint"* (P26). In teams with a high degree of masculinity, team members with the most knowledge on a topic typically makes the decision: *"At the moment it doesn't feel like willing consent from all team members, more a kind of 'I don't want to argue about it, so I'll just go with it'"* (P4). Masculinity is mostly prevalent in newly formed Agile teams but as the team matures, it often demonstrates less masculinity and instead use the method of willing consent. Masculinity also influences how conflict is resolved in South African Agile teams. Agile teams with a high degree of masculinity resolve conflicts through direct confrontation or in the presence of management: *"A conflict resolution that we had was with the Scrum Master where we suggested that we have a conversation with the each one's manager to try and resolve the conflict"* (P4). In teams where a low degree of masculinity is manifested, conflict (especially personal conflict) is avoided or resolved through conversation that the Scrum Master facilitate (P17).

The findings also reveal that different team members can demonstrate different degrees of assertiveness. In South African Agile teams, when some members are more assertive, others in the team tend to not speak up to give their opinion or ideas (P6). However, this can be circumvented if the Scrum Master ensures that all voices are equally heard. In line with the above findings, the following proposition is formulated: ***Proposition 4: In South African Agile teams, masculinity / assertiveness influence how members reach agreement and resolve conflict.***

The Scrum value of commitment proposes that team members come to an agreement on the commitments they make as a team and as individuals (Schwaber & Sutherland, 2017). The findings reveal that the national culture of masculinity (Hofstede, 2013) and assertiveness (House et al., 1999) influence the extent to which this Scrum value is adhered to. Masculinity influences the conflict resolution mechanisms in South African Agile teams. Past studies have mostly related the issue of conflict resolution to the power distance cultural dimension (Sutharshan & Maj, 2011). This study reveals that masculinity also influences how conflict is resolved, in line with Hofstede (2013) who states that masculine cultures resolve conflict by fighting.

5.5 Long-Term (Short-Term) Orientation and Agile Practices

In South African Agile teams, the long-term (short-term) orientation national culture dimension influences how members approach the retrospective meetings to improve on their work practices. In particular, the findings reveal that short-term orientated teams mostly reflect on the past sprint i.e., "what went well" and "what did not go well" during retrospective meetings. They do not necessarily focus on long-term results, future actions, or how the team can improve: *"In retrospective meetings, there is an aspect of focusing on continuous improvement but there is a larger aspect of focusing on the past. The conversations about the future become a frustration for the team because they feel that it won't change anything"* (P4). Teams with long-term orientation instead have in-depth discussions around improvements for future: *"It was very much backward-looking at first. Once we started putting measures in place, things started to change so that we focus on how we can get better going forward"* (P20). In line with the above findings, the following proposition is formulated: ***Proposition 5: In South African Agile teams, long-term (short-term) orientation influence teams' approaches to process improvement.***

The findings are in line with literature relative to long-term orientation, whereby the team members display habits that show consideration for future events by preparing for them in the present (Darwish & Henryson, 2019). Furthermore, in long-term orientated teams, members actively engage in tasks that lead to continuous improvement and are willing to brainstorm how to do things better. This is in line with literature that states that long-term orientation cultures emphasize schooling (learning) and have conversations about the effectiveness of Agile methods to deliver working software (Brockmann & Thaumüller, 2009). It can therefore be posited that long-term orientated teams are better able to adhere to the Agile principle stating that "at regular intervals, the team reflects on how to become more effective, then tunes and adjusts its behavior accordingly" (Beck et al., 2001).

5.6 Future Orientation and Agile Practices

Future orientation influences Agile practices in relation to how product backlog refinement sessions are conducted. In South African Agile teams that are future oriented, members are more forward-looking during product backlog refinement sessions. These Agile teams not only plan for the next sprint but sometimes plan for future sprints as well: *"We plan for every sprint. In some cases, we plan two sprints ahead. This depends on the PO and business because they buy into the product, so we wait for them to give us the requirements"* (P1). Future orientation traits are prevalent in mature Agile compared to novice teams, and this translates in their level of planning of the sprints. In line with the above findings, the following proposition is formulated: ***Proposition 6: In South African Agile teams, future orientation influence teams' approaches to sprint planning.***

Literature states that limiting planning to only a sprint prevents developers from thinking ahead, while planning for two or more sprints helps the developers focus on the product vision and to maintain the bigger picture (Cockton, Lárusdóttir, Gregory & Cajander, 2016). Therefore, while Scrum proposes only planning for the next sprint ahead due to the future being uncertain beyond two weeks, there is value in helping teams see the bigger picture.

5.7 Indulgence and Agile Practices

In South African Agile teams, indulgence influences Agile practices relative to whether enjoyment during Agile ceremonies is encouraged. According to the findings, teams with high degrees of indulgence are encouraged to have fun by celebrating together, playing snooker, having remote games as a team, use humor or banter during ceremonies. Humor or banter is used to ease tension and teams allocate time for fun activities during ceremonies like the retrospective meeting. This further improves team cohesion. In contrast, in teams with a low degree of indulgence, the ceremonies are formal, and members do not speak about their personal lives during meetings: *"It is always encouraged in the processes. We always start with a bit of banter. With a retro we would have some fun in the first thirty minutes and have lunch together offsite. When we were in office, we would get lunch every day and people might breakaway to do a puzzle or something like that"* (P3). In line with the above findings, the following proposition is formulated: ***Proposition 7: In South African Agile teams, the degree of indulgence influences the extent to which members are encouraged to have fun during ceremonies.***

Findings indicate that teams that emphasize indulgence, have better team cohesiveness. This agrees with literature which states that in societies with a high degree of indulgence, individuals tend to show positive attitude which helps to maintain team motivation (Ayed et al., 2017). Literature also states that teams with a low degree of indulgence display fatigue (Ayed et al., 2017). The findings reveal a similar trend where low indulgence teams do not have fun activities due to being busy with projects and not having time to build team morale. Team morale increases commitment to the Scrum team goals and the sprint goals. Therefore, teams that manifest a high degree of indulgence, are closely aligned to the Scrum value of commitment and the Agile principle of building projects around motivated individuals (Beck et al., 2001).

6. CONCLUSION

Culture can be an impediment to Agile implementations in that cultural issues can cause a lack of trust, challenges collaboration and diminishes collective ownership and team success. There exist many empirical studies that have investigated the relationship between organizational culture and the deployment of Agile. However, few studies have focused on the influence of national culture dimensions Agile Implementations, especially in the South African context. This thesis provides a useful contribution to research and practice as it provides insights into the role of a consolidated set of cultural dimensions on Agile practices.

Seven propositions have been formulated to highlight how Hofstede (2013) and GLOBE (House et al., 1999) national culture dimensions influence Agile practices. The findings reveal that various national culture dimensions influence the decision-making process, the degree of sprint interruptions, participation in Agile ceremonies, adherence to policies and prescribed Agile practices, how teams reach agreement, approaches to process improvement and sprint planning, as well as the extent to which team members are encouraged to have fun.

Although in South African culture hierarchical order is accepted to a greater extent (Hofstede, 2013), the hierarchical dynamic assisted the Scrum Master to manage novice team, give direction, and coach the team to get them back on track. In addition, the collectivist cultural trait in South Africa was found to more suitable to Agile implementations than the South African individualistic cultural trait. In collectivist South African software development teams, democratic decisions (consensus) are mostly used but over time as teams trust one another they use the method of willing consent. Therefore, the Ubuntu collectivist culture is leaner over time as collectivist teams experiment with other Agile methodologies to optimize for continuous flow, and community-orientation. Lastly, teams with low masculinity are better suited to Agile implementations in terms of the team's interactions and the team's focus on the work in the sprint and the goals of the team.

The findings not only contribute to theories around the impact of culture in Agile teams, but also provide key insights to practitioners on what cultural manifestations might be at play in their project teams. It is important to understand the cultural driving forces at play behind the challenges that they might be experiencing. The findings can help inform Agile implementations in practice, and therefore help managers and teams curate Agile teams for appropriate environments.

Most of the respondents provided input in relation to the Scrum framework. Future studies could focus on a wider sample of respondents with experience in a broader range of Agile frameworks. Future studies could also focus on the influence of national culture dimensions on Agile implementations in teams other than those in software development. A longitudinal study could be conducted to obtain deeper insights into the cultural manifestations over a longer period. This might provide more insights into how teams cultural traits changes over time as the teams mature. Further opportunities to explain the findings with other theoretical frameworks such as Complex Adaptive Theory (CAS) also exist.

REFERENCES

Ayed, H., Vanderose, B., & Habra, N., 2017. Agile cultural challenges in Europe and Asia: insights from practitioners. In 2017 IEEE/ACM 39th International Conference on Software Engineering: Software Engineering in Practice Track (ICSE-SEIP), pp. 153-162.

Aziza, R. C., 2001. The Relationship between Language use and Survival of Culture: the case of Umobo youth. Nigerian Language Studies, Vol. 4, pp. 97-111.

Beck, K., Beedle, M., Van Bennekum, A., Cockburn, A., Cunningham, W., Fowler, M., ... & Thomas, D., 2001. The agile manifesto.

Braun, V., & Clarke, V., 2006. Using thematic analysis in psychology. Qualitative research in psychology, Vol. 3, No. 2, pp. 77-101.

Brockmann, P. S., & Thaumuller, T., 2009. Cultural aspects of global requirements engineering: An empirical chinese-german case study. In 2009 Fourth IEEE International Conference on Global Software Engineering, pp. 353-357. IEEE.

Buchan, J., Bano, M., Zowghi, D., MacDonell, S., & Shinde, A., 2017. Alignment of stakeholder expectations about user involvement in agile software development. In Proceedings of the 21st International Conference on Evaluation and Assessment in Software Engineering, pp. 334-343.

Cervone, H. F., 2011. Understanding agile project management methods using Scrum. OCLC Systems & Services: International digital library perspectives.

Creswell, J. W., 2003. Qualitative, quantitative, and mixed methods approaches.

Darwish, A., & Henryson, A., 2019. How do Cultural Characteristics and Software Engineering Practices Interplay?

Etikan, I., & Bala, K., 2017. Sampling and sampling methods. Biometrics & Biostatistics International Journal,Vol.5,No.6.

Girot, E,. 2013. Practical implementation of SCRUM and associated practices.

Gregory, P., Barroca, L., Sharp, H., Deshpande, A., & Taylor, K., 2016. The challenges that challenge: Engaging with agile practitioners' concerns. Information and Software Technology, Vol. 77, pp. 92-104.

Hanges, P. J., & Dickson, M. W., 2004. The development and validation of the GLOBE culture and leadership scales. Culture, leadership, and organizations: The GLOBE study of, Vol. 62, pp. 122-151.

Hayat, F., Rehman, A. U., Arif, K. S., Wahab, K., & Abbas, M., 2019. The Influence of Agile Methodology (Scrum) on Software Project Management. In 2019 20th IEEE/ACIS International Conference on Software Engineering, Artificial Intelligence, Networking and Parallel/Distributed Computing (SNPD), pp. 145-149.

Hofstede, G., 2013. Geert Hofstede. https://geerthofstede.com/research-and-vsm/dimension-data-matrix/

Hofstede, G., Hofstede, G. J., & Minkov, M., 2005. Cultures and Organizations: Software of the Mind McGraw-Hill. New York, NY.

House, R. J., Hanges, P. J., Ruiz-Quintanilla, S. A., Dorfman, P. W., Javidan, M., Dickson, M., & Gupta, V., 1999. Cultural influences on leadership and organizations: Project GLOBE. Advances in global leadership, Vol.1, No. 2, pp. 171-233.

Joseph, N. M. C., & Santana, M. J., 2016. Agile software development and IT project performance in South Africa: a positive relationship. In The 25th International Conference for Management of Technology, pp. 335-355.

Jukich, B. L., 2018. Multicultural Understanding: Leveraging the Advantages of Diversity in Scrum Adoption.

Idang, G. E., 2015. African culture and values. Phronimon, Vol. 16, No. 2, pp. 97-111.

Iivari, J., & Iivari, N., 2011. The relationship between organizational culture and the deployment of agile methods. Information and software technology, Vol. 53, No. 5, pp. 509-520.

Mbigi, L., 2007. Spirit of African leadership: A comparative African perspective. In Diversity, pp. 294-303. Palgrave Macmillan, London.

Metz, T., & Gaie, J. B., 2010. The African ethic of Ubuntu/Botho: implications for research on morality. Journal of moral education, Vol. 39, No. 3, pp. 273-290.

Minkov, M. & Hofstede, G., 2011. The evolution of Hofstede's doctrine. Cross Cultural Management: An International Journal, Vol. 18, No. 1, pp. 10-20.

Minkov, M. and Kaasa, A., 2021. A test of the revised Minkov-Hofstede model of culture: Mirror images of subjective and objective culture across nations and the 50 US states. Cross-Cultural Research, 55(2-3), 230-281.

Misra, S., Kumar, V., Kumar, U., Fantazy, K., & Akhter, M., 2012. Agile software development practices: evolution, principles, and criticisms. International Journal of Quality & Reliability Management.

Mnkandla, E., 2013. A review of communication tools and techniques for successful ICT projects. The African Journal of Information Systems, Vol. 6, No. 1, 1.

Morse, J. M., Barrett, M., Mayan, M., Olson, K., & Spiers, J., 2002. Verification strategies for establishing reliability and validity in qualitative research. International journal of qualitative methods, Vol. 1, No. 2, pp. 13-22.

Neelima, E., & Saile, N. D. S., 2013. A Study on SCRUM Agile methodology and its knowledge management process. The International Journal of Engineering and Science, Vol. 2, No. 3, pp.22-27.

Noble, H., & Smith, J., 2015. Issues of validity and reliability in qualitative research. Evidence-based nursing, Vol. 18, No. 2, pp. 34-35.

Palokangas, J., 2013. Agile Around the World-How Agile Values Are Interpreted in National Cultures? (Master's thesis).

Schwaber, K., & Sutherland, J., 2017. The Scrum Guide. November, 6-17.

Siakas, K. V., & Siakas, E., 2007. The agile professional culture: A source of agile quality. Software Process: Improvement and Practice, Vol. 12, No. 6, pp. 597-610.

Sidky, A., Arthur, J., & Bohner, S., 2007. A disciplined approach to adopting agile practices: the agile adoption framework. Innovations in systems and software engineering, Vol. 3, No. 3, pp. 203-216.

South Africa. Statistics South Africa. 2016. Community Survey 2016. http://cs2016.statssa.gov.za/wp-content/uploads/2016/07/NT-30-06-2016-RELEASE-for-CS-2016-_Statistical-releas_1-July-2016.pdf

Sutherland, J., 2005. Future of scrum: Parallel pipelining of sprints in complex projects. In Agile Development Conference (ADC'05), pp. 90-99.

Sutharshan, A., 2013. Human factors and cultural influences in implementing agile philosophy and agility in global software development.

Tanner, M., 2009. Communication and Culture in Global Software Development: The Case of Mauritius and South Africa. Journal of Information, Information Technology & Organizations, Vol. 4.

Tanner, M. C., 2013. Social conditions leading to Scrum process breakdowns during Global Agile Software Development: a theory of practice perspective (Doctoral dissertation, University of Cape Town).

Tanner, M., & Noruwana, N., 2012. Understanding the structured processes followed by organisations prior to engaging in agile processes: A south African perspective. South African Computer Journal, Vol. 48, No. 1, pp. 41-58. doi:10.18489/sacj.v48i1.74

Wanasika, I., Howell, J. P., Littrell, R., & Dorfman, P., 2011. Managerial leadership and culture in Sub-Saharan Africa. Journal of World Business, Vol. 46, No. 2, pp. 234-241.

Ward, J. A., Brown, W. J., & Kiruswa, S., 2015. African Maasai leadership: An extension of the globe study. Journal of International Business Research, Vol. 14, No. 3, pp. 97.

West, A., 2014. Ubuntu and business ethics: Problems, perspectives, and prospects. Journal of Business Ethics, Vol. 121, No. 1, pp. 47-61.

Zhao, C., 2015. Impact of National Culture Dimensions on Scrum Implementations. (Thesis), Faculty of Computing, Blekinge Institute of Technology SE-371 79 Karlskrona Sweden.

PYRAMID MODEL – CONCEPTUALIZING AN ORGANIZATIONAL CAPABILITY TO DESIGN IT INVESTMENTS

Mikko H. Hirvonen
Lappeenranta University of Technology, School of Business and Management, Finland
P.O. Box 20, FIN-53851 Lappeenranta, Finland

ABSTRACT

In this paper, a configurational framework to conceptualize an *organizational capability*, to design IT investments, is presented. IT is seen as a main driver of productivity and an enabler of digital innovations. At the same time, companies are struggling how to design IT investments. Based on Resource Based View of the firm and Dynamic Capabilities Framework, an organizational capability is considered as a basic unit, and a building block, of a competitive advantage. By building on those theories and systems thinking, Leavitt's 'Diamond model', and Parsons' model of an organization with 'three levels of responsibility', a '*Pyramid model'* to conceptualize an organizational capability is developed. Suggested framework provides a foundation for business need-driven IT investment design at any level of an organization. In the 'Pyramid model' the recent understanding how IT can generate business value, is brought together and further developed. The model is expected to be highly valuable in practice helping to design and justify investments to drive productivity and e.g., to scale digital innovations.

KEYWORDS

IT Investment, Complementary Investments, Organizational Capability, IT Business Value (ITBV), Configurational Model

1. INTRODUCTION

Information technology (IT) has been a key driver of productivity during the last decades. In the near future, most of the productivity potential is expected to come from digital opportunities (Remes et al. 2018). The *'modern productivity paradox'* (Brynjolfsson et al. 2017), and reported challenges in scaling of innovations (McKinsey 2019) anyhow indicate, that organizations are experiencing serious challenges with IT investments.

In IT business value (ITBV) research, where ITBV is defined as IT's impact on firm performance (see e.g., Gandelman et al. 2019), there is an understanding that value is gained when IT is aligned with, or complementary to, other organizational variables (Kohli and Grover 2008). The prevailing approach has been IT-driven and *reductionistic/pairwise* (Fink 2011) where the impact of IT has been examined with complementary investments to one or a few organizational variables. The result is a field of scattered research with very limited support to practice, whereas for practical purposes, the *holistic* and *business need-driven approaches* have been recognized essential (Kohli and Grover 2008). To serve practice several configurational multivariate organizational models have been developed, but the challenge is in identification of the relevant organizational variables (Gandelman et al. 2019) and understanding of their interdependencies (Cao 2010). Typically, the models conceptualize operational level of an organization by ignoring organization's hierarchical aspect, when management and adaptation to the changing environment has got very little attention.

The *purpose* of this research is to develop a configurational framework to conceptualize a systemic and evolving *organizational capability* which can be used as a basis to design IT investments including complementary investment to organizational variables ('IT investments' from now on). An *organizational capability* is defined as the firm's ability to achieve desired goals by routinely deploying available resources (Amit and Schoemaker 1993). It is the basic unit, and a building block, of a competitive advantage, and therefore appropriate unit of analysis in this research. '*Systemic*' refers to the organizational capability as a system consisting of interconnected and interdependent system elements operating in its task environment, and '*evolving'* to its dynamic nature. Developed '*Pyramid model'* is a foundation to design an IT investments to achieve targeted *organizational capability*.

2. BACKGROUND

2.1 IT Business Value Research (ITBV)

'Invisible business value of IT' with lacking, or in many cases at least delayed bottom-line impact, led to the extensive '*productivity paradox*' discussion in 80's and 90's (Brynjolfsson 1993; Solow 1987). Although there is today a strong evidence that IT adds value (Kohli and Grover 2008) together with organizational variables, the same productivity discussion has popped up once in a while - most recently, at the eve of digitalization as a '*modern productivity paradox*' (Brynjolfsson et al. 2017).

ITBV has been recognized to manifest through *conversion processes* (see e.g., Gandelman et al. 2019) where commodity-like IT resource is converted to a synergistically operating and value enhancing asset *embedded* (Kohli and Grover 2008) to the organization and individual organizational capabilities within their context (see e.g., Schryen 2013) where *alignment* (Miller 1996) is pursued with coordinated complementary investments to adjust *organizational variables* (see review by Cao 2010). Regardless of an extensive and continuously sharpening body of research (see review e.g., by Schryen 2013) and development of several configurational multivariate organizational models (see Cao 2010), the challenge, and a research gap, is in identification of relevant organizational variables (Gandelman et al. 2019), understanding of their interdependencies (Cao 2010), and estimation of the performance impact of different configurations (Nevo and Wade 2010). Additionally, feasibility of the prevailing *reductionistic/pairwise approach*, especially in empirical investigations, has been questioned and the need for more holistic approach (Fink 2011), where ITBV is the behavior of the system (Ackoff 1999; Churchman 1971), has been emphasized.

2.2 Background Theories and Systemic Capabilities

The Resource-Based View (RBV) of the firm (Wernerfelt 1984), where the firm is seen as a bundle of resources and capabilities (Amit and Schoemaker 1993), and Dynamic Capabilities Framework (DCF)(Teece et al. 1997), have provided valuable theoretical base to investigate how IT might help to create heterogeneity and strategic value (Cao et al. 2016). Capabilities can be divided to the *potential* i.e., what could be done, and *realized* i.e., what is actually done (cf. Penrose 1959; Zahra and George 2002). *Ordinary capabilities* have been categorized to *operational capabilities* executing day-to-day activities (Winter 2003) and *managerial capabilities* to "*...run the organization and make and implement strategic and operational decisions...*" (Hugill and Helfat 2016). *Dynamic capabilities* refer to the firm's abilities to sense and seize new opportunities to develop existing capabilities, to reconfigure *resources* and capabilities, and/or to shape the task environment (Teece 2000; Teece et al. 1997). *Dynamic managerial capabilities* refer to the role and capacity of managers to orchestrate these changes (Adner and Helfat 2003; Harris and Helfat 2018). It has been also suggested, that companies possess non-routinized and less structured *improvisational / ad hoc* capabilities (Pavlou and El Sawy 2010; Winter 2003). Here an *organizational capability* is defined to consist of operational, dynamic, and managerial capabilities with varying degrees of routine.

Systems theory (ST) has been suggested as a complementary theoretical lens to the RBV and DCF to study ITBV (Cao et al. 2016; Nevo and Wade 2010). In ST, an organization is seen as a *system* consisting of system elements, composed of interrelated subsystems, where the value is the behavior of the whole system with synergies and emergent properties rather than separated parts (Ackoff 1999; Churchman 1971). To maintain *equilibrium*, a change in any of the system elements, would most probably result compensatory changes in others (1965). The compatibility and interaction, of the system elements define the performance of the system (Ackoff 1999; Galbraith and Kazanijian 1986). In this research, capabilities are considered as systemic.

2.3 Leavitt's Diamond Model

In Leavitt's (1965) '*Diamond model*' an organization is seen as a multivariate system consisting of four organizational variables. *Task* refers to an organization's *raison d'être* i.e., desired outcomes. *Structures* are formal allocations of work roles and administrative mechanisms to organize, coordinate, and control work activities, including those that cross formal organizational boundaries. They are created by management (Penrose 1959), and consist of *systems of communication, systems of authority* (roles, responsibilities and power), and *systems of workflow*. With *technology* Leavitt referred to the problem-solving inventions - mainly technical tools. *Actors* refer mainly, but not always, to the people. The variables are interdependent and consistently striving towards equilibrium. The model has been criticized of ignoring certain variables and therefore extensions has been suggested (see e.g., Davis and Olson 1985; Nograsek 2011; Scott Morton 1995). In this research, a few extensions and several specifications to the original models are done.

2.4 Parsons 'Three Levels of Responsibility and Control'

Parsons (1960) broke down the hierarchical aspect of an organization and identified three levels of responsibility and control ('level' from now on) responsible of solving different classes of problems (see also Thompson 1967a). *Operational level* is responsible of conducting operational tasks i.e., the actual 'process' where physical production of goods and/or services occurs. *Managerial level* is focused on effective performance of the operational level by organizing, coordinating, controlling and 'servicing' it (Thompson 1967a). This task can be divided to ´external relations´ i.e., mediation between the organization and the task environment, and ´internal relations´ i.e., administration of the organization´s internal affairs. From external relations point of view, the managerial system services the operational sub-organization by procuring the resources ('resource-acquisition problem' Thompson 1967b) necessary for carrying out the operational tasks, and by mediating between the operational sub-organization and those who use its products i.e., disposal of products (Parsons 1960; 'output-disposal problem' Thompson 1967b). From *internal relations* point of view management system determine topics in the operational level like scale of operations, allocation of resources, integration, coordination, as well as administration and control of the operations (Thompson 1967b). On *institutional level* an organization needs to articulate with 'organized superior' agency. The organization is part of a wider social system which is the source of the 'meaning', legitimation, and the higher-level support controlling the organization (Thompson 1967a). *Qualitative breaks* exist between levels at the point where the levels connect. The levels have two-way interaction and interchange of essential inputs and outputs including information (Thompson 1967).

3. THE 'PYRAMID MODEL'

3.1 Adjusted Capability Levels

An organizational capability consists of three interdependent and partially overlapping levels - each with its own types of responsibilities. *The operational level* is the *raison d'être* of an *organizational capability* responsible of conducting the day-to-day value adding activities i.e., physical production of goods and/or services. This is consistent with Parsons' definition.

The dynamic level is responsible of maintaining equilibrium of an organizational capability. It is partially overlapping with managerial and operational levels. Parsons recognized the dependency from environment and related uncertainty but did not explicitly include this *'system of change'* as an own level to his model. In *'Pyramid model'* the dynamic level is considered as an own level with two sub-levels: *'Dynamic operational level'* is responsible of adjusting and developing existing capabilities and *'Dynamic managerial level'* responsible of reconfiguration of resource position and capabilities, and shaping the task environment.

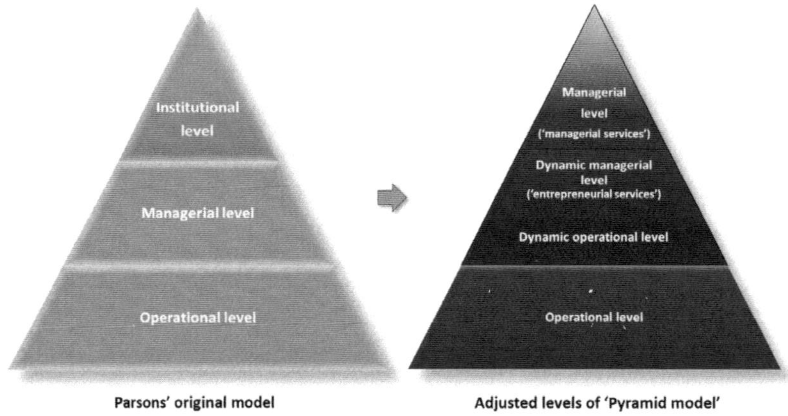

Figure 1. Original and adjusted levels of responsibility and control

The managerial level is responsible of effective performance of operational and dynamic levels, and the tasks of original *institutional level*. *'Servicing'* responsibility is divided here to the *'managerial services'* (operational managerial task) and *'entrepreneurial services'* (dynamic managerial task) accordingly (Penrose 1959). They both include the responsibility of *'leadership'* (see figure 1).

3.2 Capability Variables

A capability is defined to consists of four interdependent *capability variables*. Unlike Leavitt, an open system logic is assumed. To represent selected background theories (RBV and DCF), the variables are adjusted and further specified (see figure 2). Compatibility and interaction of capability variables, and task environment, define the performance of a capability.

Coherent '*Tasks, Abilities & Qualities'* are the starting point for defining the targeted capability, derived from the business needs. By complementing Leavitt's original model, *tasks* define the expected actual outcomes and purpose i.e., the *realized capability* (or activity). *Abilities* are potential evolution paths (Teece et al. 1997) what could be done either immediately (*potential capability*), or *readiness* to develop the capability to a certain direction (i.e., paths available to it). *Qualities* are non-functional requirements (NFR).

'*Technologies*' consist of product technology, value configuration technology (VCT) with frequency, and information systems (IS) technology (Porter 1985). The *product technology* defines the technical details of the outcome. *VCT* (see e.g., Fjeldstad and Snow 2018; Thompson 1967a) defines how resources are utilized, and inputs combined/integrated to produce the throughput. *Frequency* defines how many times it is exercised in a certain time frame. The *IS technology* defines how data and information is gathered, processed, stored, delivered/accessed, and utilized. Leavitt defined 'technologies' only as "*problem solving inventions - mainly technical tools*", which are considered here as *'resources.'*

'*Resources & Sub-capabilities'* cover all available resources and sub-capabilities forming a *resource position*. A capability is highly dependent of available resources, and their mutual compatibility and interaction i.e., potential co-specialization and fit. To align with basic postulates of RBV and DCF, *routine* is considered as a resource, defined as a patterned and repeated way to conduct one or many interconnected task(s) by an actor (*individual routine)* or by multiple actors (*organizational routine)*. Routine evolves in a continuum from weak/non-existing (i.e., improvisational/ad hoc capabilities) to strong/perfectly routinized.

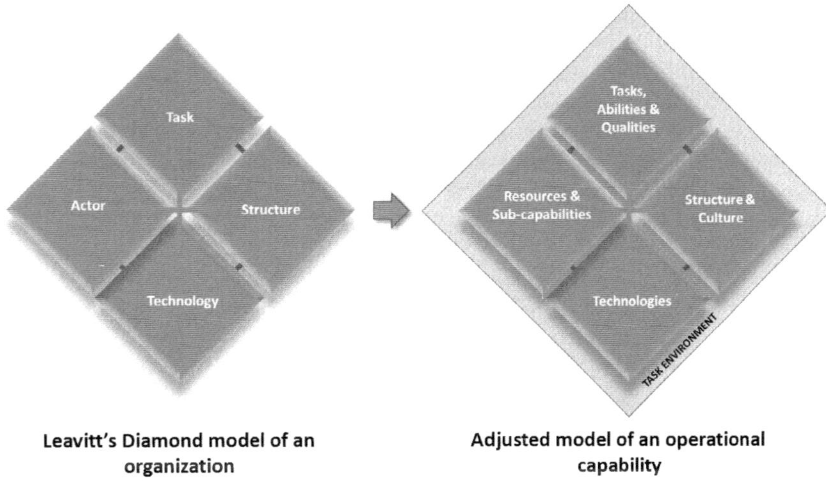

Figure 2. Leavitt's Diamond model (left) and adjusted model of an operational capability (right)

'*Structure & Culture*' is the 'administrative framework' (Penrose 1959) i.e., a formal allocation of resources and administrative mechanisms to organize, coordinate, control capabilities - including the ones that cross formal functional and organizational boundaries. To Leavitt's original definition I'm including *incentive system*, and *culture* (organizational and/or micro) referring to the values and beliefs mediating the behavior of individuals (i.e., a steering mechanism) by giving values and social order (Schein 2010).

In his original model, Leavitt assumed a closed system logic. Here, to better represent DCF, organizational rationality, and Parsons' model, an open system logic is assumed. Accordingly, capability is dependent of, and controlled by, its *task environment* (see Pfeffer and Salancik 1978) which as a wider social system gives e.g., the meaning, legitimation, and the higher-level support to the capability.

3.3 Synthesis: Organizational Capability Consists of Three Types of Capabilities

The above presented adjusted capability levels and capability variables are synthetisized to '*Pyramid model*' (see figure 3). Accordingly, an *organizational capability* consists of three interdependent and overlapping levels i.e., *types of capabilities* (operational, dynamic, and managerial), each consisting of four interconnected and interdependent capability variables ('*Tasks, Abilities & Qualities*', '*Technologies*', '*Resources & Sub-capabilities*', and '*Structure & Culture*').

Operational capability. The *task* of an operational capability is to deliver the outcome(s) expected from the organizational capability. *Abilities* are potential *evolution paths* for the future (potential capability or readiness). *'Qualities'* define the non-functional criteria for the operational capability (e.g., ecology, profitability, etc.). '*Technologies*' define the technical details of an outcome (*product technology*). *VCT* and *frequency* define how resources are used and outcomes combined, and how many times it needs to be repeated in a certain time frame. How received and generated data and information is gathered, processed, stored, delivered/accessed, and utilized is defined by *IS technology*. '*Resources & Sub-capabilities*' consist of all available internal and external resources, (outcomes of) sub-capabilities, and *routines* to combine those. '*Structure & Culture*' define how an organizational capability is organized, coordinated, and controlled; and what are the common values and beliefs impacting to the behavior.

Dynamic capability. The *task* of a dynamic level is to keep an organizational capability vital and to ensure its *evolutionary fitness* by maintaining internal and external equilibrium. Task is divided to *dynamic operative task* i.e., development and adjustment of the existing elements and their interaction of an organizational capability, and *dynamic managerial task* i.e., maintenance of an optimal resource position, capability configuration, and *fit* with task environment. *Abilities* are potential dynamic capabilities what could be utilized immediately and/or readiness to develop those to a certain direction. *Qualities* define the non-functional criteria. '*Technologies*' define the technical details of outcomes (*product technology*), how an equilibrium is maintained (*VCT*) and frequency. *IS technology* defines how data/information is gathered, processed, stored, delivered/accessed, and utilized to conduct the tasks. '*Resources & Sub-capabilities*' consist of all available resources, (outcomes of) dynamic sub-capabilities, and routines to conduct the tasks. Of these, the *dynamic operative capability* is responsible of *dynamic operative tasks* (defined above). *Dynamic managerial capability* is responsible of *capability reconfiguration* (internal domain) and *shaping of the task environment* (external domain). Dynamic capabilities include *improvisational capabilities* to handle unfamiliar ad hoc problems. *'Structure & Culture'* forms an administrative mechanism including common values and beliefs guiding development and adjustment of an organizational capability.

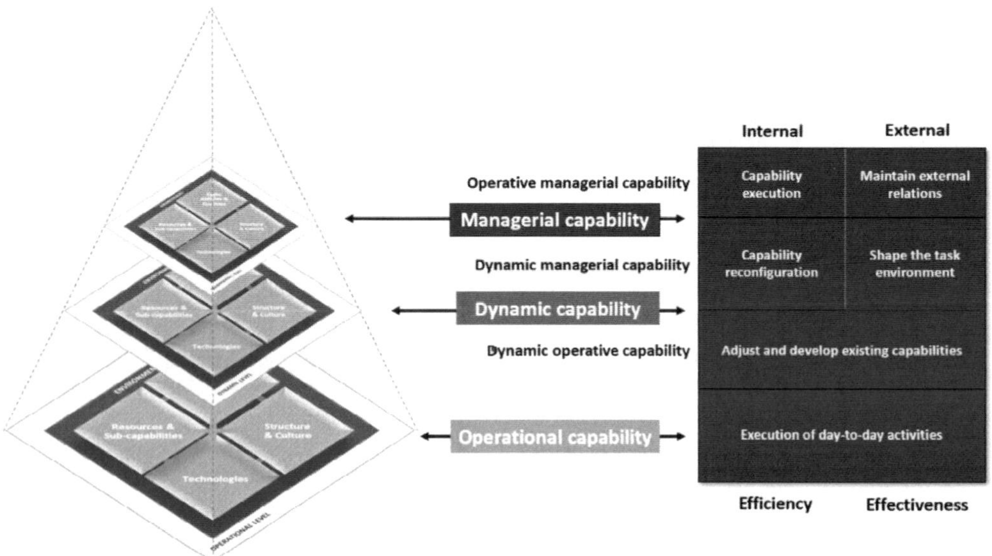

Figure 3. The 'Pyramid model', types of capabilities, and main tasks in internal and external domains

The *task* of managerial level is to ensure achievement of targeted performance (*operative managerial tasks)* and maintenance of evolutionary fitness (*dynamic managerial tasks*) of the operational capability. The first one is divided to *capability execution* and *maintain external relations* -tasks. The dynamic managerial task is overlapping part with dynamic level covered above. *Abilities* are either *potential managerial capabilities* what could be utilized, and/or *readiness* to develop those to a certain direction. *Technologies* define the technical details of managerial outcomes (*product technology*), management methods and frequency how managerial tasks are conducted (*VCT*), and how information and insights are utilized (*IS technology*). '*Resources and Sub-capabilities'* consist of all resources, outcomes of sub-capabilities and routines to conduct the managerial tasks. Managerial level is organized, coordinated, and controlled by higher level social system (their managers, business owners, and institutional structures and agencies) which together determine the '*Structure & culture'*.

3.4 Degree of Equilibrium

An organizational capability as a system of interdependency strives towards equilibrium in internal and external domains. The *degree of equilibrium* tells how well it has been achieved. An *external equilibrium* is defined as a compatibility and interaction with external environment i.e., how effectively the organizational capability interacts and is coherent with it. The higher the degree of external equilibrium, the more *effective* the organizational capability is. An *internal equilibrium* is defined as the compatibility and interaction of the levels (i.e., types of capabilities), capability variables, and elements inside the capability variables. The higher the degree of internal equilibrium, the more *efficient* the capability is.

4. CONCLUSIONS

The developed '*Pyramid model*' is a multivariate model to conceptualize an organizational capability - the building block of a competitive advantage. Based on two well accepted, but modified and combined organizational models, it represents selected underpinning theories of RBV, DCV, and ST. An organizational capability is defined to consists of three levels i.e., types of capabilities – each with own types of responsibilities. The levels consist of four interdependent *capability variables*. The tasks of each level are based on business needs and might pertain expected outcomes (*tasks*), *abilities* to do something (i.e., evolution paths), or *qualities* (how things are done). The model also recognizes hierarchical structure of capabilities. It advances the holistic view and business need-driven approach in ITBV. It is based on the concepts of *embeddedness*, *equilibrium,* and *dynamism* as key attributes of an organizational capability. To the best of author knowledge, the 'Pyramid model' is in many ways unique and more advanced than e.g., prior organizational models.

The *'Pyramid model'* with holistic approach to conceptualize a business need-driven organizational capability to design an IT-investment is expected to be highly valuable in practice. It can be applied throughout the IT investment life cycle in investment design, justification, during the transformation, and *ex post* assessments. It is expected to help to improve quality of investment initiatives, potentially leading to higher success rate and shorter periods of 'temporary productivity loss' (Brynjolfsson 1993).

The '*Pyramid model'* necessitates good understanding of the applied concepts. This is anyway a deliberate choice to get closer to the organizational rationality and complex phenomenon of IT investment with targeted ITBV. Although it provides a basis for structured way to identify required complementary investments, its application still necessitates a procedure with supporting tools, and a good understanding of the capability with constituting elements, their interaction, and the context. The model does not tell anything about the means to conduct the required adjustments nor organization's absorptive capacity (Zahra and George 2002).

The '*Pyramid model'* opens a way for testing of holistic IT investment configurations. It should be also applied with different organizational capabilities, with linked capabilities (e.g., when ITBV could be realized only through linked capabilities known as *'locus of value'* Kauffman and Weill 1989), and in capabilities of different level in an organization (e.g., on business model level) or even in wider entities (e.g., ecosystems).

ACKNOWLEDGEMENT

I wish to thank professor Mikael Collan for valuable guidance during the research process and the three anonymous reviewers for helpful comments. This research is grateful for the support received from the Strategic Research Council at the Academy of Finland project Manufacturing 4.0 #335980 and #335990.

REFERENCES

Ackoff, R. 1999. *Re-Creating the Corporation: A Design of Organizations for the 21st Century*. New York: Oxford University Press.

Adner, R., and Helfat, C. E. 2003. "Corporate Effects and Dynamic Managerial Capabilities," *Strategic Management Journal* (24:10), pp. 1011-1025.

Amit, R., and Schoemaker, P. J. H. 1993. "Strategic Assets and Organizational Rent," *Strategic Management Journal* (14:1), pp. 33-46.

Brynjolfsson, E. 1993. "The Productivity Paradox of Information Technology: Review and Assessment," *Communications of the ACM* (36:12), pp. 67-77.

Brynjolfsson, E., Rock, D., and Syverson, C. 2017. "Artificial Intelligence and the Modern Productivity Paradox: A Clash of Expectations and Statistics, Working Paper 24001," National Bureau of Economic Research.

Cao, G. 2010. "A Four Dimensional View of It Business Value," *Systems Research and Behavioral Science* (27:3), pp. 267-284.

Cao, G., Yanqing, D., Cadden, T., and Minocha, S. 2016. "Systemic Capabilities: The Source of It Business Value," *Information Technology & People* (29:3), pp. 556-579.

Churchman, C. W. 1971. *The Design of Inquiring Systems: Basic Concepts of Systems and Organizations*.

Davis, G. B., and Olson, M. H. 1985. *Management Information Systems: Conceptual Foundations, Structure and Development*, (2nd edition ed.). McGraw-Hill Books Company.

Fink, L. 2011. "How Do It Capabilities Create Strategic Value? Toward Greater Intergration of Insight from Reductionistic and Holistic Approaches," *European Journal of Information Systems* (20:1), pp. 16-33.

Fjeldstad, O. D., and Snow, C. C. 2018. "Business Models and Organizational Design," *Long Range Planning* (51:1), pp. 32-39.

Galbraith, J. R., and Kazanijian, R. K. 1986. *Strategy Implementation: Structure, Systems, and Process*, (Second edition ed.). West Publishing.

Gandelman, R. T., Cappelli, C., and Santoro, F. M. 2019. "Assessing It Business Value Using Catalogues," in: *2019 IEEE 21st Conference on Business Informatics (CBI)*.

Harris, D., and Helfat, C. E. 2018. "Dynamic Managerial Capabilities," in *The Palgrave Encyclopedia of Strategic Management,* M. Augier and D.E. Teece (eds.). Basingstoke, England: Palgrave Macmillan, pp. 452-454.

Hugill, A., and Helfat, C. E. 2016. "Managerial Resources and Capabilities," in: *The Palgrave encyclopedia of strategic management*. Springer Link.

Kauffman, R. J., and Weill, P. 1989. "An Evaluative Framework for Research on the Performance Effects of Information Technology Investments, Proceedings of the Tenth International Conference of Information Systems," Boston, MA, pp. 377-388.

Kohli, R., and Grover, V. 2008. "Business Value of It: An Essay on Expanding Research Directions to Keep up with the Times," *Journal of the Association for Information Systems* (9:1), pp. 23-39.

Leavitt, H. J. 1965. "Applied Organizational Change in Industry: Structural, Technical and Humanistic Approaches," in *Handbook of Organizations,* J.G.E. March (ed.). pp. 1144-1170.

McKinsey. 2019. "Industry 4.0: Capturing Value at Scale in Discrete Manufacturing," *McKinsey article*).

Miller, D. 1996. "Configurations Revisited," *Strategic Management Journal* (17:7), pp. 505-512.

Nevo, S., and Wade, M. R. 2010. "The Formation and Value of It-Enabled Resources: Antecedents and Consequences of Synergistic Relationships," *MIS Quarterly* (34:1), pp. 163-183.

Nograsek, J. 2011. "Change Management as a Critical Success Factor in E-Government Implementation," *Business Systems Research* (2:2), pp. 1-56.

Parsons, T. 1960. *Structure and Process in Modern Societies*. New York: The Free Press of Glencoe.

Pavlou, P. A., and El Sawy, O. A. 2010. "The "Third Hand": It-Enabled Competitive Advantage in Turbulence through Improvisational Capabilities," *Information Systems Research* (21:3), pp. 443-471.

Penrose, E. T. 1959. *The Theory of the Growth of the Firm*. London: Basil Blackwell: Oxford.

Pfeffer, J., and Salancik, G. R. 1978. *The External Control of Organizations: A Resource Dependence Perspective*. New York: Harper and Row.

Porter, M. E. 1985. *Competitive Advantage: Creating and Sustaining Superior Performance*. Free Press.

Remes, J., Manyika, J., Bughin, J., Woetzel, J., Mischke, J., and Krishnan, M. 2018. "Solving the Productivity Puzzle," McKinsey Global Institute.

Schein, E. H. 2010. *Organizational Culture and Leadership, 4th Edition*.

Schryen, G. 2013. "Revisiting Is Business Value Research: What We Already Know, What We Still Need to Know, and How We Can Get There," *European Journal of Information Systems* (22:2), pp. 139-169.

Scott Morton, M. 1995. "Emerging Organizational Forms: Work and Organization in the 21st Century," *European Management Journal* (13:4), pp. 339-345.

Solow, R. 1987. "We'd Better Watch Out. New York Times Book Review, July 12: 36,").

Teece, D. J. 2000. *Managing Intellectual Capital: Organizational, Strategic, and Policy Dimensions*. Oxford: Oxford University Press.

Teece, D. J., Pisano, G., and Shuen, A. 1997. "Dynamic Capabilities and Strategic Management," *Strategic Management Journal* (18:7), pp. 509-533.

Thompson, J. D. 1967a. *Organizations in Action*. New York: McGraw-Hill.

Thompson, J. D. 1967b. "Organizations in Action," in *Classics of Organization Theory,* J.M. Shafritz and S.J.E. Ott (eds.). Hartcourt College Publishers, pp. 268-281.

Wernerfelt, B. 1984. "A Resource-Based View of the Firm," *Strategic Management Journal* (5:2), pp. 171-180.

Winter, S. G. 2003. "Understanding Dynamic Capabilities," *Strategic Management Journal* (24:10), pp. 991-995.

Zahra, S. A., and George, G. 2002. "Absorptive Capacity: A Review, Reconceptualization, and Extension," *Academy of Management Review* (27:2), pp. 185-203.

AN OBJECTIVE-BASED APPROACH FOR DEFINING AND SELECTING THE MOST RELEVANT KPIS FOR MEASURING BUSINESS PROCESS PERFORMANCE

Amina Haouas[1], Emna Ammar Elhadjamor[2] and Sonia Ayachi Ghannouchi[1,2]
[1]*ISG Sousse University of Sousse, Tunisia*
[2]*RIADI Laboratory-ENSI, University of Mannouba, Tunisia*

ABSTRACT

The purpose of our work is to improve the performance of business processes. Our contribution consists of proposing an approach to defining key performance indicators for a set of well-defined objectives. To test our approach, we defined a set of objectives and KPIs, and then we elaborated a survey to match the objectives to different specific KPIs. This survey is applied to the case study of a COVID-19 care process and is dedicated to the members of Farhat Hached's crisis unit. In addition, we have developed a web application dedicated to the crisis unit. This application allows to: (1) add the objectives and to manage the KPIs, (2) assign the objectives to the KPIs, (3) display a comparative table of the values of the KPIs, (4) present a histogram for each KPI. Moreover, through this prototype we can (5) know the percentage of the achievement of the objectives.

Furthermore, we used the DMN, based on the Signavio tool. Indeed, the use of DMN in our work consists first in matching the objectives to the KPIs, then placing the decision rules based on the threshold values of the KPIs, entering the observed values, and finally obtaining the result about the achievement of the objectives.

KEYWORDS

Business Process Performance, KPI, BPM Approach, SMART Criteria

1. INTRODUCTION

According to (Gries and Restrepo 2011), KPIs are quantifiable measures that help an organization to measure the success of critical factors. For a company or a process, activities are conducted for achieving a set of objectives. Thus, KPIs and objectives are closely related terms, since performance measures allow to measure the achievement of objectives.

Following our study of previous works of the literature, we observed that the decisions are taken for the improvement of BP lack essential analyzes because of several reasons. First, a very large number of KPIs is defined for a business process. Second, the relation between KPIs and objectives remains unknown. Third, logs contain information that is misused to improve business processes.

We will therefore seek to answer the questions listed below, (1) How can we define KPIs and objectives? (2) How can we determine the relation between KPIs and objectives or select the most appropriate KPIs according to a well-defined set of objectives? (3) How can we know if the objectives are achieved or not?

Our work answers these questions by proposing a new approach to support the definition of key performance indicators. More precisely, our contribution consists of (1) defining a set of KPIs and objectives, (2) associating the KPIs with the objectives, (3) evaluating the degree of achievement of the objectives of the business processes through the comparison of the threshold values with the observed values and (4) improving the performance of the business processes based on the KPIs. To do this, we take the case of COVID-19 care process.

This paper is divided into 6 main sections planned as follows: section 2 presents the main concepts used in this study. Section 3 presents a literature review of existing methods for KPIs and shows clearly the need for a method that covers both KPIs and goals. In section 4, we expose the proposed approach. Then, section 5 shows the main obtained results. Finally, section 6 concludes the paper and gives directions for future works.

2. THEORETICAL FOUNDATIONS

In this section, we present the two most important concepts on which our work is based, which are business processes and key performance indicators.

2.1 Business Process

In (Hammer and Champy, 1993) a business process is defined as a set of activities that form one or more types of input that produce an output that has value to the customer. However, they do not mention any relation between these activities. While in (Davenport, 1993) this relation is taken into consideration where a business process is defined as a set of activities that are logically linked to achieving a business result defined by the customer or by the market. Based on these two definitions, in (Weske, 2007) a business process is defined as a set of activities that are performed in harmonization in an organizational and technical environment, and that achieve a business objective. In addition, each business process is implemented by a single organization, it can interact with other business processes executed by other organizations.

2.2 Key Performance Indicators

According to (Gries and Restrepo 2011), KPIs are quantifiable measures that help an organization to measure the success of critical factors, these measures must be agreed upon in advance and depend on the objectives of the organization. This is the most general definition, so it can be applied to all KPIs in all use cases.

According to (Parmenter 2015), KPIs represent a set of metrics that focus on critical aspects of organizational performance for the success of the organization.

According to (del Río-Ortega 2012), KPIs are defined for the organization as a means to measure the level of achievement of its strategic and operational objectives.

2.3 Business Process Management

According to (van der Aalst and al. 2003), Business Process Management (BPM) can be defined as a support of business processes using methods, techniques and software to design, control and analyze operational processes that involve humans, organizations, applications, documents and other sources of information.

As mentioned in (Weske 2007), the basis of business process management is the explicit representation of business processes, since it allows discovering the weaknesses of the organization of activities in order to analyze and improve them.

2.4 Decision Model and Notation

According to (Hasić and Serral 2019), Decision Model and Notation (DMN) is a recently introduced decision-modeling standard that has generated great interest in the literature. The DMN consists of two levels, which must be used, in parallel. First, the decision requirement level represented by the Decision Requirement Diagram (DRD), which describes the requirements of the decisions and the dependencies between the elements that exist in the decision model. Second, the decision logic level, which presents means for specifying the underlying decision logic.

The DMN standard uses rectangles to represent decisions and sub-decisions, and ovals to represent input data, while the decision logic level is represented as decision tables.

3. RELATED WORK

In this section, we present the various related works that are most relevant to our contribution, with particular emphasis on KPIs, objectives, and business processes.

The work of (Kbira and al. 2017), presented a procedure which consists in identifying candidate KPIs from existing sources, then defining new candidate KPIs, next, selecting the most appropriate KPIs according to the KPIs criteria. Finally, they compose a final set of selected KPIs. However, before these four steps, we must first start by establishing the objectives of the KPIs. The work of (Ponsard and Darimant 2019) provide a guide in two steps, the first approach, is an analysis of implicit goals, and the second approach, is an analysis of explicit goals. The authors used KAOS as support for modeling objectives. The work of (Baisli and al. 1994), create the GQM approach with an example of its application to an organization that can measure in an accurate and targeted manner. The work of (Ammar Elhadjamor and Ayachi Ghanouchi 2017), proposed an approach using the Analytic Hierarchical Process (AHP) method to solve multi-criteria decision-making to prioritize key performance measures of health care organizations using Expert Choice (EC) software. The work of (Cherni and al. 2019), proposed a KPI4PPI approach for process improvement by first defining and configuring target values of KPIs, then using process mining techniques to discover and analyze deviations from those values, and for each deviation, they propose improvement solutions based on BP redesign models. The work of (Simeunovic and al. 2020), proposed a new model of process performance measurement (PPM), named GPI model. The objective of this model is to help companies measure the performance of their processes, by selecting PPIs based on their strategic objectives. GPI is tested through case studies, and the results verified that the model could achieve this goal. The work of (Lamghari and al. 2018), presented a business process improvement methodology, which includes a new vision of the BPM lifecycle, including the design phase, modeling, execution, then monitoring, and ending with the optimization phase. Hence, on each phase, they define a set of improvement indicators for redefining business processes with better optimization results. The work of (Pusnik and al. 2019), mainly focus on the possibilities of optimizing the business process by analyzing and evaluating the activities of the process such as measuring the quality of existing software, introducing new information system support and risk management solutions, as well as identifying potential for optimization. The work of (Del Río-Ortega and al. 2013), proposed a PPINOT metamodel, which is a metamodel of PPIs, which is very flexible. It provides automatic semantic mapping that enables automated reasoning.

For comparing this existing works, we rely on the following criteria Proposes a life cycle of KPIs / PPIs, Integrates the life cycle of KPIs into the life cycle of BPM, Determines the correspondence between objectives and KPIs, Uses the construction of a DMN, Proposes / uses a method that determines KPIs / PPIs and / or objectives, Offers a framework and Calculation of the of KPIs / PPIs values. First, we find that none of the works fully meets all the criteria and there are three approaches that offer a KPI / PPI lifecycle. Then there are three works that integrate the proposed lifecycle into the BPM lifecycle and seven works that determine the relationship between KPIs / PPIs and goals. On the other hand, we find that all the works proposed or used a method that determine KPIs and / or objectives. However, we find only one approach that offers a Framework. We notice that only works of (Ponsard and Darimant 2019) and (Simeunovic and al. 2020) did not calculate the values of the indicators. Moreover, the strongest point of the approach we are targeting to build will be the construction of a DMN. We will ensure that our approach takes into account all the criteria mentioned in the table.

4. PROPOSED APPROACH

Through this work, we put in place an approach for defining and selecting the most relevant key performance indicators (KPIs) for a given set of objectives. To do this, first, we present our approach by introducing the different phases as well as the suggested modifications in the life cycle of BPM. The starting point of our approach is the life cycle of BPM to which we bring new sub-phases. We have adopted the BPM lifecycle described by (Weske 2007), and we add sub-phases as shown in Figure 1. The detail of these phases will be presented in the following subsections.

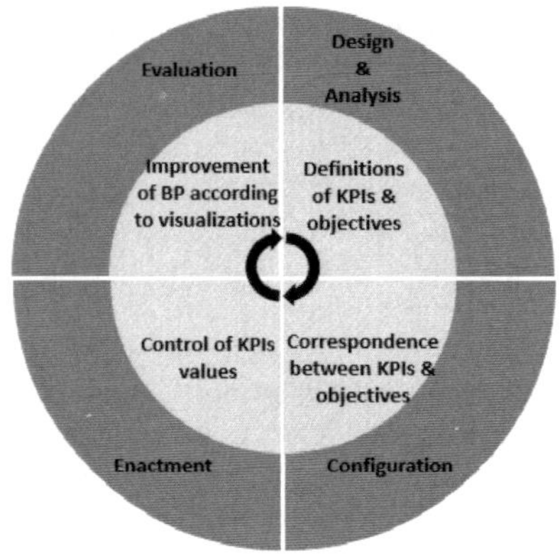

Figure 1. KPIs management lifecycle integrated into the BPM lifecycle

4.1 Design & Analysis Phase

According to (Weske 2007), the life cycle of business processes begins with the design and analysis phase. In this phase, business experts define a new business process or redefine an existing process, which is represented by a business process model.

In our approach, we propose to exploit during this phase, the Goal Question Metric (GQM) method as well as the SMART criteria. Indeed, the combination of these two methods allows us to define clear objectives as well as significant KPIs. For this, we applied the five SMART criteria (Specific, Measurable, Attainable, Realizable, and Time-bound) on the questions described in the GQM method so that the KPIs and objectives are SMART.

We start by identifying general objectives, which are: (1) ensuring the quality of the processes, this objective refers to the extent to which the process takes into account the procedures defined by the organization. (2) Ensuring quality of results, i.e. ensure all the characteristics of the product offered by the process after its execution. In addition, (3) reduce the risks; it refers to all the strategies that aim to limit the risks and damages associated with a specific area.

Then, the next step is to formulate SMART questions according to the objectives defined above and to facilitate the definition of indicators. Table 1 presents the different questions proposed as well as the corresponding KPI (s):

Table 1. SMART questions and their KPIs

Question	KPI
Is the wasted time less than the waiting time threshold at time t?	Waiting time between an event and an activity
	Waiting time in a process/process fragment
Does the duration of the activities exceed the value of the ideal duration during a specific period?	Duration of an activity
	Duration of a process fragment/process
Is the number of repetitions of activities acceptable relative to the threshold for a given date?	Number of repetitions of an activity/process fragment
Does the number of activities reach the maximum number on a specific date?	Number of activities/process fragments (in progress, completed, repeated)
Is the number of instances acceptable at time t?	Number of instances (According to progress, per unit of time, per category)
Is the number of actors participating in the process satisfactory compared to the ideal value for a given date?	Number of actors involved in a fragment of a process/process or per service
Is the place where the process is carried out adaptable for a specific period?	Number of services/locals
Are the resources used throughout the process satisfactory compared to the ideal number?	Number of information that can be produced/retrieved/used
	Number of material resources

4.2 Configuration Phase

According to (Weske 2007), in the configuration phase, the process modeled in the previous phase must be implemented. For this, the system must be configured, once the system is configured, the business process implementation should be tested. Subsequently, the system can be deployed in its target environment.

In our approach, in the previous phase, the questions asked are applied to all the objectives, this is due to the importance of the correspondence between the objectives and the KPIs, which must be made by experts in the field. Hence, during this 2nd phase, to match each objective with the appropriate KPI (s), we designed a questionnaire containing the general KPI(s) and objectives. This questionnaire is dedicated to those responsible for various processes such as the administrative process, the process of organizing an event with associations, the production process of services or products, etc.

Based on the responses collected by those responsible for the different processes, we obtained the most relevant KPIs for each objective mentioned in Table 2:

Table 2. Correspondence between general KPIs & objectives

Objective	KPI
Ensuring process quality	Waiting time between an event and an activity
	Duration of a fragment of a process/process
	Number of activities/process fragments (completed, repeated, in progress)
	Number of actors involved in a fragment of a process/process or per service
Ensuring quality of results	Waiting time between an event and an activity
	Duration of an activity
	Duration of a fragment of a process/process
	Number of activities/process fragments (completed, repeated, in progress)
	Number of instances (According to progress, per unit of time, per category)
	Number of actors involved in a fragment of a process/process or per service
	Number of services/locals
	Number of material resources
Reducing risks	Waiting time between an event and an activity
	Waiting time in a process/process fragment
	Duration of an activity
	Duration of a fragment of a process/process
	Number of activities/process fragments (completed, repeated, in progress)
	Number of instances (According to progress, per unit of time, per category)

4.3 Enactment Phase

Once the system configuration phase is complete, business process instances can be executed, during this execution, valuable execution data is usually collected, in the form of event logs (Weske 2007).

In this step, based on the log files obtained from the execution of the business process, our contribution consists in monitoring the values of the KPIs, to know whether our objectives are achieved or not. To do this, we use the DMN, more precisely we place decision rules from which we can know the outcome of the objectives (in terms of whether or not these objectives have been achieved).

4.4 Evaluation Phase

According to (Weske 2007), the evaluation phase uses the available information to evaluate and improve business process models and their implementations. Execution logs are evaluated using Business Activity Monitoring and Process Mining techniques that aim to identify the quality of the business process models.

Our contribution in this phase consists in evaluating the performance of the business process based on the result of the execution established in the previous phase. From where we bring corrective or improvement actions if there is a discrepancy between the ideal and real values of KPIs to improve the overall performance of the business process.

5. EXPERIMENTATION

In this part, we have chosen to work on a case study related to COVID-19. More precisely, we will focus on the COVID-19 health care process.

To validate our approach, we have developed a prototype intended for the different 10 experts of the crisis unit. Therefore, we applied our proposed approach to this case study. Starting with the analysis and design phase, we take into consideration the objectives proposed by the crisis unit, and from our research, we have identified a list of objectives validated by Farhat Hached's team presented in table 3.

Table 3. List of objectives

N°	Objective
1	Monitor the state of health of staff and minimize contact with the patient throughout the care process
2	Ensure patient safety as well as data integrity
3	Help decide on the most appropriate treatment for each patient
4	Strengthen human and material resources
5	Strengthen human and material resources in the event of an increase in the number of patients to be treated
6	Reduce the number of actors involved in the care of a COVID patient
7	Minimize the time taken to take care of a COVID-19 patient

In addition, we have determined a list of specific KPIs from those identified in the first sub-phase of our approach. In the second sub-phase, we matched the specific objectives to the specific KPIs that were defined in the previous step. To do this and to have quality results validated by experts, we have developed a specific questionnaire dedicated to members of the crisis unit to carry out this assignment procedure. After the matching step came the process execution step. First, we calculated the values of the KPIs and compared them to the threshold values given and validated by the members of Farhat Hached. Figure 2 presents a screenshot with a comparison of the observed values of the KPIs (Min observed value, Max observed value and Avg observed value) to the threshold values (Min value, Max value and Avg value). Indeed, this visualization offered by our prototype makes it possible to detect whether the calculated value is higher or lower than the threshold value. For example for the first KPI "Duration of the activity 'Choose COVID procedure' per patient", we notice that the three values observed (3mn, 13.88mn, 30mn) are lower than the threshold values (10mn, 20mn, 30mn) respectively. This result is acceptable because we are always looking to reduce the time, which is applicable to our case of COVID patient care process.

N°	KPI	Min value	Min observed value	Max value	Max observed value	Avg value	Avg observed value
1	Duration of the "Choose COVID procedure" activity per patient (avg, min, max)	10mn	3	30mn	30	20mn	13.88
2	Duration of the fragment from "Choose a COVID procedure" to "Monitor progress after treatment" without waiting time	5h	0 : 13 : 0	12h	145 : 22 : 0	8h	43 : 1 : 41
3	Overall length of patient stay in the infectious disease department with waiting time per patient	1d	2	14d	32	5d	10.12

Figure 2. Visualizations of KPIs values

Second, we used the DMN, through which we put decision rules.

	Inputs								Outputs
U	Duration of the "Choo...		Duration of the fragme...		Overall length of patie...		Number of serious pat...		Evaluate the objective "Minimize the ti...
	Number		Number		Number		Number		{Reached,Partial Reached,Not Reached}
1	≤	30	≤	12	≤	14	≤	10	Reached
2	≤	30	>	12	≤	14	≤	10	Reached
6	≤	30	≤	12	>	14	>	10	Partial Reached
7	≤	30	>	12	≤	14	>	10	Partial Reached
15	>	30	>	12	>	14	≤	10	Not Reached
16	>	30	>	12	>	14	>	10	Not Reached

Figure 3. Decision rules of the seventh objective

Figure 3 shows the decision rules set which are based on the threshold values. These rules concern the seventh objective "Minimize the time taken to take charge of a patient" which is associated with the first, second, third and seventh KPIs. In fact, regarding this objective we have defined 16 rules, which give three types of results “Reached”, “Partially Reached” and “Not Reached”. To fully understand these rules, if all or most of the inputs satisfy the rule then the objective is reached, otherwise if half of the inputs satisfy the rule then the objective is partially reached, however the objective is not reached in the case where the majority or all of the inputs do not satisfy the rule. In our case, rule 1 indicates if (1) the duration of the "Choose COVID procedure" activity per patient (avg, min, max) <= 30 minutes and (2) the duration of the fragment from "Choose a COVID procedure" to "Monitor progress after treatment" without waiting time <= 12 hours and (3) the overall length of patient stay in the infectious disease department with waiting time per patient <= 14 days and (4) the number of serious patients treated at the same time in the infectious disease department <=10 patients, then our objective is reached.

During this last step, and based on the following steps we obtained the result of the achievement of objectives through KPIs evaluation, this result of the objective 7 is shown in figure 4 below.

In this figure, we see that this objective is reached, in fact, the values of the KPIs “Duration of the "Choose COVID procedure" activity per patient (avg, min, max)” and “Overall length of patient stay in the infectious disease department with waiting time per patient” and “number of serious patients treated at the same time in the infectious disease department” are acceptable, while the value of the KPI “Duration of the fragment from "Choose a COVID procedure" to "Monitor progress after treatment" without waiting time” is not acceptable. Therefore, according to the rules defined previously the result gives us reached.

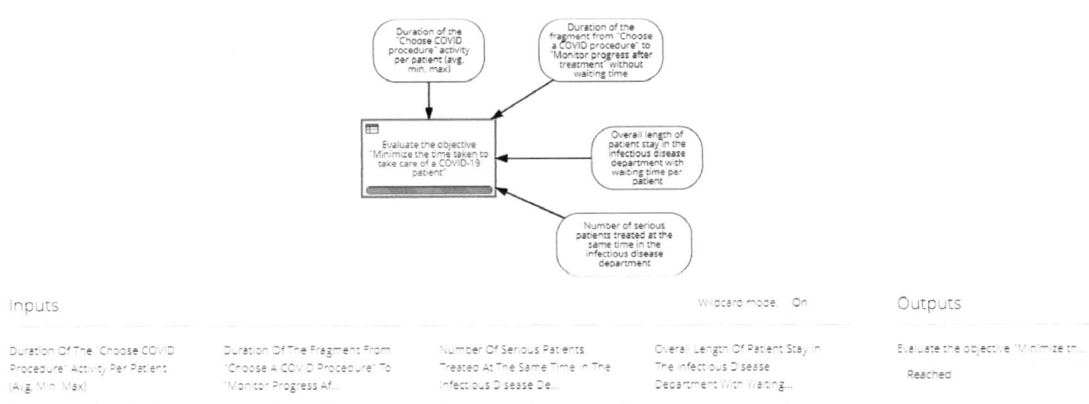

Figure 4. Decision rule results

Based on the results obtained through the questionnaire, the exploitation of the advantages of the GQM method and the SMART criteria as well as the use of a set of decision rules via the DMN, we can conclude that the addition of the proposed sub-phases offers a plus in the life cycle of BPM.

6. CONCLUSION

In this work, we proposed a new KPI management lifecycle integrated into the BPM lifecycle proposed by Weske. Secondly, we have defined a set of general objectives and KPIs. Then, we especially focused on the process of taking care of Covid-19 patients, in which we interviewed the members of the crisis unit. Finally, to experiment our solution, we proposed a prototype, which is a web application implemented by Laravel, intended for the members of the COVID crisis unit at Farhat Hached hospital in Sousse. To validate our prototype, we exploited data of COVID patients, and we evaluated the performance of their care process by analyzing the results of the KPI values displayed in a visualization table. This visualization allows displaying whether there is a difference between the values of the KPIs calculated and their threshold values, to improve the quality of the performance of the process in question. We also used the Signavio tool by introducing the objectives and their KPIs. Indeed, to help the user in the decision-making process, we put the decision rules based on the values of the KPIs to check if the objectives are reached, not reached, or partially reached. Finally, note that our work remains open to several improvements and perspectives such as exploring the correlations between KPIs by applying machine-learning techniques.

REFERENCES

Ammar El Hadj Amor E. and Ayachi Ghannouchi S., 2017. AHP Method for Selecting Emergency Care Key Performance Indicators. *International Conference on Computer Theory and Applications (ICCTA).*

Basili V., Caldiera G. and Dieter Rombach H., 1994. THE GOAL QUESTION METRIC APPROACH. *Encyclopedia of Software Engineering.*

Cherni J., Martinho R. and Ayachi Ghanouchi S., 2019. Towards Improving Business Processes based on preconfigured KPI, target values, Process Mining, and Redesign Patterns. *International Conference on ENTERprise Information Systems (CENTERIS).*

Davenport T. H., 1993. *Process innovation: reengineering work through information technology*. Harvard Business School Press, Boston, Massachusetts.

del Río-Ortega A., Resinas M., Cabanillas C. and Ruiz-Cortés A, 2013. On the definition and design-time analysis of process performance indicators. *Information Systems.*

del Río-Ortega A., 2012. *On the definition and analysis of process performance indicators*. The University of Seville.

Franceschini F., Galetto M. and Maisan D, 2019. *Designing Performance Measurement Systems: Theory and Practice of Key Performance Indicators.* Springer Nature Switzerland AG.

Gries B. and Restrepo J., 2011. KPI Measurement in Engineering Design – A Case Study. *In Proceedings of the International Conference on Engineering Design (ICED11).*

Hammer M. and Champy J., 1993. *Reengineering the corporation: a manifesto for business revolution.* Harper Collins.

Hasić F. and Serral E., 2019. Change Patterns for Decision Model and Notation (DMN) Model Evolution. *Proceedings of the 18th Belgium-Netherlands Software Evolution Workshop.*

Kibira D., Brundage M., Feng Sh. and Morris KC., 2017. Procedure for Selecting Key Performance Indicators for Sustainable Manufacturing. *Proceedings of the ASME 2017 12th International Manufacturing Science and Engineering Conference MSEC2017.*

Lamghari Z., Radgui M., Saidi R. and Driss Rahmani M., 2018. A set of indicators for BPM life cycle improvement. *International Conference on Intelligent Systems and Computer Vision (ISCV).*

Parmenter D., 2020. *Key performance indicators: developing, implementing, and using winning KPIs.* John Wiley & Sons, Inc.

Ponsard C. and Darimont R., 2019. Towards Goal-oriented Analysis and Redesign of BPMN Models. *Proceedings of the 7th International Conference on Model-Driven Engineering and Software Development (MODELSWARD).*

Pusnik M., Kous K., Godec A. and Sumak B., 2019. Process Evaluation and Improvement: A Case Study of The Loan Approval Process. *Proceedings of the SQAMIA 2019: 8th Workshop on Software Quality, Analysis, Monitoring, Improvement, and Applications.*

Simeunovic B., Tomasevic I., Slovic D. and Stojanovic D., 2020. Novel Approach to Measuring Business Process Performance. *Ekonomický časopis (Journal of Economics).*

Weske M., 2007. *Business Process Management: Concepts, Languages, Architectures*. Springer Berlin Heidelberg.

van der Aalst W. M. P., ter Hofstede A. H. and Weske M, 2003. Business process management: A survey. *International Conference on Business Process Management.*

IMPACT OF INDIVIDUAL DECISION-MAKING FACTORS ON PROJECT FAILURE

Narasimha Rao Vajjhala[1] and Kenneth David Strang[2]
[1]University of New York Tirana
Tirana, Albania
[2]W3 Research
New York, USA

ABSTRACT

There is a need for research to identify the factors contributing to the high failure rate in global projects. If individual, organizational, and global factors cannot account for why half of all projects failed, there may be hidden causes. The argument in the current study is that since the project manager (PM) is the risk decision maker, this is the best place to explain why half of all projects fail. We may posit that individual decision-making factors ought to be significant in the context of a project failure. Therefore, we should rule out other project failure predictors. This study examines whether 'a priori' individual factors, such as age, gender, PM certification, education, and experience, are related to a project outcome. The findings of this study indicate that PM experience does not play a significant role in risk decision-making because other factors may be more dominant. Education was not related to project outcome for a primary decision. Still, it was significantly and negatively associated with a biased decision. The results of this study should help understand some of the individual factors and should contribute to future studies on the influence of other factors, including PM competency that was not studied completely in this study.

KEYWORDS

Project Risk, Failure, Certification, Project Manager, Experience, Decision Making, Enterprise, Risk Management

1. INTRODUCTION

For several decades, project failure rates have been significantly high (Borbath, Blessner, and Olson, 2019, Eckerd and Snider, 2017, Strang, 2021). While several researchers have studied the causes of failures on an individual project basis, only a few empirical studies found individual project manager (PM) factors such as experience and certification were related to project success/failure (Anthopoulos et al., 2016, Laurie, Rana and Simintiras, 2017, Strang, 2021). Consequently, more research is needed to determine why so many PMs have failed to meet their scope, time, quality, and or budget mandates. Education, experience, and certification should be relevant factors, but something else is also possible. It is generally accepted in psychology that complex decision making, such as terminating a failing project, cannot be taught during training or certification, nor can these competencies be articulated in organizational procedures due to the required tacit knowledge such as perceptual skills, pattern repertoires, rich mental models, and sense-making (Akpan, 2016; Klein et al., 2016). Therefore, bias may be a cognitive PM failure factor. It is challenging to measure cognitive decision-making in a failed project because PM bias is tacit or memories fade when accessed beyond the point of failure. Another approach would be needed to determine if hidden PM decision-making factors could be why half of all PMs fail.

The rest of this paper is structured with the literature review section, followed by the research methodology, analysis of the results, followed by the limitations of this study, and the conclusion. The following section presents a literature review, including some of the recent studies and findings from seminal studies in this field.

2. REVIEW OF LITERATURE

2.1 Risk Decision Making in Projects

Doug Barlow introduced the concept of risk in 1963. This included risk management costs beyond risk transfer, including costs related to risk avoidance, risk mitigation, and risk retention (McShane, 2018). Risks are classified into four major categories: hazard, financial, operational, and strategic risks (Callahan and Soileau, 2017). Firms have experienced significant losses because of failures of their risk management strategies. Some examples include Barings Bank in 1995 and J.P. Morgan Chase in 2012 (Callahan and Soileau, 2017). Both these examples are cases of lack of appropriate enterprise risk management strategies because of which some of the employees were given excessive authority to make risky equity trades (Callahan and Soileau, 2017). According to Boncella, Reed, and Sun (2004), project managers must recognize the time, quality, and cost problems early to avoid placing the entire project in jeopardy. Some project managers identify the problems early and resolve the issues or recommend terminating failing projects before significant losses creep in. However, many project failures are not detected in time as project managers fail to evaluate the risks, especially the hazard and strategic risks. Some of these failures, such as in the examples mentioned, are because of a lack of appropriate enterprise-wide risk management strategies or the proper application. The project managers' failures to promptly detect the project's problems can also be attributed to individual risk-taking behavior and propensity. This warrants a deeper look into the unique risk decision models. Although individual risk decision models have been applied in several contexts, there is limited literature examining the project manager's risk-taking behavior and the impact on the project failure.

2.2 Enterprise Risk Management

Enterprise Risk Management Framework (ERM), created by the Committee of Sponsoring Organizations (COSO) of the Treadway Commission in 2004, provides reasonable assurance regarding the achievement of the objectives (Callahan and Soileau, 2017). The ERM-COSO framework was updated into a more detailed and complex ERM framework called ERM - Integrating with Strategy and Performance (Prewett and Terry, 2018). The main difference between the 2004 and 2017 frameworks is that the focus of the 2017 framework is on strategy-setting and performance and a more profound recognition of the role of governance and culture (Prewett and Terry, 2018). ERM focuses on a portfolio approach to risk and recognizes that most risks are correlated (Anton and Nucu, 2020). ERM is different from the classical risk management approach, where risks are managed separately in silos. ERM is also referred to as strategic risk management or integrated risk management (Anton and Nucu, 2020).

ERM also models, measures, analyzes, and prioritizes operational and reputational risk within a centralized and integrated framework (Bohnert et al., 2019). In ERM, the individual risk categories are not managed in risk silos as traditional risk management. Rather the firms implementing ERM manage a wide array of risks in an enterprise-wide and integrated fashion (Hoyt and Liebenberg, 2011). ERM proposes the integrated management of all the risks facing an organization, including aligning risk management with corporate governance and strategy (McShane, 2018). ERM can reduce the overall risk of failure and increase firm performance and shareholder value (Bohnert et al., 2019). Prewett and Terry (2018) describe the various ERM maturity levels. At the lowest maturity level, risks are managed separately in silos. At higher maturity levels, firms consider hiring a Chief Risk Officer (CRO) who reports directly to the Chief Financial Officer (CFO) or the Chief Executive Officer (CEO). At the highest maturity levels, firms have ERM integrated into their strategic processes, including long-term planning, capital allocation, and decision making. COSO-ERM framework identified the significant capabilities of an ERM, including identifying and managing multiple cross-enterprise risks, improving the development of capital, aligning risk appetite and strategy, and enhancing risk response decisions (Callahan and Soileau, 2017). ERM benefits firms by reducing external capital costs, increasing capital efficiency, and creating synergy between the various risk management activities (Hoyt and Liebenberg, 2011). Firms can improve the understanding of risk exposure by considering the interdependencies between risk positions and aggregating the risks into one risk portfolio for the enterprise (Bohnert et al., 2019, Lipovetsky, 2020).

Downside side risks are associated with insurance and hedging activities in the case of financial activities, while upside risks are focused on business strategy and development investment. ERM processes not only consider downside risk but manage upside risk as well (Callahan and Soileau, 2017). Even though several large corporations have indicated that they have implemented ERM across their organizations, the 2008 financial crisis demonstrates that either the ERM philosophy of the organizations is wrong or that the organizations have not implemented the ERM effectively (McShane, 2018). This indicates that ERM is an evolving discipline.

2.3 Individual Risk Decision-Making Models

The five main individual management decision-making models include rational, bounded rationality, implicit favorite, intuitive, and garbage-can (Hsu and Chiu, 2008). The rational decision-making model is based on the premise that individuals can fully search and process all the information required for decision-making (Hsu and Chiu, 2008). The rational decision-making model is based on six conditions that allow individuals to make the final management decisions, including defining the problem, confirming the management decision-making principles, weighing the principles in preferential order, finding out all the feasible schemes, evaluating the feasible schemes, and selecting the optimized scheme (Hsu and Chiu, 2008). The bounded rationality decision-making model is based on the premise that certain limitations confine the decision-maker. The decision-maker does not reach full rationality (Simon, 1955, Simon, 1997). The bounded rationality model is the foundation for artificial intelligence and behavioral science (Secchi, 2017). The assumption in bounded rationality is that the decision-maker is limited in the access to the external information and the way the information is processed by the decision-makers cognition (Secchi, 2017). This model also referred to as the Simon model, states that individuals cannot process information and consider all the feasible outcomes (Hsu and Chiu, 2008). As per the bounded rationality theory, the subjects rationally suboptimal decision-making within the constraints of bounded rationality (Kim, 2021).

The implicit favorite decision model is like the bounded rationality decision-making model with the premise that when a manager faces a problem, the manager's favorite solution likely appeared in his mind earlier and is derived from personal values, favors, disfavors, experience, and expectations (Hsu and Chiu, 2008, Soelberg, 1966). The intuitive decision-making model combines rationality and intuition (Simon, 1987). This model was developed after examining the job choice processes of graduating business students (Bahl and Hunt, 1984). In this model, the decision-maker identifies a favorite alternative based on two key factors: perceptual distortion of information and criteria factors (Bahl and Hunt, 1984). In the intuitive decision-making model, the decision-maker is led by sub-consciousness in making final managerial decisions (Hsu and Chiu, 2008). The biased decision then confirms the superiority of the implicit favorite. In the garbage-can decision-making model, events can be understood or predicted but not surpass the favorites (Cohen, March and Olsen, 1972). This model hypothesizes that the problem, the solution, the decision-maker, and selection opportunities are all independent (Hsu and Chiu, 2008). This model was later revised in March, Olsen and Christensen (1976), and March and Olsen (1984). The garbage can model involves three conditions, namely, problematic goals, unclear technology, and fluid participation (Fardal and Sørnes, 2008). As decision-makers often disagree about the organizational goals, it is complex for them to act on those goals in concert. Even if the decision-makers agree on the organizational goals, they still face the challenge of unclear technology (Fardal and Sørnes, 2008). The decision-makers need to arrive at an interpretation of what they are doing. Fluid participation deals with the issues of involvement of various decision-makers, considering that organizational members often change jobs or positions within the organization (Fardal and Sørnes, 2008).

Critical cognitive processes that influence individuals' decision-making include heuristics, herding, and prospect theory (Goyal, Gupta and Yadav, 2021). Heuristics refers to the reliance on mental shortcuts in decision-making. These heuristics include overconfidence, representativeness, and anchoring (Goyal, Gupta and Yadav, 2021). Jordão et al. (2020) highlight the influence of biased thinking on producing irrational decisions even when all the relevant facts are readily available to them. The impact of biased thinking, including overconfidence, optimism, and anchoring effect, can even influence intelligent and successful managers (Jordão et al., 2020). Overconfidence is considered the most significant of all the biases. The effects are dominant and destructive among all the biases and drivers for the remaining biases (Bazerman and Moore, 2013). Overconfidence refers to the tendency of the decision-makers to believe that they are better than what they are (Goyal, Gupta and Yadav, 2021). Some of the factors contributing to overconfidence include age and external factors (Goyal, Gupta and Yadav, 2021). Overconfidence affects corporate investment decisions and the performance of traders investing in markets. Despite the high failure rate, overconfidence is responsible for situations like stock market bubbles, continuous bets on acquisitions, and organizational mergers (Jordão et al., 2020). Studies have shown both positive and negative influences of overconfidence on investor returns (Goyal, Gupta and Yadav, 2021). Unrealistic optimism tends to overestimate the positivism of the future (Jordão et al., 2020). Representativeness refers to the overreliance on stereotypes influencing decision-making (Goyal, Gupta and Yadav, 2021). For instance, some investors may consider past returns to represent future performance. This can lead to investors making erroneous decisions based on a heuristic that is not essentially valid in an investment scenario (Goyal, Gupta and Yadav, 2021). Optimism bias is responsible for failures in setting deadlines and in cost-benefit analysis.

The anchoring effect is the tendency for decision makers' judgments influenced by the opinions or initial information (Jordão et al., 2020). Anchoring relies on reference points created by decision-makers to assist them in the decision-making process (Goyal, Gupta and Yadav, 2021). Age and gender were among the demographic factors that impacted the anchoring heuristic, with women and older age groups tending to have a higher degree of reliance on anchors (Goyal, Gupta and Yadav, 2021). Prospect theory (PT) (Kahneman and Tversky, 1979) is one of the most significant models of decision-making under risk (Liu et al., 2020, Tapas and Pillai, 2021). PT refers to the loss of aversion theory under which the investors exhibit different behaviors and tend to be risk-averse when it comes to gains but are risk-seekers to losses (Tapas and Pillai, 2021). In this theory, decision-making under risk is viewed as a choice between prospects or gambles (Kahneman and Tversky, 1979). According to PT, whether the decision-maker makes risk-seeking or risk-averse decisions depends on several factors, such as loss aversion, reference points, and decision weights (Yan and Liu, 2016).

Tversky and Kahneman (1992) proposed the cumulative prospect theory (CPT), extending the expected utility model and the original prospect theory by applying the cumulative function separately to gains and losses. Although individuals may claim to be logical decision-makers, individuals are susceptible to cognitive biases and overlook rational choices (Tapas and Pillai, 2021). When presented with an option, an investor tends to choose the one shown in potential gains. Another set of interesting decision-making models is classified as naturalistic decision-making models (NDM), where the focus is on expert performance and the role of intuition (Boyes and Potter, 2015). NDM relies on observations of how expert leaders make decisions in the field. NDM is performed under several conditions, including dynamic environments with evolving goals, time constraints, multiple players, and the influence of organizational goals and norms (Boyes and Potter, 2015). The recognition primed decision-making model (RPD) (Klien, 1989) is one of the key NDM models. The expertise supplemented by intuitive and analytical processing of information is used to decide. The four critical components of Klien's model (Klien, 1989) include situational recognition, situational understanding, mental stimulation, and serial evaluation. The multi-criteria evaluation approach (Samadi, Nazari-Shirkouhi and Keramati, 2014) is based on the premise that ideal risk response strategies can be formulated using the multi-criteria evaluation tools on evaluation criteria and concerning the expert judgments prioritizing risk responses (Yan et al., 2021).

3. METHODOLOGY

The study was created as a brief project document describing a significant military software development initiative, with precisely 50% of the anticipated 12-month duration completed. Participants were given ethical disclosure and consented. They were told they would receive a minimum of $10 and up to $40 depending on performance in the interviews. After the interviews, all participants were given the same $40 since the incentive scale was an illusion designed for the treatment. A project dashboard was displayed with metrics representing all the organizational and global factors to ensure no missing facts and that the contextual data would be identical for every participant. There was a statement highlighted in a bolded font that delays beyond 30 days must be presented to the gating committee for a project go/no-go decision. Instead, the PM may issue a cancellation notice. Below the dashboard, interview participants were informed a risk event had just been detected, and the PM needed to decide. Participants were told that the coronavirus COVID-19 pandemic was now impacting the team because someone had tested positive.

This first activity was a competency test to determine how accurately the PM could calculate the risk impact on the project. The risk event was that 1 of 2 senior programmers who created the online security frontend (not yet started) suddenly died due to COVID-19. The security program had the projected 5-week 30-day duration (60 effort days of 2 people) and was on the critical path to start now. There were no similar resources available on the team, so now only one programmer was available. Participants were given a short open-book style test, allowing 30 minutes to complete it, to determine their competency in calculating standard deviation risk on this revised activity. The first treatment was a no-incentive condition to see if the participant would terminate the project when they ought to due to the severity of the risk and according to the mandate above. To clarify that a severe risk event had occurred that ought to stop the project, participants were told that suddenly the second programmer also died of COVID-19. Participants were told that the system automatically recalculated all project activity effort estimates to save time. Participants were shown the project dashboard with the bolded estimate of an additional 64-day effort would be needed. The second treatment was an incentive condition. Participants were told to consider their previous answer void (never happened). Participants were asked to reconsider mitigating the risk event above due to newly available information. They were told one of the marketing directors, a key stakeholder in a different division, offered to increase the PM salary by a 400% bonus if they did not cancel the project. The marketing director suggested the PM could fast-track the hiring of several cheap but talented computer science students under the radar to program the security model in the original budget without delaying the project beyond 30 days. Participants were told to make this feel real. They would get $40 instead of the $10 if they did not cancel. With a 400% incentive, participants were asked the same question as above with the same ordinal scales. They were given 15 minutes to complete this question. Participants were then asked for their demographic data to capture important individual PM factors. Age and years of experience were stored as ratio data types in the database. Gender was indicated as 0=female, 1=male. The highest education level was recorded as an interval data type using these scales: 1=school only, 2=vocational, 3=associate, 4=bachelor, 5=master, and 6=doctorate. PM certification was created as a binary field, 1=yes, 0=no.

The confidence level was set at 95%. Since this is an exploratory study, an 80% power level was desired. Means, standard deviations (SD), and ranges were calculated for continuous data types. Normality tests were conducted for each technique as needed. It was possible the first treatment may have impacted the second. No placeboes were used. All key organization and global factors were controlled, including firm size, revenue, industry type, quality registration, maturity level, standard operating procedures, project/team context, and the risk events. The independent factors were: PM certification, PM education level, PM age, PM gender, and PM years of experience. The dependent variables formed in the study represented the likelihood to cancel a failing project, an interval data type (1 to 5), with higher values meaning a good decision - to cancel.

It is understood in the PM profession that canceling a project is not a desirable outcome, even if there would be no value prospect loss. We may posit that individual decision-making factors ought to be significant in the context of a project failure. Some factors can be easily controlled, such as the global, organizational, and project-level characteristics. Other ‘a priori’ factors such as PM gender, age, experience, education, and certification cannot be controlled, but they may be measured to ensure they do not confound other variables. Prior literature has found that experience and certification are sometimes related to project performance (Barrows, Clevenger, Abdallah, & Wu, 2020; Laurie et al., 2017; Pace, 2019; Strang, 2021). So, at this point, we can propose a set of control hypotheses to determine if ‘a priori’ factors are related to an project outcome condition, as listed below.

H1a: PM age is not related to project outcome;
H1b: PM gender is not associated with project outcome;
H1c: PM certification is related to project outcome;
H1d: PM education is not related to project outcome;
H1e: PM experience is related to project outcome.

4. DISCUSSION OF RESULTS

4.1 Preliminary Analysis

All 16 participants completed the interviews and answered all questions. The mean age was 40.6 (SD = 6.4), ranging from 29 to 55. Most (14 out of 16, 88%) were male. The average years of experience was 9.8 (SD = 2.3), which ranged from 5 to 13. All participants had at least an associate degree and this was the most common (minimum = 3, median = 3 and mode = 3). Slightly less than half (7/16, 44%) claimed to be certified. Alarmingly, less than half of participants (43%) passed the competency test.

4.2 Hypothesis Test Analysis

Correlation tests were used to test most of the hypotheses. First a Shapiro-Wilk Test (SW) was conducted to check for multivariate normality of the dependent variables (before and after the second treatment) as well as the competency score. The results indicated data were not normally distributed (SW = 0.687, $p < .001$). Additionally, since the variable types ranged from categorical to ratio, the nonparametric Spearman correlation was selected to test the relationship hypotheses. The correlation estimates are listed in table 1, with significant coefficients flagged.

Table 1. Spearman Correlations

Factor	Age	Gender	Experience	Education	Certified	Competency
Gender	0.431					
Experience	0.466	0.415				
Education	-0.052	-0.303	0.211			
Certified	-0.137	-0.048	-0.332	-0.424		
Competency	0.244	0.310	-0.041	-0.175	0.661*	
Basic Decision	0.301	0.043	0.006	-0.163	0.570	0.824***
Biased Decision	0.034	0.131	-0.303	-0.609*	0.769**	0.631**

* p < .05, ** p < .01, *** p < .001

The first desirable observation from table 1 was no significant correlation between the independent PM factors (age, gender, experience, education, and certification). This is good because it shows that the independent factors were not interfering as mediators. However, a priori literature suggested age could be positively correlated with experience. In the current study, the lack of correlation between age and experience may be that PMs often change their career or thought some pre-PM experience was not worthy of self-reporting. Another desirable result in table 1 was age was not related to project decision making at least in the sample (rho = 0.301, $p > .05$ and rho = 0.034, $p > .05$). We can accept hypothesis H1a: PM age is unrelated to project outcome. Secondly, gender was not related to project decision making (rho = 0.043, $p > .05$ and rho = 0.131, $p > .05$). This finding supports hypothesis H1b: PM gender is not related to project decision-making. Experience was not related to either decision (rho = 0.006, $p > .05$ and rho = -0.303, $p > .05$) so hypothesis H1e: PM experience is related to project outcome, was rejected. This finding suggests PM experience does not play a significant role in risk decision-making because other factors may be more dominant.

Next are the interesting correlation results with the two decision-making scenarios. First, certification was not significantly related to making a basic decision to cancel a failing project ($rho = 0.57, p > .05$). Still, certification was significantly related to the biased decision to cancel a failing project when added value prospect ($rho = 0.769, p > .01$), producing a large 59% effect size. We expected both correlations to be positively significant because higher dependent variable levels reflect correct risk decision-making. Consequently, we rejected hypothesis H1c: PM certification is related to project outcome, but the results were theoretically desirable. This interesting finding can be interpreted as PM certification not playing a significant role in making a correct basic risk decision. Still, in contrast, and of interest in the current study, certified PMs made better decisions (as compared to uncertified PMs) under biased conditions when a personal value prospect was on the table to influence them to make a bad choice. We could label this as ethical PM decision-making.

5. LIMITATIONS AND CONCLUSION

Generalizations must be cautioned because this was study had interviews with only 16 participants. Although experienced PMs were randomly selected, we must keep in mind that certification was self-reported, and competency was judged solely by the score on one open book test question to calculate risk using PERT during the study. Additionally, all organization-level factors were controlled, defined in the study according to what the authors wanted. This means the project would not necessarily be equivalent to those faced in the real world, nor would the organizational conditions be identical. Controlling the factors made the study objective and very successful but at the cost of reduced generalizability. The findings of this study indicate that PM experience does not play a significant role in risk decision making because other factors may be more dominant, education was not related to project outcome for a primary decision, but it was significantly and negatively associated with a biased decision. The results of this study should help understand some of the individual factors and should contribute to future studies on the influence of other factors, including PM competency and certification.

REFERENCES

Akpan, J.W. (2015). "Motivational Influences on Project Risk Management and Team Performance". *International Journal of Risk and Contingency Management,* Vol. 4, no. 387, pp. 34-48.

Anthopoulos, L., Reddick, C.G., Giannakidou, I. and Mavridis, N. (2016). "Why e-government projects fail? An analysis of the Healthcare.gov website". *Government Information Quarterly,* Vol. 33, no. 1, pp. 161-73. doi:10.1016/j.giq.2015.07.003.

Anton, S.G. and Nucu, A.E. (2020). "Enterprise risk management: A literature review and agenda for future research". *Journal of Risk and Financial Management,* Vol. 13, no. 11, pp. 1-22.

Bahl, H.C. and Hunt, R.G. (1984). "Decision-making theory and DSS design". *SIGMIS Database,* Vol. 15, no. 4, pp. 10–14.

Bazerman, M. and Moore, D. (2013). *Judgment in Managerial Decision Making.* 8th Edition ed., New York, NY: Wiley.

Bohnert, A., Gatzert, N., Hoyt, R.E. and Lechner, P. (2019). "The drivers and value of enterprise risk management: evidence from ERM ratings". *The European Journal of Finance,* Vol. 25, no. 3, pp. 234-55.

Boncella, R.J., Reed, G. and Sun, N. "Software Project Management: Scenarios of Failure and Potential Solutions
". Southern Association for Information Systems (SAIS)2004, *Chicago, USA*. Association for Information Systems.

Borbath, M., Blessner, P. and Olson, B. (2019). "An empirical approach to the evaluation of defence contractor performance". *International Journal of Logistics Research and Applications,* Vol. 22, no. 2, pp. 138-53, doi:10.1080/13675567.2018.1497148.

Boyes, M. and Potter, T. (2015). "The application of recognition-primed decision theory to decisions made in an outdoor education context". *Journal of Outdoor and Environmental Education,* Vol. 18, no. 1, pp. 2-15.

Callahan, C. and Soileau, J. (2017). "Does Enterprise risk management enhance operating performance?". *Advances in Accounting,* Vol. 37, pp. 122-139.

Cohen, M.D., March, J.G. and Olsen, J.P. (1972). "A Garbage Can Model of Organizational Choice". *Administrative Science Quarterly,* Vol. 17, no. 1, pp. 1-25.

Eckerd, A. and Snider, K. (2017). "Does the program manager matter? New public management and defense acquisition". *American Review of Public Administration,* Vol. 47, no. 1, pp. 36–57. doi:10.1177/0275074015596376.

Fardal, H. and Sørnes, J.-O. (2008). "IS Strategic Decision-Making: A Garbage Can View". *Issues in Informing Science and Information Technology,* Vol. 5, no. 1, pp. 553-69.

Goyal, P., Gupta, P. and Yadav, V. (2021). "Antecedents to heuristics: decoding the role of herding and prospect theory for Indian millennial investors". *Review of Behavioral Finance,* Vol. 13, no. 6, pp. 34-42.

Hoyt, R.E. and Liebenberg, A.P. (2011). "The Value of Enterprise Risk Management". *Journal of Risk and Insurance,* Vol. 78, no. 4, pp. 795-822.

Hsu, M.L. and Chiu, K.Y. (2008). "A comparison between 's early management decision-making model and western management decision-making models". *Chinese Management Studies,* Vol. 2, no. 1, pp. 52-75.

Jordão, A.R., Costa, R., Dias, Á.L., Pereira, L. and Santos, J.P. (2020). "Bounded rationality in decision making: an analysis of the decision-making biases". *Business: Theory and Practice,* Vol. 21, no. 2, pp. 654-65.

Kahneman, Y.D. and Tversky, A. (1979). "Prospect Theory: An Analysis of Decision Under Risk". *Econometrica,* Vol. 47, no. 2, pp. 263-91.

Kim, D. (2021). "Bounded rationality in a P2P lending market". *Review of Behavioral Finance,* Vol. 13, no. 2, pp. 184-201.

Klein, D.E., Woods, D.D., Klein, G.A. and Perry, S.J. (2016). "Can we trust best practices? Six cognitive challenges of evidence-based approaches". *Journal of Cognitive Engineering and Decision Making,* Vol. 10, no. 3, pp. 244-54.

Klien, G.A. (1989). *Recognition Primed Decisions.* Greenwich, CT: JAI Press.

Laurie, H.D., Rana, N.P. and Simintiras, A.C. (2017). "The changing landscape of IS project failure: an examination of the key factors". *Journal of Enterprise Information Management,* Vol. 30, no. 1, pp. 142-65. https://doi.org/10.1108/JEIM-01-2016-0029.

Lipovetsky, S. (2020). "Personalized Key Drivers for Individual Responses in Regression Modeling". *International Journal of Risk and Contingency Management,* Vol. 9, no. 38, pp. 15-30.

Liu, Y., Cai, D., Guo, C. and Huang, H. (2020). "Evolutionary Game of Government Subsidy Strategy for Prefabricated Buildings Based on Prospect Theory". *Mathematical Problems in Engineering,* Vol. 2020, p. 8863563.

March, J.G. and Olsen, J.P. (1984). *The new institutionalism organizational factors in political life.* Washington, D.C: American Political Science Review.

March, J.G., Olsen, J.P. and Christensen, S. (1976). *Ambiguity and choice in organizations.* Bergen, Norway: Universitetsforlaget.

McShane, M. (2018). "Enterprise risk management: history and a design science proposal". *The Journal of Risk Finance,* Vol. 19, no. 2, pp. 137-53.

Prewett, K. and Terry, A. (2018). "COSO's Updated Enterprise Risk Management Framework—A Quest For Depth And Clarity". *Journal of Corporate Accounting & Finance,* Vol. 29, no. 3, pp. 16-23.

Samadi, H., Nazari-Shirkouhi, S. and Keramati, A. (2014). "Identifying and Analyzing Risks and Responses for Risk Management in Information Technology Outsourcing Projects Under Fuzzy Environment". *International Journal of Information Technology & Decision Making,* Vol. 13, no. 06, pp. 1283-323.

Secchi, D. (2017). "Agent-based models of bounded rationality". *Team Performance Management: An International Journal,* Vol. 23, no. 1/2, pp. 2-12.

Simon, H.A. (1955). "A Behavioral Model of Rational Choice". *The Quarterly Journal of Economics,* Vol. 69, no. 1, pp. 99-118.

Simon, H.A. (1987). "Making Management Decisions: the Role of Intuition and Emotion". *Academy of Management Perspectives,* Vol. 1, no. 1, pp. 57-64.

Simon, H.A. (1997). *Administrative Behavior.* 4th ed., New Yok, NY: Free Press.

Soelberg, P. (1966). "Unprogrammed Decision Making". *Academy of Management Proceedings,* Vol. 1966, no. 1, pp. 3-16.

Strang, K.D. (2021). "Which organizational and individual factors predict success versus failure in procurement projects". *International Journal of Information Technology Project Management,* Vol. 12, no. 3, pp. 19-39. doi:10.4018/IJITPM.2021070102.

Tapas, P. and Pillai, D. (2021). "Prospect theory: An analysis of corporate actions and priorities in pandemic crisis". *International Journal of Innovation Science,* Vol. 12, no. 2, pp. 45-59.

Tversky, A. and Kahneman, D. (1992). "Advances in Prospect Theory: Cumulative Representation of Uncertainty". *Journal of Risk and Uncertainty,* Vol. 5, no. 4, pp. 297-323.

Yan, P., Liu, J., Zhao, X. and Skitmore, M. (2021). "Risk response incorporating risk preferences in international construction projects". *Engineering, Construction and Architectural Management,* Vol. ahead-of-print, no. ahead-of-print.

Yan, S. and Liu, S. (2016). "Multi-stage group risk decision making with grey numbers based on grey target and prospect theory". *Grey Systems: Theory and Application,* Vol. 6, no. 1, pp. 64-79.

MODELING THE SCALE OF SATISFACTION AND THE VIRTUAL PLATFORM APPLIED TO THE EXPERIENCE OF SPECIALISTS AND USERS OF HEALTH SERVICES[1]

Galba Freire Moita[1], Zulmira Hartz[2] and Galba Freire Moita Júnior[3]
[1]*Univ. Coimbra, CeBER, Faculty of Economics, Av Dias da Silva 165, 3004-512. Coimbra, Portugal and Ministério de Saúde do Brasil, Brazil*
[2]*Pos Doc, Universidade Nova de Lisboa, Lisboa, Portugal*
[3]*MBA, OmnielMaster Consultoria – Fortaleza, Brazil*

ABSTRACT

The index of people who evaluate public health negatively in Brazil reaches rates of 75% to 93% of dissatisfaction between 2012 and 2018. Moita (2019c) showed that the initiatives to measure quality and satisfaction in Brazilian health are incipient and that there is no validated scale for the national health system in Brazil (SUS), but that the Gespública initiative (Brasil, 2014) created the index had many similarities to the international SERVQUAL scale. Objective: Cross-cultural adaptation of SERVQUAL scale for the development of a virtual platform to capture the experience of SUS users. Methods: The research is observational, using a mixed method of evaluation (CAAE: 54972816.9.0000.5051). The 20 validated questions, 13 sub-dimensions and six macro-dimensions of quality/satisfaction were the basis for the development of a virtual platform (*Quality Saude™*) with online application in multicenter groups of SUS users. Flows and functionalities were structured for the development of a virtual platform pilot and its extraction, transformation and loading (ETL) processes, inserted in the Data Warehouse (DW) and BI of results visualization. Results: The scale (*Quality Saude™*) was validated with 2,574 users in 74 health units in Ceará, and the application used by 1989 users of the Eusébio (Brazil) health facilities, with easy handling and quick responses (< 4 min.). Answers were analyzed using the R software, version 3.6.3. P, Project R R (Team, 2019), through PostgreSQL-R (PostgreSQL, 2018; PostgreSQL-R, 2008). Conclusion: An innovative scale for evaluating health quality was validated, which allowed the creation of an online application (*QualitySaude™*) that analyzes the user's perception in contrast to their expectations, highlighting which points demand interventions from health managers.

KEYWORDS

Quality, Access and Evaluation of Health Care, Health Care Quality Indicators, Business Intelligence

1. INTRODUCTION

The New Public Management (NGP), or the New Managerialism, has required from public health managers efforts to monitor results, control and account for expenses (accountability), in addition to ensuring delivery, effectiveness and adequacy to the needs of users (Moita, 2019a).

In Brazil, nationally based opinion polls pointed out the population's dissatisfaction in public and supplementary health that ranged from 54 to 93%, and, also, that high percentages of Brazilians assess public health as bad or very bad, which increased from 61% to 75% between 2011 and 2018 (Moita et al., 2021; G. F. Moita et al., 2019).

Another highlight is the initiative within the Gespública initiative for the creation of the Standard Research and Satisfaction Instrument (IPPS). There are no IPPS continuity records. (Brasil, 2014).

However, robust literature reviews (Machado et al., 2013; Moita, 2019a; Volpato, 2014) showed that quality assessment in health is an incipient topic and that there is no validated scale for the Brazilian health system whose acronym in Portuguese is Sistema Único de Saúde - SUS) (2019c). Also, the bibliographic

[1] *This work has been funded by national funds through FCT – Fundação para a Ciência e a Tecnologia, I.P., Project UIDB/05037/2020*

review of the online platform for the assessment of quality and satisfaction of use relevant to Brazilian health was not located.

In the absence of quality and satisfaction measurement instruments, no SUS motive for a prior work of validation of the *Quality Saude*™ scale for or SUS (Moita & Moita Júnior, 2020; G. F. Moita et al., 2019). As a complement, this work is addressed to the elaboration of a web platform for application of the *Quality Saude*™ instrument, in addition to a use case of application in field research.

Therefore, the article develops the fundamentals of a virtual pilot platform of an online application (*Quality Saude*™) to capture the experience of SUS users, in addition to data processing and application in a multicenter exemplary case, to generate support information to decision making.

1.1 Quality Assessment and User Experience Satisfaction

There is no consensus in the literature on the scope and breadth of health assessment and monitoring, but many possible conceptual theoretical frameworks (Arah, Custers, et al., 2003; Arah, Klazinga, et al., 2003; Arah et al., 2006; Murray & Frenk, 2000). Arah et al.(2003) present a global comparison of the different theoretical and conceptual framework approaches of performance measurement systems in the United Kingdom (NHS), Canada, Australia, USA, from the World Health Report 2000 report (WHO, 2000), in addition to the 'Health at a Glance and OECD Health Data' publications of the Organization for Economic Co-operation and Development (OECD) (Development, 2001; Unit, 2001).

Vinagre (2008) emphasizes the complexity of measuring services due to the intangibility (absence of physical attributes) aspects of services (Oliver, 1980; Parasuraman et al., 1985, 1991b) and the fact that services are essentially processes, being affected by interactions and activities, that is, it depends on relational aspects between users and service providers (Grönroos, 1984, 1988; Grönroos, 1997; Oliver, 1989; Rust & Oliver, 1994; Westbrook, 1987; Westbrook et al., 1978).

In the evolution of these studies, psychometric scales for measuring perceived quality emerged, based on the *gap model* of satisfaction (Oliver, 1980; Oliver & Linda, 1981; Westbrook & Reilly, 1983), in which the position of the customer's perception of perceived service quality depends on the nature and extent of the discrepancy between service *expectation* and *perceived performance*.

Based on the *gap model*, the SERVQUAL scale was initially developed with 97 items, based on the 10 dimensions of quality (Parasuraman et al., 1988) which was validated in an instrument with 22 questions, in addition to redistributing the ten (10) dimensions originals for the current five (5) dimensions of the SERVQUAL scale (Babakus & Boller, 1992; Babakus & Mangold, 1992; Berry et al., 1994; Parasuraman et al., 1991a).

The initiative to create the Standard Survey and Satisfaction Instrument (IPPS) can be highlighted, with apparent similarities with the five proposed dimensions (Tangibility, Reliability, Responsiveness, Assurance and Empathy) and its 22 questions from the SERVQUAL scale (Parasuraman et al., 1991a). However, recent publications on the IPSS were not found, perhaps due to the discontinuity of the initiative.

Thus, the scales for measuring service quality and user satisfaction are consolidated in several fields and may be a field of interest in Brazil.

2. METHODS

The research is *observational*, *cross-sectional*, using a mixed evaluation method (Minayo et al., 2010). It was supported by a study of multiple cases, in a sample of informants selected for convenience, within the scope of the PhD of the University of Coimbra (CAAE: 54972816.9.0000.5051). The ethical rules of resolution no. 466/12 of the National Health Council (CNS - Brazil).

The scale had incremental validations with 195 professionals (from 10 Brazilian states) and 2,547 users from municipalities in Ceará, in which the answers were objects of descriptive analysis and of statistical significance. Twenty adapted questions, 13 sub-dimensions and six macro-dimensions of quality/satisfaction were validated (Moita, 2019a; G. F Moita et al., 2019), being the basis for the development of a virtual platform (*Quality Saude*™) with subsequent online application with 1,589 users of health units in Eusébio (Brazil).

We have structured flows and functionalities for the development of a virtual platform pilot and its processes of extraction, transformation and loading (ETL), inserted in Data Warehouse (DW) and results visualization BI. An analysis of responses from software R, version 3.6.3. P. O Projeto R (Team, 2019) is a programming language with a focus on statistics and graphics; um project *General Public License* (GNU) which is under the license of open code and executes a wide variety of functions (Team, 2019). These research dice are structured in a relational data bank and, for this research, are established the PostgreSQL[2] (2018), or the PostgreSQL-R (2008).

In the field of *Design Research*, an existing artifact was studied (the perception of the management of organizations and health services, structured and in operation) and an improvement solution was proposed for the following stages: i. Define a data model that allows storing collected data in an organized manner; ii. Apply collected data extraction, transformation and loading processes; iii. Keep data in a relational database; iv. Produce solutions to visualize the collected data, presenting them in a way to accurately evidence the obtained results.

3. ANALYSIS AND DISCUSSION OF RESULTS

In the analysis of the results obtained, 9,063 responses to each of the items of the scale were obtained in groups of 195 experts in pilot groups with responses from 10 Brazilian states: Bahia, Ceará, Distrito Federal, Goiás, Maranhão, Mato Grosso, Pará, Piauí, Rio Grande do Norte e Rondônia, in addition to 2,547 SUS users.

The 20 validated questions, 13 sub-dimensions and six macro-dimensions of quality/satisfaction (Moita, 2019b) were the basis for the development of a virtual platform (*Quality Saude*^{TM}) with online application in multicenter groups of SUS users.

3.1 The Construction of the Virtual Platform and Application of Business Intelligence

The *Quality Saude*^{TM} screen functionality modeling flowchart, which synthesizes the logic and diagramming of the web application, developed for user interface (Moita & Moita Júnior, 2020).

In our research, the data obtained in the first moment were not able to transmit accurate information to the interested parties, as they are often disconnected and/or inconsistent, mainly due to the lack of standardization. To avoid these inconsistencies, it was necessary to standardize the data collected so that this information could be cross-referenced, and the results obtained from the application of the scale could be outlined, which proved to be efficient because significant data and great potential for analysis were collected.

In this way, the application pilot resulted in the encapsulation of the 20 *Quality Saude*^{TM} scale questions in a responsive virtual platform (which adapted to various equipment of different models and screens). The treatment and analysis of the collected data, proposed in our study, were used as a technological support for applying the proposed models and later systematizing the results. In this case, innovation is the use of BI tools and techniques to support the application of questions.

On the initial screen of the questionnaire application, the respondent informs his basic and sociodemographic data (figure 1).

2 O PostgreSQL is an open source project coordinated by PostgreSQL Global Development Group, with support for hybrid object-relational model and Procedural Language in several languages (PL/pgSQL, PL/Python, PL/Java, PL/Perl) for Stored Procedures.

Figure 1. The Basic Data Entry Screen

From this flowchart (Moita & Moita Júnior, 2020), figure 2 shows the example of two of the screens of the virtual platform prototype for data collection of the responses of users of health services.

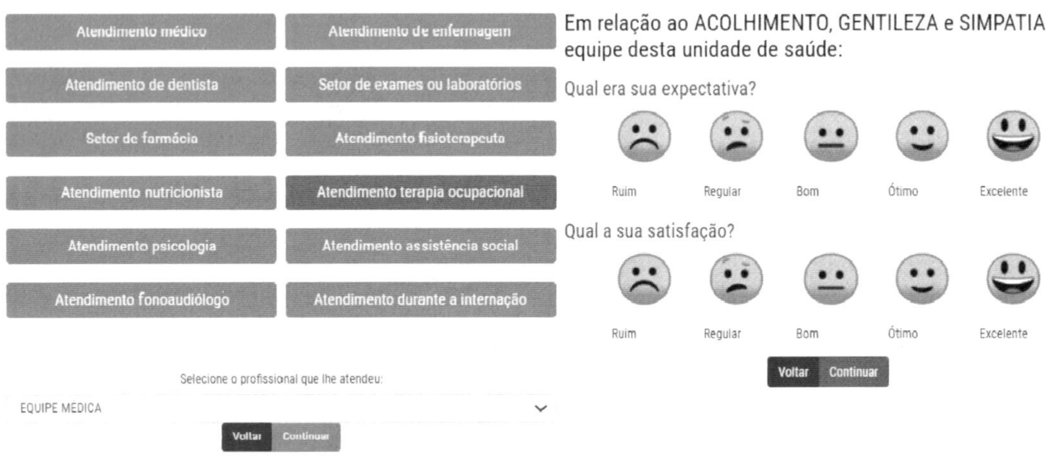

Figure 2. Selection of 12 types of services and professional teams and the model of the prototype's 20 question-scenarios screens *Quality Saúde*™

Techniques for gathering requirements and computer commands were used for the processes of extraction, transformation, and loading (ETL), insertion of data in the *Data Warehouse* (DW). For the treatment of the analyzed results, two BI tools (free license versions) were used: 1. Power Designer (Sybase, 2018) supports various activities such as business process modeling, data modeling, multidimensional data modeling, which stores and controls developed models. Power Designer brings impact analysis, design-time change management, and metadata management techniques to the user. 2. O QlikView (QlikTech, 2018), it encompasses BI techniques, allows an interactive visualization of information and can be defined as a tool for decision making.

The initial analysis demonstrated the need for data abstraction, placing the Institution table as the main entity in the model, as it ends up being related to all other entities. Subsequently, the ETL - Extraction, Transformation and Load processes were applied to the data, in the R programming language, where they were kept in the PostgreSQL database. Data extraction, data transformation imported with R, and data loading imported with R were presented in previous publications (Moita et al., 2018; Moita & Moita Júnior, 2020).

In another light, the interactive dashboards created with the QlikView BI tool *(Qlickview Personal Edition* free version 12.0.2*)*, were aligned with the features *Gartner* (2017).

Thus, the BI platform made it possible to draw comparative graphs between service units, services and evaluated teams, putting results and performance into perspectives in the 20 adapted questions, 13 sub-dimensions and the six macro-dimensions of quality and satisfaction, as a management tool on a web platform with some graphs of 483 valid responses from the 506 responding users (figure 3).

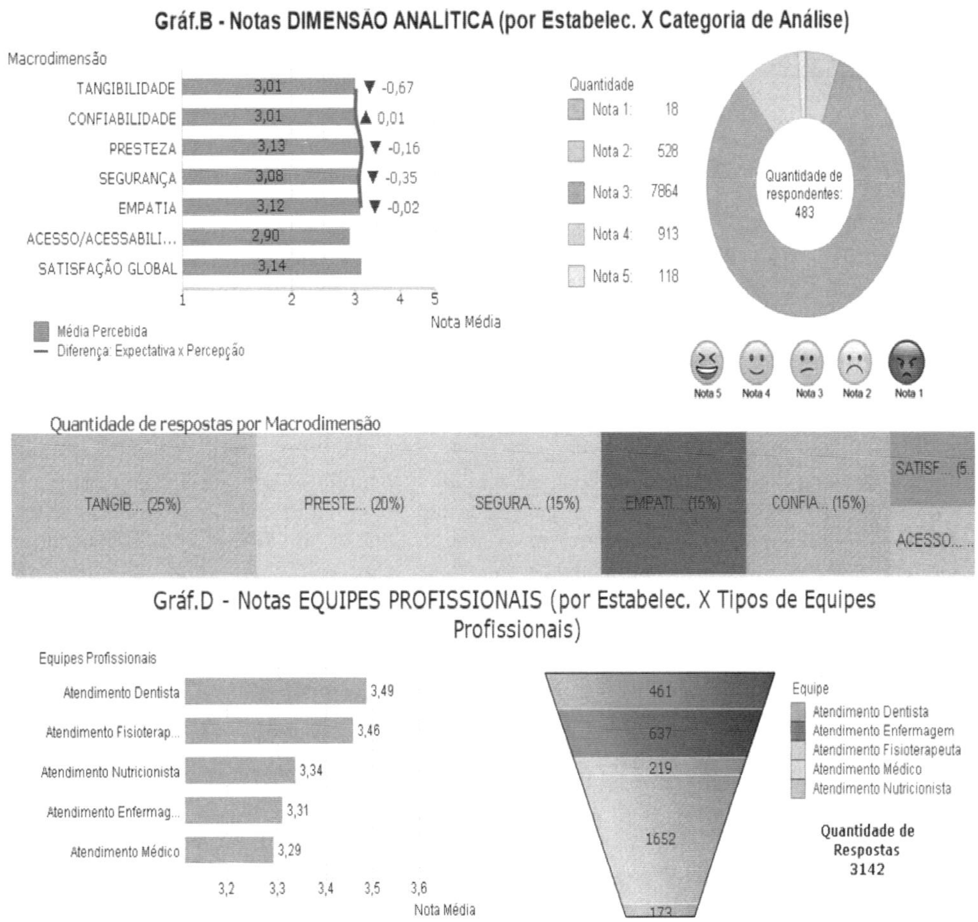

Figure 3. Comparative charts of unit results and team performance (proxy J)

In the central graph and smaller graph (figure 4), you can see the number of responses received grouped by grade, to provide a more detailed view of the data being analyzed. The home panel is the starting point for other views, functioning as an application, where the user can navigate from one screen to another using the buttons. After the initial analysis, where general data is looked at without a great deal of detail, it is possible to look at more specific data, using filters to achieve the goal. Various items can be selected in the filters, allowing the manager to view information about all institutions that interest him.

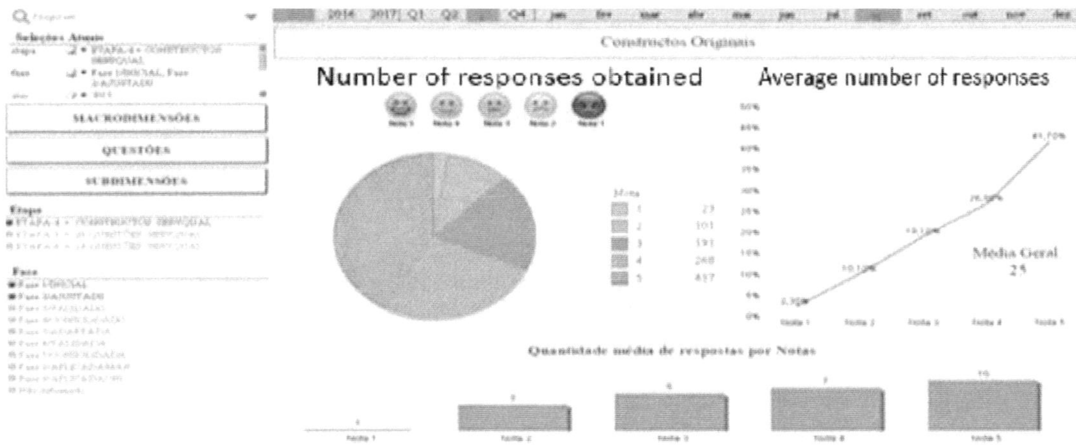

Figure 4. Dashboad 1 do QlikView – Dashboard by average obtained

Also in Figure 4, in the larger bar graph, it is possible to compare the average of grades received by institution or group of filtered institutions (overall average) in relation to the group to which it belongs, managing entity, micro-region and macro-region, grouped by macro dimensions (Tangibility, Reliability, Responsiveness, Assurance and Empathy, Access / Accessibility). The graph in the lower right corner is common to all screens as it allows you to see how many responses are being analyzed. The bar chart in the lower left corner shows the difference between grades and perceived expectations, the red line indicates this difference and represents a very important in original model of servqual (Berry & Parasuraman, 1991; Parasuraman et al., 1988, 1991a) kept in *Quality Saúde*^{TM}.

Figure 5 shows the visualization with a higher level of detail. On this screen, the averages of the grades are grouped by questions/constructions, where it is possible to see with a filter, for example, the number of grades 1 that the institution received or view without a filter.

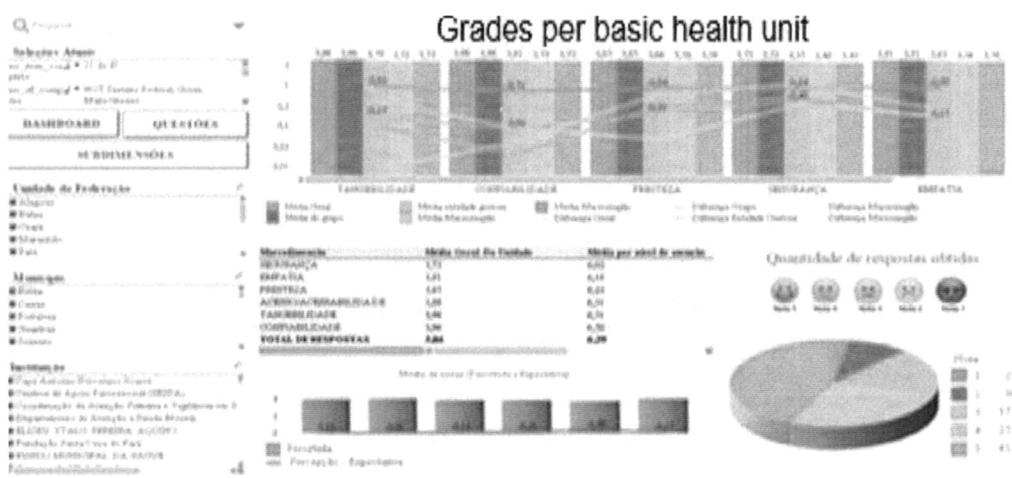

Figure 5. Dashboad 2 do QlikView - Dashboard by macro dimension

As the data refer to the number of responses for all units that belong to the stage and phase selected in the panel (figure 6), this table becomes useful when there is a greater number of responses being analyzed; in this work, with a restricted data sample, you can see a pie chart in the upper right corner, as an example.

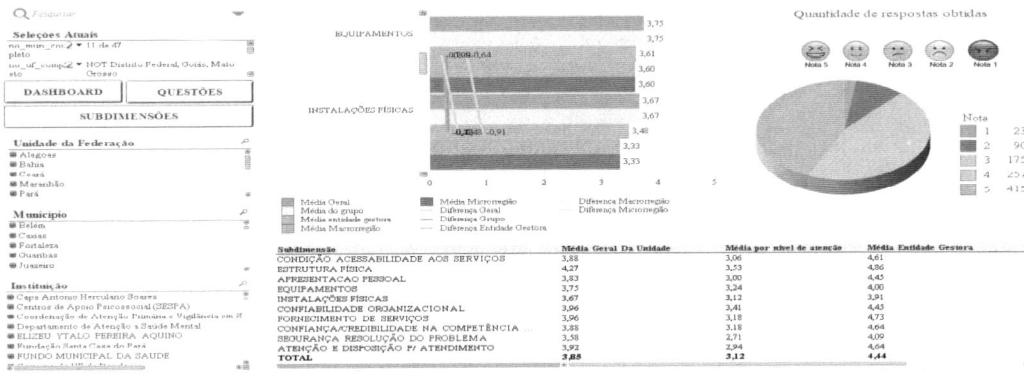

Figure 6. Dashboad 3 do QlikView - Dashboard by subdimension

In Figure 7, it is possible to observe an additional level of detail of the average grades and, in this case, the average grades obtained by one or more institutions grouped by sub-dimensions. The central graph and the table show the average of the scores in each sub-dimension, always comparing the institution with the group, managing entity, micro-region and macro-region to which the institution belongs.

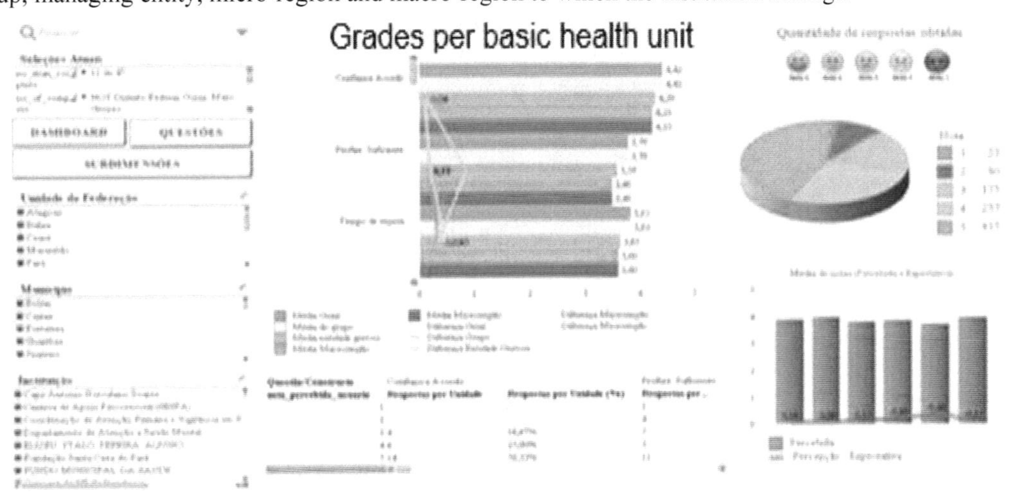

Figure 7. Dashboad 4 do QlikView - Dashboard by QualitySaude question

The artifact validated in this investigation intends to support a system of monitoring and evaluation in public health, based on results that provides crucial information about public policies or organizational performance - *results-based management* (RBM), como conceituam Morra-Imas e Rist (2009).

4. CONCLUSION

Assessing the quality of services provided to the public is extremely important, but the incipience of instruments based on scientific methods makes it difficult to define strategies to improve services.

The present work developed an application on a virtual platform, in which the extraction, transformation and loading (ETL) processes were applied, which deal with the cleaning of data from various sources to be inserted in the *Data Warehouse* (DW).

The platform proved to be efficient in extracting a relational database, whose data can be consulted in an organized, fast and mainly without the unnecessary use of repeated data, bringing integrity. The application of BI on the platform enabled the visualization of data in an analytical and synthetic way, in micro, small and macro (large) data samples.

The adaptation of the Servqual scale generated an innovative scale (*QualitySaude*^{TM}), which allows the user's perception to be seen as a counterpoint to their expectations, presenting results that really approach reality, highlighting which points require interventions by health managers (G. F Moita et al., 2019).

In this article, the foundations of a web platform were developed, in addition to the use-case application that generated a BI application on the data collected by the platform, which enabled the visualization the data in an analytical and synthetic way, in micro, small and macro (large) data samples.

Based on the analysis of these data, it is possible, for example, to invest financial resources and in areas where the average assessment was below the user's expectation, in addition to instrumentalizing the decision of managers, presenting diagnoses and emphasizing critical points that can be improved and solutions where they really need priority attention. In addition, it is possible to analyze the data in a general and grouped way, comparisons between institutions, municipalities, managing entities, macro-regions, micro-regions, among other possibilities, can be useful to assist in decision making.

Among the potential advances is the adaptation to private health and expansion to other public services, further detailing the results and graphs obtained from the analysis of the panels presented here and generating alerts, in addition to others that can be created.

REFERENCES

Arah, O. A., Custers, T., & Klazinga, N. S. (2003). *Updating the Key Dimensions of Hospital Performance: The Move Towards a Theoretical Framework* 3rd Workshop on Hospital Performance Measurement Barcelona.

Arah, O. A., Klazinga, N. S., Delnoij, D. M. J., Asbroek, A. H. A. T., & Custers, T. (2003). Conceptual frameworks for health systems performance: a quest for effectiveness, quality, and improvement *International Journal for Quality in Health Care*, *15*(5), 22. https://doi.org/10.1093/intqhc/mzg049

Arah, O. A., Westert, G. P., Hurst, J., Niek, S., & Klazinga, N. S. (2006). A conceptual framework for the OECD Health Care Quality Indicators Project *International Journal for Quality in Health Care*, 9. https://doi.org/10.1093/intqhc/mzl024

Babakus, E., & Boller, G. W. (1992). An empirical assessment of the SERVQUAL scale. *Journal of Business Research*, *24*, 16.

Babakus, E., & Mangold, W. G. (1992). Adapting the SERVQUAL scale to hospital services: an empirical investigation. *Health Services Research*, *26*(6), 20.

Berry, L. L., & Parasuraman, A. (1991). *Marketing services: competing through quality* (F. Press, Ed.).

Berry, L. L., Parasuraman, A., Zeithaml, V., & Adsit, D. (1994). Improving service quality in America: Lessons learned; Executive commentary. *The Academy of Management Executive*, *8*(2), 21.

Brasil. (2014). *Governos Estaduais no Federalismo Brasileiro*. Brasilia: Instituto de Pesquisa Econômica Aplicada

Development, O. f. E. C. a. (2001). OECD Health Data 2001. In. Paris: Organisation for Economic Cooperation and Development

Gartner. (2017). *Gartner Recognizes Qlik® as a Leader in BI and*
Analytics - Magic Quadrant for Business Intelligence and Analytics Platforms . https://community.qlik.com/docs/DOC-18134

Grönroos, C. (1984). A service quality model and its marketing implications. *European Journal of Marketing*, *18*(4), 9.

Grönroos, C. (1988). Service Quality: the six criteria of good perceived service. *9*(3), 4.

Grönroos, R. (1997). Value-driven relational marketing: from products to resources and competencies. *Journal of Marketing Management*, *13*(5), 13. https://doi.org/10.1080/0267257X.1997.9964482

Machado, J. P., Martins, A. C. M., & Martins, M. S. (2013). Avaliação da qualidade do cuidado hospitalar no Brasil: uma revisão sistemática. *Cad. Saúde Pública*, *29*(6), 20.

Minayo, M. C. S., Assis, S. G. d., & Sousa, E. R. (2010). *Avaliação por triangulação de métodos - Abordagem de programas sociais* (F. O. Cruz, Ed.). Fundação Oswaldo Cruz.

Moita, G. F. (2019a). *Avaliação integrativa de performance multidimensional e decisão multicritério: um proxy de painel de indicadores de eficiência, efetividade e qualidade para governança de organizações hospitalares e serviços de saúde no Brasil* [Doctoral, Universidade Federal de Minas Gerais]. Belo Horizonte. http://hdl.handle.net/1843/32451

Moita, G. F. (2019b). *Avaliação integrativa de performance multidimensional e decisão multicritério: um proxy de painel de indicadores de eficiência, efetividade e qualidade para governação de organizações hospitalares e serviços de saúde no Brasil* [Doctoral, Universidade de Coimbra]. Coimbra. http://hdl.handle.net/10316/88714

Moita, G. F. (2019c). *Avaliação Integrativa de Performance Multidimensional e Decisão Multicritério: Um Proxy de Painel de Indicadores de Eficiência, Efetividade e Qualidade para Governação de Organizações Hospitalares e Serviços de Saúde no Brasil [Integrating Evaluation of Multidimensional Performance and Multicriterary Decision: A Panel Proxy of Efficiency, Effectiveness and Quality Indicators for Governance of Hospital Organizations and Health Services in Brazil].* [Doctoral, Universidade de Coimbra]. Coimbra.

Moita, G. F., Bernardo, C. G., Costa, J. C., & Azevedo, D. A. (2018). Business Intelligence application in adaptation of Servqual scale at brazilian health system. Proceedings of 11th IADIS International Conference Information Systems, Lisbon, Portugal.

Moita, G. F., Hartz, Z. M. A., & Moita Jr., G. J. (2021). *QualitySaude – aplicativo web de avaliação de qualidade e de desempenho de equipes na experiência de usuários do SUS* I Congresso Internacional de Auditoria em Saúde
II Congresso Latinoamericano de Auditoria em Saúde
V Congresso Brasileiro de Auditoria em Saúde, Fortaleza, Ceará, Brasil. https://congresso.abeabrasil.com.br/

Moita, G. F., & Moita Júnior, G. F. (2020). Quality scale adaptation applied to a communication platform for primary health care analysis. Proceedings of 13th IADIS International Conference Information Systems, Sofia, Bulgaria.

Moita, G. F., Raposo, V. M. R., & Barbosa, A. C. Q. (2019). Quality Saúde – uma adaptação transcultural multicêntrica dos constructos da escala Servqual de satisfação para o SUS, por translação de conhecimento de especialistas e usuários. *Rev. Serv. Público*, *70*(2), 40. https://doi.org/10.21874/rsp.v70i2.3142

Moita, G. F., Raposo, V. M. R., & Barbosa, A. C. Q. (2019). Reliability and validity analyzes of constructs and dimensions scale of measurement of quality and satisfaction of public health users in Brazil. *X Congreso Internacional en Gobierno, Administración y Políticas Públicas #GIGAPP 2019*, Madrid.

Morra Imas, L. G., & Rist, R. C. (2009). *The Road to Results Designing and Conducting Effective Development Evaluations*. The Wolrd Bank.

Murray, C. J. L., & Frenk, J. (2000). A framework for assessing the performance of health systems *Bulletin of the World Health Organization*, *78*(6), 15.

Oliver, R. L. (1980). A Cognitive model of the antecedents and consequences of satisfaction decisions. *Journal of Marketing Research*, *17*(4), 10. https://doi.org/10.1177/002224378001700405

Oliver, R. L. (1989). Processing of the satisfaction in consumptions a suggested framework and research propositions. *Journal of Consumer Satisfaction*, *2*, 16.

Oliver, R. L., & Linda, G. (1981). Effects of satisfaction and its antecedents on consumer preference and intention. *Advances in Consumer Research*, *8*, 6.

Parasuraman, A., Berry, L. L., & Zeithaml, V. A. (1985). A Conceptual model of service quality and its implications for future research. *Journal of Marketing*, *49*, 41-50.

Parasuraman, A., Berry, L. L., & Zeithaml, V. A. (1988). SERVQUAL: a multiple-item scale for measuring consumer perceptions of service quality. *Joumal of Retailing*, *64*, 29.

Parasuraman, A., Berry, L. L., & Zeithaml, V. A. (1991a). Refinement and reassessment of the SERVQUAL scale. *Journal of Retailing*, *67*(4).

Parasuraman, A., Berry, L. L., & Zeithaml, V. A. (1991b). Understanding costumer expectation of service. *Sloan Management Review*, *31*, 10.

PostgreSQL. (2018). *The PostgreSQL global development group*. In (Version 9.6.11) http://www.postgresql.org/files/documentation/pdf/8.3/postgresql-8.3-A4.pdf

PostgreSQL-R. (2008). *PostgreSQL Global Development Group*. In *Postgres-R: a database replication system for PostgreSQL* Ronja Wanner. http://www.postgres-r.org

QlikTech. (2018). *Introdution to QlikView*. In https://www.qlik.com/pt-br/products/qlikview

Rust, R. T., & Oliver, R. L. (1994). Service quality: insights and implications from the frontier service quality. In Sage (Ed.), *New Directions in Theory and Practice*.

Sybase. (2018). *Enterprise Architecture tools for digital transformation success*. In https://www.sap.com/products/powerdesigner-data-modeling-tools.html

Team, R.-C. (2019). *R: A language and environment for statistical computing*. In https://cran.r-project.org/bin/windows/base/old/

Unit, O. H. P. (2001). Health at a Glance. In. Paris: Organisation for Economic Co-operation and Development

Vinagre, M. H. (2008). *A satisfação de utentes de serviços públicos de saúde: preditores e mediadores* [Doctoral, Instituto Superior de Ciências do Trabalho e da Empresa-ISCTE]. Portugal: Lisboa.

Volpato, L. F. (2014). *Utilização de uma ferramenta para análise da qualidade nos serviços públicos de saúde* [Doctoral, Universidade estadual de campinas]. Piracicaba

Westbrook, R. A. (1987). Product/consumption based affective responses and postpurchase processes. *Journal of Marketing Research*, *24*, 13. https://doi.org/10.1177/002224378702400302

Westbrook, R. A., Newman, J. W., & Taylor, J. R. (1978). Satisfaction/dissatisfaction in the purchase decision process: are consumers really as dissatisfied as many studies claim? *Journal of Marketing*, *42*(4), 7. https://doi.org/10.2307/1250086

Westbrook, R. A., & Reilly, M. D. (1983). Value-percept disparity: an alternative to the disconfirmation of expectations theory of consumer satisfaction. *Advances in Consumer Research*, *10*(1), 6.

WHO. (2000). *The World Health Report 2000. Health Systems: Improving Performance* Geneva: World Health Organization.

A GRAMMAR FOR INFORMATION SYSTEMS AND TECHNOLOGY COMPETENCIES

Fábio Longo De Moura and Filipe De Sá-Soares
Centro ALGORITMI – University of Minho – Guimarães, Braga, Portugal

ABSTRACT

The description of Information Systems and Technology professional competencies requires the articulation of various concepts in an integrated structure. The definitions for these concepts are not consensual and the instantiations of the concepts are written in non-standard ways. This ambiguity can have a negative impact on the characterization and evaluation of professional attributes. This work carries out an analysis of several competency frameworks and proposes the application of grammatical classes for the concepts that make up the competency structure, aiming at greater transparency and clarity in the use of the concepts. To this end, a Backus-Naur Form grammar is proposed to standardize the writing of concepts. Seeking to validate the competency grammar, Information Systems and Technology professionals reported attributes of their occupations, observing the proposed grammatical rules. Afterwards, the exercise was replicated with practitioners from four other professional areas.

KEYWORDS

Competency, Information Systems and Technology, Information Systems and Technology Competency, Competency Grammar, Backus-Naur Form

1. INTRODUCTION

Addressing the concept of competency in scientific investigations has been increasingly challenging, as it may be found by the number of scientific publications that refer to this concept. With a proliferation of studies on a topic, it might be expected that the more a concept is referenced, the greater the rigor in its use. However, in what concerns competency, this does not necessarily mean higher levels of maturity or standardization in the employment of the concept. Indeed, Ferrari (2012) notices the existence of a "jargon jungle not easy to breach" (p. 11), Janssen *et al.* (2013) observe that "concrete elaborations [*of digital competence*] vary depending on the context and the particular 'language' used," (p. 473), and Oberländer *et al.* (2020) highlight the prevalence of "many different labels" (p. 4), frequently "used interchangeably, as synonyms, describing the same concept", but where "definitions and intended meanings are rather imprecise and depend on the context of use." (p. 4).

This perceived lack of rigor when applying the word "competency" and other terms that are often treated as synonyms for competency, such as, skill, knowledge, ability, and proficiency, or that are closely related to competency, such as, posture, behavior, disposition, and attitude, conveyed the opportunity for this work.

By studying several well-known Information Systems and Technology (IST) competency-focused frameworks in the search for definitions of competency-related concepts, we found that different concepts form the structure of those frameworks. The lack of rigor when applying the concepts related to the competencies of individuals led us to resort to dictionaries, seeking primary definitions for the concepts. In an effort to obtain a unified approach to the variety of concepts addressed in this work, as well as to grasp better ways to formulate (writing) them, we advanced revised definitions for the concepts, based on the reviewed literature. This allowed us to structure the construct of competency in the realm of IST professional area.

In this paper, we argue that one way to distinguish the attributes characterizing professionals' competencies is the way of writing the attributes that compose the competency construct. We advocate that the attributes associated to job competencies, such as, expected actions from a professional, knowledge requirements, individuals' features, or even job-related objects, may have their writing standardized, and that this will assist in their classification in one of the main concepts reviewed in this work. To this end, we propose that Backus-Naur Form (BNF), a meta-syntax notation, can be used to define criteria – a grammar – to govern the writing of concepts that composes the competency construct. Thus, the research question that this work aims to answer is the following: Is a Backus-Naur Form competency grammar able to assist in the identification, classification and writing of IST professional attributes? Aiming to answer the research question, IST professionals were involved in this work, having used the BNF competency grammar to map the responsibilities assigned to them in the workplace in order to meet the daily demands of their job functions.

We delineated the competency-related concepts based on several competency frameworks and grounded in definitions found on dictionaries. In the next section of the paper, we summarize the literature review, briefly describing the competency frameworks, and identifying the dictionaries that provided support material for the definition of concepts. The main concepts are also presented, with BNF being introduced as the notation for specifying the rules of writing the instantiations of the concepts involved. After the literature review, the section on competency grammar sets forth the writing rules for each of the reviewed concepts. Also in that section, we propose a decision tree to aid in the classification of words or sentences related to the practice of professionals. In the final section, conclusions, limitations of the study and ideas for future work are pointed out.

2. LITERATURE REVIEW

The definition of the concepts was considered a requirement to start this work. In what concerns the competency frameworks, it was noted that these references approach the concepts differently, resulting in different definitions for the same concept, as well as different concepts with the same definition. Aiming more consistency to the path that led to the definition of concepts, it was also necessary to use dictionaries, given that the definitions present in these references were not influenced by the specific purposes or central themes that guided the frameworks reviewed.

The following subsection addresses the competency frameworks reviewed in this work, paying special attention to the approach to competency adopted in each framework and to its respective central theme.

2.1 Competency Frameworks

The O*NET framework is supported by the United States Department of Labor (2020), receiving constant updates. This framework has professional occupation as its central theme, but it involves several other concepts that refer to characteristics and attributes expected to be found in professionals. Some complementary concepts are based on the RIASEC concept (Realistic, Investigative, Artistic, Social, Enterprising, and Conventional) proposed by Holland (1997). With similar characteristics, there is the Répertoire Opérationnel des Métiers et des Emplois (ROME) (ETALAB, 2020), provided by the French government. This framework also uses the RIASEC concept, but it constrains the concept addressed to its central theme, namely occupation. Assigning the concept of competency as the central theme of the framework, the European e-Competence Framework (ECF) (European Union, 2016), specifically aimed at the area of IST, sets forty different competencies.

Assuming skill as the central theme, there are the Skill Framework for the Information Age (SFIA) (SFIA Foundation, 2015, 2018) and the i-Competence Dictionary (iCD) (Hayashiguchi, Endou and Impagliazzo, 2018), both specific to IST professional area. The support provided by SFIA is based on the mapping of 112 skills, grouped into 17 subcategories and 6 categories. The iCD, although having skill as its central theme, proposes a different approach that lists the tasks associated to each individual's skill. This framework includes 84 skills, divided into 14 classifications and four categories.

In this work, seven competency frameworks were analyzed, each one composed by different concepts that make up what the authors of the frameworks define as competency. Through the proposal of a definition for the competency construct and an associated set of rules for expressing instances of the component concepts (the grammar), we hope to increase the maturity and rigor with which these matters are dealt with.

In the next subsection, we present the main concepts in the aforementioned frameworks and advance definitions that will be useful for the standardization of the concepts involved in this study.

2.2 Main Concepts

Considering that IST was the main area under study in this work, in the beginning we sought for concepts defined and applied specifically in IST, and the references that initially contributed to the study were ECF and SFIA, and later iCD. Considering the structure of each framework, the definitions for the concepts are contrasting. When comparing SFIA and ECF, for example, a common concept is that of skill, however, its application is different. In ECF, skill is one of the elements that support the existence of a competency, while in SFIA skill is related to a professional area. Also present as central to iCD, the concept of skill is referred as a group of expected functions that the professional performs. Although these frameworks, as mentioned, pertain to the area of IST, the results of the relationship between these frameworks had some commonalities with the structure of broad non-specific frameworks, such as O*NET and ROME.

According to ECF definition, the competency concept can be defined as a demonstrated ability to apply knowledge, skills, and attitudes for achieving observable results. In this definition, some concepts are pointed out that need special attention, such as ability, knowledge, skill, and attitude. The ECF notes that competency is a holistic concept, being related to workplace activities, and incorporating behaviors expressed as embedded attitudes.

In addition to the frameworks mentioned before, we also reviewed the IT2017 (IT2017, 2017) and MSIS2016 (Topi *et al.*, 2017), two curriculum guidelines that provide support in the design of programs at graduate and undergraduate levels for IT and Information Systems (IS), respectively. Building on the concept of competency, both documents lay out professional profiles for the IST area, defining skills, tasks, and levels of difficulty related to the functions performed by IT and IS professionals.

When recurring to some dictionaries, for the term competency or competence, the Oxford (2014) registers "the ability to do something successfully or efficiently", very close to Collins' entry "the ability to do something well or effectively" (Collins Dictionary, 2017), but different from Cambridge's explanation as "an important skill that is needed to do a job" (Cambridge, 2020) or APA's definition of "one's developed repertoire of skills, especially as it is applied to a task or set of tasks" (APA Dictionary, 2018). From the competency frameworks, groups of tasks are assigned to a competency, which can be segregated into abilities, which correspond to different levels of proficiency. These levels of proficiency involve a combination of knowledge and skills that will enable the professional to perform the tasks inherent to its abilities. The analysis of the IST frameworks also suggested that professional practice, regardless of the possession of abilities, is conditioned to the professional's posture, which may be formed by the behavior and disposition elements.

In this work, we consider that competency has two pillars that support it, namely ability and posture. Ability has levels of proficiency, that express the complexity of the knowledge and skill associated to an ability. Since the combination of knowledge and skills indicate a level of complexity for a given ability, there is also the possibility of measuring the complexity to perform a given task, making evident the relevance of the ability element in this competency structure. For each task, there may be a set of tools necessary for its execution. The other pillar that supports competency goes beyond technical factors, addressing personal factors, which are equally relevant to competency. The professional's posture is something that can be identified through attributes and characteristics observed in the work environment, which are the dispositions that, in turn, support the occurrence of certain behaviors by the professional and that enact his/her competency. The definitions proposed for the competency construct and competency-related concepts are now presented, built upon IST and general competency frameworks, as well as entries from dictionaries:

- Competency: [1]It refers to a combination of abilities and postures at the individual level to solve a given task at a specific time. [2]It must be related to a professional area where individuals employ their abilities.

- Ability: [1]It refers to the condition that indicates someone can perform a certain task, having a degree of proficiency in the use of resources, which at the individual level refers to the possession of knowledge and skills. [2]It has great proximity to the definition of a position to be held by a professional.

- Posture: 1Classifier of the recurrent behavior observed in the individual. 2It characterizes the moment when the individual responds to a stimulus received, influenced by his/her disposition in the face of an event, which leads to the execution of specific behaviors.

- Disposition: 1It refers to an inclination or tendency to favor an alternative over other(s), which results in one or more behaviors, supporting an individual's characteristic posture. 2It specifically addresses inclinations, individual preferences.

Table 1. Concepts and Their Relationships with Framework

Concept	Related Concepts	Example
Competency	①Dimension 2	Information Systems and Business Strategy Alignment
	②Category	Strategy and architecture
	④Areas	Business Continuity and Information Assurance
	⑤Career Pathway	Programming and Software Development
	⑥Professional Domain	Études et développement Informatique
	⑦Skill Classification	(Development) System architecting technology
Posture	⑤Work Values	Achievement; Independence
Disposition	⑤Interests	RIASEC
	⑥Personality Type	RIASEC
Behavior	①Behavior	Transforming, making decisions, applying, organizing
Task	③Essential IT Domains	Use a risk management framework
	⑤Tasks	Coordinate installation of a software system
Tool	⑤Tools Used	Computer servers
Ability	②Subcategory	Information strategy
	⑥Occupation	Software Developers
	⑦Skill Item	System development management technology
Proficiency	①Dimension 3	Level 1 – Level 5
	②Levels of responsibility	Follow, Assist, Apply, Enable, Ensure, Initiate, Inspire
	④Levels of competence	Awareness; Novice; Supporting; Independent
	⑦Skills Proficiency	Level 1 – Level 7
Knowledge	①Dimension 4	Business strategy concepts
	⑥Savoirs	Algorithmique
Skill	①Dimension 4	Review and analyze the effects of implementations
	④Foundational Competences	Critical Thinking, Creativity, Leadership
	⑤Skill	Speaking, Coordination, Monitoring, Writing
	⑥Savoir-faire	Installer un équipement informatique
	⑦Skill Item	Software construction technology

- Behavior: [1]It is what can be observed as the result of a stimulus received by the individual, depending on the environment in which he/she is located. [2]It is influenced by the beliefs and experiences that the individual has and contributes to the evolution of knowledge at the individual level. [3]It is the immediate response to a stimulus.

- Task: [1]Something that can be performed by the individual, in fulfilling a demand or attending to the solution of a problem, requiring the use of one or more abilities and one or more postures for its full fulfillment, as expected. It is possible that, for its execution, it is necessary to use one or more tools. [2]It is something that can be fulfilled by employing (posture) the individual's abilities.

- Tool: [1]Auxiliary technological resource that can be used to accomplish a given task. A tool can be involved in different tasks, just as a task can demand different tools for its execution. [2]It is something that can be mobilized during the employment (posture) or ability as a support for the completion of a task.

- Proficiency: [1]It indicates the level by which the individual is trained, considering the resources possessed (knowledge and skills) and the results that can be obtained when putting them into practice (posture). [2]The proficiency of an individual must indicate the result that he/she must deliver when acting professionally.

- Skill: [1]It is one of the elements that make up the ability of the individual and may be carried by the individual's posture (along with knowledge). [2]It refers, in some situations, to the application of knowledge acquired, and in other situations, it refers to the application of natural knowledge, both intending to solve some demand in the professional scope. [3]Some skills support the execution of other skills, that is, one skill may depend on another to be applied. It is important to emphasize that having skills is a necessary condition for the professional to be able to perform tasks.

- Knowledge: [1]It sustains the individual's action in the execution of his/her skills or in the conduct of the professional position he/she holds. [2]It is what can be acquired through experience and study; thus, the sources of knowledge acquisition are the practice of the individual's abilities and the individual's participation in training and qualification courses. [3]It is considered that knowledge is improved through its practice (posture), forming the beginning or basis of an ability formation process. [4]There is knowledge that supports the acquisition of another knowledge. This means that for acquiring some specific knowledge it may be necessary the existence of some previous knowledge.

Table 1 covers the concepts, the framework to which they referred to, and how the concept was addressed in that framework. Frameworks are signaled by numbers, identified as ①ECF, ②SFIA, ③IT2017, ④MSIS2016, ⑤O*NET, ⑥ROME, and ⑦iCD. Analyzing the provisions in Table 1, although we have equivalent examples related to the same concept, having different sources, we note the absence of criteria for its writing. Establishing criteria for writing the attributes that make up the competency construct can provide some advantages, such as classifying the element according to the concept; establishing dependencies between competency attributes, indicating an evolutionary path for the professional, and raising the maturity of a particular professional area.

Considering what has been portrayed regarding the difficulties involved in investigating the subject of competency, and avoiding being limited to an isolated research initiative, a step to standardize the application of competency in future studies on the subject is suggested in this work. This possibility concerns the use of BNF as a resource for the definition of writing standards for the concepts related to the competency construct, such as those present in this subsection, considering their definitions and correspondence with other reviewed frameworks. Next, we provide a brief overview of BNF.

2.3 Backus-Naur Form

BNF is one of the most used methods for writing syntax for context-free grammars (McCracken and Reilly 2003). The origin of the name comes from the creators of BNF, John Backus and Peter Naur. The first incarnation of BNF was used to describe the syntax of the programming language ALGOL 60, in 1960. In the following years, updates to the BNF notation were made.

In this proposal, we will use BNF, because we believe is the form that allows a better understanding of the writing pattern, even for non-IST professionals. According to Sebesta (2011), there are three advantages when opting for the use of BNF: clarity and conciseness of the BNF description; the possibility to use BNF as a basis for a parser; and the BNF-based implementations being relatively easy to maintain due to their modularity. From a standardization point of view, it is desirable that meta-syntaxes, such as BNF and its variants, possess a set of characteristics (ISO, 1996), like: conciseness, precision, formality, naturality, generality, simplicity, self-describing, and linearity. In practical terms, considering BNF as a standard for writing, we can define transparent delimitations and rules, that mitigate the mishmash associated to definitions of competency.

To write a grammar in BNF, one uses the set of symbols from the BNF notation. The symbols needed to understand the competency grammar that will be presented in the next section are now addressed.

The symbols "<" and ">", respectively used before and after a word, define BNF classes, allowing values to be assigned to the class. The value is assigned by using the symbol "=" followed by the value one wants to assign, forming an expression such as: <class> = "xpto".

The symbol "+" serves to complement information that will be assigned to a class, such as: <class> = "xpto" + 123. In this example, "<class>" will have the assigned value "xpto123".

Another important symbol is "|", which is equivalent to the logical operator "or". It means that the <class> may have one or another value, such as: <class> = "xpto" | "123"

When using BNF notation, classes can be assigned to the values of another class. The next example, which contains five lines, consists of a sequence of value assignments. The value that "<mainclass>" may have is either "XPTO" or "xpto" or "1234".

```
<mainclass> = <text> | <number> + "4"
<text> = <capital> | <tiny>
<capital> = "XPTO"
<tiny> = "xpto"
<number> = "123"
```

In BNF notation, there are so-called terminals and non-terminals. Non-terminals will always be between "<" and ">", while terminals are those that never appear on the left side of the "=" symbol.

3. COMPETENCY GRAMMAR

In view of the scenario described for the concept of competency, we propose a BNF grammar that establishes the syntactic rules for writing competencies, as well as the elements that make up its structure. These rules aim to prevent the undisciplined use of competency related concepts, by reducing the variations in the application of these elements and, therefore, heading towards a more mature state in approaching the competency construct. For each component of the construct, a syntax with specific rules to its writing is proposed, so that to maintain and strengthen the writing pattern proposed.

```
<competency> = <expr>
<posture> = <adjective>
<disposition> = <action verb>
<behavior> = <action verb> + <expr>
<ability> = <expr>
<task> = <action verb> + <expr>
<tool> = <expr>
<proficiency> = "1" | "2" | "3" | "4" | "5"
<skill> = <expr>
<knowledge> = <substantive> + <expr>
<expr> = <part> | <expr> + <part>
<part> = <substantive> | <preposition> | <article>
<adjective> = TEXT
<action verb> = TEXT
<substantive> = TEXT
<preposition> = TEXT
<article> = TEXT
```

Figure 1. Syntactic structure of Competency Grammar

The main goal is that different people involved in a professional occupation, such as trainers, contractors, and workers, may "speak the same language". This makes the competency approach more direct, accurate, and independent on interpretations among those involved in the professional environment to determine requirements for a profession or specialty. Once the composition of competency has been defined, a set of specific knowledge and skills is established, which may form the requirements for the professional to exhibit that competency. Through this set of requirements, it is possible to identify the sources that may provide the opportunities for professionals to acquire a certain competency, such as training courses or experiences to which the professionals need to be exposed. The syntactic structure proposed for the way of writing the elements that make up the competency construct is shown in Figure 1.

In order to assist in the classification of the attributes of a professional area according to the structure of the competency construct, we designed an instrument in the form of a decision tree. This instrument starts with a single node (root), dividing into possible results, following a sequence of questions. These questions create branches with possible answers. The tree includes eight questions (Q), positioned in the nodes that build the branch of the decision tree. The initial node corresponds to Q1, while the following decision nodes address the other issues. The branches that connect the nodes carry the values that guide the user of the decision support mechanism, based on the issues present in the internal nodes. These questions lead the user of the decision tree to classify the word or phrase according to the concept under analysis. The paths that lead to the classification of any word or sentence related to the competency construct are shown in Figure 2. The tree also includes brief explanations to the eight questions. The concept of proficiency is not part of the scheme; since it does not have a script that can be interpreted (we propose the scale 1–2–3–4–5 to capture the values of proficiency levels).

When using this instrument to support the classification of a sentence or word that is related to the context of a profession, it is expected that the user will be able to classify it in one of the concepts covered by the competency construct, bearing in mind the definition proposed for the concepts. Afterwards, the sentence formulating the professional attribute must be written according to the proposed BNF rule.

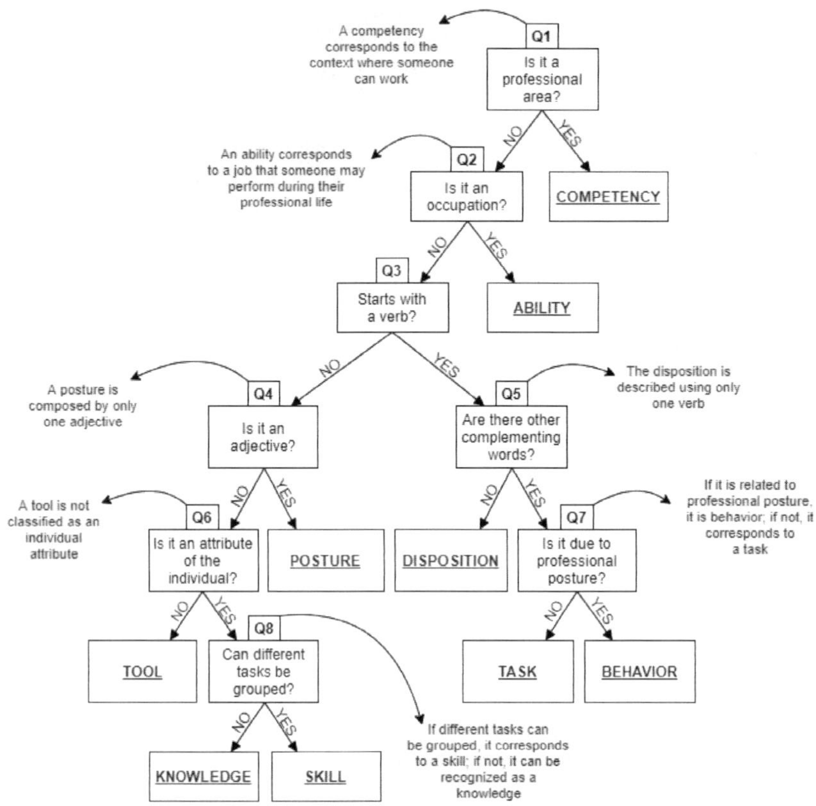

Figure 2. Decision Tree to Concepts Classification

4. VALIDATING THE COMPETENCE GRAMMAR

Seeking to validate the rules of writing the competency related concepts, eight IST professionals of three different abilities ("Software Developer", "Tester", and "Data Engineer") were asked to indicate attributes that they consider necessary in their current occupation, given the demands inherent to the environment in which they operate. The respondents had between five and seven years of experience in the IST job market, attending to the role they currently perform; six (75%) were graduated in Information Systems (Bachelor), and two (25%) were graduated in Computer Engineering (Licensed).

As shown in Table 2, 361 attributes were informed by eight respondents about their professional occupation. After reclassification, changes in writing, identification of duplicates, and the separation of some that added more than one attribute in just one sentence, 273 records remained. Respondents justified such changes, stating they considered behavior to be "behavioral skills". However, the authors argued that considering the existence of the behavior concept in the proposal, the skill concept refers to the means for the application of knowledge, such as system documentation, or functionality implementation, each of which will group a set of associated tasks. At the end of the interviews, after the analysis performed, the respondents reviewed all the records and endorsed the classifications.

Table 2. Synthesis of Collected Data

		Reclassification										
Concept	Collected	Skill	Knowledge	Task	Tool	Posture	Disposition	Behavior	Correct	Repeated	Separated	Final
Skill	62 (17%)		7	13	0	0	0	16	22	6	6	26 (10%)
Knowledge	51 (14%)	3		0	0	0	0	0	46	11	0	43 (16%)
Task	55 (15%)	1	1		0	0	0	1	60	7	5	66 (24%)
Tool	73 (20%)	0	0	0		0	0	0	64	11	0	59 (22%)
Posture	34 (9%)	0	0	0	0		0	0	28	12	0	18 (7%)
Disposition	35 (10%)	0	0	0	0	0		0	29	11	0	18 (7%)
Behavior	51 (14%)	0	0	5	0	0	0		53	14	0	43 (16%)

Considering that the study also looked at frameworks related to other areas of professional activity, the opportunity to test the rules and standards in different areas was seized. Thus, five professionals from other professional areas (Biology, Human Resource Management, Psychology, and Veterinarian) performed the procedure of filling out the forms with attributes inherent to their current professional occupations. Afterwards, a process for the collection, analysis, and validation of data similar to the one applied to IST professionals was conducted. In the end, 184 attributes were obtained, properly classified in the concepts addressed in this work.

5. CONCLUSION & FUTURE WORKS

In an attempt to standardize the approach to the notion of competency and related concepts, some challenges were faced. These challenges, for the most part, related to the perceived low rigor in the application of the concepts. Hence, in an initial phase of this study, adjustments in the definition of the concepts were made by the authors, in an attempt to clarify and support the differentiation of professional attributes among the range of concepts involved.

There is a variety of frameworks related to the theme of competency, specifically focused on IST, which organize professional attributes. This variety may be related to the pace of growth of the IST area, where a myriad of different activity sectors employs IST professionals. Since IST play an important role in all professional areas that require the use of information processing of any nature, IST professionals are required to operate in diverse environments. This gives rise to a number of IST job specificities, according to particular contexts of activity, such as health, logistics, education, government, and business. The pervasiveness of the IST profession and the need to broaden the perspective on competency, justified the analysis of general competency frameworks to find out their approach to the topic of competency, in comparison to the IST frameworks.

However, it is necessary to consider the limitations of this work. One refers to the number of participating IST professionals. Our test sample involved a small group of IST professionals, and we strongly believe that extending the process with different professionals in future works would put the grammar to a stress test, eventually revealing the need for adjustments in the rules of the grammar. A second limitation regards the type of individuals that participated in this study, namely IST professionals. It also makes sense to involve IST recruiters and IST leaders to validate the professional attributes informed by the respondents, making this inquiry a new phase of the grammar validation process. Along the same line, the participation of IST educators and trainers would provide further indications on the validity and usefulness of the grammar. Although laborious, these are essential steps for the refinement of the competency grammar and for increasing the confidence in its practical application.

To improve and supplement the data on IST competencies, structured according to the competency construct and formulate observing the competency grammar, more work is required. Besides enhancing the characterization of the IST competencies versed in this work, there is a need to start collecting and organizing attributes pertaining to other IST competencies. After reaching a certain level of maturity in the description of an IST competency, or even in an ability, it becomes possible to move on to the next stage. This stage would involve the definition of the degree of difficulty of the ability, mapping it to the levels of proficiency proposed in this study, as well as pointing out dependencies between professional attributes. To this end, it is deemed necessary to engage professionals, both to define the degree of difficulty and to point out the dependencies. This work would provide guidance of great relevance for professionals who wish to evolve in their careers.

The generalization of this proposal is envisaged as a future endeavor. The idea is to involve researchers from different professional areas to collaborate in the data collection, analysis, and validation of the process for defining competency profiles, using the same set of rules–the competency grammar–presented in this work.

REFERENCES

APA Dictionary (2018) *Competence*. Available at: http://dictionary.apa.org/competence.

Cambridge (2020) *Competency*. Available at: https://dictionary.cambridge.org/pt/dicionario/ingles/competency.

Collins Dictionary (2017) *Competence*. Available at: https://www.collinsdictionary.com/dictionary/english/competence.

Department of Labor (2020) *O*NET OnLine*. Available at: https://www.onetonline.org/.

ETALAB (2020) *Répertoire Opérationnel des Métiers et des Emplois (ROME) - data.gouv.fr*. Available at: https://www.data.gouv.fr/fr/datasets/repertoire-operationnel-des-metiers-et-des-emplois-rome/.

European Communities (2008) *The European Qualifications Framework for Lifelong Learning (EQF) European Qualifications Framework*. Bruxelas: European Communities.

European Union (2016) *European e-Competence Framework 3.0*. Available at: http://ecompetences.eu/wp-content/uploads/2014/02/User-guide-for-the-application-of-the-e-CF-3.0_CEN_CWA_16234-2_2014.pdf.

Ferrari, A. (2012) *Digital Competence in Practice: An Analysis of Frameworks*.

Hayashiguchi, E., Endou, O. and Impagliazzo, J. (2018) 'The "i Competency Dictionary" Framework for IT Engineering Education', *EDUNINE 2018 - 2nd IEEE World Engineering Education Conference: The Role of Professional Associations in Contemporaneous Engineer Careers, Proceedings*, pp. 1–6.

Holland, J. L. (1997) *Making vocational choices : a theory of vocational personalities and work environments*. 3rd edn. Odessa, FL: Psychological Assessment Resources.

ISO (1996) *ISO/IEC 14977: 1996, Information technology - Syntactic metalanguage - Extended BNF*. Available at: https://www.iso.org/standard/26153.html (Accessed: 13 January 2020).

IT2017 (2017) *Information Technology Curricula 2017: Curriculum Guidelines for Baccalaureate Degree Programs in Information Technology*. Association for Computing Machinery.

Janssen, J. *et al.* (2013) *Experts' views on digital competence: commonalities and differences*.

Oberländer, M., Beinicke, A. and Bipp, T. (2020) 'Digital competencies: A review of the literature and applications in the workplace', *Computers & Education*, 146.

OXFORD (2014) *Competency*. Available at: https://en.oxforddictionaries.com/definition/competency.

Sebesta, R. W. (2011) *Conceitos de Linguagens de Programação*. 9th edn. Edited by Bookman. Porto Alegre.

SFIA Foundation (2015) *SFIA 6 - The complete reference guide*. Available at: http://www.sfia-online.org/en.

SFIA Foundation (2018) *SFIA 7 - The complete reference guide*. Available at: http://www.sfia-online.org/en.

Topi, H. *et al.* (2017) 'MSIS 2016: Global Competency Model for Graduate Degree Programs in Information Systems', *Communications of the Association for Information Systems*, 40(January), p. 117.

VALUE AND BENEFITS OF PROJECT MANAGEMENT CERTIFICATIONS - AN EMPIRICAL ASSESSMENT

Georg Disterer and Andreas Daum
University of Applied Sciences and Arts Hannover, Germany

ABSTRACT

All tasks in project management will continue to gain in importance, while the supply and demand for certifications in project management is large and increasing. This raises the question of value and benefits of certifications in project management. More than 3,600 IPMA-certified project management professionals in Germany were surveyed on this matter. They were asked about what motivations they had in having a certificate in project management. These motivations are compared with the value and benefits that are actually perceived by them years later. As a result, the motivations "personal challenge", "skill improvement", and "professional progress" make significant contributions to the motivation to seek certification. Overall, the participants attach considerable value to their certificates and consider their commitment and effort for certification to be worthwhile. More than 80% of the participants recommend to colleagues to obtain a certificate.

KEYWORDS

Project Management, Certificate, Certification, Value, Benefits, Empirical Study

1. PROJECT MANAGEMENT CERTIFICATION

Defined certification programs have existed in project management for about 40 years. In recent years, the interest in certifications has increased both among people looking for further education and training and among employers looking for qualified personnel. The range of different certificates is growing and certification program providers are expanding their activities to more and more countries. Between the years 2007 and 2017, the number of certificates issued in project management by the world's two leading providers increased approximately tenfold.

As a result, the supply and demand for certifications in project management is significant and on the increase. In general, a number of different benefits are ascribed to certificates; however, a selection of slightly abbreviated titles of relevant research contributions over the past few years indicates that the value and the benefits of certificates in project management or similar fields of work in science and actual practice are being called into question (Catanio et al., 2013; Farashah et al., 2019; Cegielski, 2004; Coes and Schotanus, 2009; Mateyaschuk, 1998; Joseph and Marnewick, 2018):

Effects of Project Management Certification
Exploring the Value of Project Management Certification
Who Values Certification?
Certifications: Who Dares?
Certification Pays Off!
Certification: Do Organisations Get their Money's Worth?

The central assumption regarding the value and the benefits of certifications in project management is that certified persons perform better in project management. However, so far there is only rudimentary evidence which suggests this (Catanio et al., 2013; Farashah et al., 2019; Coes and Schotanus, 2009; Joseph and Marnewick, 2018; Starkweather and Stevenson, 2011; Morris et al., 2006; Crawford, 2005; Fertig, 2009; Costello, 2009; Robin, 2011). A number of substantive and methodological problems make it difficult to prove value and benefits, such as questions like: What is "performance"? How can performance be measured? Similarly, studies have also found that:

„... project performance was not influenced by project management certification presence." (Joseph and Marnewick, 2018)

"… current … certifications are of no value to IT-related projects." (Joseph and Marnewick, 2018)

"… uncertified project managers perform their duties as well as certified project managers." (Catanio, 2013)

Nevertheless, assumptions about the relationship between a person's certification and his or her performance in managing projects are important for employees, employers, providers of training and courses, and professional associations acting as professional organizations. If these assumptions can no longer be defended, then certifications would only be considered as a ticket to enter the labor market for newcomers and would hardly have any effect beyond that (Fertig et al., 2009; Blomquist et al., 2018).

Because of the above-mentioned substantive and methodological problems, a different approach is used here. The aim is to investigate the advantages and disadvantages that people perceive when they obtained a certificate, what motivated them to obtain certification and what benefits they subsequently derived from it. In this way, the perceived value is taken to identify intrinsic and extrinsic motivations that explain why people strive to obtain a certificate in project management.

2. OBJECTIVE OF THE STUDY AND RESEARCH QUESTIONS

The basic tasks of project management, i.e. the planning, management and control of projects, will become even more important in the future (Crawford, 2005; Remer and Ross, 2014; Whitley, 2006; Bredin and Söderlund, 2011; McHugh and Hogan, 2009) because companies will organize work in the future more often in project form in order to be able to cope with rapid change. It has been observed for many years that company environments are becoming more complex and at the same time changed more often. Customer requirements change frequently, processes and workflows are frequently reorganized, stake holder of different requirements have to be considered, the competition between companies is increasing, and the pressure to innovate is growing. That is why it is often necessary to implement change projects. In addition, companies must take into account developments like increasing complexity of supply chains and growing and more extensive use of information technology, which make projects and project management (even) more important.

As a result, continuing education and training in project management will also become more important. The world's two leading providers of certification programs in project management are International Project Management Association (IPMA) and Project Management Institute (PMI). These two providers have issued more than one million certificates worldwide as of 2019, mostly at the respective entry level (Farashah et al., 2019; Blomquist et al., 2018). An increase in these numbers is expected (Farashah et al., 2019; Blomquist et al., 2018; Loufrani-Fedida and Saglietto, 2016).

The key stake holder interested in certification in project management include:

- Employees who acquire knowledge and skills in project management in the course of further education or training programs and who want to receive a certificate to prove knowledge and skills
- Employers who need qualified personnel for their projects. Certifications support in the recruitment process of qualified personnel
- Providers of training programs and training courses in project management that prepare participants for the final assessment. Their business model is based on revenues from participation fees for training courses and examinations
- Professional societies in the function of professional or specialized associations of people professionally interested in project management (such as IPMA or PMI). They organize a professional exchange between the members, define the professional profiles and develop curricula based on current knowledge and methods in project management

The main aim of this study is to analyze how people who have acquired knowledge and skills in project management and have received certifications to prove this, assess the value and benefits of these certificates. Therefore, the perceived value is measured in order to identify fulfillment of intrinsic and extrinsic motivations. There is a variety of motivations, e.g. personal challenge in striving for a professional examination, increase and confirmation of professional knowledge, professional prestige and recognition, opportunities for advancement, access to a broader range of activities, access to more demanding activities, better earning potential, greater job satisfaction. In this respect, the study is based on previous work by other authors (Farashah et al., 2019; Fertig et al., 2009; Blomquist et al., 2018); motivation theory was used as the theoretical basis, in particular self-determination theory (SDT) (Deci et al., 2017).

As a result, the following research questions are addressed: What value is attached to a certification in project management by the people who have obtained one? What personal advantages and disadvantages do they attribute to a certification? The results offer important support to all the above-mentioned groups of interested parties:

- Employees who want to acquire knowledge and skills in project management and receive a certificate as a proof of this. What are their intrinsic and extrinsic motivations?
- Employers who need qualified personnel to carry out projects: How can qualified persons be addressed and motivated?
- Providers of training courses in project management, who, with a better understanding of the motivations, are able to better adapt the contents of the training and to take a more targeted approach.
- Professional associations that build and maintain communities of people interested in project management. Better knowledge of the motivations makes it easier to address interested people.

3. COLLECTION AND RECORDING OF EMPIRICAL DATA

In order to empirically investigate the value and benefits of project management certificates perceived by people who have obtained a certificate, different formulations of value and benefit effects were developed on the basis of the literature. In doing so, it was possible to build on studies that have also examined issues related to certification in project management (Farashah et al., 2019; Blomquist et al., 2018), and other studies that focused on certifications in other professional domains, such as for nurses (Henderson et al., 2019; Ward et al., 2019; Gulick and Halper, 2016; Niebuhr and Biel, 2007; Gaberson et al., 2003; Sechrist et al., 2006) or for human resources professionals (Lester and Dwyer, 2021; Hsu and Yancey, 2015; Putka et al., 2015). All the formulations of the questions – particularly for measuring the value and benefits of certifications – are checked in preliminary investigations and pretests in order to secure that the measures are reasonable and suitable. Suggestions of a number of people who are personally known to one of the authors from training courses and who have taken part in a pilot test were especially helpful.

The research questions were investigated by means of a large-scale survey of professional project manager who had acquired knowledge and skills in training courses and who received a certificate after an assessment. Access to the participations of the study was achieved in cooperation with the support of the professional society German Association for Project Management (GPM), through which all the persons who had received IPMA certificates in project management in Germany between 2011 and 2020 (September) were contacted by e-mail. The survey was conducted in a structured manner and administered using an electronic platform on the WWW. The participants were contacted personally, and their answers were collected, stored and analyzed anonymously, so it is not possible to draw conclusions on individuals.

A total of 3,623 completed questionnaires suitable for evaluation were returned from participants in Germany in the period between November 10 and December 20, 2020. Participants received their certificates in the period from 2011 to 2020. Using 33,304 addresses, 3,623 completed questionnaires results in a response rate of 10.9%. Taking into consideration that many of the participations had received their certificate several years ago, the response rate is high and indicates a high level of interest with the study. The interest is also indicated by the fact that 10% of the participants registered separately to be sent the results.

Additionally, some sociodemographic characteristics of the participants and their job situations are collected and analyzed anonymously. For example, data about the number of years the participants have work experience, the number of days they are working in projects per week, and the type of projects they work in.

At the time of the survey, the 3,623 participants were on average 42 years old; at the time of their certification, they were 39 years old. Of the participants, 31% are women. Participants are individuals with significant work experience: Excluding periods of training/study and taking part-time employment into account on a pro-rata basis, participants have an average of 16 years of professional work experience at the time of the survey, of which they have been working in projects for 11 years. The vast majority of projects the participants have worked are in the realm of software development and implementation, IT concepts, change management and process improvement.

Since experience and competence in project work are of particular importance in this study, the intensity of project work was questioned separately. Figure 1 shows that 78% of the participants were working in projects at least 3 days per week during the past 3 years. 3,016 of the participants (83%) have been in charge of projects or subprojects during the past 3 years.

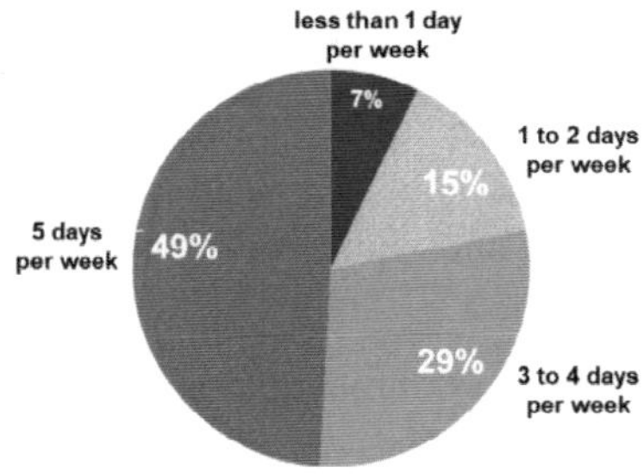

Figure 1. Intensity the participants worked in projects in the past 3 years; source: 3,623 participants

All participants obtained internationally recognized IPMA certificates, 68% of them an entry-level certificate as "Project Management Associate" (Level D), 32% obtained certificates of higher levels like "Level C" through "Level A"; Figure 2. As a result, the participants can be regarded as qualified and experienced project staff. The evaluations of the sociodemographic data as well as the job situations do not show any anomalies.

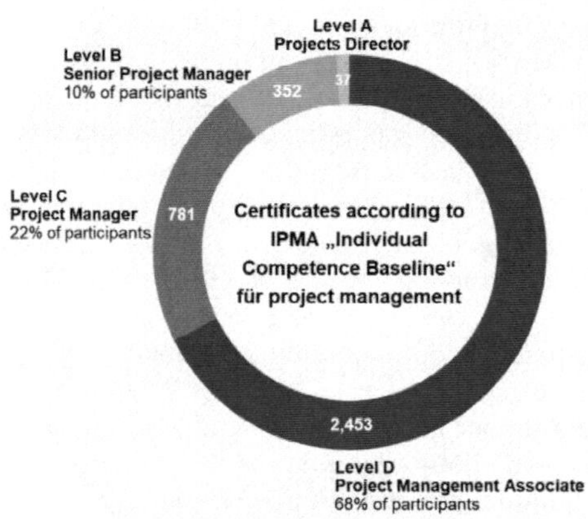

Figure 2. Participants' certificates according to IPMA „Individual Competence Baseline"; source: 3,623 participants

4. MEASURING MOTIVATIONS AND BENEFITS

The survey instruments to measure motivations as well as perceived benefits are tested with explorative factor analyses (maximum likelihood with varimax rotation). In the preparation, Bartlett's chi-square tests for sphericity show that the correlations observed in the sample are significant, i.e. not random. The Kaiser-Meyer-Olkin test procedure for suitability of the data for factor analysis ("Measurement of Sampling Adequacy" MSA) is > 0.7 for the variables, which are considered "fairly good" ("middling") (Backhaus et al., 2018). The details are given in Figure 3, as well as the results for explanatory power and for loading and reliability (Cronbach's alpha), which are to be regarded as "good" according to conventional standards.

	Motivations			Benefits		
	Loading	Cronbach's Alpha	Composite reliability	Loading	Cronbach's Alpha	Composite reliability
personal challenge		0.694	0.660		0.751	0.690
(1)	0.781			0.740		
(2)	0.618			0.711		
skill improvement		0.767	0.737		0.817	0.748
(3)	0.483			0.468		
(4)	0.904			0.929		
(5)	0.667			0.680		
professional network		0.751	0.731		0.807	0.786
(6)	0.652			0.913		
(7)	0.858			0.686		
professional progress		0.825	0.813		0.862	0.836
(8)	0.850			0.869		
(9)	0.721			0.796		
(10)	0.723			0.710		
	KMO = 0.755; Bartlett's test < 0.000; 60.6 % explained variance			KMO = 0.796; Bartlett's test < 0.000; 67.2 % explained variance		

Figure 3. Factor analysis on motivations and benefits

During the course of the factor analyses, some items had to be excluded because they did not show sufficient loading and reliability – see on Figure 4 the final items on motivations - for benefits the items were formulated accordingly and almost identically. As a result, a solution with four factors was determined, since it has suitable results and provides good explanations of the variances in the sample for both motivations and benefits. The items are developed with reference to studies that have also been conducted on certificates in project management (Blomquist et al., 2018) or on certificates in other domains (Henderson et al., 2019; Lester and Dwyer, 2012; Hsu and Yancey, 2015; Putka et al., 2015). The four-factor solution provides a suitable and usable instrument for motivations and perceived benefits. The four factors are named as follows: (1) personal challenge, (2) skill improvement, (3) professional network and (4) professional progress. The factors are identical for motivations and benefits, which allows evaluation and comparison.

personal challenge
(1) Certification is a challenge to me to meet officially recognized requirements of project management.
(2) Certification is a chance to have my skills independently assessed.
skill improvement
(3) Certification is a chance to increase my knowledge and my skills in project management.
(4) Certification is a chance to work more autonomously and independently in projects.
(5) Certification is a chance to take on more demanding and more important activities in projects.
professional network
(6) Certification is a way to network with other project managers.
(7) Certification is a way to meet new people.
professional progress
(8) Certification is a chance to earn a promotion or to improve my career respectively.
(9) Certification is a chance to make more money.
(10) Certification is a chance to become more marketable for other jobs.

Figure 4. Questionnaire items to measure motivations

5. EMPIRICAL FINDINGS

The measurement concept used allows to analyze the motivations of people who want to obtain a certificate in project management and enables to compare and to interpret. The motivation to obtain a certificate is 3.2 for all participants. This result can be broken down into the four explanatory components as shown in Figure 5 (left side). The components "personal challenge", "skill improvement" and "professional progress" clearly contribute positively to motivation. In contrast, an improvement in the "professional network" makes only a minor contribution, i.e. the participants had no great expectations of improving their professional network by obtaining a certificate.

The items of the questionnaire (Figure 4) show that the factors of "personal challenge" and "skill improvement" and "professional network" comprise intrinsic motivations, while the factor "professional progress" describes an extrinsic motivation (Deci et al., 2017; Hsu and Yancey, 2015). Intrinsic motivations stem from inner drive, such as personal interest and enjoyment in a task, from the inner striving for achievement or the realization of one's own ideas as well as personal goals (Deci et al., 2017; Hsu and Yancey, 2015). In this respect, the behavior aims at personal well-being at work as well as the development and expansion of knowledge and skills. In summary, this is also referred to as striving to "be good" (Fertig et al., 2009; Blomquist et al., 2018). In contrast, people act from extrinsic motivations when they hope to gain such advantages as material incentives, promotion, better employment, greater prestige, or recognition and appreciation from their environment (Deci et al., 2017; Hsu and Yancey, 2015). This striving to make a good impression on others is referred to as striving to "look good" (Fertig et al., 2009; Blomquist et al., 2018) and is also considered as "dark side of certification" (Fertig et al., 2009). The context and technical content of project management then plays a minor role; the focus is on those effects that are ignited in the context of "impression management" (Fertig et al., 2009). These effects can lead to improvements of the existing employment relationship or to better chances on the labor market. The "professional progress" factor included in the measurement concept is to be assigned to behavior based on extrinsic motivations (Deci et al., 2017; Hsu and Yancey, 2015).

Overall, the participants assigned a level of 3.2 to motivation in obtaining the certificate (Figure 5). The intrinsic factors of "personal challenge" and "skill improvement" are attributed a positive motivational effect, as is the extrinsic factor of "professional progress", measurement generated by the results of the factor analysis. In contrast, the intrinsic factor of "professional network" has only a minor motivational effect.

The benefits currently perceived by participants as a result of obtaining a certificate is 3.2 and can be broken down into four components as shown in Figure 5 (right). The motivations and expectations of the participants for certificates in project management are actually perceived as benefits, i.e. the expected "personal challenge" is perceived, "skill improvement" is noticeable and "professional progress" is observed. The intensity of these benefit effects with regard to "personal challenge" and "skill improvement" roughly corresponds to the motivations and expectations, while the effects with regard to "professional progress" fall somewhat short. The low expectations regarding the "professional network" tend to be overfulfilled.

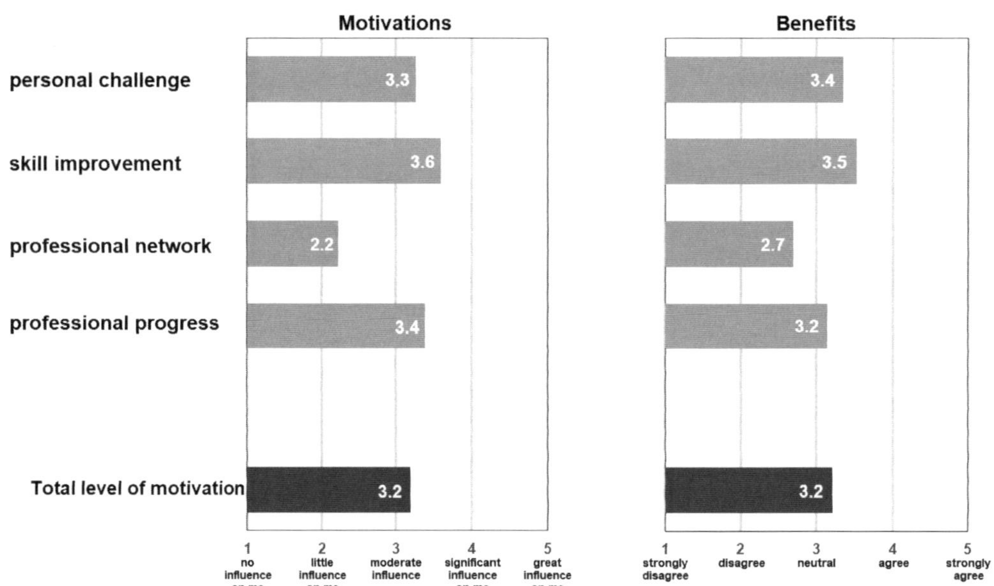

Figure 5. Motivations for and benefits from project management certification; source: 3,521 to 3,545 participants

Studies in other domains indicate that certificates are used to pursue intrinsic rather than extrinsic motivations and corresponding benefits; intrinsic motivations outweigh extrinsic motivations (Hsu and Yancey, 2015). This is not shown by the results on certificates in project management, because the extrinsic motivation factor of "skill improvement" is of high significance. Overall, the motivations – at the time of certification – and the currently perceived benefits are well balanced among the participants. Consequently, they consider their commitment and their efforts in the course of the training and the final certification to be worthwhile.

The participants received their certificates in the period from 2011 to 2020. This enables us to compare whether differences in motivations and perceived benefits have occurred over the years. An analysis of the motivations and benefits does show changes over the years. The motivations of "personal challenge", "skill improvement" and "professional network" have almost the same level, but "professional progress" is a significantly more important motivation for obtaining a certificate for participants with later certificates. In terms of perceived benefits, the explanatory components of "personal challenge", "skill improvement" and "professional progress" play a recognizable and significantly greater role for participants with later certificates.

This development in recent years can be attributed in part to the fact that in mid-2018, GPM adapted its continuing education and training programs as well as assessments for certification to the new version of its standard for individual competence ICB 4 (Individual Competence Baseline, Version 4.0). Certifications are being conducted according to this new training and examination standard from mid-2018 (GPM, 2018).

Because the conversion to ICB 4 were made in the middle of 2018, Figure 6 eliminates participants with certificates from 2018 in order to be able to delineate "before / after" the conversion to ICB 4. Participants with certificates from 2019 and later have significantly higher motivation and perceived benefits than participants from years prior. When surveying motivations for certification, the different time intervals – less than 2 years versus more than 3 years to fill out the questionnaire – can influence participants recall differently. However, memory effects will not play a role in assessing the current benefits of certification. As a result, it can be concluded that the increase in perceived benefits – from 3.16 among participants with certificates through 2017 to 3.30 among participants with certificates beginning from 2019 and later – is also attributable to the interim conversion to ICB 4. This means that the conversion to ICB 4 have increased the perceived benefits among participants to some extent.

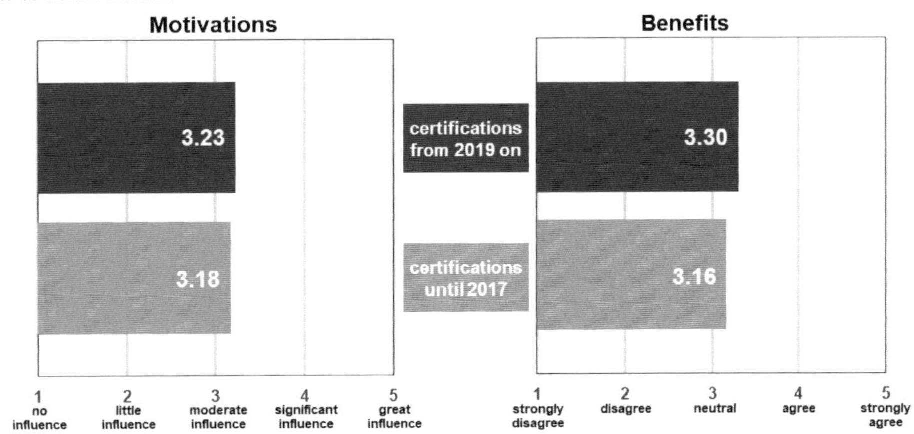

Figure 6. Motivations and benefits over time, source: 1,336 participants until 2017 and 1,606 participants from 2019 on

These findings differ from other studies that, for example, identify a decline in motivation for a certificate in project management with two surveys at the time of 2014 and 2019; concurring that the importance of the "looking good" motivation increases over time (Blomquist et al., 2018).

6. SUMMARY

The supply and demand of advanced training and continuing education in project management, as well as for certificates attesting knowledge and skills, are large and growing. This is because the importance of managing projects will continue to increase. The motivations that lead people to seek a certificate in project management are examined here. These motivations are compared to the benefits these individuals perceive from holding their certificate years later. The study is based on a large-scale, anonymous survey of certified project manager who obtained their IPMA certificates in Germany between 2011 and 2020.

As a result, motivations bundled into "personal challenge", "skill improvement" and "professional progress" make significant contributions strive for a certificate. In contrast, an improvement of the "professional network" makes only a minor contribution. Consequently, the participants had no great expectations that obtaining a certificate would improve their professional network. Years later, the participants did perceive benefits from the certificate, i.e. the expected "personal challenge" was felt, "skill improvement" was noted and "professional progress" was observed. Overall, the motivations existing at the time of certification and the perceived benefits after a few years later are in a balanced relationship. According to this, the participants consider their commitment and effort in the course of further training or education and the final certification to be worthwhile. Complementary to the measurement of perceived benefits, the participants were also whether they would recommend a certification in project management. The question was framed in a job-related and realistic situation of advising a "junior employee with less experience in project management" to strive for a certificate in project management – or not. Well over 80% of the participants would make a recommendation ("definitely yes," or "rather yes"). This result is stable despite all sociodemographic characteristics, such as gender, age, year of certification, only a share of approx. 8% would not recommend a certificate in project management.

Basically, 84% of the participants expressly agree that the content of a certificate includes special knowledge in project management, while just under 5% reject a corresponding statement. At the same time, however, the participants gave quite clear indications that the current topics for certification in project management also has gaps compared with current professional practice in project management. In particular, approaches and methods that are currently labeled "agile" are missing from the range of topics covered by project management certificates. The use of agile approaches and methods is clearly increasing in the professional practice of project management, agility is clearly gaining momentum in project management (Disterer and Daum, 2021). Among participants with profound project experience, only 25% assume that in 3 years projects will continue to be carried out using traditional, classic approaches to project management. In contrast, a very clear majority is convinced that traditional and agile approaches must be combined to form "hybrid" approaches (Disterer and Daum, 2021). Thus, many statements made by participants in the free texts suggest that agile approaches are widespread and that their use is expected to increase in future. Hence, a number of statements on the subject-specific focus of certificates in project management can be bundled into "... not agile enough ..." or "... agility is more important than project management ...". The current roles of the participants in actual practice in project management are more likely to be characterized as "agile coach" or "scrum master" than as "project manager" or "subproject manager", and recertification after the expiration of a certificate is called into question because of a "... lack of consideration of agile approaches ...".

For the providers of certificate schemes, the indications of content-related gaps, which can be outlined using the term "agile", are important indicators of the need for further development of the training programs and assessments. Even for the near future, the participants already expect that agile approaches will have to be used in the majority of projects in order to be able to meet the requirements for flexibility and speed (Disterer and Daum, 2021). As a result, traditional and agile approaches will also have to be combined to form "hybrid" approaches in the certificates for project management. If these content-related gaps are not addressed, the providers of certification schemes run the risk that the central assumption of a positive correlation between a person's certification in project management and actual performance in project management (see Section 1) will be abandoned in the professional community. This would considerably reduce the value of certificates in project management (Fertig et al., 2009; Blomquist et al.; 2018).

The extrinsic motivation of "professional progress" plays an important role for the participants, especially if the certificates were obtained in the recent past. Giving excessive importance to this "impression management" (Fertig et al., 2009) causes the risk that certifications in project management will lose their effectiveness. If "looking good" comes too much to the fore, then certifications will only be seen as a ticket to entry into the job market for junior staff and will hardly develop any effect beyond that (Blomquist et al., 2018).

REFERENCES

Backhaus, K. et al., 2018. *Multivariate Analysemethoden - Eine anwendungsorientierte Einführung*, 3rd ed., Springer, Berlin.

Blomquist, T. et al., 2018. Feeling good, being good and looking good: Motivations for, and benefits from, project management certification. *International Journal of Project Management*, 3, pp. 498-511.

Bredin, K. and Söderlund, J., 2011. The HR quadriad: a framework for the analysis of HRM in project-based organizations. *International Journal of Human Resource Management*, 10, pp. 2202-2221.

Catanio, J. et al., 2013. The Effects of Project Management Certification on the Triple Constraint. *International Journal of Information Technology Project Management*, 4, pp. 93-111.

Cegielski, C. G., 2004. Who Values Technology Certification? *Communications of the ACM*, 10, pp. 193-105.

Coes, G. and Schotanus, K., 2009. Certifications: Who Dares? *IT Professional*, 5, pp. 50-52.

Costello, T., 2009. Certifications: Does the Emperor Have Any Clothes? *IT Professional*, 9, pp. 63-64.

Crawford, L., 2005. Senior management perceptions of project management competence. *International Journal of Project Management*, 1, pp. 7-16.

Deci, E. L. et al., 2017. Self-determination theory in work organizations: the state of a science. *Annual Review of Organizational Psychology and Organizational Behavior*, 1, pp. 19-43.

Disterer, G. and Daum, A., 2021. Agilität nimmt weiter Fahrt auf im Projektmanagement. *Projektmanagement Aktuell*, 2, pp. 52-57.

Farashah, A. et al., 2019. Exploring the value of project management certification in selection/recruiting. *International Journal of Project Management*, 1, pp. 14-26.

Fertig, J. et al., 2019. Building internal motivation for worker competency certifications: a critique and proposal. *Human Resource Development Review*, 2, pp. 197-222.

Gaberson, K. B. et al., 2003. The perceived value of certification by certified perioperative nurses. *Nursing Outlook*, 6, pp. 272-276.

GPM Deutsche Gesellschaft für Projektmanagement (Eds.), 2018. Eine neue Ära in der Projektmanagement-Weiterbildung, www.gpm-ipma.de/weiterbildung/aktuelles/detail/eine_neue_aera_in_der_projektmanagement_weiterbildung.html [15.11.2021].

Gulick, E. E. and Halper, J., 2014. Value, challenges, and satisfaction of certification for multiple sclerosis specialists. *International Journal of MS Care*, 2, pp. 83-90.

Henderson, J. et al., 2019. Perceived Value of Certification - The 2019 ABNS PVCT Study. nursingcertification.org/resources/conference/2019fall/session4.pdf. [15.11.2021].

Hsu, Y. and Yancey, G. B., 2015. The benefits of human resources certification. *Emporia State Research Studies*, 1, pp. 1-10.

Joseph, N. and Marnewick, C., 2018. Investing in project management certification: Do organisations get their money's worth? *Information Technology and Management*, 1, pp. 51-74.

Lester, W. and Dwyer, D. J., 2012. Motivations and benefits for attaining HR certifications. *Career development international*, 7, pp. 584-605.

Loufrani-Fedida, S. and Saglietto, L., 2016. Mechanisms for Managing Competencies in Project-Based Organizations: An Integrative Multilevel Analysis. *Long Range Planning*, 1, pp. 72-89.

Mateyaschuk, J., 1998. Certification Pays Off. *Information Week*, 26.10.1998, p. 110.

McHugh, O. and Hogan, M., 2007. Project Managers - Do They need to be Certified?, in: Barry, C. et al. (Eds.), *Proc. of the 16th Int. Conf. on Information Systems Development*, Springer, Berlin, pp. 795-808.

Morris, P. et al., 2006. Exploring the role of formal bodies of knowledge in defining a profession: the case of project management. *International Journal of Project Management*, 8, pp. 710-721.

Niebuhr, B. and Biel, M., 2007. The value of specialty nursing certification. *Nursing Outlook*, 4, pp. 176-181.

Putka, D. J. et al., 2015. An Evaluation of the Value of HR Certification. HumPRO HR Research Organization (Eds.), Alex.

Remer, D. S. and Ross, E. M., 2014. Review of Project and Engineering Management Certifications Offered by Professional Organizations. *Engineering Management Journal*, 4, pp. 3-12.

Robin, G. J., 2011. Do Companies Look for Education, Certifications or Experience: A Quantitative Analysis. *Proc. of SIGMIS-CPR*, San Antonio (Texas), pp. 1-5.

Sechrist, K. R. et al., 2006. Perceived value of certification among certified, noncertified, and administrative perioperative nurses. *Journal of Professional Nursing*, 4, pp. 242-247.

Starkweather, J. A. and Stevenson, D. H., 2011. PMP Certification as a Core Competency: Necessary But Not Sufficient. *Project Management Journal*, 1, pp. 31-41.

Ward, R. C., et al., 2019. The Perceived Value of Certification in Nonsurgical Pain Management. *American Association of Nurse Anesthetists Journal*, 1, pp. 29-36.

Whitley, R., 2006 Project-based firms: new organizational form or variations on a theme. *Industrial Corporate Change*, 1, pp. 77-99.

CLINICAL PATHWAY – TO FOLLOW OR NOT TO FOLLOW

Päivi Ovaskainen[1], Jouni Alin[2], Seija Arve[1], Reima Suomi[3] and Pirkko Nykänen[4]
[1]*Faculty of Medicine, University of Turku, Finland*
[2]*Deloitte and Touche Limited, Finland*
[3]*Turku School of Economics, University of Turku, Finland*
[4]*Faculty for Information Technology and Communication Sciences, Tampere University, Finland*
Nelson Mandela African Institution of Science and Technology, Tanzania

ABSTRACT

Rationale, aims and objectives: Clinical Pathways are expected to make health care delivery more efficient and effective. Yet we have very little research on how Clinical Pathways are followed. This study assesses the functioning of a Clinical Pathway for elderly people in a Finnish case. At the same time it documents the hardships of getting information on the patient flows in a Clinical Pathway.
Method: The data on all patients aged 75 years or more who had visited the emergency unit of the city hospital in 2006–2008 was collected. The study sample comprised 24,195 admissions. The flow of patients after the first care at the emergency unit was analyzed, collecting data from various scattered sources.
Results: The results show that the planned Patient Pathways seem not to be followed always. Yearly about 17% of the patients were referred to the university hospital, the more expensive care, but about 74% of these referrals did not follow the agreed procedure. The excess costs of referring patients to a non-standard, more expensive Clinical Pathway were 2,57 Million Euros over a period of three years for the studied population of 24,195 admissions, also averaging 106 Euros per admission.
Conclusion: Clinical Pathways were not followed in the case as planned and expected. Reasons for this should be better understood and studied in more depth. In addition, follow-up information of Clinical Pathway flows is often hard to collect because of fragmented information systems, that are not designed to document patient flows in Clinical Pathways.

KEYWORDS

Clinical Pathways, Information Systems, Health Care, Aged Patients

1. INTRODUCTION

Clinical Pathways are tools used to guide evidence-based healthcare that have been implemented internationally since 1980s (Kinsman et al., 2010). Clinical pathways (CPWs) are a common component in the quest to improve the quality of health. CPWs are used to reduce variation, improve quality of care, and maximize the outcomes for specific groups of patients (Lawal et al., 2016) .According to the European Pathway Association (EPA) (2020) "a care (clinical) pathways is a complex intervention for the mutual decision making and organization of care processes for a well-defined group of patients during a well-defined period". It is worth noting that the use of the term "Care Pathway" extends the use of the term "Clinical Pathway" to areas outside core medicine, such as social care.

McGraw-Hill Concise Dictionary of Modern Medicine (McGraw-Hill Concise Dictionary of Modern Medicine, 2002) defines a clinical pathway as "a standardized algorithm of a consensus of the best way to manage a particular condition".

Kinsman & al (2010) found after a literature review five characteristics that are typical for Clinical Pathways: (1) the intervention was a structured multidisciplinary plan of care; (2) the intervention was used to channel the translation of guidelines or evidence into local structures; (3) the intervention detailed the steps in a course of treatment or care in a plan, pathway, algorithm, guideline, protocol or other 'inventory of actions'; (4) the intervention had timeframes or criteria-based progression (that is, steps were taken if designated criteria were met); and (5) the intervention aimed to standardize care for a specific clinical problem, procedure or episode of healthcare in a specific population.

According to EPA (European Pathway Association, 2020) characteristics of care pathways include: (1) An explicit statement of the goals and key elements of care based on evidence, best practice, and patients' expectations and their characteristics; (2) the facilitation of the communication among the team members and with patients and families; (3) the coordination of the care process by coordinating the roles and sequencing the activities of the multidisciplinary care team, patients and their relatives; (4) the documentation, monitoring, and evaluation of variances and outcomes; and (5) the identification of the appropriate resources.

Lawal (2016) found four common definitions for clinical pathways: (1) the intervention was a structured multidisciplinary plan of care; (2) the intervention was used to translate guidelines or evidence into local structures; (3) the intervention detailed the steps in a course of treatment or care in a plan, pathway, algorithm, guideline, protocol or other 'inventory of actions' (i.e. the intervention had time-frames or criteria-based progression); and (4) the intervention aimed to standardize care for a specific population.

Despite the common agreement by both academics and practitioners, it is very common that clinical pathways are not always adhered to. Indeed, there exists doubts about the studies that have documented the (good) effects of Clinical Pathways. El Pax & al (2007) evaluated 115 publications reporting the effects of utilizing Clinical Pathways. They classified just 33 percent of the papers as having good quality, and 67 percent as displaying bad quality. In general it is thought that non-adherence to Clinical Pathways leads to deterioration of case quality: Negative variation in the management of patients with the same clinical condition is frequent, and affects quality of care (Caminiti et al., 2005). Vanhaect & al (2009) found in a self-assessment exercise supported by the Care Process Self Evaluation Tool (CPSET) that care processes supported by Clinical Pathways had the highest CPSET scores, were also self-evaluated by hospitals and their staff as better care processes than the ones for which Clinical Pathways were not defined.

There is a research gap concerning empirical the adherence of medical professionals to defined clinical pathways. Although implementations of clinical pathways have reduced medical errors, lowered costs, and improved patient outcomes, monitoring whether a patient is following the intended pathway is problematic (Konrad et al., 2013). Some results anyway exist. Mohn & al (Moth et al., 2008) studies asthmatic children care pathway adherence in Denmark, and found that care was in accordance with guidelines in all three indicators of quality only in 7% of the Hospital specialists provided care in accordance with guidelines nine times more often compared with GPs, but still only one quarter of these children had pathways in accordance with guidelines. to different care pathways.

Different methods have been proposed to monitor and add to adherence of clinical pathways. Konrad & al (2013) propose the use of HL7 messages to perform monitoring. Maheshwari & al (2019) tested the use of machine intelligence to form patient groups and monitor their Clinical Pathway adherence with good results. Already in year 2006 Vanhaecht & al (2006) found 15 clinical pathway audit tools, and analyzed seven of them in detail. Ovaskainen et al (Ovaskainen, 2005; Ovaskainen et al., 2007; Ovaskainen et al., 2004) found by analyzing CPWs comparisons can be made between medical care at different hospitals, between municipalities and between the expenditure patterns.

This study interrogates adherence to a Clinical Pathway defined for elderly care in a Finnish middle-sized city with 170 000 inhabitants. In addition to finding the the low adherence to the planned Clinical Pathway, it contributes to the understanding of the hardships of distilling Clinical Pathway adherence information from standard patient records. In the case information had to be collected from two separate electronic patient records.

The article unfolds further as follow. In the next section we introduce the study setting in more detail. Then the data collection sources and methods are discussed in more detail. Then the detailed results of our data analysis are discussed. The article ends with conclusions, including assessment of the study and recommendations for further research.

2. STUDY SETTING

2.1 The Clinical Pathway for Elderly Patients

This study was performed to test the adherence to clinical pathway specifications designed for elderly patients arriving to emergency care in City of Turku, Finland (195 500 inhabitants). The study focused on inhabitants aged 75 years or more. In 2006 they numbered 15 196 inhabitants, in 2007 they were 15 381, and in 2008 they were 15 481.

The city has two publicly funded hospitals where patients from emergency care can be further transferred: the university hospital (run by a health district comprising of municipalities in the area) and the city hospital run by city of Turku (Figure 1). The university hospital specializes in treating critically ill patients and the city hospital specializes in general practice and rehabilitation. Both hospitals receive patients directly from home or nursing homes to the emergency unit.

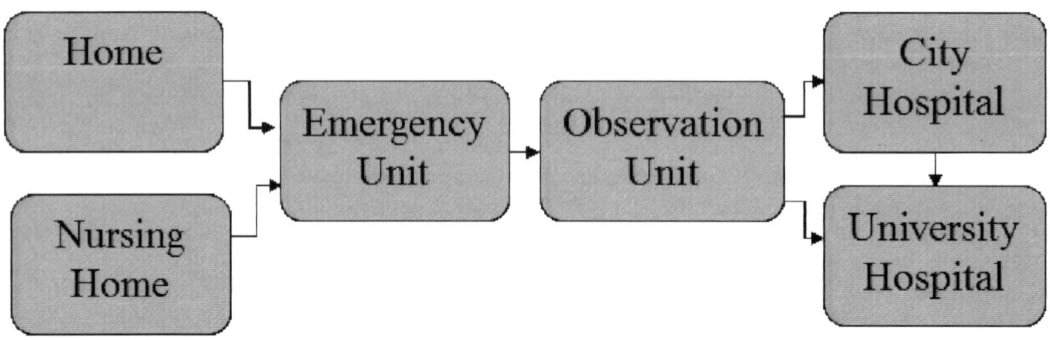

Figure 1. The core patient's pathway from home to emergency department via the observation unit to the city or the university hospital

The hospitals have an agreement that patients with stroke or acute myocardial ischemia or who require surgery are treated at the university hospital, while all other patients are treated at the city hospital, unless their clinical condition demands treatment in the university hospital. Due to cost issues there is a need at the emergency and observation units to be restrictive in sending patients to the university hospital.

The use of different electronic health record systems in the two hospitals, which makes patient transfers and their follow-up difficult. It would be important that the healthcare managers get real-time information about the patients' pathways. They should be provided with visual reports about the financial effects and be alerted immediately if the pathways are not adhered to as planned.

The purpose of this study was to assess the adherence to the clinical pathway designed for the elderly patients coming to emergency care and then needing further care (elderly critical pathway, ECP). Electronic patient record information from both involved hospitals were used for this assessment.

2.2 Data and Methods

The study population consisted of inhabitants in the city of Turku, Finland, aged 75 years or more who visited the health care center or social services in 2006–2008. In total 11 360 persons met the criteria and were selected for observation over the study period. In total 24 195 ECP episodes were recorded for the study during the study time 2006–2008 (Table 1), also 2.13 episodes per patient.

Data was collected from the two different electronic medical record systems (Pegasos® and Miranda®). and inserted to a temporary Research Data Mart (RDM). The RDM contained information on each ECP episode for each individual patient in chronological order. Only the information on complete pathways (i.e., those that ended in patient discharge) was included in the RDM. Information on the incidents was identified from the patient documentation files, and information on waiting list placement for further care place was retrieved from the SAS Pro Consona program.

Statistical analyses and data integration were performed with SAS® software release 9.2 (SAS Institute Inc, Cary, NC, USA). The analysis of referral amounts was based on number of monthly referrals analyzed with a regression model with first-order autoregressive errors.

All data was in operative and transactional form. It consisted of encrypted patient information, and included demographic variables, diagnoses, admission, and discharge information. The data was anonymized after the health care data of two hospitals had been combined with the same algorithms. The following pieces of information were collected of the individuals of the study population: diagnoses, age, gender, and habitation. Additional general background information was also collected: size of the age groups, number of people treated by the home care service, estimated amount and cost of use of health care facilities used. The cost estimate was grouped by year, day and incident. All data of a single pathway was combined using the patient's anonymized identification code and date of admission as key identifiers.

The data from different source systems was first transformed into a common structure by patient and date and then, if available, by date of the assumed logical direction (arrival, health care center emergency unit, university hospital emergency unit, care periods). Timestamp and 'send to / arriving from' information was also used.

Clinical pathways were conformed into ordered and transformed data by applying the following principle. The first pathway starts from the earliest observation of patient data, observations of individual patients from the same date are referred to the same pathway, full care periods in the hospitals are included. Outpatient observations connected with the care periods at the time are connected to the same pathway. The more complete patient flow diagram where also ECP takes place is depicted in Figure 2.

Table 1. ECP episodes per year studied

Year	**Episodes**
2006	7 710
2007	8 014
2008	8 471
Total	24 195

Data was collected from the two different electronic medical record systems (Pegasos® and Miranda®) and inserted to a temporary Research Data Mart (RDM). The RDM contained information on each ECP episode for each individual patient in chronological order. Only the information on complete pathways (i.e., those that ended in patient discharge) was included in the RDM. Information on the incidents was identified from the patient documentation files, and information on waiting list placement for further care place was retrieved from the SAS Pro Consona program.

Statistical analyses and data integration were performed with SAS® software release 9.2 (SAS Institute Inc, Cary, NC, USA). The analysis of referral amounts was based on number of monthly referrals analyzed with a regression model with first-order autoregressive errors.

All data was in operative and transactional form. It consisted of encrypted patient information, and included demographic variables, diagnoses, admission, and discharge information. The data was anonymized after the health care data of two hospitals had been combined with the same algorithms. The following pieces of information were collected of the individuals of the study population: diagnoses, age, gender, and habitation. Additional general background information was also collected: size of the age groups, number of people treated by the home care service, estimated amount and cost of use of health care facilities used. The cost estimate was grouped by year, day and incident. All data of a single pathway was combined using the patient's anonymized identification code and date of admission as key identifiers.

The data from different source systems was first transformed into a common structure by patient and date and then, if available, by date of the assumed logical direction (arrival, health care center emergency unit, university hospital emergency unit, care periods). Timestamp and 'send to / arriving from' information was also used.

Clinical pathways were conformed into ordered and transformed data by applying the following principle. The first pathway starts from the earliest observation of patient data, observations of individual patients from the same date are referred to the same pathway, full care periods in the hospitals are included. Outpatient observations connected with the care periods at the time are connected to the same pathway. The more complete patient flow diagram where also ECP takes place is depicted in Figure 2.

In cases where arrival information was not available it was assumed that it was from "home or home-like conditions" if the departure from the same or a previous pathway of the same patient was "home or home-like conditions". By applying this logic, in cases where departure information was not available it was assumed that it was "home or home-like conditions" if the "arriving from" information was "home or home-like conditions" in the same or next patient flow for the same patient. These two sets of logics where applied to 13 ECP episodes in order to fill data gaps. In this way we established the first arrival and last departure information for each ECP episode.

Cost analysis of different ECP variations was based on selecting the year 2007 as the reference year with the following key indicators:

1. number of pathways episodes
2. percentage of pathways to the university hospital
3. percentage of these without justified diagnosis
4. average number of days spent in the university hospital.

These four figures were retrieved from the RDM and combined with the official population forecasts (Statistics Finland) of elderly people in city of Turku.

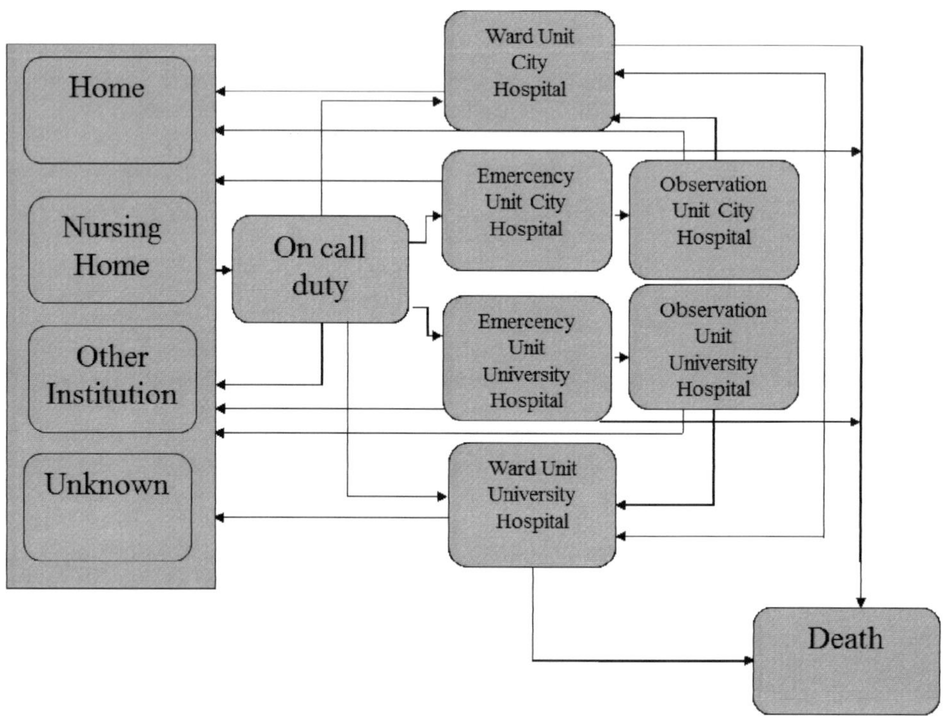

Figure 2. A detailed illustration of possible patient flows in elderly care

3. RESULTS

3.1 Patient Flows

Of the patients who were sent directly from the emergency or observation unit to the university hospital, 29% (2006), 27% (2007), and 22% (2008) had a diagnosis based on an agreement, while 71% (2006), 73% (2007), and 78% (2008) did not (Table 2).

Table 2. Patient pathways from emergency and observation unit to a nursing home, the city hospital, or the university hospital in 2006–2008

Target point after the emergency and the observation unit	Not recorded diagnosis or diagnosis without based on an agreement			The diagnosis based on an agreement			Total number of the pathways		
	2006	2007	2008	2006	2007	2008	2006	2007	2008
Home or nursing home							5055 66%	5172 65%	5545 65%
Turku city hospital	1120	1442	1630	32	47	43	1152 15%	1489 19%	1673 20%
University hospital	1065 71%	992 73%	974 78%	***438 29%***	***361 27%***	***280 22%***	1503 19%	1353 17%	1253 15%
Total	2185	2434	2604	470	408	323	7710 100%	8014 100%	8471 100%

The trend of justified transfers to the university hospital over time is shown in Figure 3. As seen, the proportion of appropriate transfers decreased towards the end of the observation period.

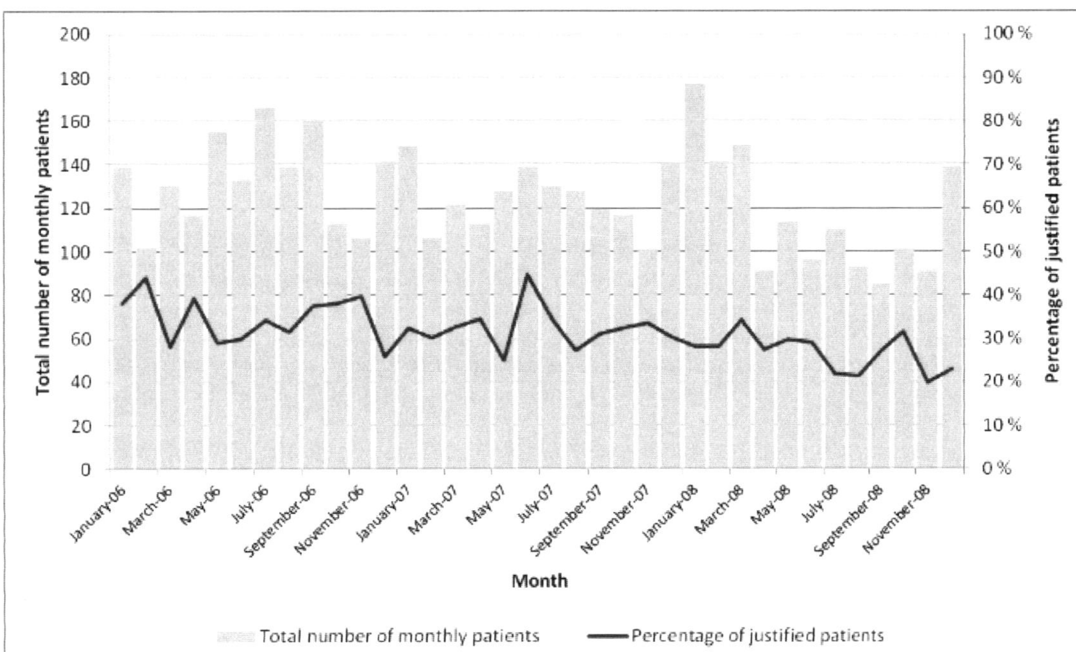

Figure 3. Number of patients directed from the city hospital emergency unit to the university hospital, and percentage of patients with a diagnosis justifying the transfer (black line)

Figure 4 shows the total amount of EPC transfers from City Hospital to University Hospital, and the percentage of transfers that were not having a diagnosis justifying the transfer. Starting from an average of 825 monthly referrals in 2006, there was a decrease to 723 average referrals in 2007 and an increase to an average of 763 monthly referrals in 2008. As it comes to the transfers without a diagnosis, the amount sharply rose during the study period.

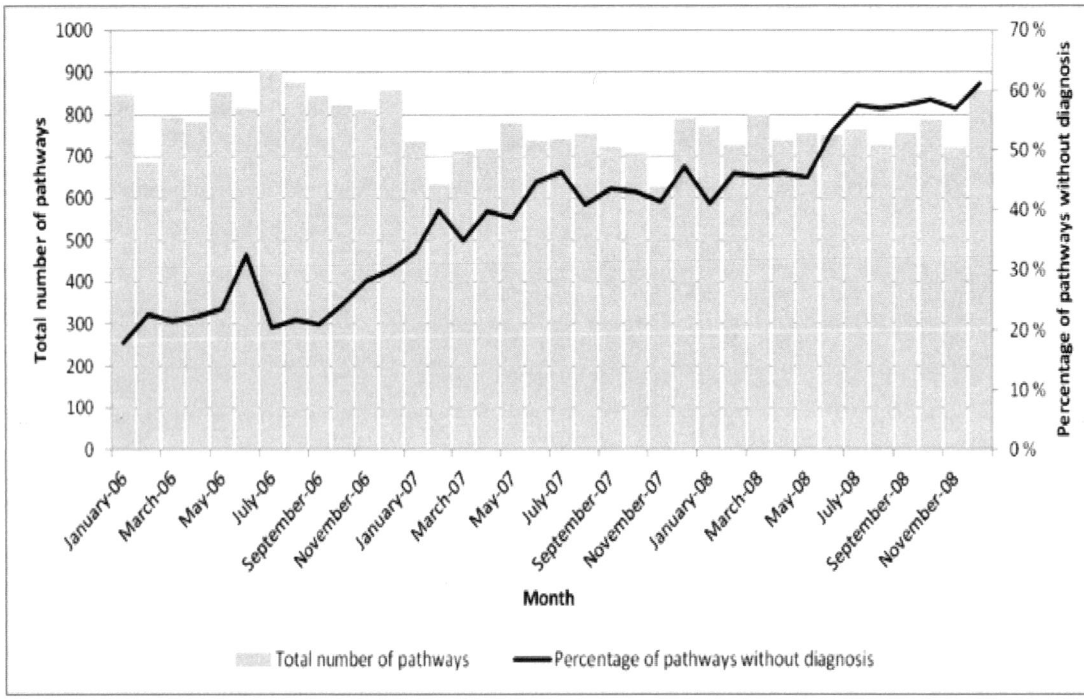

Figure 4. Patient pathways from emergency and observation unit to a nursing home, the city hospital, or the university hospital in 2006–2008, and percentage of patients without a diagnosis justifying the transfer (black line)

3.2 Cost Considerations

The year 2007 was selected as the reference year to provide a forecast platform to evaluate the cost associated with referring patients inappropriately (against the agreement made) to the university hospital. This year represented approximately the median number of inappropriate referrals.

The excess average cost of unjustified acute care is about 180 € per day, since the cost per day of acute care in the university hospital is approximately 500 €, and the corresponding cost in the city hospital or the health care center is 320 €.

The total excess costs were €1.15M in 2006, €0.78M in 2007, and €0.64M in 2008, and the full acute care day costs €13.79M, €11.46M, and €10.34M, respectively (Figure 5). The excess hospital days associated with referring the patients without the proper to the university hospital were on average 5.73 days in 2006, 4.04 days in 2007, and 3.14 days in 2008.

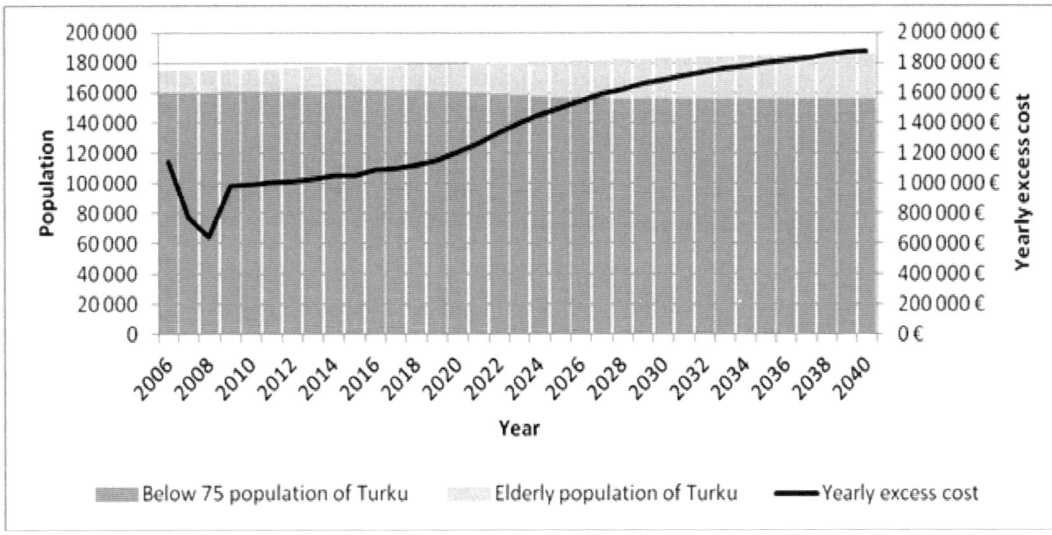

Figure 5. Yearly actual (2006–2008) and forecast (2009–2040) excess cost of the unjustified patient transfers to university hospital in the ECP and the population distribution of Turku

In 2006–2008, the average number of ECP episode with respect to the population size was calculated to be 60%, i.e., approximately 60 ECP episodes a year for every 100 elderly citizens and 6 of them displaying unjustified transfer to the university hospital. The population size was taken from the official statistics and the forecasts of Statistics Finland. Costs were assumed constant. With these assumptions, the estimate graph in Figure 5 was created for the years 2006–2040.

The calculations infer that the saving of taxpayers' money in the city of 175 570 inhabitants would have been at least one million Euros annually, if information about ECP episodes had been recorded and used properly. Upscaling this to the total Finnish population (5,5 million inhabitants) the yearly saving would be at least 35 million Euros.

4. DISCUSSION

In 2006–2008 there was a decreasing overall trend of referring patients to the university hospital but an increasing trend of referring patients based on an agreement between the local hospitals and the university clinic. Still, most of the patients referred to the university hospital did not have a diagnosis as stipulated in the agreement defining the ECP. Such referrals were often followed by further treatment in the city hospital or the health care center.

It was astonishing to see how many patient transfers happened without any diagnosis, this was even a growing trend during our study period. In a busy emergency room or similar setting it is not, understandably, always possible to obtain a full diagnosis, especially if no radiology or laboratory facilities are available. However, a suspected diagnosis should be recorded at the very least. The clinicians must understand the importance of documentation. Ovaskainen et al. studies (Ovaskainen, 2005; Ovaskainen et al., 2007; Ovaskainen et al., 2003; Ovaskainen et al., 2004) suggest that with CPWs may be used as predicting and planning tools as well as financing tools when municipalities and hospitals draw up contracts for health services. If clinical pathway decisions are to be made based on diagnosis (even maybe preliminary), there is little possibility to make clinical pathway decisions in the case of this central piece of information missing. Diagnosis has important implications for patient care, research, and policy. Public policy decisions are often influenced by diagnostic information, such as setting payment policies, resource allocation decisions, and research priorities. (Committee on Diagnostic Error in Health et al., 2015)

There might have been situations where the patient's condition would have demanded care at the university hospital even if the patient had some other condition than the agreed ones, but our data did not allow us to evaluate this. The methods of analyzing narrative text are not very efficient and outside the scope of this research, and hence we had to use the available structured records. One potential discussion item of course is, if the agreement on the pathways is not up-to-date to best medical knowledge, and if there are plenty of other conditions not identified in the agreement that demand university hospital level treatment. The emergence of a multitude of new rare diseases (Groft, 2010) might contribute to this potential conclusion.

Health service planning needs data of high quality. If information is poor or lacking, it is impossible to evaluate the efficacy of treatment and the delivery of health services (Weiskopf et al., 2013; Weiskopf & Weng, 2013). Electronic health records have the potential of improving the efficiency and effectiveness of healthcare delivery. The use of patient data may be used to aggregate data for providing systematic answers to clinical and policy questions (Kuperman, 2011; Reed et al., 2008). Databases may be exploited to improve patient care and for cost-effective operative decision making (Dixon et al., 2013; Kuperman, 2011; Øvretveit et al., 2007). The sharing of information between organizations is particularly important for delivering highly coordinated health care services and for a better understanding of clinical pathways (Cegarra-Navarro & Cepeda-Carrión, 2010). Electronic health records improve the efficiency of making admission decisions and reduce the number of admissions of patients that may be managed in open care (Ben-Assuli et al., 2015).

For analysis of health care processes, the EHRs of different organizations should be synchronized so that the information follows the patient through the whole clinical pathway (Ishikawa et al., 2007). This calls for centralized systems capable of integrating and combining any kind of information in any structured or unstructured format from various different operational systems. Such centralized systems must also be able to take into account the data quality and analyze the combined data in real-time if they are to support timely and proactive decision making and management of the health care processes. At present, we are far from that. However, basic interconnectivity is provided by the national Kanta-service , but the service does not contain all details of care activities. Several systems also have connectivity at a bigger data detail level, but so far, they are rather isolated islands of integration rather than widely available solutions. There are attempts to form one national warehouse, but the quality of the recorded data must improve remarkably before harmonized analyses are possible. The results of this study call for fast development of uniform and compatible information processing systems.

Information about patients' clinical pathways is often lost, unavailable, or unused (Bryan & Boren, 2008). That was also the case in the present study concerning the clinical pathways of the elderly. The health care managers are entitled to demand reliable and relevant information and usable software to support key decision-making. Information technology has great potential for improving the quality of health care data as well as for creating new service innovations.

In order to be able to analyze the health care processes, the electronic patient records of different departments should be synchronized so that the information of the records follows the patient through the whole clinical pathway (Øvretveit et al., 2007). Information on patients in the information systems should be transferred from the home care to hospital care and back again. The responsibility lies with the health care personnel to record the information about the patient in the system, from where it then becomes available for experts, decision makers and everyone in the care process. This means that the patient flow need to be directed according to agreed rules, which take into consideration the resources defined by the taxonomy of care interventions (Ben-Assuli et al., 2015). For this, the management need to construct an information system for the personnel from where to get visual, up to date reports on resources and inpatients, as well as predictive information on future patient volumes (Davenport et al., 2010).

5. CONCLUSIONS

Our study documents that an analysis can be made on the adherence to Clinical Pathways, even in demanding circumstances where data is scattered in different system of rather low quality and data parsing must be done in great amount.

We were able to show that the ECP in city of Turku did not function as planned in years 2006–2008. However, we are not able to witness whether the ECP is designed well or badly, and subsequently whether it is odd or natural that it is not being followed. The difficulty of evaluating a digital pathway is also well documented in (El Baz et al., 2007).

Our study shows the potential for generating substantial savings through alert monitoring of the function of Clinical Pathways. It is also imperative that Clinical Pathways must be evident-based and reflect needs of reality. They cannot be based on local arrangements mainly based on cost considerations. Clinical pathways can never completely catch the complicated reality of human health. The clinical condition of the patient should be the most important argument when referring patients to the appropriate hospital, not financial considerations. This is both humane and at the long term most cost effective.

This analysis was not without limitations. The quality of data is essential if management in health care is to be effective (Weiskopf & Weng, 2013). The quality of data available for this study was moderate, in line with the normal state of the art (Reed et al., 2008). Not all diagnoses were recorded in the electronic medical record systems. In many cases, the only diagnosis recorded by the attending physician was a diagnosis of 'observation for suspected disease or condition', not a complete final diagnosis. Securing that the identified EPC episodes were complete and contained all stages of care was challenging. The financial calculations have to be made based on simplified average assumptions: in real life ECP episodes take many and complicated ways, resulting in many unforeseen costs. It is most likely that our calculations of possible savings are rather moderate. Unfortunately, there are no common agreed nor fixed standards for health economic analysis covering the multiple dimensions of health care, and considering the limited capacity of related information technology to document the reality (Luzi et al., 2016).

The digital health care institutions which belong to the digital public health service are more cost-efficient than the earlier traditional hospitals and health care centers and they aim at the better exactness and to capacity in the health care processes and in the diagnosing of illnesses. The digital hospital environment utilises digital electronic health records which are one, it the most central functions. This study shows that the data from two hospitals with different patient data systems can be combined due to the national harmonized data model for patient documentation. Both hospitals have made the huge investments in electronic health records. As technology continues to upgrade in this digital landscape, most hospitals and other healthcare providers of various sizes have invested a lot of time and money in boosting operational efficiencies while minimizing costs. For all these reasons, Enterprise Resource Planning technology (ERP) has come into play.

REFERENCES

Ben-Assuli, O., Shabtai, I., & Leshno, M. (2015). Using electronic health record systems to optimize admission decisions: The Creatinine case study. *Health informatics journal, 21*(1), 73-88.

Bryan, C., & Boren, S. (2008). The use and effectiveness of electronic clinical decision support tools in the ambulatory/primary care setting: a systematic review of the literature. *Journal of Innovation in Health Informatics, 16*(2), 79-91.

Caminiti, C., Scoditti, U., Diodati, F., & Passalacqua, R. (2005, Sep 19). How to promote, improve and test adherence to scientific evidence in clinical practice. *BMC Health Serv Res, 5*. https://doi.org/10.1186/1472-6963-5-62

Cegarra-Navarro, J. G., & Cepeda-Carrión, G. (2010). How to implement a knowledge management program in hospital-in-the-home units. *Leadership in Health Services, 23*(1), 46-56.

Committee on Diagnostic Error in Health, C., Board on Health Care, S., Institute of, M., The National Academies of Sciences, E., & Medicine. (2015). In E. P. Balogh, B. T. Miller, & J. R. Ball (Eds.), *Improving Diagnosis in Health Care*. National Academies Press (US). https://doi.org/10.17226/21794

Davenport, T. H., Harris, J. G., & Morison, R. (2010). *Analytics at work: Smarter decisions, better results*. Harvard Business Press.

Dixon, B. E., Siegel, J. A., Oemig, T. V., & Grannis, S. J. (2013). Electronic health information quality challenges and interventions to improve public health surveillance data and practice. *Public Health Reports, 128*(6), 546-553.

El Baz, N., Middel, B., van Dijk, J. P., Oosterhof, A., Boonstra, P. W., & Reijneveld, S. A. (2007, Dec). Are the outcomes of clinical pathways evidence-based? A critical appraisal of clinical pathway evaluation research. *J Eval Clin Pract, 13*(6), 920-929. https://doi.org/10.1111/j.1365-2753.2006.00774.x

European Pathway Association. (2020). *Care pathways*. Retrieved 20.2.2020 from http://e-p-a.org/care-pathways/

Groft, S. C. (2010). Rare diseases-avoiding misperceptions and establishing realities: the need for reliable epidemiological data. *Advances in experimental medicine and biology, 686*, 3-14.

Ishikawa, K., Ohmichi, H., Umesato, Y., Terasaki, H., Tsukuma, H., Iwata, N., Tanaka, T., Kawamura, A., Sakata, K., & Sainohara, T. (2007). The guideline of the personal health data structure to secure safety healthcare: The balance between use and protection to satisfy the patients' needs. *International Journal of Medical Informatics, 76*(5-6), 412-418.

Kinsman, L., Rotter, T., James, E., Snow, P., & Willis, J. (2010). What is a clinical pathway? Development of a definition to inform the debate. *Bmc Medicine, 8*(1), 31.

Konrad, R., Tulu, B., & Lawley, M. (2013). Monitoring adherence to evidence-based practices: a method to utilize HL7 messages from hospital information systems. *Appl Clin Inform, 4*(1), 126-143. https://doi.org/10.4338/ACI-2012-06-RA-0026

Kuperman, G. J. (2011). Health-information exchange: why are we doing it, and what are we doing? *Journal of the American Medical Informatics Association, 18*(5), 678-682.

Lawal, A. K., Rotter, T., Kinsman, L., Machotta, A., Ronellenfitsch, U., Scott, S. D., Goodridge, D., Plishka, C., & Groot, G. (2016). What is a clinical pathway? Refinement of an operational definition to identify clinical pathway studies for a Cochrane systematic review. *Bmc Medicine, 14*(1), 35.

Luzi, D., Pecorado, F., & Tampuris, O. (2016). Economic evaluation of health IT. In E. Ammerwerth & M. Rigby (Eds.), *Evidence-based Health Informatics* (pp. 165-180). IOS Press.

Maheshwari, K., Cywinski, J., Mathur, P., Cummings, K. C., 3rd, Avitsian, R., Crone, T., Liska, D., Campion, F. X., Ruetzler, K., & Kurz, A. (2019, Aug). Identify and monitor clinical variation using machine intelligence: a pilot in colorectal surgery. *J Clin Monit Comput, 33*(4), 725-731. https://doi.org/10.1007/s10877-018-0200-x

McGraw-Hill Concise Dictionary of Modern Medicine. (2002). The McGraw-Hill Companies, Inc.

Moth, G., Schiotz, P. O., & Vedsted, P. (2008, Jun 12). A Danish population-based cohort study of newly diagnosed asthmatic children's care pathway - adherence to guidelines. *BMC Health Serv Res, 8*, 130. https://doi.org/10.1186/1472-6963-8-130

Ovaskainen, P. (2005). *Follow-up of utilisation and prediction of primary health care and hos-pital care from the municipality point of view* University of Turku]. Turku.

Ovaskainen, P., Rautava, P., Ojanlatva, A., & Kortekanga, s. P. (2007). Health care planning in Finland using databases. *Futura, 26*(2), 67-77.

Ovaskainen, P., Rautava, P., Ojanlatva, A., Päkkilä, J., & Päivärinta, R. (2003). Analysis of primary health care utilisation in south-western Finland—a tool for management. *Health Policy, 66*(3), 229-238.

Ovaskainen, P., Rautava, P., Ojanlatva, A., Päkkilä, J., & Päivärinta, R. (2004). Analysing the use of hospital care services in Finland. *The International journal of health planning and management, 19*(3), 287-297.

Reed, V., Schifferdecker, K., & Homa, K. (2008). Improving information management in primary care: the proof is in the pudding. *Journal of Innovation in Health Informatics, 16*(3), 213-220.

Vanhaecht, K., De Witte, K., Panella, M., & Sermeus, W. (2009, Oct). Do pathways lead to better organized care processes? *J Eval Clin Pract, 15*(5), 782-788. https://doi.org/10.1111/j.1365-2753.2008.01068.x

Vanhaecht, K., Witte, K. D., Depreitere, R., & Sermeus, W. (2006). Clinical pathway audit tools: a systematic review. *Journal of nursing management, 14*(7), 529-537.

Weiskopf, N. G., Hripcsak, G., Swaminathan, S., & Weng, C. (2013). Defining and measuring completeness of electronic health records for secondary use. *Journal of biomedical informatics, 46*(5), 830-836.

Weiskopf, N. G., & Weng, C. (2013). Methods and dimensions of electronic health record data quality assessment: enabling reuse for clinical research. *Journal of the American Medical Informatics Association, 20*(1), 144-151.

Øvretveit, J., Scott, T., Rundall, T. G., Shortell, S. M., & Brommels, M. (2007). Improving quality through effective implementation of information technology in healthcare. *International Journal for Quality in Health Care, 19*(5), 259-266.

RESEARCH ON THE WILLINGNESS OF USERS' PRIVACY CONCERNS TO USE EPIDEMIC PREVENTION TECHNOLOGY UNDER THE BACKGROUND OF THE NEW CORONAVIRUS EPIDEMIC

Chensang Ye, Jinjing Yang, Miaomiao Zheng and Cong Cao*
School of Management, Zhejiang University of Technology
288 Liuhe Road, Xihu District, Hangzhou City, Zhejiang Province, China
**Corresponding author*

ABSTRACT

Nowadays, governments worldwide use artificial intelligence (AI), big data, cloud computing, and other technologies to control the spread of the epidemic. These measures significantly improve the efficiency of virus tracking. Nevertheless, such digital defences have also raised concerns about privacy leaks. Privacy concerns and use intention have been studied in several areas in the existing literature, but few have been explored in-depth based on epidemic prevention. Therefore, this paper focuses on the background of the novel coronavirus epidemic and constructs a structural equation model based on the theory of privacy concern and technology acceptance model. The research studies the influence of privacy concerns, perceived risk, and other factors on users' willingness to use new technologies. Based on 132 samples, the results show that privacy concerns significantly impact perceived risk. Perceived trust has significant positive impacts on self-disclosure intention. This study discusses individual self-disclosure intention in the field of public security from multiple perspectives. The research results extend the relevant theories on adopting and using emerging technologies. This study provides ideas on how to alleviate residents' privacy concerns in practice and helps government departments to carry out better prevention work.

KEYWORDS

Epidemic Prevention Technology, Privacy Concerns, Self-Disclosure Intention, Use Intention, Structural Equation Model

1. INTRODUCTION

Since the novel coronavirus epidemic (COVID-19) in 2019, governments have effectively improved the efficiency of epidemic monitoring and virus tracking with artificial intelligence (AI), big data, and cloud computing. However, related digital epidemic prevention measures have also attracted people's privacy. The risk of privacy disclosure affects users' willingness to use epidemic prevention technology and hinders the implementation of government epidemic prevention measures. From the perspective of privacy concern and privacy perception, some scholars have studied users' willingness to use in e-commerce (Gefen et al., 2003), mobile medical (Guo et al., 2016), and mobile social (Chang et al., 2016) to explore the key factors affecting use intention. Although there are many studies on use intention from the perspective of privacy, few studies are deeply explored in new epidemic prevention technologies. Information asymmetry and peer pressure in the context of the novel coronavirus epidemic make users' privacy sensitivity and privacy perception different. For example, user privacy sensitivity may change due to the epidemic environment and legal policy (Koohikamali et al., 2019).

Therefore, this paper will focus on the background of the COVID-19 combined with theories such as privacy concerns and the technology acceptance model. This paper constructs a user intention model of epidemic prevention technology driven by privacy concerns. This study discusses self-disclosure intention in specific public safety and health fields from the perspectives of risk, benefit, trust, and control. The findings extend theories related to the adoption and use of emerging technologies. This study provides practical ideas on how developers of epidemic prevention technology can alleviate residents' privacy concerns and help government departments to carry out their epidemic prevention work better.

The paper describes the current state of digital prevention of governments and then reviews the relevant research on privacy theory and the influencing factors of new technologies' use intention. We set out the relevant assumptions in section 3. We constructed a research model and conducted an empirical study on the effect of privacy concerns on use intention through questionnaire analysis. The paper concludes with a discussion of the contributions and limitations of the study and future research directions.

2. LITERATURE REVIEW

Information Privacy is the ability of an individual or group to control the circumstances, persons or systems that can collect and disseminate information about themselves (Burgoon et al., 1989). Scholars argue that information privacy refers to the right of individuals to autonomously determine the time, scope, means, and extent of the dissemination of private information (Awad and Krishnan, 2006, Culnan and Bies, 2003, Jiang et al., 2013). People can judge whether their privacy has been violated based on their own experience and take appropriate measures to protect their privacy. Privacy concerns are one of the core concepts in information privacy. In the online environment, privacy concerns refer to consumers' voluntary or unconscious disclosure of personal information to websites, triggering consumers' concerns about the loss of privacy (Dinev and Hart, 2005). Related scholars have demonstrated that privacy concerns are a crucial factor influencing trust and willingness to disclose personal information (Bansal et al., 2016). Based on previous studies, some scholars have further demonstrated that a higher level of privacy concerns can significantly reduce the willingness to share personal information and knowledge (Baruh et al., 2017). Based on privacy concerns studies, scholars have also proposed the concept of privacy sensitivity. Consumer data privacy sensitivity refers to consumers' perceptions of the potential harm caused by their data being used by others or organizations in various ways (Martin et al., 2017). Different consumers have different privacy sensitivities. Consumers with high privacy sensitivity are more likely to perceive privacy security problems. Therefore, they are unwilling to expose more information further. They even take privacy protection measures and defensive behaviour out of privacy concerns (Lwin et al., 2016). Consumers with low privacy sensitivity cannot easily perceive personal privacy security issues, so they do not care whether to expose information.

Davis (1989) proposed the Technology Acceptance Model (TAM), which mainly includes a series of external variables, perceived usefulness, perceived ease of use, attitude, use intention, and actual use. The use intention is the focus of TAM research, which plays an essential role in the actual use of users. Generally speaking, the higher the use intention is, the more likely it is to prompt consumers to use new technologies. Scholars have conducted various analyses on the influencing factors of use intention and found more influencing factors. Turel (2015) shows that satisfaction with hedonic information systems affects the formation of habits and confirms that personal habits are negatively correlated with non-sustainable use intention. However, habits can also promote individual addiction to the system, resulting in guilt and reducing use intention (Turel, 2015). Scholars also found that users' perceived value and satisfaction will directly affect users' behaviour intention (Chen and Lin, 2015). In addition, switching costs significantly impact switching intentions (Quoquab et al., 2018).

Scholars have gradually studied how privacy concerns affect use intention in recent years. However, these studies still have many limitations. On the one hand, based on privacy concerns, scholars mainly study use intention in e-commerce, online reading, social media, and other fields. There is a lack of research on individual privacy in public safety and health. On the other hand, scholars are not deep enough about how privacy concerns affect intention. In the context of the electronic society, an in-depth discussion of privacy concerns is of great significance to the study of use intention. Therefore, this study will construct the structural equation model (SEM) under the guidance of TAM. The impacts of risks, benefits, security, trust, and control on individuals' willingness to disclose information in specific public security and health fields are discussed from multiple perspectives. This study can further expand the relevant theories on adopting and using emerging technologies and put forward social suggestions.

3. THEORETICAL BACKGROUND AND HYPOTHESES

Users will measure their willingness to use a new technology based on the perceived trust, risks, benefits, information control, and other privacy factors. Users with high privacy concerns are more sensitive. When disclosing personal information, they will consider privacy security issues and may have negative emotions such as anxiety and suspicion. Privacy-sensitive users tend to protect personal data due to privacy risks (Kruikemeier et al., 2020). Trust in this study refers to the user's trust in the effect of new technologies and privacy. The user believes that the collected information is strictly confidential and helps improve the effect of epidemic prevention. Some studies suggest that although mobile health apps require users to provide sensitive information such as personal medical history, users will not produce resistance despite high privacy concerns. That is because users trust the app (Chen et al., 2018). Perceived benefits are the benefits that individuals expect to receive in exchange for the private information they provide (Jiang et al., 2013). The higher the user's privacy concerns, the stronger the effect of perceived usefulness on their willingness to use social networks (Tan et al., 2012). Perceived privacy control reflects the user's grasp of the privacy boundary. When users are unwilling to disclose privacy, they often think that they cannot control personal information. Based on this, we propose the following hypothesis:

H1a: *Privacy concerns have a significant positive effect on perceived risk.*

H1b: *Privacy concerns have a significant adverse effect on perceived trust.*

H1c: *Privacy concerns have a significant adverse effect on perceived benefits.*

H1d: *Privacy concerns have a significant positive effect on perceived privacy control.*

Privacy disclosure refers to the intentional or voluntary disclosure of personal information in interpersonal relationships (Lowry et al., 2011). Studies have shown that the perceived privacy risk of mobile location App users negatively affects their willingness to use mobile location Apps (Wang and Lin, 2017). Perceived privacy risk reflects users' concerns about their information security. When users worry that their personal information will be abused, they will intentionally reduce the disclosure of personal information. Thus, it is hypothesized that:

H2: *Perceived risk has a significant negative effect on self-disclosure intention.*

Trust is an essential condition for disclosure. In the experimental study of clinical patients, it was found that patients' trust in clinicians was proportional to their willingness to share personal health information (Teixeira et al., 2011). Trust leads users to believe in the benefits of new technologies and be more willing to use them, thereby facilitating user privacy disclosure. Therefore, the following hypothesis is proposed:

H3: *Perceived trust has a significant positive effect on self-disclosure intention.*

Privacy computing theory suggests that users calculate their risks and benefits when deciding whether to expose their private information, leading to a privacy paradox. Although users are concerned about their privacy risks when the perceived benefits are high, the privacy disclosure is also enhanced (Awad and Krishnan, 2006). According to the exchange theory, privacy computing can be interpreted as exchanging personal privacy information for high-quality services (Culnan and Bies, 2003). If the theory is applied to the epidemic prevention technology, the user's willingness to disclose information is in exchange for protecting public safety. Hence, we propose the following hypothesis:

H4: *Perceived benefits have a significant positive effect on self-disclosure intention.*

Users' attitudes are affected when perceived privacy risks exceed their control. If the new technology collects and uses data more transparently, it can improve user perception of information control (Wang et al., 2016). Users often feel they have better control over their private information and are more willing to disclose personal information if they are fully informed of what the information will be used for. Therefore:

H5: *Perceived privacy control has a significant positive effect on self-disclosure intention.*

Relevant studies have found that consumers are willing to disclose privacy, such as personal information and behavioural preferences, to obtain emotional support or decision-making advice from other users (Ooi et al., 2018). Studies have also suggested that since users see travel websites as valuable tools, they are willing to consistently create travel-related posts despite their privacy concerns (Lee and Cranage, 2011). This phenomenon also exists in the use of epidemic prevention technology. When users use new epidemic prevention technologies, they inevitably need to reveal their health status and other information for public safety and self-health, but this usually does not prevent users from using the technology. Hence:

H6: *Self-disclosure intention has a significant positive effect on use intention.*

Users' willingness to use epidemic prevention technology under the background of the novel coronavirus epidemic may be affected by many factors. This study mainly focuses on the mediating effect of perceived risk, perceived trust, perceived benefits, perceived privacy control, and self-disclosure willingness on the relationship between user privacy concerns and willingness to use new technologies. To further understand the internal influence mechanism of privacy concerns on the willingness to use new technologies. Therefore, this study uses TAM. The model considers that system use is determined by an intention to use, and behavioural intention is determined by attitude to use and perceived usefulness. Therefore, the model of user privacy concerns on the willingness to use epidemic prevention technology' constructed in this paper is shown below. Privacy concern, perceived risk, perceived trust, perceived benefits, perceived privacy control, and self-disclosure intention are the variables of user attitude. This paper studies the impact of these factors on users' willingness to use new technologies.

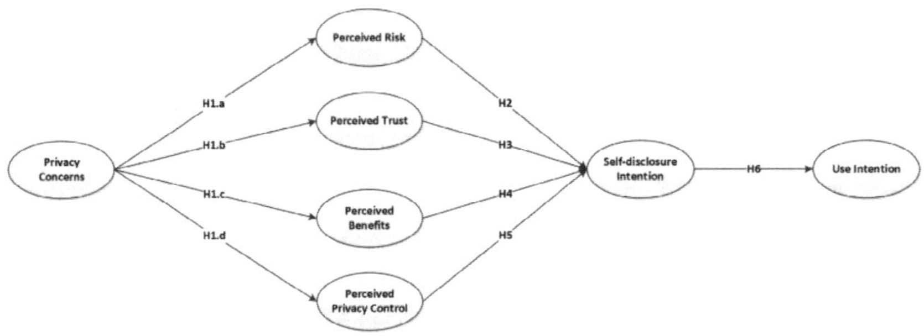

Figure 1. Research Model

4. RESEARCH METHODOLOGY AND DATA ANALYSIS

4.1 Research Method

The online questionnaire was conducted for data collection in this study, and 171 sample data were recovered. Excluding invalid samples due to too short answer data and excessive topic answers, the effective samples were 132. The partial least squares structural equation modelling (PLS-SEM) has good explanatory power in the case of a small sample size. It also does not require the normal data distribution, so this approach is utilised to test the research model and hypotheses proposed herein. This study used the SmartPLS 3.3.3 software to test the data reliability and validity.

The demographic characteristics of respondents to the questionnaire are shown in the following. The male sample reached 79, accounting for 59.8%, and 53 of the women sample. The age distribution of samples varied significantly: 18 to 25 years, 44.7%, 25.8% from 26 to 30, 15.9% from 31 to 35, 9.85% from 36 to 40, and over 40 is 3.79%.

4.2 Measurement Model

In this study, Cronbach's alpha was used for the reliability test of the scale data. Cronbach's α (CA) is the most widely used reliability test. When this coefficient is greater than 0.6, the internal consistency between the scale observations and the classification variables is higher, the higher reliability. The reliability test results in Table 1 show that all Cronbach's α are greater than 0.8, which shows that the measurement model has good reliability.

Table 1. The Descriptive Statistics for the Constructs

	CA	CR	AVE
Use Intention (Inte)	0.939	0.961	0.892
Self-disclosure Intention (Self)	0.942	0.958	0.852
Perceived Risk (Risk)	0.906	0.942	0.843
Perceived Trust (Trus)	0.886	0.929	0.815
Perceived Benefits (Bene)	0.889	0.931	0.818
Perceived Privacy Control (Priv)	0.978	0.985	0.957
Privacy Concerns (Conc)	0.931	0.956	0.878

The validity test, used to measure the actual measurement degree of the classified variables, is mainly divided into convergence validity test and discrimination validity test. Usually, the results of integrated Loading, Composite Reliability (CR), Average Variance Extracted (AVE) to evaluate the convergence validity. The data is generally considered more reliable when CR is greater than 0.7 and AVE is greater than 0.5. Furthermore, the square root of AVE shall be larger than the correlation coefficient of other latent variables. As shown in Table 1, Table 2 and Table 3, the loading of the measurement model is above 0.800, CR is greater than 0.9, and AVE and its square root also fully meet the requirements. It shows that the measured variables can well explain the latent variables.

Table 2. The Factor Loadings and Cross Loadings

	Inte	Self	Risk	Trus	Bene	Priv	Conc
Inte.1	**0.949**	0.666	-0.291	0.821	-0.035	-0.579	-0.388
Inte.2	**0.958**	0.693	-0.407	0.829	0.046	-0.479	-0.427
Inte.3	**0.926**	0.644	-0.314	0.758	0.064	-0.505	-0.358
Self.1	0.684	**0.939**	-0.319	0.760	0.303	-0.065	-0.200
Self.2	0.655	**0.913**	-0.304	0.718	0.310	-0.088	-0.150
Self.3	0.661	**0.921**	-0.360	0.735	0.327	-0.074	-0.194
Self.4	0.609	**0.920**	-0.405	0.721	0.349	0.055	-0.145
Risk.1	-0.351	-0.358	**0.932**	-0.420	-0.182	-0.205	0.357
Risk.2	-0.356	-0.341	**0.945**	-0.389	-0.156	-0.265	0.382
Risk.3	-0.275	-0.334	**0.876**	-0.381	-0.233	-0.250	0.308
Trus.1	0.851	0.792	-0.390	**0.941**	0.063	-0.340	-0.211
Trus.2	0.698	0.636	-0.398	**0.859**	0.066	-0.236	-0.232
Trus.3	0.744	0.714	-0.386	**0.905**	0.126	-0.303	-0.198
Bene.1	0.008	0.320	-0.221	0.080	**0.932**	0.164	-0.042
Bene.2	0.052	0.336	-0.189	0.126	**0.876**	0.146	-0.005
Bene.3	0.009	0.286	-0.144	0.043	**0.905**	0.125	-0.078
Priv.1	-0.569	-0.072	-0.235	-0.343	0.158	**0.980**	0.283
Priv.2	-0.554	-0.061	-0.277	-0.333	0.135	**0.984**	0.246
Priv.3	-0.496	-0.006	-0.256	-0.286	0.176	**0.972**	0.291
Conc.1	-0.434	-0.243	0.380	-0.267	-0.066	0.278	**0.957**
Conc.2	-0.383	-0.150	0.411	-0.219	-0.057	0.245	**0.961**
Conc.3	-0.339	-0.120	0.263	-0.164	0.011	0.269	**0.891**

Notes: Bold number indicate item loading on the assigned constructs.

Table 3. The Correlation between the Dimensions

	Inte	Self	Risk	Trus	Bene	Priv	Conc
Inte	**0.944**						
Self	0.707	**0.923**					
Risk	-0.358	-0.375	**0.918**				
Trus	0.851	0.795	-0.432	**0.903**			
Bene	0.027	0.349	-0.206	0.094	**0.904**		
Priv	-0.551	-0.047	-0.261	-0.327	0.161	**0.979**	
Conc	-0.415	-0.187	0.382	-0.235	-0.044	0.281	**0.937**

Notes: Boldface values on the diagonal are the square root of the AVE.

4.3 Structural Model

In this study, the degree of fit between the observed indicators of the model and the categorical variables was assessed using the coefficient of determination (R^2). The closer the R^2 is to 1, the model is more valuable for the interpretation of the assumptions. In this research, the degree of explanation of the model by user's use intention is 0.500, which means the explanatory power of this model can meet the requirements. Figure 2 is the significance test of the model path coefficient performed in this study with the t-value test. The nine hypotheses were established in this study, seven hypotheses have passed the significance test.

4.4 Summary of the Results

This study combines the theory of privacy concerns and the technology acceptance model to construct the structural equation model. The empirical research is conducted through questionnaire analysis. The research conclusions and test results are as follows:

First, privacy concerns significantly positively impact perceived risk and perceived privacy control. Privacy concern has a significantly negative impact on perceived trust. This finding verifies the hypothesis. Thus, when users are highly concerned about privacy issues, they will assess risks more carefully, and there will be more mistrust and doubt about new technologies. At the same time, the higher users' privacy concerns, the better control they feel they have over their private information. In contrast to the hypothesis, privacy concerns do not significantly impact perceived benefits.

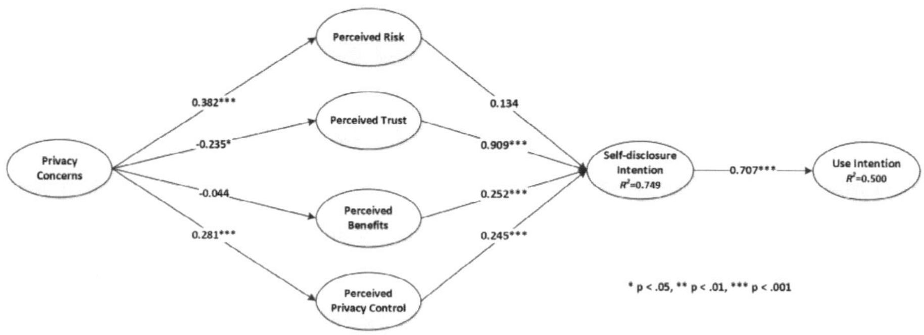

Figure 2. The Path Coefficient of Research Model

Second, there is no significant adverse effect of perceived risk on self-disclosure intention. The potential cause could be due to the specificity of the epidemic context. Even though users will inevitably reveal private information about their health status, access to places when using epidemic prevention technology, however, as this better maintains public safety, users tend to use this technology at the cost of privacy.

Third, perceived trust has a significantly positive impact on self-disclosure intention. For users, perceived trust reflects their recognition and dependence on technology, so they are willing to disclose sensitive information such as their health status and geographical location. Moreover, users feel that the new technology provides them with the necessary security and reduces their concerns about privacy breaches.

Fourth, perceived benefits have a significantly positive impact on self-disclosure intention. The primary purpose of epidemic prevention technology users is to maintain public safety and cooperate with government epidemic prevention initiatives. Technologies such as artificial intelligence and big data can effectively improve the efficiency of virus tracking and ensure public safety. When the capabilities of these technologies allow users to perceive benefits, they will increase their self-disclosure intention despite the risk of privacy breaches.

Fifth, perceived privacy control has a significant positive impact on self-disclosure intention. Users tend to be more willing to disclose personal information when they believe they have reasonable control over it. If epidemic prevention technology is more transparent in collecting and using data, it can improve users' perceived control of information and thus their willingness to disclose.

Sixth, self-disclosure intention has a significant positive impact on the use intention. As can be seen from the previous conclusions, high user willingness to self-disclose means that users' perceived trust, perceived benefits are higher. Therefore users tend to be more willing to use new technologies.

In addition to the questionnaire survey, we also conducted interviews with new technology users to further understand the impact of privacy concerns on the willingness to use epidemic prevention technology. The interviews showed that some interviewees felt they had a high level of privacy concerns. When referring to new epidemic prevention technologies, respondents also showed trust in them, believing they could help the government better control the epidemic. When asked if there was any concern about privacy disclosure in using new technologies, some respondents admitted that there was indeed a concern about privacy disclosure. Especially the disclosure of their health status and travel locations makes them feel that new technologies have certain risks. However, people will cooperate with government regulations, actively use epidemic prevention technology, and show a high willingness to disclose themselves. We believe that this result may be due to the epidemic context. On the one hand, users are trying to better protect public safety and their health. On the other hand, the government's credibility has led to epidemic prevention technology suppressing users' privacy needs and reducing their risk perceptions, which in turn has increased their willingness to use it. However, users are still more concerned about privacy in the general environment.

5. DISCUSSION AND CONCLUSION

First of all, based on privacy concerns, most scholars mainly study the use intention in e-commerce, online reading, social media, and other fields. However, there is a lack of research on individual privacy in public security and health. Therefore, this study explores users' privacy concerns under the influence of the novel coronavirus epidemic in China. On the other hand, scholars' discussion of how privacy concerns affect intention is not deep enough. Usually, scholars do not add intermediary variables to the research but directly study the relationship between the two. Such research is not apparent enough to reveal the profound relationship between the two. In the context of electronic society, in-depth study of privacy concerns on the user intention is significant. Therefore, this paper adds mediating variables in the study of privacy concerns on user intention. In this way, we can further study the impact of privacy concerns on users' willingness to use.

This study finds many factors that affect users' willingness to use epidemic prevention technology. This finding provides a new idea for helping the government carry out more effective epidemic prevention and helping users use epidemic prevention technology more assuredly. First, the government can reduce the user's perceived risk and increase trust through prior commitment. Governments can make commitments to users before using epidemic prevention technology. The government can promise users that the collected user information will only be used for epidemic prevention purposes and will not use for other purposes and leak personal privacy. This approach can increase users' trust in epidemic prevention technologies, thereby increasing their willingness to self-disclosure and technology use; second, the government can explain to users the importance of epidemic prevention technologies to society and individuals. The original intention of using epidemic prevention technology was to prevent the spread of the epidemic and maintain social stability. When users understand that epidemic prevention technology maintains public security, their perceived benefits will significantly improve. Therefore, their willingness to self-disclosure and technology use will also increase. Finally, the government can let users freely choose to disclose the epidemic prevention information, which is not critical. This unimportant information does not help prevent and control the epidemic, but it can increase users' perception of their privacy control and increase intention.

This study still has the following limitations. First, the number of samples in this research meets the minimum requirement for sample size, but a larger sample size can increase the accuracy of model testing and estimation accuracy. Second, this study is particular in the context of public security incidents of epidemic prevention and control. Therefore, it is uncertain whether the results have reference significance in the ordinary environment. In the future, the impact of these variables can be studied in the general environment. Third, the original version of TAM is still used in this study. Therefore, more accurate measurement methods and theoretical models can be used in the future.

ACKNOWLEDGEMENT

The work described in this paper was supported by grants from the Zhejiang University of Technology Humanities and Social Sciences Pre-Research Fund Project (GZ21731320013), the Zhejiang University of Technology Subject Reform Project (GZ21511320030), and China's National Undergraduate Innovation and Entrepreneurship Training Program (202110337006X).

REFERENCES

Awad, N. F. & Krishnan, M. S. 2006. The Personalization Privacy Paradox: An Empirical Evaluation of Information Transparency and the Willingness to Be Profiled Online for Personalization. *MIS Quarterly*, 30, 13-28.

Bansal, G., Zahedi, F. M. & Gefen, D. 2016. Do context and personality matter? Trust and privacy concerns in disclosing private information online. *Information & Management,* 53, 1-21.

Baruh, L., Secinti, E. & Cemalcilar, Z. 2017. Online Privacy Concerns and Privacy Management: A Meta-Analytical Review. *Journal Of Communication,* 67, 26-53.

Burgoon, J. K., Parrott, R., Le Poire, B. A., Kelley, D. L., Walther, J. B. & Perry, D. 1989. Maintaining and Restoring Privacy through Communication in Different Types of Relationships. *Journal of Social and Personal Relationships,* 6, 131-158.

Chang, S. E., Shen, W.-C. & Liu, A. Y. 2016. Why mobile users trust smartphone social networking services? A PLS-SEM approach. *Journal of Business Research,* 69, 4890-4895.

Chen, S.-C. & Lin, C.-P. 2015. The impact of customer experience and perceived value on sustainable social relationship in blogs: An empirical study. *Technological Forecasting and Social Change,* 96, 40-50.

Chen, Y., Yang, L., Zhang, M. & Yang, J. 2018. Central or peripheral? Cognition elaboration cues' effect on users' continuance intention of mobile health applications in the developing markets. *International Journal of Medical Informatics,* 116, 33-45.

Culnan, M. J. & Bies, R. J. 2003. Consumer Privacy: Balancing Economic and Justice Considerations. *Journal of Social Issues,* 59, 323-342.

Davis, F. D. 1989. Perceived Usefulness, Perceived Ease of Use, and User Acceptance of Information Technology. *MIS Quarterly,* 13, 319-340.

Dinev, T. & Hart, P. 2005. Internet Privacy Concerns and Social Awareness as Determinants of Intention to Transact. *International Journal of Electronic Commerce,* 10, 7-29.

Gefen, D., Karahanna, E. & Straub, D. W. 2003. Inexperience and experience with online stores: the importance of TAM and trust. *IEEE Transactions on Engineering Management,* 50, 307-321.

Guo, X., Zhang, X. & Sun, Y. 2016. The privacy–personalization paradox in mHealth services acceptance of different age groups. *Electronic Commerce Research and Applications,* 16, 55-65.

Jiang, Z., Heng, C. S. & Choi, B. C. F. 2013. Research Note—Privacy Concerns and Privacy-Protective Behavior in Synchronous Online Social Interactions. *Information Systems Research,* 24, 579-595.

Koohikamali, M., French, A. M. & Kim, D. J. 2019. An investigation of a dynamic model of privacy trade-off in use of mobile social network applications: A longitudinal perspective. *Decision Support Systems,* 119, 46-59.

Kruikemeier, S., Boerman, S. C. & Bol, N. 2020. Breaching the contract? Using social contract theory to explain individuals' online behavior to safeguard privacy. *Media Psychology,* 23, 269-292.

Lee, C. H. & Cranage, D. A. 2011. Personalisation–privacy paradox: The effects of personalisation and privacy assurance on customer responses to travel Web sites. *Tourism Management,* 32, 987-994.

Lowry, P. B., Cao, J. & Everard, A. 2011. Privacy Concerns Versus Desire for Interpersonal Awareness in Driving the Use of Self-Disclosure Technologies: The Case of Instant Messaging in Two Cultures. *Journal of Management Information Systems,* 27, 163-200.

Lwin, M. O., Wirtz, J. & Stanaland, A. J. S. 2016. The privacy dyad: Antecedents of promotion- and prevention-focused online privacy behaviors and the mediating role of trust and privacy concern. *Internet Research,* 26, 919-941.

Martin, K. D., Borah, A. & Palmatier, R. W. 2017. Data Privacy: Effects on Customer and Firm Performance. *Journal of Marketing,* 81, 36-58.

Ooi, K.-B., Hew, J.-J. & Lin, B. 2018. Unfolding the privacy paradox among mobile social commerce users: a multi-mediation approach. *Behaviour & Information Technology,* 37, 575-595.

Quoquab, F., Mohammad, J., Yasin, N. M. & Abdullah, N. L. 2018. Antecedents of switching intention in the mobile telecommunications industry. *Asia Pacific Journal of Marketing and Logistics,* 30, 1087-1111.

Tan, X., Qin, L., Kim, Y. & Hsu, J. 2012. Impact of privacy concern in social networking web sites. *Internet Research,* 22, 211-233.

Teixeira, P. A., Gordon, P., Camhi, E. & Bakken, S. 2011. HIV patients' willingness to share personal health information electronically. *Patient Education and Counseling,* 84, e9-e12.

Turel, O. 2015. Quitting the use of a habituated hedonic information system: a theoretical model and empirical examination of Facebook users. *European Journal of Information Systems,* 24, 431-446.

Wang, E. S.-T. & Lin, R.-L. 2017. Perceived quality factors of location-based apps on trust, perceived privacy risk, and continuous usage intention. *Behaviour & Information Technology,* 36, 2-10.

Wang, T., Duong, T. D. & Chen, C. C. 2016. Intention to disclose personal information via mobile applications: A privacy calculus perspective. *International Journal of Information Management,* 36, 531-542.

DIGITAL TRANSFORMATION: COMPLEXITY AND NEED FOR A FRAMEWORK FOR ITS MANAGEMENT

Omar Gaidi and Salah Baïna
ENSIAS, Mohammed V University in Rabat, Morocco

ABSTRACT

Digital Transformation has become an imperative for most organizations. It is a journey that has been induced by the accelerated pace of technological developments (Data, Cloud, IA, ML, RPA, Agility, ...). The integration of these technologies in almost every industry has fundamentally changed the operational processes of companies. It impacts business levels, starting with business models and ending with the customer journey. The adoption of these technologies has also offered an opportunity for these companies to grow, increase agility, strengthen governance models by eliminating traditional silos and ensure better knowledge and proximity to the customer.
This theme, "Digital transformation", has been very widely covered in recent years, it has aroused great interest in research both in academia and in practice and has been the subject of several studies. This is a very complex subject and many question marks remain, particularly on the definition of digital transformation, we have identified more than 100 definitions spread over time and between sectors of activity. To approach it properly, it is essential to define or describe the Digital Transformation well first.
The main objective of this article is to give a general review of the systematic literature on Digital Transformation, to bring together the different definitions given and to propose a metamodel to explain this notion and show the interactions between the different concepts concerned by this concept. Through this metamodel, we will show the complexity of this transformation and the need to use a Framework for the management of the Digital Transformation.

KEYWORDS

Systematic Literature Review, Digital Transformation Definition

1. INTRODUCTION

Due to democratization, the rapid adoption and massive use of new information and communication technologies, consumption habits have changed a lot. Organizations are adopting these emerging technologies such as Cloud, ML, Big Data, AI, ... (Heilig et al., 2017; Nwankpa et al., 2017; Wiesboeck et al., 2019) to improve their operational processes, their operating models, their customers' journey, thus contributing to the creation of values (Heilig et al., 2017; Hartl et al., 2017; Hausberg et al., 2018; Horlacher et al., 2016; Iansiti et al., 2014; Ismail et al., 2017; Mhlungu et al., 2019; Morakanyane et al. 2017; Paavola et al., 2017; Reis, 2018; Schallmo et al., 2017; Singh, 2017; Wiesboeck et al., 2019). This is called "Digital Transformation".

In its October 2020 edition, the IDC (International Data Corporation, the world's leading consulting and research group on information technology markets) forecast the digitization of 65% of global GDP by the end of 2022. In parallel, we are seeing a sharp increase in the number of publications on Digital Transformation. Several studies have been conducted or are underway to demonstrate how organizations are adopting these technologies to succeed in their transformation projects. According to some authors (Berghaus et al., 2016; Hinings et al., 2018), the main opportunities of Digital Transformation are : (i) the development of innovation in the service of strategy, (ii) the creation of new business models ; (iii) improvement of the customer experience; (iv) improvement of operational processes and (v) employee motivation and organizational agility.

Despite the growing interest in this topic, we have noticed that several questions remain unanswered. The articles collected as part of this Digital Transformation literature review indicate a multitude and diversity of definitions or descriptions of Digital Transformation as well as a lack of universal and complete understanding of this concept. The question of what Digital Transformation really is and how we should conceptualize it remains. Moreover, our experience has confirmed this observation. Different stakeholders in Digital Transformation project use this term inconsistently to describe various activities.

Some authors consider that a simple technological change such as the implementation of a new ERP system or a new website, or the simple use of technology to improve business performance (Westerman et al., 2011) is a Digital Transformation. Others believe that Digital Transformation is an evolutionary process that harnesses digital capabilities and technologies to enable business models, operational processes and customer experiences to create value (Morakanyane et al., 2017). It is difficult to find "a unified" definition of Digital Transformation, it is a transversal, complex and mobilizing project. To ensure its good design, management and success, the use of certain techniques, methodologies or framework is essential.

Section 2 describes the research methodology. Section 3 presents the results and the discussion. Finally, the conclusion and some directions for future research.

2. METHODOLOGY

To carry out this literature review, we referred to the Okoli protocol (Okoli et al., 2010), considered to be a rigorous and standardized methodology for the systematic review of the literature, especially for IS researchers, the approach taken to relieve this SLR is shown in Figure 1 below.

To have a global understanding, the method consists of a search based on a set of keywords to review the maximum number of articles referenced. In our research, published between 2000 and 2020 (At the start of this research, we did not specify the start date, we noticed that the first documents dealing with this type of subject start from 2000, hence the choice of the start date). This research identified and selected a set of relevant and valid articles for analysis. To carry out this research, we relied on a set of tools. The main one was Google Scholar and Scopus. "Publish or Perish" was used to facilitate the processing of search results.

Figure 1. A Systematic literature review method

2.1 Research Question

Through this research work, we will try to answer the questions indicated in the Table 1 below.

Table 1. List of questions asked

N°	Question
Q1	**What are the different definitions of "Digital Transformation" throughout history ?**
Q2	**What are the axes common to these definitions ?**
Q3	**Can we propose a new definition based on the above ?**
Q4	**Is it important to be based on an enterprise architecture framework ?**

2.2 Research Strategy

The objective of this phase is to develop a relevant, comprehensive and repeatable strategy that will be used to retrieve all of the necessary documentation. At this stage, it is a matter of listing the electronic databases used and identifying the fields searched for in each database. In order to assess the majority of the scientific evidence, we have chosen to conduct a broad search by processing a fairly large history. The parameters used to carry out this research are indicated in Table 2 below.

Table 2. Identification of search parameters used for retrieving documentation

Search criteria	Wanted value
Search engine	**Google scholar, Scopus, All fields, documents in English, Published studies**
Period	**Between January 2000 and December 2020**

2.3 Research Strategy

The objective of this phase is to identify the keywords and the compositions that will be used to carry out the documentary research. Table 3 below lists the compositions of the keywords used in this search.

Table 3. Identification of keywords used for retrieving documentation

Keywords used	The compositions used	
Digital transformation	- (1) : **"Digital Transformation Definition"**	- (4) : **"Digital Transformation History"**
Definition	- (2) : **"Define Digital Transformation"**	- (5) : **"Digital Transformation Framework"**
Literature Review	- (3) : **"Digitization Definition"**	

2.4 Inclusion and Exclusion Criteria

The inclusion and exclusion criteria that were applied to all references retrieved from electronic databases so that irrelevant references can be excluded are described in Table 4 below.

Table 4. Inclusion and exclusion criteria used for triage of documentation

Factor	Inclusion criteria	Exclusion criteria
Language	**The language used is English**	**Any other language except English**
Report type	**Complete articles. Original research works. Authoritative statement (articles published by a credible scientific body)**	**Books, Summaries, Patents, Quotes or anecdotes published**
Source	**Research should come from trusted resources and journals**	**Published in a non-peer reviewed source (internet reports, journal and journal articles)**
Nature	**Scientific publication directly related to Digital Transformation. The publication must have a transparent methodology**	**The publication is an editorial, a keynote, an opinion, a tutorial, a workshop, a summary report, a poster and books**

2.5 Extraction

The goal of this phase is to implement the search strategy uniformly for all electronic databases, keep a record of all retrieved documentation before sorting it, and organize retrieval of documentation in a systematic manner. Then, it is a question of identifying and eliminating the references cited in duplicate, to exclude the references which, according to their titles, in-depth analysis of the abstracts and the purposes or the complete text, meet the exclusion criteria or do not meet the criteria of inclusion specified before. Finally, to identify the references retained after reading the summaries first, then those that are retained after reading the texts. The evolution of the number of references retained through the different phases is indicated in Table 5 below.

Table 5. Documentation sorting results - Summary

Composition used	Initial number of references	Number of references after elimination of duplicates	Number of references after analysis of abstracts	Number of references after analysis of the texts
(1)	**83**	**72**	**11**	**4**
(2)	**237**	**190**	**57**	**7**
(3)	**69**	**64**	**12**	**3**
(4)	**46**	**33**	**7**	**4**
(5)	**402**	**332**	**72**	**12**
Total	**837**	**691**	**159**	**30**

3. RESULTS AND DISCUSSION

In this part, it is about analyzing the results obtained and trying to answer the questions asked initially.

3.1 Breakdown of Definitions by Year

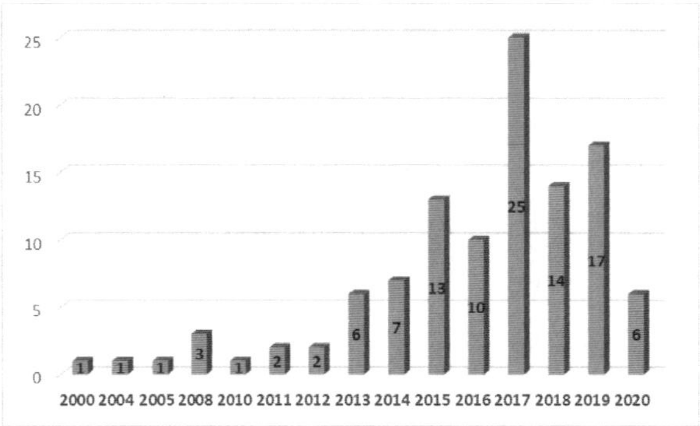

Figure 2. Documentation sorting results - Summary

By referring to the 30 documents selected, we have identified 108 definitions of "Digital Transformation". The graph in Figure 2 above shows the distribution of the number of these definitions between 2000 and 2020. We noticed that the "Digital Transformation" made its first appearance under this name in 2000 (Patel et al., 2000). The number of definitions did not change much between 2000 and 2012. It was not until 2013 that the subject started to gain momentum. Several authors have started to take an interest in the topic. Definitions have also changed a lot. The pace remained practically the same during the period 2015-2020.

3.2 Summary of Definitions

By analyzing the words and terms used in the 108 definitions collected, we were able to identify some common concepts. These concepts are : (1) Strategy & Innovation, (2) Business Models, (3) Customer Experience, (4) Operational Processes, (5) Employees, Culture & Organization and (6) Technology & Data. The distribution of these concepts among the 108 definitions is shown in Table 6 below.

Table 6. Distribution of concepts by definition

Year	1. Strategy and Innovation	2. Business Models	3. Customer Experience	4. Operational Processes	5. Employees, Culture & Organization	6. Technology & Data	**Total**
2000							**0**
2004					**1**	**1**	**2**
2005				**1**		**1**	**2**
2008	**1**			**1**		**2**	**4**
2010						**1**	**1**
2011			**1**	**2**	**1**	**2**	**6**
2012							**0**
2013	**1**	**1**	**2**	**2**	**2**	**2**	**10**
2014	**2**	**4**	**3**	**3**	**3**	**5**	**20**
2015	**1**	**6**	**4**	**3**	**1**	**8**	**23**
2016	**3**	**3**	**1**	**6**	**3**	**10**	**26**
2017	**4**	**9**	**11**	**14**	**7**	**20**	**65**
2018	**2**	**6**	**6**	**7**	**7**	**7**	**35**
2019	**3**	**7**	**2**	**11**	**6**	**10**	**41**
2020				**2**		**2**	**4**
Total	**17**	**36**	**30**	**52**	**31**	**71**	**237**

The use of "technology and data" is by far the most common concept. It was cited in 71 definitions, followed by "operational processes", cited in 52 definitions, "business models" in third position, it was cited in 36 definitions, "employees, culture & Organization" in fourth position where it was cited in 31 definitions, "Customer experience" in 30 definitions and "strategy & innovation" in 17 definitions.

In addition, the definition of Digital Transformation has also undergone several changes over the past 20 years. Between 2000 and 2012, the concepts most used in the definition were (4) Operational Processes, (5) Employees, Culture & Organization and (6) Technology & Data. The other concepts only appeared from 2013 and 2014. In what follows, we will limit our analysis only to definitions that contain at least 4 concepts. The summary table is as follows. Of the 108 definitions collected initially, we will only retain 19. They are grouped together in the Table 7 below.

Table 7. List of definitions with more than 4 concepts

Year	Author	Definition
2013	Fitzgerald et al.	The use of new digital technologies (social media, mobile, analytics or embedded devices) to enable major business improvements (such as enhancing customer experience, streamlining operations or creating new business models).
2014	Iansiti & Lakhani	The digitization of previously analog machine and service operations, organizational tasks, and managerial processes. It changes a business model is in two ways: how the organization creates value for its customers (the customer value proposition) and how it captures that value (how it makes money).
2016	Berghaus & Back	Technology-induced change on many levels in the organization that includes both the exploitation of digital technologies to improve existing processes, and the exploration of digital innovation, which can potentially transform the business model.
2016	Horlacher & Hess	The use of new digital technologies, such as social media, mobile, analytics or embedded devices, in order to enable major business improvements like enhancing customer experience, streamlining operations or creating new business models.
2017	Haffke, Kalgovas, and Benlian	Digital transformation encompasses the digitization of sales and communication channels, which provide novel ways to interact and engage with customers, and the digitization of a firm's offerings (products and services), which replace or augment physical offerings. Digital transformation also describes the triggering of tactical or strategic business moves by data-driven insights and the launch of digital business models that allow new ways to capture value.
2017	Hartl & Hess	The IT-enabled change in organizations through digitalization of products, services, core processes, customer touch points and business models. It distinguishes itself from previous IT-enabled business transformations in terms of velocity and its holistic nature.
2017	Hess et al.	Digital transformation is concerned with the changes digital technologies can bring about in a company's business model, which results in changed products or organizational structures or in the automation of processes. These changes can be observed in the rising demand for Internet-based media, which has led to changes in entire business models.
2017	Ismail, et al.	We define it as the process through which companies converge multiple new digital technologies, enhanced with ubiquitous connectivity, with the intention of reaching superior performance and sustained competitive advantage, by transforming multiple business dimensions, including the business model, the customer experience (comprising digitally enabled products and services) and operations (comprising processes and decision-making), and simultaneously impacting people (including skills talent and culture) and networks (including the entire value system).
2017	Morakanyane, et al.	An evolutionary process that leverages digital capabilities and technologies to enable business models, operational processes and customer experiences to create value.
2017	Nwankpa and Dappa	Digital business intensity is a measure of the level of strategic organizational investments in emergent and innovative digital technology such as analytics, big data, cloud, social media, and mobile platforms in order to engage customers, connect people, place, and information in a seamless and economically sustainable model of operation.
2017	Paavola et al.	The use of digital technology, in order to enable major business improvements in operations and markets such as enhancing customer experience, streamlining operations or creating new business models.
2017	Schallmo et Williams	The implementation of technologies in business processes is only a small part of digitally transforming a business. Moreover, digital technologies need to create additional value for the customers, the business itself, and other essential stakeholders

2017	Singh and Hess	Use of new digital technologies, such as social media, mobile, analytics or embedded devices, in order to enable major business improvements like enhancing customer experience, streamlining operations or creating new business models.
2017	Solis	The investment in and development of new technologies, mindsets, and business and operational models to improve work and competitiveness and deliver new and relevant value for customers and employees in an ever-evolving digital economy.
2018	Bloomberg	The customer-driven strategic business transformation that requires cross-cutting organizational change as well as the implementation of digital technologies. DT requires the organization to deal better with change overall, essentially making change a core competency as the enterprise becomes customer-driven end-to-end.
2018	J. Reis et al.	Digital Transformation may be categorized into three distinct elements: (1) Technological – Digital Transformation is based on the use of new digital technologies such as social media, mobile, analytics or embedded devices; (2) Organizational – Digital Transformation requires a change of organizational processes or the creation of new business models; (3) Social – Digital Transformation is a phenomenon that is influencing all aspects of human life by, e.g., enhancing customers experience
2018	Liere-Netheler et al.	The use of new digital technologies (social media, mobile, analytics, or embedded devices) to enable significant business improvements (such as enhancing customer experience, streamlining operations, or creating new business models).
2019	Chanias et al.	A Digital Transformation Strategy is supposed to coordinate, prioritize, and implement a pre-digital organization's transformation efforts and, as a long-term objective, to govern its journey to achieve the desired future state of being digitally transformed. Its scope goes beyond the digitization of resources and involves the transformation of key structural and organizational aspects, the use of advanced information technologies (IT) or aspects of value creation including key products and services, leading to adjusted or completely new business models.
2019	Wiesboeck and Hess	Digital transformation has been defined as the use of new digital technologies, such as mobile, artificial intelligence, cloud, blockchain, and the Internet of things (IoT) technologies, to enable major business improvements to augment customer experience, streamline operations, or create new business models.

Based on all of the above, we can ask ourselves the question about the evolution of the definition of digital transformation. It is a very complex concept, which will certainly evolve further, especially with the acceleration of technological developments. Proceeding from there we can deduce that "Digital Transformation" is a process brought about by technological changes, which, thanks to their development and their accessibility, make it possible to better exploit the explosion in the mass of data. These two factors have led to a radical and permanent change in the consumption habits of customers and stakeholders. These changes in consumption habits necessarily and deeply impact the company's strategy, its business model, its culture, the profile of its employees, its organization and its governance and obliges it to be more innovative in order to better differentiate itself through compared to the competition. These changes also allow the company to be more agile in order to promote overall cohesion and provide the conditions for the development of collective intelligence.

This agility and overall cohesion will allow the company to improve its profitability and generate more profit. These profits will finance the acquisition and adoption of new technologies, allowing better adoption of new technologies, better use of data, better knowledge of customers and their journeys in order to offer them more suitable products and services. Then we can represent this description by the metamodel shown in Figure 3 below. the objective of the proposed metamodel is to show the interactions between the concepts concerned by the digital transformation, to show the complexity of the subject and above all the fact that it is a continuous cycle over time as technology is developing.

It is clear that this is a very complex transformation which takes into account several factors which determine the sustainability of the company. Faced with this complexity, it is very important to be based on a Framework capable of piloting this "Digital Transformation" project.

The Enterprise Architecture (EA) provides the tools and approaches to manage the complexity of digital transformation.

It is a major lever for managing these transformations, thanks in particular to its methods, its Frameworks and its tools. They facilitate communication between stakeholders and the sharing of a common transversal vision. EA provides a holistic view that enables the organization to leverage resources as a lever for transformation. It consists of a set of reference frameworks, which allow in particular:

- To develop project management principles, models on which to build information systems, norms, rules and standards;
- To position the projects in an overall perspective;
- To anticipate opportunities for sharing and reuse;
- To ensure that all information systems are interoperable, while maintaining the appropriate levels of security.

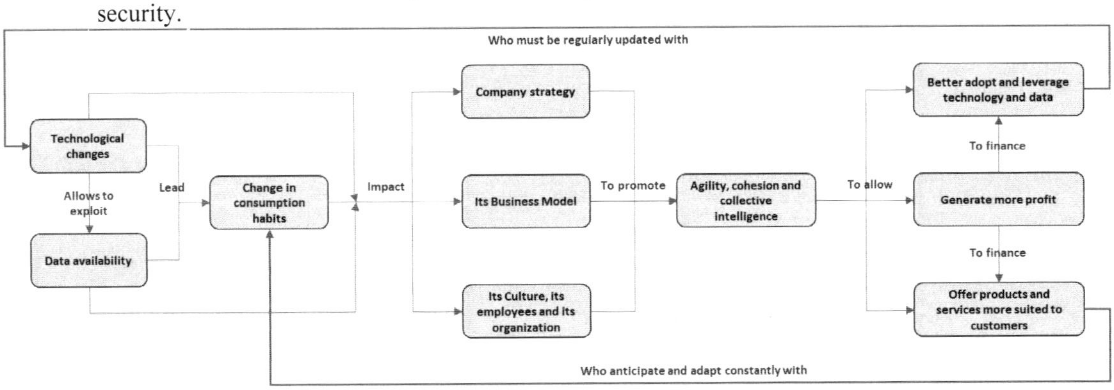

Figure 3. Metamodel for "Digital Transformation"

4. CONCLUSION

Digital transformation is a subject that has evolved well in recent years, the results of this study show that there is still a limited number of articles exploring the implementation of Digital Transformation. Thus, the analysis of the literature review only allowed us to shed light on certain concepts.

Digital transformation is a real challenge for almost the majority of organizations in all sectors. In the academic world, this is a subject that has evolved a lot in recent years. The analysis of the literature review only allowed us to clarify certain concepts. The results of this study show that there are still areas to be clarified. Admittedly, a limited number of articles were explored, but it still allowed us to propose a new metamodel of Digital Transformation. The most important thing for us was to be able to demonstrate, through the proposed metamodel, the complexity of this subject. Hence the need to use a solid framework to drive this transformation.

We then asked the question about the contribution of Enterprise Architecture to the success of the Digital Transformation.

REFERENCES

Berghaus, S., Back, A. (2016). *Stages in Digital Business Transformation: Results of an Empirical Maturity Study* [Conference paper]. Mediterranean Conference on Information Systems (MCIS), 1–17.

Bloomberg, J. (2018). Digitization, digitalization, and digital transformation: confuse them at your peril. *Forbes*, 28.

Chanias, S., Myers, M.-D., Hess, T. (2019). Digital transformation strategy making in pre-digital organizations: the case of a financial services provider. *The Journal of Strategic Information Systems* January, 1–17. doi: 10.1016/j.jsis.2018.11.003

Fitzgerald, M., Kruschwitz, N., Bonnet, D., Welch, M. (2014). Embracing digital technology: a new strategic imperative. *MIT Sloan Manag, Rev*, 55 (2), 1.

Haffke, I., Kalgovas, B., Benlian, A. (2017). Options for Transforming the IT function using bimodal IT. *MIS Quarterly Executive*, 16(2), 101–120.

Hartl, E., Hess, T. (2017). *The role of cultural values for digital transformation: insights from a delphi study* [Conference]. The Americas Conference on Information Systems: A Tradition of Innovation. AMCIS.

Hausberg, J. -P., Liere-Netheler, K., Packmohr, S., Pakura, S., Vogelsang, K. (2018). *Digital Transformation in Business Research: A Systematic Literature Review and Analysis* (April 26, 2018). DRUID18, Copenhagen Business School, Copenhagen, Denmark. URL: https://ssrn.com/abstract=3169203

Heilig, L., Schwarze, S., Voß, S. (2017). *An analysis of digital transformation in the history and future of modern ports* [Conference]. Proceedings of the 50th Hawaii International Conference on System Sciences.Waikoloa Beach: HICSS. 1341-1350.

Hess, T., Matt, C., Benlian, A., Wiesboeck, F. (2016). Options for formulating a digital transformation strategy. *MIS Quarterly Executive*, 15(2), 123–139.

Hinings, B., Gegenhuber, T., Greenwood, R. (2018). Digital innovation and transformation: An institutional perspective. *Information and Organization*, 28(1), 52–61. URL : https://doi.org/10.1016/j.infoandorg.2018.02.004

Horlacher, A., Hess, T. (2016). *What does a chief digital officer do? Managerial tasks and roles of a new C-level position in the context of digital transformation* [Conference paper]. The 49th Annual Hawaii International Conference on System Sciences, HICSS.

Iansiti, M., Lakhani, K. -R. (2014). Digital ubiquity: how connections, sensors, and data are revolutionizing business. *Harvard Business Revue*, 92 (11), 19.

Ismail, M. -H., Khater, M., Zaki, M. (2017). Digital business transformation and strategy: What do we know so far. *Cambridge Service Alliance*, 10.

Korachi, Z., Bounabat, B. (2020). General Approach for Formulating a Digital Transformation Strategy. *J. Comput. Sci*, 16, 493-507.

Mahraz, M. -I., Benabbou, L., Berrado, A. (2019). *A Systematic literature review of Digital Transformation*.

Mhlungu, N. -S., Chen, J. -Y., Alkema, P. (2019). The underlying factors of a successful organisational digital transformation, *South African Journal of Information Management*, 21(1), 1-10.

Morakanyane, R., Grace, A., O'Reilly, P. (2017). *Conceptualizing Digital Transformation in Business Organizations: A Systematic Review of Literature*. BLED. 21, 426-444.

Nwankpa, J. -K., Datta, P. (2017). Balancing exploration and exploitation of IT resources: the influence of digital business intensity on perceived organizational performance. *European Journal of Information Systems*, 26(5), 469–488.

Okoli, C., Schabram, K. (2010). *A Guide to Conducting a Systematic Literature Review of Information Systems Research.*

Paavola, R., Hallikainen, P., Elbanna, A. (2017). *Role of middle managers in modular digital transformation: the case of Servu* [Conference paper]. The 25th European Conference on Information Systems, ECIS.

Patel, K., McCarthy, M. -P. (2000). *Digital Transformation: The Essentials of E-Business Leadership 1st*.McGraw-Hill Professional.

Reis, J. (2018). *Digital transformation: A literature review and guidelines for future research*. Intelligent Systems and Computing. 745, 411-421. ISSN 21945357. doi : 10.1007/978-3-319-77703-0_41

Schallmo, A., Daniel, R., (2018). *Digital Transformation Now! Guiding the Successful Digitalization of YourBusiness Model.* Springer. URL: https://doi.org/10.1007/978-3-319-72844-5

Schallmo, D., Williams, C. (2017). Digital Transformation of Business Models – Best Practice, Enablers and Roadmap. *International Journal of Innovation Management*, 21(8): 1740014.

Singh, A., Hess, T. (2017). How chief digital officers promote the digital transformation of their companies. *MIS Quarterly Executive*, 16(1), 1–17.

Solis, D. (2017). *Digital Transformation–The six stages of digital transformation*.

Veldhoven, Z. -V., Vanthienen, J. (2019). *Designing a Comprehensive Understanding of Digital Transformation and its Impact.*

Westerman, G., Calméjane, C., Bonnet, D., Ferraris, P., McAfee, A. (2011). *Digital transformation: A roadmap for billion-dollar organizations.* MIT Center for Digital Business and Capgemini Consulting, 1–68.

Wiesboeck, F., Hess, T. (2019). Digital innovations embedding in organizations. *Electronic Markets*, 30, 75–86. URL: https://doi.org/10.1007/s12525-019-00364-9

Zaouia, F., Souissi, N. (2020). *Roadmap for digital transformation: A literature review.* URL: https://doi.org/10.1016/j.procs.2020.07.090

SHORT PAPERS

FOSTER TRUST IN INDUSTRIAL QUALITY CONTROL BY INTRODUCING SMART CONTRACTS

Markus Nöbauer
InsideAx GmbH
Kramlehnerweg 1a, 4061 Pasching, Austria

ABSTRACT

Quality control is a key process for goods-producing companies. Its purpose is to verify that the produced goods meet the desired quality. Data collected during this process is used for internal controlling purposes as well as for external customer-facing communication. While some customers require access to the collected data during and after the production process, it is also used to convince prospects of the high quality of goods. Publishing such information comes with two major challenges. First, how can the recipient be convinced that data was not altered to be hidden? Second, how the risk of information disclosure be mitigated? One way to address these challenges is to digitalize the production and quality control processes and apply data management techniques to the collected data. Blockchain technology can be used to foster trust in the collected and later shared information. In this paper, we present our approach to mapping production orders on Ethereum based Smart Contracts.

KEYWORDS

Blockchain, Smart Contract, Trust, Plastic Production, Quality Control

1. INTRODUCTION

Quality Control is a key process for most goods-producing companies to ensure that the goods satisfy a certain quality standard before they are shipped. Typically, a set of examples is selected from the finished goods. For each example, a set of checks must be performed. Monitoring the production environment also provides valuable information. Such data serves multiple purposes. First, it can trigger immediate actions on the production process e.g., adjusting machine settings like temperature, pressure, etc. Second, it can be used for process optimization. Third, it is part of documentation which is often required by customers.

To automate the data collection and analysis, data needs to be available in a digital format. For example, in a database, file export from production control systems, APIs of machine control units, etc. According to a study in order by the Austrian Ministry for Digital and Economic Affairs (KANTAR, 2022), about 60% of all production is either fully automated (7%), digitally connected (16%), or digitally controlled (37%). This provides a good foundation for digitalization projects. However, in most cases, additional work is required to collect and integrate production and quality control data.

Digital data is easier to process but also easier to manipulate than paperwork. Many techniques have been developed to ensure and validate the correctness of digital data. For example, public key infrastructure (Adams, 2003) (PKI) uses certificates to protect transmitted information in a computer network. Signing is also used to verify the origin of a document and that it was not modified. Document management system often uses write-once-ready-many (Möller, 2003) (WORM) hardware devices to guarantee that documents (e.g., invoices) have not been modified or deleted. All these techniques are well established but also have downsides. PKI and document signing relies on a central certification authority. If the chain of trust breaks, the signed documents can no longer be validated by a third party. WORM hardware guarantees that initial written data is not modified. But production and quality control are highly dynamic scenarios and require data management like sorting, filtering, aggregation, and separation.

In general, blockchains are transaction-oriented distributed systems that support the transfer of value between accounts and guarantee correctness by using a consensus mechanism. Such a consensus mechanism makes it hard for blockchain participants to manipulate data on the blockchain. First-generation blockchains like Bitcoin are mainly designed to transfer value in a quick and secure way and use proof-of-work as a consensus mechanism. Second-generation blockchains like Ethereum also support the execution of program code on the blockchain. A Smart Contract combines data and program logic on a blockchain. (Vogshmgir, 2019)

InsideAx is an Austrian SME software company and Microsoft Gold Partner for Dynamics 365 Enterprise Resource Planning (ERP) systems. We have teamed up with one of our customers working in the area of plastic production in an innovation project to foster trust in quality control data. We created the foundation for a digitally integrated production and quality control process. Moreover, we have realized an approach that hosts production orders as Smart Contract on an Ethereum Blockchain. Our approach ensures that gathered data is provided to internal and external stakeholders in a trustworthy way.

We present the project goals and research questions in section 2. In section 3 we discuss the conceptual solution. Section 4 provides a summary.

2. PROJECT GOALS AND RESEARCH QUESTIONS

Our goal was to provide a trustworthy platform for quality control data. The project addressed three types of stakeholders. Internal stakeholders like production and quality control managers and company management. The second group is customers who request access to quality control data related to their production orders. The third group is potential customers who shall be convinced of the quality of goods produced. We identified the following research questions:

RQ1: Which data needs to be collected to provide meaningful information for the three groups of stakeholders? Different stakeholders have different requirements regarding the type, details, and accuracy of production and quality control data. Especially data for external stakeholders like customers must be prepared to avoid leaking company secrets.

RQ2: Can we collect data that is required but not available from existing data sources? Production and quality control is a highly dynamic process and involves different software systems, machines, and humans. Static information like orders and material can easily be accessed in ERP and Production Planning (PP) systems. However, we also need to acquire data from the machines used in production and from the workers performing quality control tests.

RQ3: How can we manage, store and provide data for the three groups of stakeholders? Different stakeholders shall have different views on the data. The provided data shall be accurate and requires updates and changes, but it shall also be trustworthy. For example, legal requirements like the General Data Protection Regulation (GDPR) (EU, 2016) require the deletion of person-related data.

3. BLOCKCHAIN BASED QUALITY CONTROL

This project was conducted as 2 years applied research project. We decided to use the action research (Johanneson, 2014) approach. It is an iterative approach that supports incremental improvement steps. We conducted three iterations to establish and improve our approach to the customer. In the first iteration, we focused on the identification and collection of existing data. The second iteration was used to implement a mobile application for production workers to document the production and quality control process. We finalized the Smart Contract and integration within the customer's process in the third iteration.

We conducted multiple workshops with customer's key users to identify relevant data for the three stakeholder groups. Therefore, we invited production and quality control managers, accountants as well as sales and marketing experts. In these workshops we identified three types of data:

Static meta data: This group of data mainly consists of ERP and PP data. For example, the customer, sales order, production order, item attributes, raw material, and associated quality control measures. All this data was accessible via the company's software systems.

User-generated data: Quality orders and quality control tasks were automatically generated and assigned to QS workers. However, these orders were printed on paper and the results from the quality check were also noted down on paper. It showed that we had to transform the quality control process from a paper-oriented one to a digital process. We developed an app for android tablets that presented the quality control tasks to the QS employee. Instead of writing the results down, they typed it in and we could easily access the data.

Machine data: The customer is using a range of different machines for plastic production. We found that processing information like spiral speed, water temperature, saw length, etc. should be recorded. Machine setup and conditions under which a good was produced can be valuable information for the later quality investigation. We followed the IOT Reference architecture (Microsoft, 2022) to collect on-premises machine data. Sorting and aggregation were done in the Microsoft Azure cloud.

3.1 Data Classification

In order to address the three stakeholder groups (Internal, Customers, Marketing) we introduced a data classification framework. Data in our understanding are records e.g., Production Order and Documents. We introduced a classification vector with 4 Boolean elements. The first three elements indicate if the data is relevant to the stakeholder group. The fourth record indicates if it is protected which means it must be deleted in the future. The value 1 indicates that it is relevant for the stakeholder.

Documents were classified as a whole, not particular paragraphs. For records, we had to drill down to individual table fields because a single record very likely contains fields that can be shared with external stakeholders while others are only relevant for internal stakeholders. Table 1 shows three examples:

Table 1. Examples for data classification

Data	Vector	Meaning
ProductionOrder.CustomerName	<1,0,0,1>	Name of the Customer can be used for internal purposes. It must not be used for external use and will be deleted in the future
ProdutionOrder.ItemName	<1,1,1,0>	The item name is relevant for all three stakeholder groups and will not delete in the future.
Factsheet Item 123.pdf	<0,1,1,0>	The factsheet is not relevant for internal stakeholders, but for customers and in marketing. There is no policy that requires the deletion of the fact sheet.

3.2 Smart Contract

We use an Ethereum based Smart Contract to cover the production process and related quality control tasks. We are using a private Ethereum blockchain because its technology is already established, and tools are available. In particular, we use a consortium as a consensus mechanism. Ethereum is a transaction-oriented blockchain and not designed to receive very frequent IOT calls. It is also not designed to store a vast amount of binary data e.g., documents. We also had to keep in mind that some data must be deleted in the future and therefore we cannot store it on a blockchain e.g., the name of the QS worker is person-related data and protected by the GDPR. Therefore, our approach uses a combination of on-chain storage for production order meta data and off-chain storage for collected quality-control data and documents.

Whenever a production order is created within the customer's ERP system, a corresponding Smart Contract is automatically deployed to the blockchain. A new Smart Contract contains the corresponding production order number from the ERP System, the item ID, and the planned quantity. The Smart Contract also stores hash values for the off-chain data. By calculating hashes, we can verify that the off-chain data has not been changed. The address of the Smart Contract is stored within the ERP system and linked to the production order.

Off-chain is stored in a cloud storage account. For each production order, a folder is created containing three subfolders for the three stakeholder groups. Based on the earlier defined classification vectors, the data is copied to the corresponding folders. For example, a fact sheet that is classified as relevant for external stakeholders will be copied into the folder for external stakeholders. We are aware that this approach generates duplicate data if it is relevant for more than one stakeholder, but since cloud storage is available at a low cost, we don't see this as a problem.

Each folder is consecutively filled with ZIP files containing collected quality control data. For example, when the machine setup was finished the meanwhile collected data is classified, zipped, and uploaded to the folders of the production order. After data was uploaded to the cloud storage, an MD5 hash value is calculated for the complete folder. The Smart Contract stores the actual hash values for the three folders. Validating the data in the cloud storage can be done by calculating an MD5 hash value and comparing it with the hash value in the Smart Contract. If both values are the same, the data has not been modified.

4. SUMMARY

We have developed an approach to foster trust in quality control data by mapping production orders on a Smart Contract. Our approach uses on-chain and off-chain storage. Data that is required to identify the production order are stored on-chain. Data collected during the production and quality control process are stored off-chain. The Smart Contract contains the hash values for the off-chain data. We learned that collecting and classification of data is the most time-consuming part of such a project. It required process changes and employee training to establish the foundation for the blockchain project.

We received positive feedback from the QS workers. Especially the app to document quality control was very welcome because it replaced paperwork. Moreover, employees reported they felt more valued by getting equipped with modern devices and apps developed for their needs. Production and quality control managers liked the fact that they can now access all relevant data on a digital platform. However, the blockchain and Smart Contract integration didn't provide values for them. Sales and marketing management was impressed by the fact that blockchain technology was put to use in their company. They argue that it will take some discussions to explain the benefit to their customers.

ACKNOWLEDGEMENT

This project was partially funded by the Austrian Research Promotion Agency (FFG, 2022).

REFERENCES

Adams C., Lloyd S., 2003. Understanding PKI: concepts, standards, and deployment considerations, Addison-Wesley

FFG, Austrian Research Promotion Agency Project Database https://projekte.ffg.at/projekt/3157985

Johanneson P., Perjons E., 2014, An Introduction to Design Science, Springer International Publishing, Switzerland

KANTAR TNS, Digital-Dossier, 2018, Online (23.01.2022), Initiative D21 e.V., https://www.bmdw.gv.at/DigitalisierungundEGovernment/Documents/DigitalDossier.pdf

Microsoft, IOT Reference Architecture, Online (23.01.2022), https://docs.microsoft.com/en-us/azure/architecture/reference-architectures/iot

Möller, S., Perlov, C., Jackson, W. et al. A polymer/semiconductor write-once read-many-times memory. Nature 426, 166–169 (2003). https://doi.org/10.1038/nature02070

REGULATION (EU) 2016/679 OF THE EUROPEAN PARLIAMENT AND OF THE COUNCIL of 27 April 2016 on the protection of natural persons with regard to the processing of personal data and on the free movement of such data, and repealing Directive 95/46/EC (GDPR)

Vogshmgir S., 2019. Token Economy: How Blockchain and Smart Contracts Revolutionize the Economy, BlockchainHub, Berlin, Germany.

ANALYSIS OF A DISTRIBUTED HYBRID MAS APPROACH FOR INFORMATION SYSTEM DEVELOPMENT

Agnese Salutari[1,2] and Laura Tarantino[2]
[1]*Reiss Romoli s.r.l., Via Enrico Berlinguer 3, 67100 L'Aquila, AQ, Italy*
[2]*Università degli Studi dell'Aquila, Via Vetoio 1, 67100, L'Aquila, AQ, Italy*

ABSTRACT

The choice of proper technologies and frameworks – generally facing tradeoff involving costs, resources, performances and innovation – is a crucial point in Information Systems Development (ISD), necessary to make the system effective, maintainable and easy to develop. In this direction, in this paper we analyze the results achieved with the adoption of a novel Distributed Hybrid System approach blending Multi-Agent Systems programming with Object and Event Programming techniques, used to manage asynchronous events, communication between different modules, and data flows within the refactoring and the expansion of an e-learning application. In particular, we analyze architectural and technology choices with respect to benchmark aspects typically faced in ISD, including integration of research and practice, ease of installation in pre-existing environments, security, data modeling, error correction, cost, multi-tenancy requirements, and computational and memory load. The achieved results demonstrate the success of the hybridization choices for ISD and of the fruitful bridging of research and practice.

KEYWORDS

Design and Development Methodologies and Frameworks, Multi-Agent Systems, E-learning, Agile Methodologies

1. INTRODUCTION

The choice of appropriate technology is recognized as a key aspect in every ICT and Information Systems (IS) project, particularly when the design involves the development of innovative products and services, determining tradeoff among costs, resources, performances and innovation. Cost, for example, is considered so determinant that some studies suggest delaying the start of the project until a new, less-costly technology is available (Benaroch and Kauffman, 2000) even if such decision can reduce the project benefits, particularly when the project involves the launching of an innovative technology that can bring competitive advantage only to first movers (Sanchez et al. 2017). Organizations must also evaluate the risk of potential losses that technology uncertainty can cause (Fichman et al. 2005), as analyzed also in (Tatikonda and Rosenthal 2000), who studied the relationships between typical characteristics of product development project, including technology, novelty and project outcomes. Innovation objectives would ideally imply to bridge the gap between academic and industrial interests and to advance both academic and practical/industrial knowledge., Anyhow the goal of advancing practice with the benefits of research findings has often been difficult to achieve (Taylor et al. 2012), and research findings have to be transformed into practices while taking into account industrial expectation, for example as to integrability, scalability, modularity, resistance to change, and security.

In this bridging direction, in (Salutari et al. 2021) we introduced a novel *Distributed Hybrid System* (DHS) approach to Information System Development (ISD), *blending Multi-Agent System (MAS) programming with Object and Event Oriented programming* to take the best from each one and to manage IS aspects such as asynchronous events, communication between different modules, and data flows that need to be treated as big data. Indeed, MASs promise to offer efficient development approaches (Batkovskiy et al. 2019, Giannakis and Louis 2016), based on the integration of cooperating autonomous intelligent agents, and offer the advantage of distributing computational effort and of increasing overall robustness (Costantini 2016). On the other hand, though largely used for simulations in academic contexts (e.g., Costantini 2017, Costantini 2020), they have the disadvantage to be very often closed systems, e.g., programmed in logic programming languages like

Prolog, Datalog or their derivatives, and it may be burdensome integrating and managing MASs in real systems, especially after production.

In this paper we discuss the advantages of our DHS approach through a case study related to the industrial project CyberTrainer, currently under refactoring and expansion, aimed at developing a Cyber Security e-learning platform. The project derived from an academic pilot, thus bridging research and development by its very nature. In the remainder of the paper, after summarizing architectural and technological choices, we analyze them with respect to the following benchmark aspects, typically faced in ISD: (A1) *integration of research and development*, (A2) *ease of installation in pre-existing environments*, (A3) *security*, (A4) *data modeling*, (A5) *error correction*, (A6) *cost*, (A7) *multi-tenancy requirements*, (A8) *computational and memory load.* The achieved results demonstrate the success of the two-fold hybridization, on the one hand bridging research and practice and on the other hand integrating diverse technologies and methods.

2. ANALYSIS OF ARCHITECTURAL AND TECHNOLOGY CHOICES

CyberTrainer is an in-progress industrial project by Reiss Romoli s.r.l., aimed at developing a *Cyber Security e-learning platform* where users attend Courses, carry out laboratory activities, and participate in Team Challenges. Team Challenges are hacking competitions in which users are divided into two teams, attackers and defenders. In these challenges, users' and network machines are virtual machines hosted on servers, like for Laboratories. The CyberTrainer life cycle (design, developing, testing and release) is based on the integration of research and development. As to the choice of analytics and business intelligence platforms, we initially considered the acquisition of commercial platforms, which, besides purchasing costs, has the disadvantage of requiring the installation of additional software (e.g., Power BI requires Microsoft OS on the hosting server). We hence opted for a development approach based on an ad-hoc novel solution to be internally developed, discussed in the following with reference to the Report module.

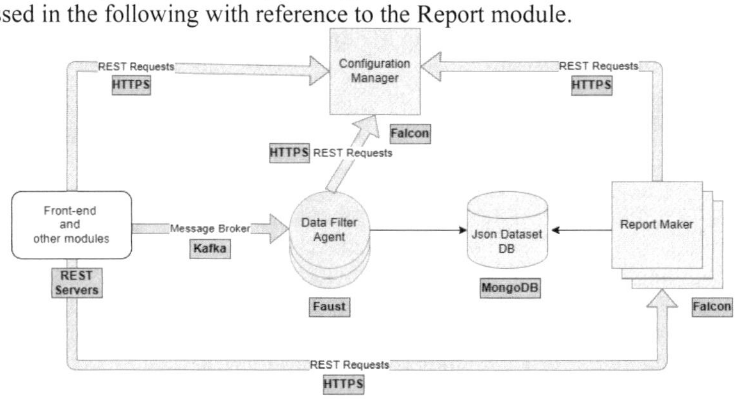

Figure 1. The DHS-based Report module architecture

Architectural and technological choices. The *Report module* is a recently developed part of CyberTrainer that had to be integrated with pre-existing modules, required to be resistant to changes, easily integrable, performing, modular, portable and secure. Figure 1 illustrates the architecture of the module, based on our DHS approach, showing submodules and adopted technologies. In particular, the MAS-based submodule "Data Filter Agent" is developed in Python3, using the stream processing library Faust (https://faust.readthedocs.io/en/latest/) running on Kafka broker (https://kafka.apache.org/) for data filtering and inferences by events, while the REST server submodule "Report Maker" is developed in Python3, using the Falcon minimalist WSGI library (https://falconframework.org/). The Report Maker is actually realized as a set of servers (one on each tenant) for aggregating MAS's results and providing output to the system in the proper format, sharing the MongoDB database with the MAS-based submodule. The Configuration Manager is a Falcon-based submodule in charge of managing all the configurations that can be shared by the system modules, allowing them to share the same updated configurations at runtime. In the following we analyze this DHS-based architectural and technology choices with respect to benchmark aspects A1-A8 introduced in the Introduction, also summarized in Table 1.

Table 1. Analyzing the Report module with respect to (A1) integration of research and development, (A2) ease of installation in pre-existing environments, (A3) security, (A4) data modeling, (A5) error correction, (A6) cost, (A7) multi-tenancy requirements, (A8) computational and memory load

Architectural and technological aspects	Involved benchmark aspects
Integration of research and development	**A1**
Ad-hoc analytics and business intelligence platforms	**A6**
Centralized shared and secure configuration	**A4, A5, A6**
Faust over Kafka broker with Json messages	**A2, A3, A4, A5, A6**
Faust data casting	**A1, A2, A3, A7**
Integration of batch and real-time processing	**A4, A5, A8**
Mongo DB No-SQL database	**A1, A3, A4, A6, A7**
Distributed approach	**A1, A2, A6, A8**

Centralized shared and secure configuration. Starting from the Configuration Manager, we observe that, thanks to the architectural and technological choices, shared configurations are always aligned and updated for everyone, so to avoid misconfiguration errors and redundancy. Furthermore, configurations are stored in Json format, and are therefore compatible with all system's modules, including the Report module with its MAS. All system modules can require the set of their special configurations by using a bearer token authentication. Tokens are no longer valid after a configured number of requests and the last new token is available in the response, as in line with the latest security trends **(Ref: A4, A5, A6)**.

Faust over Kafka broker with Json messages. The choice of using Faust over Kafka broker with Json messages for the communication between the agents and the back-end, exchanging data with the front-end in turn, made our module extremely easy to install in the pre-existent environment. Kafka is revealed to be secure, thanks to SSL encryption, and effectively brings the advantage of managing messages storage and delivery by itself, lightening up us from solving problems related to common network related error, like messages resending in case of network connections failure **(Ref: A2, A3, A4, A5, A6)**.

Faust data casting. Another advantage of that decision is the messages casting performed by Faust, increasing security and helping data modelling. This approach is surely very performing in IoT contexts for data exchange with the different microservices, maybe enriching agents with pre-trained neural networks properly programmed or given by providers, hosted onboard or on different machines. Other CyberTrainer modules interacting with the MAS are pure REST servers, so, in our case, it is still good but has the disadvantage of requiring other applications to push data on the broker instead of performing REST requests. This can be partially mitigated by Faust basic REST requests management feature (**Ref: A1, A2, A3, A7**). For the sake of completeness, it has to be observed that in other contexts less secure than ours, a possible disadvantage is that the addition of a message broker can increase the border of eventual attacks: for cyber-security, every additional item is one more item one has to defend. For that reason, one has to make the broker not too exposed, avoiding interaction with many other modules. An effective protection can be reached by installing the broker in a Docker container (https://www.docker.com/), maybe accessed by some delegated back-end modules only. This would help in clustering between different tenants, having a containerized Kafka instance for each tenant instead of using a different topic only.

Integration of batch and real-time processing. With the aim of error correction, the integration of batch agents in the MAS resulted useful. Those agents, running in background in predetermined time slots, can reprocess MAS inputs in order to detect and correct eventual agents' errors, repairing the resulting data on the database. This combines the enjoyable user experience coming from other always updated data available for the users from the other agents with the precision typical of batch processing **(Ref: A4, A5, A8)**.

Mongo DB No-SQL database. At the beginning, we decided to use Couchbase, a NoSQL database, to store Json data. Lately, after clients' request for a multi-tenancy feature because of security constraints, we decided to change the database using MongoDB, which is very similar to Couchbase but is economically more affordable (**Ref: A1, A3, A4, A6, A7**).

Distributed approach. Our distributed approach, finally, helped to redistribute the computational and memory load over the different servers, while modularity and portability made the difference with reinstalling on new machines (**Ref: A1, A2, A6, A8**).

3. CONCLUSION

In this paper we discussed our DHS approach to ISD, blending Multi-Agent Systems with Object and Event Oriented programming to overcome issues typically related to the integration with possibly pre-existing modules. In particular, we described the main features of the Reporting MAS module of the CyberTrainer system, and discussed results observed during a year of work of our module in a real-world environment with respect to a set of benchmark aspects typically addressed by ISD, showing how the hybridization choices turned successful. The module is currently in expansion for the next release. Future extensions will be focused on the analysis on users' preferences, in order to add user profiling capability, and on the introduction of a recommender system. Furthermore, Machine Learning techniques will be added, together with ad-hoc agents, in order to make the system able to make predictions and classifications over data.

ACKNOWLEDGEMENT

This work is partially supported by Reiss Romoli S.R.L.

REFERENCES

Batkovskiy, A.M. et al., 2019. Sustainable Project Management for Multi-agent Development of Enterprise Information Systems. *In Entrepreneurship and Sustainability*, Vol. 7, pp. 278-90.

Benaroch, M., and Kauffman, R.J., 2000. Justifying Electronic Banking Network Expansion Using Real Options Analysis. *In MIS Quarterly*, Vol. 24, No. 2, pp. 197-225.

Costantini, S. et al., 2016. Context and Action: A Unitary Vision Within A Logic-based Multi-agent Environment. *Digitally Supported Innovation*. Lecture Notes in Information Systems and Organisation, Vol 18. Springer, Cham, pp. 97-111.

Costantini, S. et al., 2017. Dali For Cognitive Robotics: Principles and Prototype Implementation. *Proceedings of International Symposium on Practical Aspects of Declarative Languages*. Springer, Cham, pp. 152-162.

Costantini, S. et al., 2020. Proposal of an Empathic Multi-agent Robot Design Based on Theory of Mind. *Proceedings of cAESAR 2020 - Workshop on Adapted intEraction with SociAl Robots*, Cagliari, Italy.

Delone, W.H. et al., 2016. Information Systems Success Measurement. *In Foundations and Trends® in Information Systems*, Vol. 2, No. 1, pp. 1-116.

Fichman, R.G., et al., 2005. Beyond Valuation:" Options Thinking" in It Project Management. *In California Management Review*, Vol. 47, 74–96.

Giannakis, M. and Louis, M., 2016. A Multi-agent Based System with Big Data Processing for Enhanced Supply Chain Agility. Journal of Enterprise information Management, Vol. 29, No. 5, pp. 706-727.

Hassan, N.R. and Mathiassen, L., 2018. Distilling a Body of Knowledge for Information Systems Development. *In Information Systems Journal*, Vol. 28, No. 1, pp. 175-226.

Salutari, A. et al., 2021. The Hybrid MAS Approach for Information System Development in "Cyber Trainer", *Proceedings of 14th IADIS International Conference Information Systems 2021*, IADIS Press, pp. 275-281.

Sanchez, O.P. et al., 2017. Cost and Time Project Management Success Factors for Information Systems Development Projects. *In International Journal of Project Management*, Vol. 35, No. 8, pp. 1608-1626.

Taylor, H. et al., 2012. Information Technology Project Risk Management: Bridging the Gap between Research and Practice. *In Journal of Information Technology*, Vol. 27, No. 1, pp. 17-34.

Tatikonda, B.K and Stephen R Rosenthal, S.R., 2000. Successful execution of product development projects: Balancing firmness and flexibility in the innovation process. *In Journal of Operations Management,* Vol. 18, No. 4, pp. 401-425.

DATA PROTECTION AND PRIVACY DETERMINANTS OF E-GOVERNMENT ADOPTION IN NIGERIA

Joshua Chukwu, Marc Conrad and Tess Crosbie
University of Bedfordshire, Luton Campus, UK

ABSTRACT

The global recurring news about data scandals, the sale of customer data and revealing employee records intensify concerns of citizens over protecting their privacy and personal data. This paper aims to systematically review literatures and discuss how data protection and privacy influences e-government adoption in Nigeria. Based on an extensive review of literature the paper provides a structured empirical findings and theoretical perspectives relating to impact of data protection and privacy on e-government adoption.

KEYWORDS

E-Government, Adoption, Data Protection and Privacy

1. INTRODUCTION

This study is designed to understand the impact of data protection and privacy in e-government adoption in Nigeria. It explores issues that influence e-government in developing countries like Nigeria. The focus of the research is on Nigerian perception of data protection and privacy in relation to the adoption of e-government services. Data protection and privacy have drawn researchers' attention as a concern. However, there are only a few studies that have attempted to comprehensively explore the link between data protection and privacy in one study (Carter & McBride, 2010; Belanger & Hiller, 2006; Agyei-Bekoe, 2013). No research study was found to have taken a holistic view of data protection and privacy in e-government in West African countries such as Nigeria, nor offer guidelines on how to evaluate citizen expectations against the government expectations of what constitutes good practice in terms of data protection and privacy; this has contributed to an ever-widening gap in e-government adoption resulting in lesser government online integration and transformation. This study seeks to fill that knowledge gap by investigating the impact of data protection in the adoption of e-government, especially in a country that has recently been identified as the major center for online criminal activity (OCCRP, 2019; FBI, 2017).

The increasing popularity of data protection and privacy in recent years is not without reasons in the adoption of e-government. The global recurring news about data scandals, the sale of customer data and revealing employee records intensify concerns of citizens over protecting their privacy and personal data. This paper aims to systematically review literatures and discuss how data protection and privacy influences e-government adoption in Nigeria. The review will afford the researcher the opportunity to suggest promising possibilities for increasing the success rate of data protection and privacy in Nigeria. Heeks and Bailur (2007) argue that there are various insights and a range of evidence on e-Government that are yet unexplored because of the lack of critical work.

Nigeria is a significant choice for this study for different reasons. In recent years, Nigerian governments have tapped into the potential of information and communication technology (ICTs) to transform and improve government service delivery. Government at all levels are expected to improve the efficiency of their services and also provide the citizen with reliable and up-to-date information (Adeyemo, 2011). The framework covering the use of ICT in governance in Nigeria is not based on an integrated system but various policies which include: the information policy, supervised by the national media commission; the telecommunications policy, regulated by the national communication commission (NCC); and the ICT policy which is overseen by national information technology development agency (NITDA) (Adeyemo, 2011).

It is for this purpose this study seeks to investigate the impact of data protection and privacy on e-government adoption, especially in a country that has recently been identified as the primary center for online criminal activity (OCCRP, 2019; FBI, 2017).

2. DATA PROTECTION AND PRIVACY

The increase and modification of information system technology with its ability to collect data, analyse and disseminate information raises concern for data protection and privacy legislation. This is a result of new developments across various field like telecommunication, advanced transportation system, and financial transfers that interconnect people and increase the level of information generation. However, there is a major concern from an opinion poll over privacy and data protection violation (Banisar & Davis, 1999). From background study, privacy is the actual right of individuals and organizations to control the collection, use, and distribution of their data, as well as giving consent to ways they are managed and stored. In the past, data protection and privacy were centered just on personally identifiable information, consent choice on the bases. But with the increasing sophistication of information technology with enhancing capacities, ICT firms and government agencies are integrating more targeted privacy notice and control over their products and services, because data protection and privacy are no longer based on personally identifiable information. Instead, it is about risks and threats against a broader set of personal information and recognizing that all information can carry different levels of risk (Ruivo et al., 2014).

Investigating the impact of data protection and privacy on e-government adoption requires the identification of the root cause of data protection and privacy concerns (Phelps et al., 2000). However, because of the complexity in measuring and defining data protection and privacy, this study focuses on the ability for an individual or organization to manage, control the collection, use, and distribution of their data, as well as giving consent to ways they are managed and stored. As background studies show that the ability to control and manage the release and dissemination of personal information is one of the key factors that provide the greatest degree of explanation for data protection and privacy concerns (Dinev & Hart, 2004).

3. THE FUNDAMENTAL OF E-GOVERNMENT DATA PROTECTION AND PRIVACY

Lack of data protection and privacy are critical obstacles in e-government adoption and implementation. They can delay progress towards realizing the promise of e-government (OECD, 2003). The certainty of an appropriate level of protection and privacy regarding personal information and respect over rights to control personal data from unauthorized access is essential to e-government adoption (Basu, 2004). Therefore, the government has an obligation as an institution that provides e-government services to provide full data protection and privacy assurance (Sharma & Gupta, 2003). E-government should be approached based on quality assurance for data protection and privacy. Both technical and policy responses may be necessary when addressing their impact on e-government adoption. Therefore, there is a need to manage data protection and privacy risk, and it is necessary to know how to classify information and recognize data linkages in order to increase citizen confidence in the use of e-government services (Alshehri & Drew, 2010).

The center of most e-government projects depends on the collection and management of large quantities of citizen's information such as names, addresses, phone numbers, employment history, date of birth, and medical records. As a result, citizens are genuinely concerned because today, data protection and privacy are no longer about personally identifiable information mentioned above. Instead, it is about recognizing that all information can carry different levels of risk depending on a variety of factors (Belanger & Crossler, 2011). The significance of data protection and privacy in e-government adoption and implementation cannot be overlooked, as it deals with processes that involves safeguarding important information from corruption, compromise, or loss. The UN e-government survey report (2018), emphasized that data protection and privacy is a great influence on e-government adoption. Comparing Data protection and privacy perception of developed countries like South Korea, the United Kingdom, and United States may not be realistic with developing countries as a result of the economic situation, cultural norms, literacy, and lack of enforceable data protection laws (Kumara Guru & Schdeva, 2013).

A study conducted in 2019 asked 28,000 EU citizens what they think about data protection and privacy (European Union, 2019). The report contained actual disclosure of personal information, awareness and perceived control over personal data, and data protection regulation. From the survey, 9 out 10 Europeans believe that it is important to allow individuals to have full control of their data regardless of where and who is providing the service. The report shows, there is a widespread concern in EU countries about the consequences of their data being misused.

A research study conducted by Adelola et al. (2015) focused on data protection and privacy perception of Nigerians. The research contained a survey and a brief interview. The study revealed that respondents were comfortable sharing their Facebook address, mail address, but they were least comfortable disclosing their bank account details, passport Number, Debit card numbers, and medical history. 41% of the respondents had never read the privacy policy on any website they had interacted with before sharing their personal information.

4. RESEARCH METHODOLOGY

Different data sources provided the input for this paper one of which is government information quarterly, information system research, international journal of electronic government research, journal of MIS and MIS quarterly. The articles targeted are articles published from the year 2000 to date. The literature search covered 620 articles published between 2000 to 2021 on e-government adoption, impact and challenges of e-government. The search employed a drill down approach by specifically focusing on finding topics related to e-government adoption.

The researcher used systematic literature review to collate and synthesize evidence on the existing impacts of data protection and privacy on e-government adoption. Several methods like Cochrane Anderson et al. (2016), and Kitchenham et al. (2016) were considered. However, according to Lyzara et al. (2019), shows that the guideline from Kitchenham et al. (2016) is most suitable method for performing a systematic literature review in e-government studies. The guideline covered three areas which are methodology planning, conducting and reporting.

5. PLANNING THE REVIEW

The research started from the introduction of research question and objectives applicable to the research goal, it enabled the researcher to identify preconditions, methods and made outcomes of participation to be consistent with e-government benefits and motivation, the challenges and barriers as argued by Axelsson et al. (2010). Therefore the primary objective of this paper are to:

1. Identify how data protection and privacy affects e-government adoption in Nigeria
2. Conduct a critical evaluation of the provision of e-government services in Nigeria and identify the current situation and progress made in the provision of e-government services in the country.
3. Make recommendations aimed at addressing constraints and risk inherent in the process of e-government adoption in an information and communication technology (ICT) environment in Nigeria.

In order to archive the above objectives, the researcher developed the following research questions:

1. To what degree is data protection and privacy relevant to e-government adoption in a developing country like Nigeria?
2. What are the functions of the government and the citizens in e-government adoption?

Considering the scope of the study the researcher examine data protection and privacy factor impacting on e-government adoption with the guidelines of Kitchenham et al. (2016). After clarifying research objectives and questions, research strategy was used to investigate relevant empirical studies corresponding to the objectives of the study. The process of forming for the search strategy was based on consistent search electronic databases such as Government information quarterly, information system research, international journal of electronic government research, journal of MIS and MIS quarterly ACM, IEEE, Springer link and Sciencedirect with conference papers. After several test in relevant databases key words were combined about e-government, data protection and privacy in two groups and through an "AND" conjunction. First was government information quarterly and the search yielded 124 hits and international journal of electronic government research was the second which yielded 415 articles. The both databases allowed a complete view of journal articles and conference proceedings with relevant e-government tracks.

The selected articles were all published in English and contained relevant discussions about e-government adoption and impact of data protection and privacy. Publications that focused on internet usage and intention to use e-services were all left out other exclusion were articles without data protection and privacy approach.

6. DISCUSSION AND CONCLUSION

After analysing the selected articles according to the research themes, it was established that data protection and privacy is the actual right of individuals and organizations to control the collection, use, and distribution of their data, as well as giving consent to ways they are managed and stored. In the past, data protection and privacy were centred just on personally identifiable information, consent choice on the bases. But with the increasing sophistication of information technology with enhancing capacities, ICT firms and government agencies are integrating more targeted privacy notice and control over their products and services, because data protection and privacy are no longer based on personally identifiable information. Instead, it's about risks and threats against a broader set of personal information and recognizing that all information can carry different levels of risk (Ruivo et al., 2014).

Nigeria, as a developing country, appears to be left out as many Nigerians have expressed concern about the lack of data protection and privacy legislation in Nigeria Adelola et al. (2015). In order to compete with other developed countries, The realities on the ground mandate both technical and policy responses to manage data protection and privacy risk, it is mandatory to know how to classify information, recognize data linkages for the purpose of increasing citizen confidence in the use of e-government services (Bernard & Timothy, 2015). Countries with legislation for data protection and privacy have remained committed to improving their e-government services. The GDPR known as European general data protection regulation is new legislation on data protection as a result of new technologies creating an increasing amount of data. There was need to legislate policy for the emerging trends from information communication technology with the understanding that ordinary laws made for regular offline interaction are not adequate to accommodate the challenges of e-government (Addis & Kutar. 2018). However, the present global trend in the protection of individual online data and privacy demands real legislative enactments to strengthen data protection regulations. As a result, citizens are concerned because today, data protection and privacy are no longer about personally identifiable information. Instead, it is about recognizing that all information can carry different levels of risk depending on a variety of factors (Belanger & Crossler, 2011).

7. RECOMMENDATIONS

This paper assessed the impact of data protection and privacy on e-government adoption in Nigeria through existing practices of EU GDPR. The finding shows that there is no comprehensive law that provides Nigerians with online data protection, unlike countries like the United Kingdom, South Korea, and Germany that favour a comprehensive regulatory approach to data protection (Aliyu, 2016). Which implies that, there is need for the Nigerian government to establish national regulation practice to manage data protection and privacy risk, which will enable organizations to know how to classify information, recognise data linkages. There is also a need for structural collaboration between state government and federal government towards data protection and privacy.

Data protection and privacy should be considered a significant factor in the design of an information system and the adoption of e-government. The Government, therefore, should create and enforce data protection and privacy legislation to protect e-government users. This findings may be generalizable to other West African countries which have similar social-cultural characteristics and share English as official language. Clearly many of this countries have similar experience and also surfer from related low development of human and organizational resources that makes e-government users more vulnerable to manipulations like the sale of customer data, revealing employee records.

For future research, more studies should be directed towards data protection and privacy regulations in Nigeria. Ability for an individual or organization to manage, control the collection, use, and distribution of their data, as well as giving consent to ways they are managed and stored should be the baseline to ensure conformance with applicable government regulations.

REFERENCES

Addis, M., and Kutar, M. (2018) March. The general data protection regulation (GDPR), emerging technologies and UK organizations: awareness, implementation and readiness. In *UK Academy for Information Systems Conference Proceedings*.

Adelola, T., Dawson, R. and Batmaz, F. (2015) Nigerians' perceptions of personal data protection and privacy.

Adeniran, A.I. (2008) The Internet and Emergence of Yahooboys sub-Culture in Nigeria. *International Journal of Cyber Criminology*, *2*(2).

Adeyemo, A.B., (2011). E-government implementation in Nigeria: An assessment of Nigerias global e-gov ranking. Journal of Internet and Information Systems, 2(1), pp. 11-19.

Agyei-Bekoe, E., (2013). Empirical Investigation of the Role of Privacy and Data Protection in the Implementation of Electronic Government in Ghana.

Aliyu, A.S., (2016). The Nigeria Data Protection Bill: Appraisal, Issues, and Challenges. *Peer-reviewed academic journal Innovative Issues and Approaches in Social Sciences*, p. 1961.

Alshehri, M., Drew, S., Alhussain, T. and Alghamdi, R. (2012) The Effects of Website Quality on Adoption of E-Government Service: AnEmpirical Study Applying UTAUT Model Using SEM. *arXiv preprint arXiv:1211.2410*.

Andersen, K.V. and Henriksen, H.Z., 2006. E-government maturity models: Extension of the Layne and Lee model. *Government information quarterly*, *23*(2), pp. 236-248.

Basu, S., (2004). E-government and developing countries: an overview. *International Review of Law, Computers & Technology*, *18*(1), pp. 109-132.

Bélanger, F. and Crossler, R.E., (2011). Privacy in the digital age: a review of information privacy research in information systems. MIS quarterly, 35(4), pp. 1017-1042.

Belanger, F. and Hiller, J.S., (2006). A framework for e-government: privacy implications. *Business process management journal*, *12*(1), pp. 48-60.

Bernard, O. & Timothy, I. A., (2015). Regulations or legislation for data protection in nigeria?. Global Journal of Politics and Law Research, Volume 3(4), pp. 1-16.

Carter, L. and McBride, A. (2010) Information privacy concerns and e-government: a research agenda. *Transforming Government: People, Process and Policy*, *4*(1), pp. 10-13.

Davis, F.D. (1989) Perceived usefulness, perceived ease of use, and user acceptance of information technology. *MIS quarterly*, pp. 319-340.

Dinev, T. and Hart, P., (2004). Internet privacy concerns and their antecedents-measurement validity and a regression model. *Behaviour & Information Technology*, *23*(6), pp. 413-422.

EU, C. (2019). Ega.ee. Available at: https://ega.ee/wp-content Final-Report-Research-analysis-guidelines-and-roadmap-for-full-deployment-of-e-governance-systems-in-Af.pdf [Accessed 26 Nov. 2019].

Gupta, S. and Kumaraguru, P., 2013. *OCEAN: open-source collation of eGovernment data and networks* (Doctoral dissertation).

Heeks, R. and Stanforth, C., (2007). Understanding e-Government project trajectories from an actor-network perspective. *European Journal of Information Systems*, *16*(2), pp. 165-177.

Kitchenham, B., and Charters, S. (2007). "Guidelines for performing Systematic Literature Reviews in Software Engineering," Engineering (2), p. 1051

Layne, K., and Lee, J. (2001). "Developing fully functional E-government: A four stage model," Government Information Quarterly (18:2), pp. 122–136

OECD, O.E., (2003) Government Flagship Report "The E-Government Imperative". *Public Management Committee, Paris: OECD.*

Ruivo, P., Santos, V. and Oliveira, T., (2014) Data protection in services and support roles–a qualitative research amongst ICT professionals. *Procedia Technology*, *16*, pp. 710-717.

Sharma, S.K. and Gupta, J.N., (2003). Building blocks of an e-government: A framework. *Journal of Electronic Commerce in Organizations (JECO)*, *1*(4), pp. 34-48.

Whitty, M.T. and Ng, M. (2017) Literature Review for understanding West African culture to prevent cybercrimes. Report for the National Cyber Security Centre as part of a group of studies funded in the Research Institute in Science of Cyber Security.

FACTORS AFFECTING TREND INTENTION IN YOUTUBE VIDEOS

Endrit Ajrulla, Marika Apostolova and Lejla Abazi-Bexheti
South East European University
ul. Ilindenska n.335, 1200, Tetovo, Macedonia

ABSTRACT

With hundreds of videos being uploaded to the video platform YouTube each second, many of these uploaded videos are lost in the sea of content never to be discovered by the potential audience it targets with only a select few becoming trending and reaching their potential audience. Now there are many factors that come into play when video becomes trending. The goal of this research is to understand what makes a video become trending on YouTube. The research has two essential parts: data mining and visualizing the collected data. Due to the vast amount of content uploaded to this platform this paper will focus on the Balkan countries. The result of this research shows how video makers that want to establish themselves on YouTube can use data mining and visualization to predict what videos can become trending and to understand the patterns of already trending videos.

KEYWORDS

YouTube, Video, Trend, Factors, Data Mining, Visualization

1. INTRODUCTION

YouTube is one of the biggest video sharing sites in the world. With up to 500 hours of video being uploaded each minute. YouTube officials put out the information that with over 2 billion monthly logged-in users, YouTube provides a lot of opportunities to content creators of all levels from amateur to professional or even people that are not content creators to generate income and pursue such a career.

However, it is not only people that are trying to make a career out of this that benefit from such a platform, but all kinds of content creators can also benefit from YouTube`s platform ranging from people trying to establish a career in content creation through YouTube, a business trying to maintain or gain customers through YouTube, even a corporation can benefit from YouTube`s gigantic user base. One the greatest tools that YouTube has provided to small channels or just people starting on YouTube is the opportunity to get on the front page through the trending tab. Now what is the trending tab YouTube defines the trending tab as: Trending helps viewers see what's happening on YouTube and in the world. Trending aims to surface videos that a wide range of viewers would find interesting. Some trends are predictable, like a new song from a popular artist or a new movie trailer. Others are surprising, like a viral video, based on trending information published on YouTube.

Several researches were performed on this problematic. Some analysis done by Alyousfi in 2020 on trending videos in the US with up to 70,000 videos, showed that if a video was on trending for 3 days it would have more worth than 1-day old trending video. Few years before this, Barjasteh in 2014 analyzed the trending videos and non-trending videos to find out the differences with up to 8,000 videos being analyzed, The research last 9 months. Apart from this analysis, in this research the authors analyzed the channels that had trending videos in their lists and channels with non-trending videos. The research that used the biggest data set with data sets ranging from 2017 to 2019 with 110,000 videos being analyzed in total is performed by Gayakwad and others in 2020. Apart from the biggest data set, this research lasted 2 years. All these research focus on trending videos globally or trending videos in US. The purpose of this research is to understand what makes a video trend in the Balkans, if it is any different from the global trending tab or maybe it is the same. The findings from this research can shed some light on the unknown and prove to be useful to all kinds of content creators in understanding what is needed for a video to become viral and to give them the knowledge to predict if a video will become viral or not.

2. METHODOLOGY

YouTube is one of the worlds' biggest video sharing platform and individuals or companies are seeing the potential in advertising their brand through it. But because of the size of the platform, with hundreds of hours of content being uploaded each second, new channels face great difficulties in forming an audience and maintaining one. Due such difficulties YouTube provides a lending hand through the trending tab which gives a boost to these new channels or already existing ones.

The primary data for this research were collected through a python script using the YouTube API to fetch the information needed such as video length, title, tags, comments, likes and dislikes etc.

The research questions that were taken into a consideration are: what category a video should be uploaded to, to reach trending; how long a video can remain trending; and what is the lowest number of views needed to reach trending.

By Statista, YouTube unlike other online platforms is growing fast and has not slowed down at all making the competition fiercer than ever. Compared to 5 years ago, when the total number of users was 1.4 billion and compared to today it is over 2 billion because of such a huge growth there are more opportunities for new channels but also there is more competition involved.

Apart from the new competition channels also face the already established channels which have built their audience and hold the bigger part of the pie. With YouTube showing no signs of slowing down its growth this means two things for new channels, more opportunities but also more competition for them. Going into this environment new channels will need all the tools they can get just to survive and if possible, to succeed.

Decisions on what to upload and for what demographic to upload to nowadays are done with an objective point of view, compared to in the past where it was more subjective and based on experience rather than data. However due to the growth in competition and the risks of losing an audience more and more people are turning to data and analytics in making such decisions.

2.1 Tools

The main tools used to make this research: Data Mining and Data Visualization. SAS Institute analytics recognized data mining as a process of finding anomalies, patterns, and correlations within a large data set to predict an outcome. This process allows us to gain better understanding of already existing data that we have with modern technology data mining has been made extremely easy and convenient where we can analyze datasets in mere seconds. Through data mining it has become much easier to find patterns within the data and there are many algorithms that can be used to provide better understanding of them. Data Visualization is the representation of data through visual elements such as charts, graphs and maps, such visualizations provide an easy way to see patterns in data. In such types of research, Data visualization is extremely important in getting the point across, as analyzed by the Michigan State University.

2.2 Data Collection

As mentioned before the data collected for this research is made possible by the public API provided by YouTube, through this API we can collect public statistics related to trending videos and the channels that upload them. On average 200 videos a day are extracted by the API. It is important to state that the data collected was done in a small timeframe specifically 1.5 months starting from March to April 2021.

In this research the data was first gathered, pre-processed, analyzed and then at the end the results were visualized. Data Visualization was made possible with seaborn and matplotlib libraries present within the "The Jupyter Notebook" environment. Jupyter Notebook is an open-source web application that allows you to transform and visualize data. The datasets that were imported into Jupyter were in .csv format.

2.3 Data Analysis and Discussion

The dataset contains over 60,000 trending videos in the Balkans (Figure 1), the time-frame of the dataset spans from March 9th 2021 till April 29th 2021 collected through a python script that collects that days trending YouTube videos based on country and this case specifically it collects from Balkan countries.

```
Int64Index: 61453 entries, 0 to 196
Data columns (total 19 columns):
 #   Column              Non-Null Count  Dtype
---  ------              --------------  -----
 0   video_id            61453 non-null  object
 1   title               61453 non-null  object
 2   publishedAt         61453 non-null  datetime64[ns, UTC]
 3   channelId           61453 non-null  object
 4   channelTitle        61453 non-null  object
 5   categoryId          61453 non-null  int64
 6   trending_date       61453 non-null  object
 7   tags                61453 non-null  object
 8   view_count          61453 non-null  int64
 9   likes               61453 non-null  int64
 10  dislikes            61453 non-null  int64
 11  comment_count       61453 non-null  int64
 12  thumbnail_link      61453 non-null  object
 13  comments_disabled   61453 non-null  bool
 14  ratings_disabled    61453 non-null  bool
 15  description         61055 non-null  object
 16  video_length        61453 non-null  object
 17  publishing_day      61453 non-null  object
 18  publishing_hour     61453 non-null  int64
```

Figure 1. The dataset of trending videos in the Balkans

The majority of these videos have less than 20 million views when they become trending more accurately when these videos hit the trending tab over 91% of these videos have less than 10 million views and 99% had less than 100 million views. The next matter is how many views did these videos have before entering the trending tab. So, over 90%t of videos entered the trending tab when they had less than 2,908,699 views. The minimum number views a video had before entering trending was 12,969 views. The average number of views a video had before entering the trending tab was 1,371,304 views and the 50th percentile was 250,803 views. Each video enters the trending tab, but some stay longer than others with some cases ranging from a few weeks to some remaining trending for months. Also was found that the videos can remain trending for long periods of time and most of these videos belong in the Music category followed by the Entertainment category and the longest trending video was in the trending tab for 216 days (7.1 months).

Titles are very important to a video's popularity. The three most common terms found in the titles of these trending videos are: The Turkish term 'Bölüm' which episode can be seen 5625 times; the term 'Official' comes in second which is seen 5009 times; and finally, the third most popular term the current year we are in '2021' is seen 4063 times.

How long is the average the title length of a trending video is crucial. The most trending videos have a title length between 36 and 67 characters. The average length of a title is 52 characters. The maximum length is 100 characters, and the minimum is 4 characters.

Which channels produced the highest number of videos that entered trending tab, can be seen from the following Figure 2.

From this can be understood that the top 3 channels boast over 500 trending videos. The channel with biggest amount of trending videos was the Turkish channel "Legacy" with 609 trending videos, followed closely by the joint top 2 and 3 "Диана Схов" and "Zadruga Official" both with 546 videos.

Categories play quite a role if a video will enter the trending tab. The most dominant category is Entertainment with 23,527 videos (38% of trending videos). After Entertainment there is Music with 13,806 videos (22% of trending videos). Then finally the third category Sports with 4979 videos (8% of trending videos).

The top 2 days edge out the rest of days but not by a lot, with Saturday (10,202) and Friday (10,008) being neck and neck and with Sunday (9,078) coming in third in this chart while day with the lowest number of videos uploaded is Tuesday (7,274).

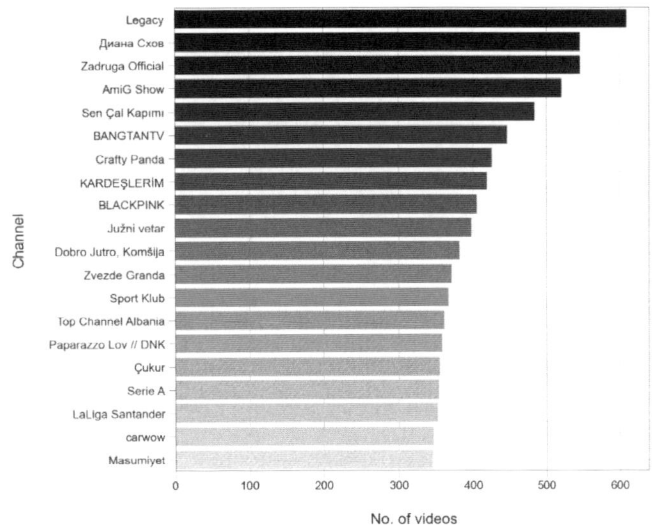

Figure 2. The channels produced the highest number of videos

The hour of the day when the trending videos published at is also something that worth analyzing. The biggest chunk of videos as seen on the chart are uploaded during 17:00 (5,669 videos) and 18:00 (5,657 videos) and in the third place 21:00 (4,861 videos).

Regarding the comments on how active a video is, it was found that most trending videos, 97% to be more precise, have less than 100,000 comments. The average amount of comments was 20,876 and the maximum 2,541,506. There is a big difference before and after a video enters the trending tab, over 90% of videos that enter the trending tab have less than 7,322 comments and 99% of videos had less than 71,781 comments.

How many likes do trending videos receive, is another parameter that we observed. We get that the most videos more exactly 93% of videos have less than 500,000 likes and 99% of videos have less than 5,000,000 likes. The video with the biggest number of likes belongs to the channel "BLACKPINK" the video is titled "ROSÉ - 'On The Ground' M/V" the video has 7,953,055 likes.

We observed the like distribution of videos before they enter the trending. So, over 90% of videos before entering the trending tab have 82,222 likes. The lowest amount of likes a video received before entering the trending tab was 19 likes and it was on the trending tab for a single day.

Compared to likes there is a big contrast in the dislikes where 99% of videos have less than 100,000 dislikes. The video with the most dislikes belongs to the channel "LilNasXVEVO" with the video "Lil Nas X - MONTERO (Call Me By Your Name) (Official Video)" having 645,865 dislikes. The dislikes distribution is also quite low and as it can be seen over 90% have 2,444 dislikes before entering the trending tab.

Furthermore, over 90% of videos have descriptions with less than 2,000 characters with only 2,4% of videos having descriptions that are above 3,000 characters, and on the right side, it can be spotted that the average number of tags is 18 tags, over 11% have no tags.

The minimum number of tags that a video has is 0 and the maximum that it has is 81.

2.3.1 Data Correlation

The kind of metrics correlation in trending videos, is presented via the heat chart on Figure 3. In this heatmap darker colors represent a stronger correlation and lighter shades mean a weaker correlation and for the highest positive value it is 1 whilst the lowest negative value is -1. The heatmap shows a strong correlation between views and likes (0.88) and a strong correlation between views and dislikes (0.78) and in top 3 of the strongest correlation is comments (0.72) these 3 correlations show how important views, likes, dislikes and comments are to a video's success.

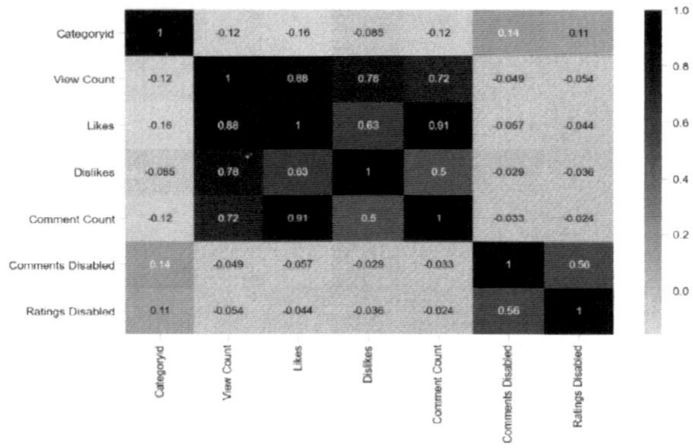

Figure 3. The correlation in trending videos

3. CONCLUSION

YouTube like any other platform has evolved through the years and one of the steps it has taken in its evolution is introducing the trending tab. Through this tab many youtubers have gained an advantage which allows them to reach new audiences and help them maintain already existing ones. Through the data collection and data analysis done through Jupyter notebook some conclusions were achieved:

- The most popular video category is Entertainment with up to 38% of trending videos being uploaded on that category.
- Videos can remain trending for months with the longest trending video trending for 216 days (7.1 months).
- A video can enter the trending tab with only 12,969 views.
- Terms such as “Bölüm”,”Official”,”2021”,”Music”,”Highlights” were the most common terms throughout.
- Almost all trending videos have tags.
- Uploading on Saturday, Friday and Sunday yields the best results.
- Uploading from 17:00 till 18:00 is the most dominant uploading hour.
- Videos before entering the trending tab on average had 4,895 comments.
- Most Title lengths of videos are between 36 and 67 characters.

REFERENCES

Alyousfi, A. 2020. Analysis of YouTube Trending Videos of 2019 (US). Link: https://ammar-alyousfi.com/2020/youtube-trending-videos-analysis-2019-us#summary-of-some-key-results-of-the-analysis

Auxier, B. and Anderson, M. Social Media Use in 2021. Pew Research Center. 2021. Link: https://www.pewresearch.org/internet/2021/04/07/social-media-use-in-2021/

Barjasteh, I. et al, 2014. Trending Videos: Measurement and Analysis. 2014; Computer Science; ArXiv 2014 https://www.researchgate.net/publication/266262149_Trending_Videos_Measurement_and_Analysis

Gayakwad, S. et al, 2020. Analysis on YouTube Trending Videos. International Research Journal of Engineering and Technology (IRJET). Volume: 07. Link: https://www.irjet.net/archives/V7/i8/IRJET-V7I8732.pdf

Michigan State University. 4 Types of Data Analytics and How to Apply Them. Business analytics. Link: 2019. https://www.michiganstateuniversityonline.com/resources/business-analytics/types-of-data-analytics-and-how-to-apply-them/

SAS Institute analytics. Data Mining, what it is and why it matters. 2021. Link: https://www.sas.com/en_us/insights/analytics/data-mining.html

Statista. Forecast of the number of Youtube users in the World from 2017 to 2025. 2021. Link: https://www.statista.com/forecasts/1144088/youtube-users-in-the-world

YouTube officials. Trending on YouTube. Link: https://support.google.com/youtube/answer/7239739?hl=en

Youtube officials. YouTube for Press. Link: https://blog.youtube/press/

AN IT-GRC APPROACH IN SME

Nico Deistler and Christopher Rentrop
HTWG Konstanz, Fakultät Informatik, Konstanz, Germany
Alfred-Wachtel-Straße 8, 78462 Konstanz

ABSTRACT

The digital transformation of business processes and the integration of IT systems leads to opportunities and risks for small and medium-sized enterprises (SMEs). Risks that can result in a lack of IT compliance. The purpose of this research-in-progress paper is to present the current state of a IT-Governance-Risk-Compliance (IT-GRC) research-project. First, the results of an already conducted literature research will be discussed, combined with qualitative interviews (expert survey) of persons close to IT compliance. In the context of this paper, a first design approach will be developed by selecting relevant existing frameworks and standards and the identification of SME-specific conditions. The first design is intended to contribute a further artefact conception of tailoring approaches and standards and the creation of a guidance.

KEYWORDS

IT-GRC, IT-Compliance, SME, DSR

1. INTRODUCTION

Small and medium-sized enterprises (SMEs) are known for their innovative strength and are increasingly confronted with the challenges of digitalization. In order to maintain or expand their competitive advantages, they are forced to actively address this development. The digital transformation of business processes and the greater integration of IT systems generate both, opportunities, and risks. Risks that can result in a lack of IT compliance, for example with regard to information security and data protection.

A literature analysis conducted (Deistler and Rentrop 2020) revealed that previous best-practice-approaches and standards are largely not suitable for SMEs and are therefore not widespread among German SMEs. The results of a survey of IT compliance managers show that the reasons for this status quo are excessively high costs for IT, limited employee resources, lack of expertise and frameworks that do not fit the structures in SMEs. As a result, companies do not implement a holistic approach, but only individual technological measures. Furthermore, digitalization, EU-DSGVO, cloud applications and cybersecurity already play a major role as drivers (Deistler and Rentrop 2022).

The purpose of this research-in-progress paper is to present the current state of the research-project. First, the results of an already conducted literature research will be discussed, combined with qualitative interviews (expert survey) of persons close to IT compliance. This forms the basis for conducting further research using the methodology of design science research approach based on Peffers et al (2008). In the context of this paper, a first design approach will be developed by selecting relevant existing frameworks and standards and the identification of SME-specific conditions. Due to the heterogeneity it is not reasonable to adapt one of the common standards for all SMEs (Beißel 2017). Instead, general SME-relevant competencies should be abstracted, and a guideline should be provided for choosing the appropriate standards, such as "BSI Grundschutz Basis" or "Cobit 2019 Focus area SME". The first design is intended to contribute a further artefact conception of tailoring of frameworks and standards.

2. STATUS QUO AND RELATED WORK

To identify relevant prior research, the literature on IT-Compliance was systematically reviewed (Webster and Watson 2002). For this purpose, the relevant scientific Internet databases were consulted, with a focus on journals, conferences, and monographs from German-speaking countries as well as selected international journals (Senior Scholar's Basket of IS Journals) in the field of Information Systems (IS). In the first step, the relevant literature was examined according to Webster and Watson using the search words compliance, IT compliance, SMEs, and mid-sized companies. From this list, more than 100 publications have been extracted. In the next step, the articles were examined for actual compliance relevance and thematic groupings were formed. In the further course, publications were identified that describe specific topic areas of IT compliance in connection with SMEs.

Contributions focus on the topics of IT risk management, IT security, cloud computing, IT governance and the implementation of reference models. Particularly in the case of contributions in connection with SMEs, it is apparent that these relate almost exclusively to the topics of digitalization and compliance-management-systems. However, the willingness in companies to actively address measures for IT compliance and IT security is low despite an increasing perception of risk (Hillebrand et al. 2017). The reasons and motives for this are, on the one hand, the perceived high costs associated with external expertise or the development of in-house staff, who are also scarce on the labor market (Deistler and Rentrop 2022). In addition, the frameworks do not fit the structures in SMEs, which was also described by Johannsen and Kant (2020).

There are barriers to the implementation in small and medium-sized enterprises, especially with more complex frameworks such as COBIT. These lie in the fact that parts of the approach, such as the seven "enablers", still have to be largely specified by the SME, and comprehensive requirements and process recommendations have to be handled (Beißel 2017).

Recent empirical evidence shows different approaches for SMEs. Henschel and Heinze (2016) present a GRC approach for SMEs, but this approach largely ignores the specific requirements and the extent of the digital transformation that has now also reached SMEs. Knoll and Strahringer (2017, p. 2) define IT-GRC as an integrated planning and control view of a company's opportunities and risks arising from the use of information as a production factor in the "age of digitalization". Their approach provides a good orientation, but still requires tailoring for SMEs. Beißel (2017) uses the example of the area of IT risk to show how existing frameworks can be meaningfully differentiated. Johannsen and Kant (2020) developed a competence-oriented approach for the perception, measurement and control of IT governance, risk and compliance management in SMEs.

This research aims to develop a guideline to choose the appropriate standards by abstracting SME-relevant competencies and tailoring existing approaches and standards to the defined competencies. With this, the following research question should be answered: How can an IT-GRC approach be designed to leverage existing frameworks and address specific needs of SMEs?

3. RESEARCH APPROACH

This chapter describes the theoretical background for designing the method to handle IT-GRC in SME. It presents similarities of IT-GRC and organizational structures and information systems and explain the connection to governance, risk and compliance management. Furthermore, it presents the applied design science research approach based on a literature review and case study's and show that this methodology is appropriate.

The study will be conducted according to Hevner´s design science research approach (Hevner et al. 2004). The primary goal is to develop a new artefact and thereby to address the research questions. The process of building artefacts in terms of a prescription-driven research is applicable to solve management problems (Van Aken 2004; Gregor and Jones 2007). By demonstrating procedural steps and measures, the proposed IS artefact represents a method focusing on an organizational issue (Braun et al. 2005). The artificial process behind the method construction follows the approved paradigm of design theory (March and Smith 1995; Peffers et al. 2008). The goal of the artefact is to specify the needs in order to solve the identified problem, to design a method, and to demonstrate and evaluate it (Figure 1).

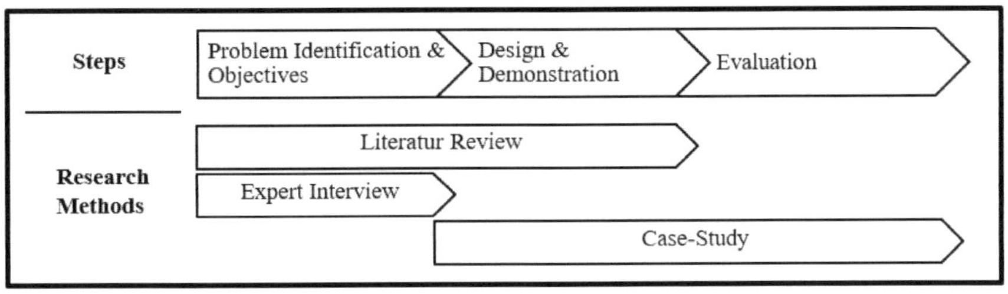

Figure 1. Research Methodology: Design Science Process based on Peffers et al. (2008)

The described status quo on IT-Compliance outlines the problem identification and objectives. Design and demonstration of the research will be reached out by using a theoretical foundation and exploratory evidences from a case study (Yin 2014). Due to the complexity of the topic, iterations of more case studies could be necessary, starting with a prototype method based on prior research and the working experiences of the authors with IT-Compliance (Flick 2009). In the end, the method is evaluated using qualitative evidences to prove its utility, quality and efficacy (Hevner et al. 2004). Following this process, we aim to ensure the conduction of good method design. Figure 2 summarizes the research foundation based on the design science research cycle model of Hevner (2007).

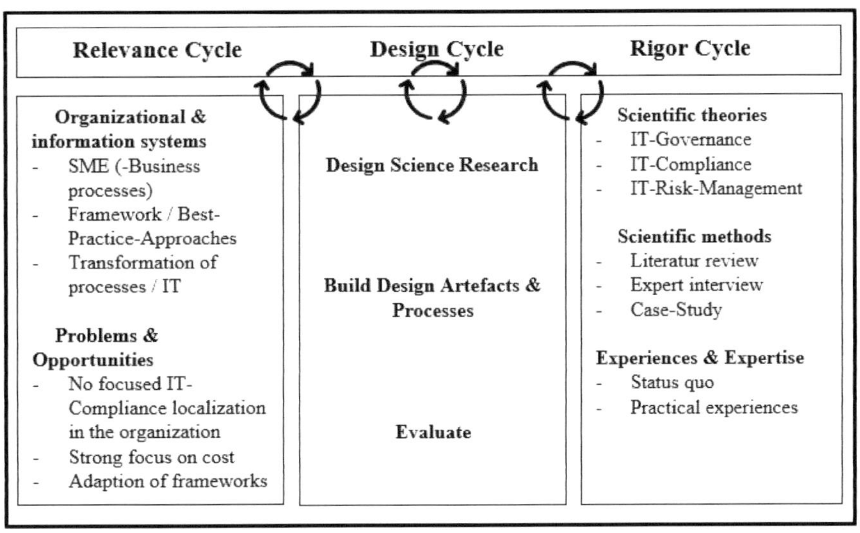

Figure 2. Research Foundation: Design Science Cycles based on Hevner (2007)

4. FIRST DESIGN APPROACH

Based on the problem identification in the status quo, this section presents the procedure of the first steps of the design process. Since this is a research-in-progress paper, representing the current state, no complete artefact is presented. The current work also serves as a proof-of-concept (Peffers et al. 2008) and are applied for the subsequent evaluation in further research. The first step was to identify the frameworks and standards relevant to this paper based on the conducted literature research and the qualitative expert interviews. This procedure already resulted in a pre-selection of standards since the focus of the paper was particular on SMEs. The selection is intended to be a representative group of heterogeneous frameworks without providing a complete coverage of all available frameworks. The approaches represent reference models/frameworks, developed by institutional and private organizations. Using the aforementioned approach, the following standards were identified as relevant: ISO/IEC 27001, ISO 20001, COBIT 2019, BSI IT-Grundschutz, ISIS12, and ITIL.

Based on the established and continuously revised COBIT 2019 Framework, this forms the basis for further research. COBIT 2019 includes a process reference model that defines and describes in detail a set of governance and management processes. All processes that are typically present in a company with regard to IT activities are represented in this model. Accordingly, the model divides into two essential process domains: Governance and Management (ISACA 2018). In this context, the COBIT 2019 framework simply provides a regulatory framework. However, the relevant design factors, especially with regard to SMEs, are not sufficiently addressed and defined. For this reason, COBIT 2019 is difficult to apply from the perspective of SMEs and justifies the need for further research, as described above. Nevertheless, the process reference model should serve as a frame of reference, which is used for structuring and mapping other standards. Mappings have already been performed in COBIT 2019 for some of the frameworks mentioned above (ISACA 2018). These are to be built upon. Within the scope of the project, the missing mappings are to be identified and supplemented on the basis of the reference model. Thus, a comparability of the different frameworks should be worked out in this form and answer the first part of the research question.

In the next step, a further classification is made based on SME-relevant competencies abstracted from the literature research and expert interviews. The already known approaches from IT risk management, IT governance and IT compliance are used. Factors according to which a distinction should be made is

- the IT organizational model, which in SMEs should be designed to be a lean organization,
- the uniqueness of the IT environment and
- the associated IT sourcing strategy from the governance perspective (Schwarze and Dillmann 2012).

Furthermore, current trends and developments are to be considered. These are, not yet conclusively evaluated, information security awareness, cyber security, cloud compliance, governance structures and data protection (Deistler and Rentrop 2022).

In further steps, the approach should be classified according to industries as well as small and medium-sized enterprises, since here there are once again significant differences. With this, the second part of the research question should be answered.

5. SUMMARY AND EXPECTED CONTRIBUTION

We have concluded the first step, problem identification and objectives, of our research on developing a guideline for IT-GRC in SMEs and briefly presented the results. The second phase, developing and evaluating the artefact, is still going on.

While we are sure that our contribution will add to theory and practice around IT-GRC in SME, we also foresee some limitations to the full coverage of the guideline.

Because of the large number of frameworks, not all of them can be included in the analysis. In addition to the competencies described, a company may need to consider other individual criteria. In summary, the contribution can be an enabler for SMEs to increase their awareness in terms of IT-GRC and provides recommendations for action to an adjusted minimum level on IT-GRC.

REFERENCES

Beißel, S. 2017. Differenzierung von Rahmenwerken des IT-Risikomanagements. *In HMD Praxis der Wirtschaftsinformatik*, Vol. 1, pp 54:37–54.

Braun, C., et al, 2005. Method construction - A core approach to organizational engineering. *Proceedings of the 2005 ACM symposium on Applied Computing, H. M. Haddad, A. Omicini, R. L. Wainwright, and L. M. Leibrock (eds.)*, Santa Fe, NM, pp. 1295-1299.

Deistler N, Rentrop C. 2020. IT-Compliance in KMU – State of the art. *In HMD Praxis der Wirtschaftsinformatik*, Vol. 57, pp 1047-1057

Deistler, N., Rentrop, C. 2022. IT-Compliance in KMU – Experteninterviews zum Status quo. *In Wirtsch Inform Manag* https://doi.org/10.1365/s35764-021-00380-5.

Falk, M., 2012. *IT Compliance in der Corporate Governance. Anforderungen und Umsetzung*. Springer, Wiesbaden, Germany.

Flick, U., 2009. *An introduction to qualitative research (4th ed.)*. Sage Publications, Los Angeles, USA.

Gregor, S., and Jones, D. 2007. The Anatomy of a Design Theory. *Journal of the Association for Information Systems*, (8:5), pp. 312-335.

Henschel T, Heinze I. 2016. *Governance, Risk und Compliance im Mittelstand, Praxisleitfaden für gute Unternehmensführung*. Erich Schmidt Verlag, Berlin, Germany.

Hevner, A. et al, 2004. Design Science in Information Systems Research. *In MIS Quarterly* (28:1), pp. 75-105.

Hevner, A. R. 2007. A Three Cycle View of Design Science Research. *Scandinavian Journal of Information Systems*, (19:2), Article 4, pp. 1-6.

Hillebrand A, et al, 2017. Aktuelle Lage der IT-Sicherheit in KMU.*WIK Wissenschaftliches Institut für Infrastruktur und Kommunikationsdienste GmbH*. https://www.wik.org/fileadmin/Sonstige_Dateien/IT-Sicherheit_in_KMU/WIK-Studie_Aktuelle_Lage_der_IT-Sicherheit_in_KMU_Langfassung__2_.pdf. (Accessed: 28. Nov. 2020).

ISACA, 2018. *Cobit 2019: Einführung und Methodik.* ISACA.org, USA

Johannsen A, Kant D. 2020. IT-Governance, Risiko- und Compliance-Management (IT-GRC) – Ein Kompetenz-orientierter Ansatz für KMU. *In HMD Pracis der Wirtschaftsinformatik*, Vol. 57, pp. 1058–1074.

Knoll M, Strahringer S. 2017. IT-GRC-Management im Zeitalter der Digitalisierung. *In: Knoll M, Strahringer S (Hrsg) IT-GRC-Management – Governance, Risk und Compliance. Grundlagen und Anwendungen*. Springer Vieweg, Wiesbaden, Germany, pp 1–24.

March, S. T., and Smith, G. F. 1995. Design and natural science research on information technology. *In Decision Support Systems* (15:4), pp. 251-266.

Peffers, K. et al, 2008. A Design Science Research Methodology for Information Systems Research. *Journal of Management Information Systems* (24:3), pp. 45-77.

Schwarze L, Dillmann C. 2012. Einflussfaktoren für IT-Governance oder „Gibt es das richtige Governance-Modell?". *In IT-Governance*. UVK, Konstanz, pp 41-45.

Van Aken, Joan E. 2004. Management research based on the paradigm of the design sciences: The quest for field-tested and grounded technological rules. *In Journal of Management Studies* (41:2), pp. 219-246.

Webster J, Watson R. 2002. Analyzing the past to prepare for the future:writing a literature review. *In MISQ* 26(2): xiii–xxiii.

Weill P, Ross JW. 2004. IT governance: how top performers manage IT decision rights for superior results. *In Harvard Business Review Press*, Boston, USA.

Yin, R. K, 2014. *Case study research: Design and methods (5th ed.)*. Sage Publications, Los Angeles, USA.

DATA COLLECTION IN HOSPITAL EMERGENCIES: A QUESTIONNAIRE SURVEY

Nouha Mhimdi[1], Wahiba Ben Abdessalem Karaa[2] and Henda Ben Ghezala[1]
[1]*National School of Computer Sciences Tunis, RIADI-GDL laboratory, ENSI, University of Manouba, Tunisia*
[2]*High Institute of Management of Tunis, University of Tunis, RIADI-GDL laboratory, ENSI, University of Manouba, Tunisia*

ABSTRACT

In order to provide data in the process of decision making, data collection is the first step. Currently, there are several methods of data collection that have been used such us questionnaires, surveys, focus group interviews. Or the collection of poor-quality data resulting, for example, from poorly designed questionnaires, the absence of good translators or interpreters, and the incorrect recording of data allow conclusions to be drawn that are not supported by the data or to focus only on the average effect of the program or policy. There are several solutions to avoid or minimize the most frequent errors, including obtaining expert advice on the design or adaptation of data collection instruments; or use technologies allowing better "anonymity" in the responses.

KEYWORDS

Data Collection, Survey, Database, Data Analysis, Hospital Emergencies

1. INTRODUCTION

Nowadays, a voluminous size of data is stored every day in data warehouses. The mass collected is from different sources, on the other hand, it is necessary to collect relevant, subject-oriented, integrated, non-volatile, historical and summary data, which will then help in the process of decision-making. The global volume of data will be multiplied by further than 3.7 between 2020 and 2025, then by 3.5 every five years until 2035, to reach the dizzying sum of 2.142 zettabytes (Kerlink and al., 2021). However, several problems are encountered, we can cite, for example, the difficulties in extracting information (Feng and al, 2021) and/or knowledge, the increase in knowledge generation time from the warehouses, the information obtained is no longer usable, also the performances obtained are insufficient (Hensen and al, 2021), (Rosenthal and al, 2020). This is due to the wrong choice of methods in data collection and analysis.

In fact, in the medical field, the existing data are confidential or protected by copyright, it is a question of inadequacy of the available data (bad resolution, lack of adequate report). Also, collecting data for the benefit of hospital emergencies becomes necessary to mitigate the problems encountered there. In this context, we opted to collect relevant data, by carrying out an extensive survey based on developing a questionnaire containing targeted and practical questions.

This paper is organized as follows: Section II provides a brief overview of the work related to data collection; the proposed approach is described in Section III. Finally, in Section IV, the simulation and the results are presented, and then a conclusion and future work are given at the end of this article.

2. LITERATURE REVIEW

In the literature, many limitations were identified, for example, complications in transcribing recordings of groups made up of several participants and unnecessary discussions between participants, which wasted a lot of time. Similarly, (Skhiri and al, 2012) carried out a cross-sectional study in the emergency departments of four hospitals in Tunisia. This involves collecting data from a questionnaire from a sample of 1058 patients of both sexes, aged 18 and over. The objective was to collect information concerning the socio-demographic characteristics of responders, the motivations for choosing the emergency service, the time and reason for consultation, the diagnosis, and the severity of the state of health. The study aimed to analyze the reasons for resorting to emergency services and the seriousness of the patient's state of health. The advantage is that the questionnaire is tested beforehand and administered by nursing investigators, the survey is systematic from the registration register by including prospectively the patients whose number is odd, and until the expected number of workers is reached, with stratification on the time slots. The downside is that using a face-to-face questionnaire to collect data near hospital emergencies can influence the quality of the obtained data (Braekman and al, 2020)

In the current research landscape, more and more researchers are using the online survey to collect data, disseminating it to relevant associations, the media, and interested individuals. The researchers noted several advantages: low cost, time-saving in data collection, reduction in errors during data entry, greater freedom of the respondent, large-scale survey dissemination (Braun and al, 2020).

2.1 Problem Description

Choosing to collect data not explicitly related to the critical evaluation questions will result in inadequate information and reporting. The online survey data collection method requires familiarity with computers and requires dexterity in handling the material (Johnson and al, 2012). It is more difficult for respondents to distinguish spam or advertising from serious mail. Some people are therefore suspicious of solicitation e-mails; others are also suspicious of computer security and fear viruses (Lindhjemand and al, 2011). These elements make the selection of respondents even more complex and certainly affect response rates. Likewise, online surveys are generally non-probabilistic and uncontrolled; one cannot distinguish respondents from others.

2.2 Objective Work

Overcrowding and tension have become a real problem in the health system nowadays; insufficient human and material resources manifest them. Likewise, emergency physicians denounced flaws in the hospital system, mainly due to a lack of resources (Tpisheh and al., 2019). This leads to increased wait times that can worsen the condition of patients, causing dissatisfaction with patients, physicians, and increase the risk of mortality.

Our objective is to solve the problems afore mentioned to improve the quality of emergency services by carrying out a study allowing the collection of coherent, and interesting data, and to set up a process allowing their cleaning, their transfer between the different types of software analysis, and their availability, and accessibility at all times for verification purposes.

3. THE EVOLUTIONARY APPROACH

In all health systems, the emergency structure represents an important link in the chain of patient care. However, the number of arrivals to emergencies continuously increased, and enormous organizational problems were caused and negatively influenced the quality of services (Asheim and al, 2019). To remedy the problems that have been caused by the massive influx of emergency room visits, we propose an approach founded on a data collection system. The latter is based on a survey made using a questionnaire near hospital emergencies. Figure 1 summarizes the steps to create a new database gathering the data necessary for optimized emergency management.

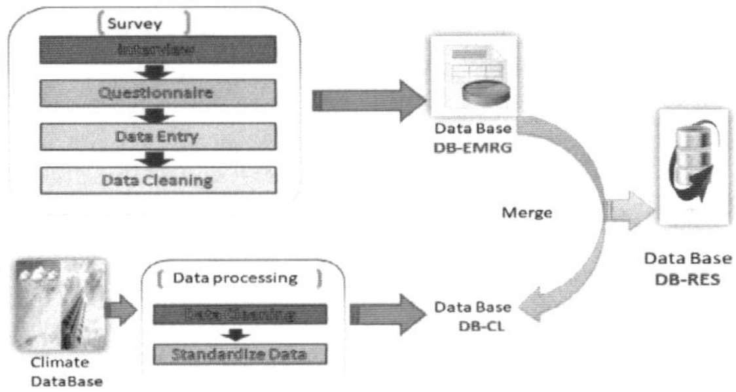

Figure 1. Approached data collection DC-EMRG: Database creation DB-RES

3.1 Phase1: Creation of the DB-EMRG Database

3.1.1 Interview

This step begins by determining the data collection problems and the tasks carried out to obtain quality data and clear and precise information. To this end, it might be useful to interview individuals affected by this study, such as emergency physicians, nurses, and patients visiting emergency departments.

Then, we collected a set of data after the interviews, we had a whole set of points of view, opinions, gaps, missing needs. We identified the set of requirements, on one hand, for the medical staff, and on another hand for the patients. Therefore, this step is considered as preparation for the next step.

3.1.2 Questionnaire Survey

Our work begins by first determining a sample of interviewees: We opted for a large sample size to achieve satisfactory results: 8829 individuals. We reached out to the population of northern Tunisia given the geographic, economic, and social specificities common to this region. We proposed short, understandable, and targeted questions to allow respondents to respond more spontaneously to the questionnaire. The choice of question type will also affect the survey results; for this, we used qualitative questions based on impressions, and opinions to collect information intended to describe the topic rather than quantitative measurement questions used to collect raw, concrete data, in digital form. We used different types of questions: closed single-choice questions, closed-ended multiple-choice questions, open-ended questions and ordered qualitative questions.

3.1.3 Data Entry

Collected answers following the paper questionnaire must be entered carefully to avoid double entry. Therefore, we used the online platform Google Sheets (Tim and al., 2018) that allows adding lines of answers. This step consists of adding to the online database the responses relating to minors, children, the elderly, and those who cannot answer the online questionnaire. Once the questionnaire has been entered, it must be classified and highlighted with a perceptible color.

3.1.4 Data Cleaning

If the data are not clean, decisions based on those data might be wrong and affect the results (Chu and al, 2016). Therefore, to have a consistent, useful, and reliable database, we processed the responses line by line to correct errors, examine incomplete data and erroneous data. In addition, in this step, we have merged the columns concerning people who give answers instead of children or instead of individuals who do not have access to the internet. Also, the answers to qualitative questions are transformed into quantitative data to be represented in the database.

3.1.5 Creation of the DB-EMRG

The result of the presented steps is a DB-EMRG database gathering structured, coherent data, useful in the third phase of the proposed approach. This database contains a set of data relating to hospital emergencies in Tunisia, which will help to alleviate existing and future problems in emergencies.

3.2 Phase2: Creation of the DB-CL Database

The second phase consists of building the DB-CL database gathering the climate values for 2020.

1) Download the existing national climate database: This database brings together Tunisian climate data (temperature, humidity, visibility, heat index, weather conditions, etc.)
2) Clean the data: To keep only useful data, needed for this study and remove the unnecessary data. Also, correct some errors, get rid of inconsistent data, and delete missing values.
3) Standardize the data: put the values in a standard format, for example, put the dates in standard format (dd-mm-yyyy), all decimal numbers of the same format, and all integers of the same format.
4) Create a database that we named DB-CL, gathering all the necessary and useful meteorological values needed in our study.

3.3 Phase 3: Creation of the DB-RES Database

This phase is the final step of our proposed approach to merge the two created databases DB-EMRG and DB-CL, after putting the data in a standard format. We named the resulting database DB-RES: it contains 49 variables and 8829 structured rows, ordered and sorted in ascending order of the date. Besides, the database obtained will then be merged with the data collected from the emergencies existed in the registers grouping the informations of the patients such as the number of visits to the emergencies and in which period, the service consulted, the patient's health.

4. SIMULATIONS CONDITION AND RESULTS

We have opted for the analysis of our data obtained in the database DB-CL by using the programming language R and the IBM SPSS statistical software to ensure advanced statistical analysis. In the DB-RES Database, for example, the number of male patients is higher than that of women for ages between 35 and 45 years and those between 55 and 65 years, which explain that the undercurrent health problems generally affecting men, such as digestive problems, respiratory problems due to frequent smoking, cardiovascular problems, and pain from work accidents or road accidents. This appeared in particular periods; for this, we have represented the distribution of patients per month, we notice that the activity peaks in emergencies in particular periods; the curve reaches its limits in March and April, between May and June, August, and December. This comes down to several external factors such as climate change which makes you feel bronchitis and flu, the appearance of an epidemic such as COVID-19 and school holidays which influence the number of accidents on the road.

In order to validate the data collected, we used the statistical measure such as the confidence interval shown in the table bellow Table 1. it concern the period when the patient visit the emergencies hospital.

Table 1. Confidence interval regarding the period of visiting day

	Estimation	Standard error	confidence interval 95%	
			Inferior	Superior
morning	2777,000	43,632	2691,471	2862,529
noon	1642,000	36,562	1570,330	1713,670
evening	4410,000	46,984	4317,900	4502,100
Total	8829,000	0,000	8829,000	8829,000
morning	31,5%	,5%	30,5%	32,4%
noon	18,6%	,4%	17,8%	19,4%
evening	49,9%	,5%	48,9%	51,0%
Total	100,0%	0,0%	100,0%	100,0%

According to the confidence measure, the error rate is negligible which involves the performance of data collected. So that, in a future work, this data will be used in the anticipation of the tension in the hospital emergencies and in the decision related to the management of human and material resources.

5. CONCLUSION AND FUTURE WORK

Guaranteeing good quality data collection is becoming necessary given the large mass of data that appears every day and comes from several sources: messages, signals, climate information, recording, video, etc. (Gauthier and al, 2016). Furthermore, the management of emergencies becomes one of the main missions of health establishments that must respond to an exponential demand for unscheduled care, which has posed the problem of dimensioning the structure and its resources (Brown and al, 2020). In this context, we proposed an approach for data collection to address existing problems and gaps. Our idea consists of creating a new database, the DB-RES database resulting from merging of the two databases named DB-EMRG and DB-CL, created in the whose creation steps are presented in this paper. The database obtained DB-RES can be used in future work to resolve the problems generated in the health system such as the anticipation of tension in hospital emergencies, also we can use the data collected for the optimized management of material and personal resources in hospital emergencies.

REFERENCES

Asheim A. et al,2019. *Real-time forecasting of emergency department arrivals using prehospital data.* BMC Emergency Medicine volume 19, 42, 2019

Braun V., et al, 2020. The online survey as a qualitative research tool, *International Journal of Social Research Methodology.*

Brown A., et al, 2020. Emergency Medicine: Diagnosis and Management, Taylor *& Francis Group,* ISBN036746991X, 9780367469917.

Chu X., et al, 2016. Data Cleaning: Overview and Emerging Challenges'', *SIGMOD '16: Proceedings of the 2016 International Conference on Management of Data June*, Pages 2201–2206.

Feng Y. et al, 2021, *Data collection methods for studying pedestrian behaviour: A systematic review*. Building and Environment Volume 187, 107329.

Gauthier B., et al, 2016. *de la problématique à la collecte des données*, Presses de l'Université du Québec, ISBN276054396X, 9782760543966.

Guo J., et al., 2020. *COVID-19: a novel coronavirus and a novel challenge for oral healthcare*, Clinical Oral Investigations volume 24, pages 2137–213.

Hensen B. et al, 2021, *Remote data collection for public health research in a COVID-19 era: ethical implications, challenges and opportunities,* Health Policy and Planning, Volume 36, Issue 3, Pages 360–368.

Johnson S., et al, 2012. *Survey Mode Effects on Data Quality: Comparison of Web and Mail Modes.* a US National Panel Survey. Social Science Computer Review 30 (2): 212-228.

Jribi S., et al, 2020. *COVID-19 virus outbreak lockdown: What impacts on household food wastage*, Environment, Development and Sustainability volume 22, pages3939–3955.

Kerlink et al., 2021.Les infographies Statista pour JDN, HTTPS://WWW.JOURNALDUNET.COM/STATISTA/

Lindhjemand H. et al, 2011. *Using Internet in Stated Preference Surveys: A Review and Comparison of Survey Modes.* International Review of Environmental and Resource Economics (Forthcoming).

Rosenthal K. et al, 2020. Modeling Difficulties in Data Modeling, *International Conference on Conceptual Modeling*, pp. 501-511.

Skhiri H., et al, 2012. Motifs du recours aux services d'urgence des principaux hôpitaux du Grand Tunis. *Eastern Mediterranean Health Journal*, 10.26719.

Tim L., et al., 2018. Googling your hand hygiene data: Using Google Forms, Google Sheets, and R to collect and automate analysis of hand hygiene compliance monitoring. *American Journal of Infection Control* Volume 46, Issue 6, Pages 617-619.

Tpisheh G.,et al., 2019. Challenges for Hospital Resilience in Emergencies and Disasters: A Qualitative Study in Iran. *Journal of Clinical & Diagnostic Research.*Vol. 13 Issue 9, p1-8. 8p, 2019

DOCTORAL

EXPLORING STRATEGIC ALIGNMENT OF BUSINESS AND INFORMATION SYSTEMS/TECHNOLOGY STRATEGIES USING A MIDDLE MANAGEMENT PERSPECTIVE

Thokozani Kachale
PhD student
School of Computing, Edinburgh Napier University, 10 Colinton Road, EH10 5DT, Edinburgh, United Kingdom

ABSTRACT

Information Systems/Information Technologies (IS/IT) have become an integral part of modern organisations. However, there are still challenges presented to business leaders on how they may achieve strategic alignment (SA) of business and IS/IT strategies. It is commonly agreed that SA is positively correlated to organisational performance. Achieving sustainable SA is a challenge for many business leaders. The literature reviewed suggests that there is a paucity of studies on SA using a Middle Management (MM) perspective which is the focus of this study. This paper starts by clarifying the distinction between corporate and business strategies before proceeding to look at the strategic role MM plays through sensemaking and issue selling. Crucially, attention is drawn to Luftman's alignment model because of its claims as focusing on the dynamism of SA rather than conceptualisation of SA as a static end state which does not render very well to operationalisation.

KEYWORDS

Middle Management, Business Strategy, IS/IT Strategy, Strategic Alignment

1. INTRODUCTION

This is a brief overview of literature for a doctoral research study being conducted by a second-year student regarding the strategic alignment of business and IS//IT strategies from a MM perspective in the banking sector in Malawi. The literature reviewed, based on corporate and business strategy, middle management, and SA streams, shows that although both SA and MM have been topics of interest for several decades, there is a paucity of research on these topics from the developing world. The literature was identified by using terms such as "strategic alignment", "middle management" and variations on journals such as: "The Journal of Strategic Information Systems", "MIS Quarterly", and other peer-reviewed journals.

The study will seek to answer the following research questions (RQs). RQ2 and RQ3 are sub questions to RQ1:

RQ1 – How do MM contribute to business, IS/IT strategies, and their SA?
RQ2 – How do MM perceive their influence on business, IS/IT and their SA?
RQ3 – How do MM participate in practices that ensure sustainability of SA?

The next section is a brief overview of the literature for this study.

2. LITERATURE OVERVIEW

This section briefly discusses some of the literature which have guided the formulation of the RQs based on corporate strategy, business strategy, MM perspective, and SA streams. There is a growing interest to understand the role that middle managers play in the formulation of strategies (Baker & Singh, 2019; Caffrey

& McDonagh, 2017; Darkow, 2015; Jansen Van Rensburg et al., 2014; Milovich et al., 2015; Rezvani & Hudson, 2021).

Many studies do not distinguish between corporate strategy and business strategy (Reynolds & Yetton, 2015) so that the role of MM in business strategy formulation and SA is obscured. Andrews (1971) defined corporate strategy as "… the pattern of decisions in a company that determines and reveals its objectives, purposes, or goals, produces the principal policies and plans for achieving those goals, and defines the range of business the company is to pursue …" p.13. Business strategy is defined as "…the determination of how a company will compete in a given business and position itself among its competitors …" (ibid.: p.13). Reynolds and Yetton (2015, p. 103) state that "… corporate strategy specifies how to compete as an organisation, including the choice of markets in which to compete, and the level and nature of the shared capabilities across the organisation …". Therefore, corporate strategy "… seeks to address a … core question: how managers set and oversee the scope of their firms — that is, how do managers determine which businesses belong within their firms and which do not …" Feldman (2020, p. 182). Business strategy pertains to a particular business function or business unit (Lyneis, 2013) within the company such as marketing, production, and/or human resources management overseen by MM (Netland, Powell, & Hines, 2020). Feldman (2020) recognises that business functions are interdependent constituent parts of firms.

Rezvani (2017) acknowledges that researchers have not been able to formulate a universally accepted definition for MM. The criteria used in the definition of MM include their positions, functional roles, and researchers' preference based on factors such as organisational size, organisational form, and industry. Netland et al. (2020) suggest that there are commonly accepted three levels of management. Namely: top management, middle management, and frontline management. Top management comprises of the team of managers at the top and close to the top of the apex (the chief executive officer and senior executive managers) with the most concentration of power, who report to the boards of directors. Immediately below this team are middle managers with specific responsibilities over plants, factories, or departments.

MM are strategically important owing to their situation as a bridge between top management and the lower levels of the organisation (Tarakci et al., 2018). The activities of MM may lead to realisation of divergent strategies due to imperfect communication, or understanding (Baker & Singh, 2019; Balogun, 2006), or self-interest (Ates, 2014; Gibson & Groom, 2021; Wooldridge et al., 2008). Although the latter might appear politically incorrect, sometimes the divergent actions of MM may lead to an overall improvement in the competitive position of an organisation (Baker & Singh, 2019). From the viewpoint of formulation and implementation of business and IS/IT strategies, and their SA it is important to note these will usually be agreed by top management. Once they have been approved, it is the middle managers who have the responsibility to oversee that these are implemented in their business units (Netland et al., 2020). Through sensemaking and issue selling MM exert strategic influence from the bottom (Balogun, 2006) in a feedback loop. Sensemaking is concerned with interpretation of top-down intended corporate strategies into relevant business strategies for their business units. Where there is self-interest, misunderstanding, or misinterpretation, top management strategic goals may not be implemented as intended within business units. Sometimes, when business units notice that intended corporate strategies are not in synch with customer expectations, or not yielding intended results, they may have to improvise or raise issues for consideration of top managers which are routed through MM in what is called issue selling (Balogun, 2006). Top management may consider some of these issues and subsequently amend corporate strategies to reflect the recommendations from the bottom.

One business unit in which the role of MM cannot be overstated is the IS/IT function of any modern organisation. This has moved from providing administrative support to become a business unit of strategic importance (Torres-Moreno & Aponte-Melo, 2021). This growth in importance makes the study of SA imperative considering that the there is agreement that it has a positive correlation with performance, and that there are constant changes in the business environment, as well as increasing innovation (Baker & Singh, 2019; Benbya et al., 2019; Coltman et al., 2015; Peppard & Ward, 2016; Sinz & McDonagh, 2019). On one hand, if top managers do not pay attention to SA as an important aspect of the organisation, there is a risk that investments may be made in IS/IT that fail to support the strategic and operational objectives for their organisations. On the other hand, if there is SA, it is expected that organisations will realise positive returns on their investments in IS/IT. From the issue selling perspective senior managers should be able to listen to MM from business units to establish whether investments have been made in IS/IT that provide adequate coverage that results in attainment of overall strategic objectives, achievement of competitive advantage, and facilitate organisational agility during turbulent times.

Coltman et al. (2015), posit that a multiplicity of terms ('matched with', 'in harmony with', 'complement each other', 'contingent upon', and 'congruent with' or more simply as 'aligned', 'fit', 'support', 'integrated', 'synergy', 'linked', or 'co-aligned') has been used to conceptualise SA but there is an apparent lack of practical guidance on how these terms could be usefully operationalised. SA operational ambiguities arise where a single state fit is used to measure a static 'fit' by simply comparing contents of business strategies and IS/IT strategies (Luftman et al.,2017). A Strategic Alignment Maturity Model (SAM) that "... provides a comprehensive vehicle for organisations to evaluate business-IT alignment in terms of where they are and what they can do to improve alignment ..." (Luftman, 2000, p. 4) promises to overcome the issues of static conceptualization of SA. Much of the current stream of research in strategic alignment emphasises on a top-down conceptual approach of SA without consideration of the dynamic behavioural bottom-up effects (Baker & Singh, 2019; Luftman et al., 2017). The SAM advocates for business leaders to consider the two-way dynamism between business units and IS/IT function and vice versa to enable managers assess the level of SA relative to their capabilities and adjust accordingly. The SAM model identifies precedents of SA: IS/IT-business communications; use of value analytics; approaches to collaborative governance; nature of the affiliation/partnership; scope of IS/IT initiatives; and development of IS/IT skills (Luftman et al., 2017). For example, it is apparent that the contents and quality of communication between MM from business units, IS/IT and top managers have a direct bearing in the bridging role that MM play.

Other issues that have emerged in SA studies include the problem of its measurement (Avison et al.,2004; Belfo & Sousa, 2012); misalignment or strategic drift (Baker & Singh, 2019); perception of SA as an end state (Luftman et al., 2017); alignment paradox (Tallon, 2003) or rigidity trap(Coltman et al., 2015), and ways in which SA can be sustained (Luftman, 2000; Peppard & Breu, 2003).

3. CONCLUSION

SA has continued to be a topical issue among practitioners and scholars. Although many studies have established a positive correlation between SA and organisational performance, its achievement remains elusive for many practitioners. One of the issues identified by this study is the paucity of SA research from an MM perspective to inform practice of SA. This study is aimed at contributing to this area. The literature overview highlights the role that MM can play in the formulation of business strategy, IS/IT strategy, and their SA through a sensemaking of top-down strategic objectives and issue selling of emergent bottom-up realities. The Luftman's (2000) SAM plays an important role in understanding such dynamic interaction between IS/IT and other business units to measure different levels of SA maturity which can help identify areas that practitioners need to focus on to attain sustainable SA.

Although a lot of care was taken to ensure that issues concerning SA from the MM were covered, this overview is limited by the available space. It should also be noted that this is a work in progress and will be the subject of revision as the study proceeds.

REFERENCES

Andrews, K. R. (1971). *The Concept of Corporate Strategy (Third ed.).* Richard D. Irwin, Inc., United States of America.

Ates, N. Y. (2014). The Strategy Process: A Middle Management Perspective. (Doctor of Philosophy). *Erasmus Research Institute of Management*, Retrieved from http://hdl.handle.net/1765/50365

Avison, D., Jones, J., Powell, P., & Wilson, D. (2004). Using and validating the strategic alignment model. *The Journal of Strategic Information Systems*, 13(3), 223-246. doi: https://doi.org/10.1016/j.jsis.2004.08.002

Baker, J., & Singh, H. (2019). The roots of misalignment: Insights on strategy implementation from a system dynamics perspective. *The Journal of Strategic Information Systems*, Volume 28 (Issue 4). doi: https://doi.org/10.1016/j.jsis.2019.101576

Balogun, J. (2006). Managing Change: Steering a Course between Intended Strategies and Unanticipated Outcomes. *Long Range Planning*, 39(1), 29-49. doi: https://doi.org/10.1016/j.lrp.2005.02.010

Belfo, F., & Sousa, R. D. (2012). A Critical Review of Luftman's Instrument for Business-IT Alignment. *MCIS 2012 Proceedings. Paper 6.* http://aisel.aisnet.org/mcis2012/6

Benbya, H., Leidner, D. E., & Preston, D. (2019). MIS Quarterly research curation on Information Systems alignment. *MIS Quarterly* (Research curations), 1-19.

Caffrey, E., & McDonagh, J. (2017). A Perspective on the Roles of Middle Managers in Aligning Strategy and Information Technology in Public Service Organizations. In L. Rusu & G. Viscusi (Eds.), *Information Technology Governance in Public Organizations: Theory and Practice* (pp. 59-83). Cham: Springer International Publishing.

Coltman, T., Tallon, P., Sharma, R., & Queiroz, M. (2015). Strategic IT alignment: twenty-five years on. *Journal of Information Technology*, 30(2), 91-100. doi:10.1057/jit.2014.35

Darkow, I.-L. (2015). The involvement of middle management in strategy development —Development and implementation of a foresight-based approach. *Technological Forecasting & Social Change*, 101, 10-24. doi: 10.1016/j.techfore.2013.12.002

Feldman, E. (2020). Corporate Strategy: Past, Present, and Future. *Strategic Management Review*, 1, 179-206. doi:10.1561/111.00000002

Gibson, L., & Groom, R. (2021). Understanding 'Vulnerability' and 'Political Skill' in Academy Middle Management During Organisational Change in Professional Youth Football. *Journal of Change Management*, 21(3), 358-382. doi:10.1080/14697017.2020.1819860

Jansen Van Rensburg, M., Davis, A., & Venter, P. (2014). Making strategy work: The role of the middle manager. *Journal of Management & Organization*, 20(2), 165-186. doi:10.1017/jmo.2014.33

Luftman, J. N. (2000). Assessing Business-IT Alignment Maturity. *Communications of Association of Information Systems*, 4, 14.

Luftman, J. N., Lyytinen, K., & Zvi, T. b. (2017). Enhancing the measurement of information technology (IT) business alignment and its influence on company performance. *Journal of Information Technology*, 32(1), 26-46. doi:10.1057/jit.2015.23

Lyneis, J. M. (2013). Business Policy and Strategy, System Dynamics Applications to. *Encyclopedia of Complexity and Systems Science*, 179-207. doi:10.1007/978-1-4939-8790-0_45

Milovich, M., Leidner, D. E., & Preston, D. S. (2015, 5-8 Jan. 2015). The Influence of Middle Management on Information Technology Alignment. *Paper presented at the 2015 48th Hawaii International Conference on System Sciences.*

Netland, T. H., Powell, D. J., & Hines, P. (2020). Demystifying lean leadership. *International Journal of Lean Six Sigma*, 11(3), 543-554. doi:10.1108/IJLSS-07-2019-0076

Peppard, J., & Breu, K. (2003). Beyond Alignment: A Coevolutionary View of The Information Systems Strategy Process. *Twenty-Fourth International Conference on Information Systems.*

Peppard, J., & Ward, J. (2016). The Strategic Management of Information Systems: Building a Digital Strategy. Wiley, United Kingdom.

Reynolds, P., & Yetton, P. (2015). Aligning Business and IT Strategies in Multi-business Organizations. *Journal of Information Technology*, 30(2), 101-118. doi:10.1057/jit.2015.1

Rezvani, Z. (2017). Who is a Middle Manager: A literature Review. *Journal of Family Business Management*, 1(2), 1-9.

Rezvani, Z., & Hudson, P. (2021). How do middle managers really make decisions within the oil and gas industry? *Safety Science*, 139, 105199. doi: 10.1016/j.ssci.2021.105199

Sinz, S., & McDonagh, J. (2019). Strategic Alignment: Towards a Holistic Perspective Embracing Complexity – Advancing the Research Agenda. *UK Academy for Information Systems Conference Proceedings 2019*, 21.

Tallon, P. P. (2003). The Alignment Paradox: It's not always the case that better IT alignment leads to business gains. Avoid creating information backbones too inflexible to embrace marketplace change. *CIO Insight*, 1(32), 75.

Tarakci, M., Ates, N., Floyd, S., Ahn, Y., & Woolidge, B. (2018). Performance Feedback and Middle Managers' Divergent Strategic Behavior: The Roles of Social Comparisons and Organizational Identification. *Strategic Management Journal,* 39(4), 1139-1162. doi:10.1002/smj.2745

Torres-Moreno, M. E., & Aponte-Melo, J. H. (2021). Assessing Business-IT Alignment Maturity at a Colombian University. *Journal of Cases on Information Technology*, 23. doi: 10.4018/JCIT.20211001.oa8

Wooldridge, B., Schmid, T., & Floyd, S. W. (2008). The Middle Management Perspective on Strategy Process: Contributions, Synthesis, and Future Research. *Journal of Management*, 34(6), 1190-1221. doi:10.1177/0149206308324326.

AUTHOR INDEX

International Association for Development of the Information Society (IADIS)
Rua Sao Sebastiao Da Pedreira
No. 100, 30, 1050-209
Lisbon, Portugal

ISBN 978-1-7138-5789-1

CURRAN ASSOCIATES INC.
proceedings.com